CHRISTMAS
—— YET TO ——
COME

A Timeline for the End Times and Second Coming of Christ

Kevin D. Perdue, M.D.

WESTBOW
PRESS®
A DIVISION OF THOMAS NELSON
& ZONDERVAN

This book is a work of non-fiction. Unless otherwise noted, the author and the publisher make no explicit guarantees as to the accuracy of the information contained in this book and in some cases, names of people and places have been altered to protect their privacy.

WestBow Press books may be ordered through booksellers or by contacting:

WestBow Press
A Division of Thomas Nelson & Zondervan
1663 Liberty Drive
Bloomington, IN 47403
www.westbowpress.com
844-714-3454

Unless otherwise indicated, all Scripture taken from the King James Version of the Bible.

Scripture quotations marked (NASB) taken from the (NASB®) New American Standard Bible®, Copyright © 1960, 1971, 1977, 1995, 2020 by The Lockman Foundation. Used by permission. All rights reserved. www.lockman.org

ISBN: 978-1-6642-7390-0 (sc)
ISBN: 978-1-6642-7391-7 (hc)
ISBN: 978-1-6642-7389-4 (e)

Library of Congress Control Number: 2022913947

Print information available on the last page.

WestBow Press rev. date: 08/15/2022

CONTENTS

ACKNOWLEDGMENTS

I would first like to thank my wife Sara for all her support throughout the writing of this book. How many times she heard my frustration in trying to make sense and order of the end time's timeline. How many times she heard me say I was giving up or that I was done writing. Thank you for your patience and endurance.

Thank you also to my neighbor and good friend Dr. Charley Carlson and my sister-in-law Dr. Laura McCammon for their input and many hours of work, helping to edit this manuscript.

A big thanks to the great Bible scholars whose thoughts, writings, and videos have made it possible for me to arrive at most of the conclusions in this book. Many thanks to Hal Lindsey who started me on this journey so many years ago. A great big SHOUT OUT to Nelson Walters for his many insightful and new ways of interpreting Bible prophecy. A giant nod of appreciation goes out to Joel Richardson for helping shape my thoughts on the Antichrist and Christ's second coming, as well as the Christian walk in general. Likewise, I'd like to thank David Rosenthal especially for his insights on Mystery Babylon; Alan Kurschner for helping solidify my beliefs and understanding of a prewrath rapture timing; Travis Snow for his enlightening thoughts on the end time's second exodus; and Ed Knorr, PhD whose online material provided so much back ground material on Bible prophecy throughout the book. Without these scholars, none of this would have been possible.

A special thanks goes out to Tim Warner whose book *The Time of the End* made me think that maybe it is possible to know when that end time is.

Finally, I'd like to thank the only source of truth, Jesus Christ. I hope that this book is a source of truth as well as a basis of anticipation and hope that whoever reads this will develop a hunger for His second coming, a Christmas yet to come.

PREFACE

The idea for this book began back in the 1960s when I was in junior high school growing up in a Pentecostal church. We were known as holy rollers and any friends that we invited to church certainly understood where that name came from. Many of the popular sermon topics at that time seemed to rely on the Book of Revelation with the theme that Jesus was coming back soon… at any moment. This message was accompanied with plenty of fire and damnation which was a great motivator, at least for me, to accept Christ as my savior at an early age. The church leaders all seemed so sure that Jesus' second coming could happen at any time.

This fear of Christ's imminent return had a different effect on my younger brother. It created what is now called FOMO, a fear of missing out. His primary love at that time was football, and the thought that the end of the world was near made him think that he might miss out on playing football, not to mention the fire and brimstone that he might have to endure in hell just for having such thoughts.

Fast forward a few years to the 1970s, and still there was no return. My brother did get his chance to play football. College came along with some travel that provided opportunities to learn that some people actually had other ideas about God and about prophecy. I suppose a little bit of enthusiasm for Christ's return lessened during that time, but then a book called *The Late Great Planet Earth* by Hal Lindsey took the world by storm. Once again, I knew that the rapture and the end of the world must be near.

Fast forward again to the early 2000s. Still no return. Like most of the world it's easy to get discouraged. He said that He was coming back, but it'd been 2000 years. Could it really be any time soon? Many people had predicted times and dates in the past that had proven to be false. Yet, I knew that the Bible had predicted His first coming in scripture and that scripture had foretold when that time would be. In fact, scholars today have gone back and determined that scripture had prophesied the exact day of Jesus' first coming hundreds of years before it had occurred. So, why wouldn't the time of His second coming also be prophesied in the Bible?

That was when I read another book written by Tim Warner called *The Time of the End*. In this book he outlines a timeline from creation to the establishment of God's kingdom on earth. This kingdom is something we pray for every time we recite the Lord's prayer. And it is this kingdom that his book predicted is coming soon. New hope was rekindled in me at that time.

So, I decided to research whether a specific date for Christ's return could be confirmed in scripture and a timeline for the end times established. It couldn't be that difficult. For certainly, there must be an abundance of information from Bible scholars on this topic. Unfortunately, although there were a lot of generalities regarding Christ's second return, there was not much in the way of specifics, which I believe is due to fear of being wrong and being labeled by the Christian society as a "date setter". Obviously, since everyone that has tried to set a date for Christ's return has been wrong and criticized for it, few would want to attempt predicting the timing of His second coming. Although fear can be a healthy emotion at times, I believe, that in this instance, it has stymied the Church from being prepared for that very time.

They say that in your twenties, you care about what everybody thinks of you. When you are in your forties, you don't care about what people think of you, and when you are in your sixties, you realize that people were never really thinking of you. Not to give away my age, but I'm not too concerned about whether people criticize me and condemn the timeline for the end times presented here. What I am concerned with is that people and the Church are awake to the fact that Jesus is returning soon, and they need to be prepared.

Unlike my early experience, not much is heard in the Church today about fire and brimstone, perhaps because much emphasis is placed on the importance of being non-judgmental and tolerant of the world. The Church needs to remember that it may be "in the world" but is not "of the world". The FOMO of what the world has to offer needs to be replaced instead with a FOMO on Christ's second coming. It is my hope and purpose that by writing this that myself, my brother, my friends and family, the Church, and the world will not worry about missing out on football or what the world itself has to offer but will know that Christ is returning soon and will be ready and waiting.

As will be emphasized later, I am not claiming absolutely to know that this is the exact timeline for the end times, just that in my mind it is simply one theory that to my knowledge has not yet been proposed but seems to align most with Bible prophecy and is pointing to a near fulfillment. Obviously, it is difficult to be fully confident of a timeline like this, and the later chapters on Wars and Judgment are even more difficult to understand and predict. Despite these difficulties, I hope that you enjoy the ideas presented here, that it awakens you to the fact that Christ's second coming is coming soon, and that it encourages you to study the Word, so that you will be prepared for the hard times that are coming soon.

CHAPTER 1

Date Setting and the Tribulation

The word *Christmas* comes from the two words *Christ* (the anointed one) and *mass* (the celebration of communion). So, although literally it means "the celebration of Christ's communion", Christmas commonly refers to the birth and first appearance or advent of Jesus Christ. The timing of that first Christmas was prophesied throughout the Old Testament, the Hebrew Bible called the *Tanakh*. Many Bible chronologists have studied and used those prophecies to declare that Jesus was not only the promised, anointed one but that he appeared precisely at the time that was foretold throughout scripture. Assuming that they are correct and that Jesus' first appearance was forecast to the exact day, then it would seem likely that God would also supply the necessary information to determine the timing of His second appearance, a Christmas yet to come. Like Christmas Future in Charles Dicken's novel *A Christmas Carol*, this Christmas yet to come is prophesied to include death and destruction but ultimately will end in restoration and eternal life for mankind.

Indeed, there is an abundance of scripture that gives specific days, months and years regarding the chronology of the end times. In fact, there is more prophecy concerning Christ's second coming than there is for his first. It is the hope here to show you a possible, if not probable, timeline developed based solely on God's holy word. There is a majority of opinion that "no one can know the day or the hour" of Jesus' second coming and that this is clearly stated in the Bible. So, one primary concern is whether or not an attempt should even be made to determine when this Christmas yet to come, Christ's second return, could occur. Again, there are many verses in the Bible related to the end times, and many of these provide specific dates and times. Consequently, it only seems reasonable that these specifics were put there for a reason.

However, the most frequently cited objection to seeking a more exact timing to Jesus' return is one verse.

> But of that day and hour no one knows, not even the angels of heaven, but My Father only. Matthew 24:36

It is just assumed that because this verse states "no one knows", that no one **will ever** know. Yet, Jesus never reprimanded his disciples for wanting to know the time of the end but actually encouraged them to seek it.

> Watch therefore, for you do not know what hour your Lord is coming. But know this, that if the master of the house had known what hour the thief would come, he would have watched and not allowed his house to be broken into. Therefore, you also be ready, for the Son of Man is coming at an hour you do not expect. Matthew 24:32

In fact, He actually rebuked the Jewish leaders of the time of His first coming for **not** knowing the time of that first appearance.

> For days will come upon you when your enemies will build an embankment around you, surround you and close you in on every side, and level you, and your children within you, to the ground; and they will not

leave in you one stone upon another, **because you did not know the time of your visitation.** Lk 19:43-44

Since there are about five hundred prophecies in the Old Testament that refer to Christ's Second Coming; and, one out of every twenty-five verses in the New Testament deals with the return of Christ [Reagan, 2011][1], it would seem wise to examine and study God's word thoroughly in order to establish as closely as possible the time of His next appearance.

The phrase "the day or hour" implies that although the exact specific time may not be known, it does not prevent us from knowing the general time frame of his second coming. In addition, this phrase is known to refer to a specific feast day in the Jewish culture, the Feast of Trumpets, one of the main Jewish holidays that occurs in the Fall. Because the Feast days are based on a lunar calendar and rely on the presence of a new moon, it is difficult to determine the exact day of most of the Feast Days, including the Feast of Trumpets. Many believe that because of this phrase ("of that day and hour no one knows"), it will be on a Jewish feast day that Jesus will make His second appearance on earth.

Now, if it is not wrong to seek the time of His coming, the next question is whether it is even possible to determine when that time takes place. Certainly, many men have tried to set specific dates, and all have failed, going down in history, to the glee and mocking of doubters, as failures and often referred to in a derogatory manner as "date setters".

Of course, many in the past have thought that their time on earth was **the** "time of the end". The Early Church Fathers thought that Jesus was coming back soon. Our grandfathers and our fathers have been calling for the return of Christ in their lifetime. Yet, still it has not happened. Will it happen in our lifetime?

These past failures and subsequent ridicule by not only non-Christians but also by brothers and sisters in Christ certainly make it difficult for anyone to even want to make an attempt at timing Christ's second return. Satan surely likes to discourage with failure. Enough failures in date setting and surely no one would be foolish enough to try again, i.e., the "boy that cried wolf" syndrome.

Even so, I believe, God has provided all the information in scripture that is needed to ascertain the time of His second coming. If He was faithful to supply enough information to calculate the exact day of His first coming, as many Bible scholars claim, then He should be faithful and able to give us the required data in His scripture to reckon the time of His second coming.

> And he said, "Go your way, Daniel, for the words are closed up and sealed till the time of the end. Many shall be purified, made white, and refined, but the wicked shall do wickedly; and none of the wicked shall understand, but **the wise shall understand**." Daniel 12:9-10

God has not left us in darkness.

> But concerning the times and seasons, brethren, you have no need that I should write to you. For you yourselves know perfectly that the day of the Lord so comes as a thief in the night. For when they say, "Peace and safety!" then sudden destruction comes upon them, as labor pains upon a pregnant woman. And they shall not escape. But you, brethren, are **not in darkness**, so that this Day should overtake you as a thief. You are all sons of light and sons of the day. We are not the night nor of darkness. Therefore, let us not sleep, as others do, but **let us watch and be sober**. 1 Thessalonians 5:1-6

Satan likes to divide and conquer the Church on relatively less important issues. Although the topic of the return of Christ is very important, there is quite a bit of disagreement among Bible scholars as to when and how these end time events will play out. In fact, there is much divisive dissention on this topic within the Church that often splits and weakens believers in their faith and fellowship. Although there are issues and doctrines that can divide the Church, this should not be one of them. Unity within the Church is of paramount importance as emphasized by Jesus and the Early Church Fathers.

> Endeavouring to keep the unity of the Spirit in the bond of peace. There is one body, and one Spirit, even as ye are called in one hope of your calling; One Lord, one faith, one baptism, One God and Father of all, who is above all, and through all, and in you all. Ephesians 4:3-6

It is vital to remember what holds us together, and that is the unwavering love of the Father and His Son. If we continue to put our trust in Him and remain obedient to His commandments to love one another, then these other issues will eventually work themselves out.

Nevertheless, there are many views on the timing of end times events, but most fall into two groups depending on how you view the Bible and interpret prophecy. The first view is amillennialism, which takes an allegorical or symbolic view of Bible prophecy. This is the belief that there will not be a future literal one-thousand-year reign of Jesus Christ on the earth. Taking a more historical approach, those who take this view believe that Christ has already returned and is ruling his kingdom from heaven in this present Church age. Additionally, they consider the one thousand years to be symbolic, not literal. According to them, it simply refers to a long period of time that is simply allegorical.

The second view is called premillennialism, a belief that Jesus is physically going to return to the earth before the Millennium begins and that he is going to rule and reign sometime in the future on this earth for one thousand years (the Millennium). The reason they believe this way is that they interpret Bible prophecy literally and not allegorically. In this camp are other subdivisions including pretribulationalism, midtribulationalism, posttribulationalism, and more recently a prewrath view. All of these take a literal approach to the Bible. It is not the purpose here to discuss in depth each of these views but to give you an explanation that seems to best align with what the Bible supports. This view (the prewrath view) uses the most literal interpretation of the Bible possible without ignoring much of the symbolism and allegory that is obviously present within prophecy.

The most popular premillennial understanding today is the pretribulation view, which states that the Church will be raptured or removed from the earth before or at the beginning of the tribulation and the last seven years. This view was detailed in the 1800's by John Darby. It has since been popularized by Hal Lindsey in his book *The Late Great Planet Earth* and more recently by the *Left Behind* Series of fiction novels by Tim LaHaye and Jerry Jenkins.

More recently a new concept of a prewrath rapture of the Church has been presented by Marvin Rosenthal in his book appropriately entitled *The Pre-Wrath Rapture of the Church*. This view holds that believers do go through the tribulation but do not experience the wrath of God. Although seemingly a new concept that is lately gaining traction, it is not a recent concept but was the primary teaching of the Early Church Fathers. This is unlike the pretribulation view that in fact is a relatively new idea. It is the prewrath view that seems to most align with God's word and the timeline for the last seven years that will be presented. For more on the prewrath view I would refer you also to *Prewrath, A Very Short Introduction* by Alan E. Kurshner.

Utilizing the prewrath view, one possible outline for the timing of the end times and the 70th Week of Daniel will be provided here. Many timelines were considered and examined before arriving at this specific order and timing of events. Like scientists who consider a hypothesis and then conduct experiments to determine if the results match that hypothesis, various timelines were considered and the variables of scripture were used to determine if that timeline was valid. If scripture contradicted that timeline, then it was clearly eliminated as an option. Additionally, if that scripture seemed to be "forced" or had to be manipulated in order to support that timeline, then that timeline was also discarded as a possibility. People, places, and events related to Biblical eschatology (the study of end time events), including the Tribulation, the Two Witnesses, the Antichrist, the Second Coming of Christ, and others, were examined and applied to this timeline. Each of these will be explored in separate chapters in detail to demonstrate that the timing aligns with the proposed order of events.

In some cases, it does require a new perspective on interpreting scripture that does not align with preconceived notions or well held beliefs (for example, the pretribulational view of the end times and a Revived Roman Empire concept for the Antichrist). So, for those who hold strongly to these traditional viewpoints, this will contain some challenging viewpoints that may open your eyes to a different way of thinking or perhaps reinforce what you already hold to be true. Nevertheless, as scripture states:

> Study to shew thyself approved unto God, a workman that needeth not to be ashamed, rightly dividing the word of truth. 2 Timothy 2:15

Our study should become more fervent as we come closer to the end times. In fact, God promises that our understanding of scripture will become clearer and sharper as we near those end times.

> The anger of the LORD shall not return, until he have executed, and till he have performed the thoughts of his heart: **in the latter days ye shall consider it perfectly.** Jeremiah 23:20

And if we are nearing the latter days, then our understanding of end times prophecy should be becoming more perfect.

Signs of the Times

So, how can we know that we are in those latter days? What are the "Signs of the Times", that we are in a unique position compared to previous generations? What are the indicators that demonstrate we are in or approaching the end times when our understanding will become clearer and show that we may actually see the return of Jesus Christ in our lifetime?

God always provides notice and warnings before sending judgment on people and places. For example, in the days of Noah, God warned of coming judgment for a hundred and twenty years. In the days of Sodom and Gomorrah, God gave notice through Abraham of impending judgment. Likewise, Jonah warned the city of Nineveh. The people then repented, and God relented from His judgment. And God used His prophets to repetitively warn His nation Israel before sending the Assyrians and Babylonians to carry them off into captivity. Similarly, God has been warning the world through His word and has provided many signs that we are nearing the return of Jesus Christ and God's judgment.[1]

Although a specific end time's timeline is provided here, it is speculation, and we cannot be absolutely certain of the exact date of Christ's return. Yet, there are signs that suggest His second coming is near. For example, there are many prophecies in Scripture which could not have been fulfilled in the past; however, in our modern generation, these prophecies have been realized or are at least capable of being realized. Jesus himself told us that there would be signs that His coming was near. In the Olivet Discourse in Matthew 24 Jesus stated:

> And as he sat upon the mount of Olives, the disciples came unto him privately, saying, Tell us, when shall these things be? and what shall be the sign of thy coming, and of the end of the world? And Jesus answered and said unto them, Take heed that no man deceive you. For many shall come in my name, saying, I am Christ; and shall deceive many. And ye shall hear of wars and rumours of wars: see that ye be not troubled: for all these things must come to pass, but the end is not yet. For nation shall rise against nation, and kingdom against kingdom: and there shall be famines, and pestilences, and earthquakes, in divers places. All these are the **beginning of sorrows**. Then shall they deliver you up to be afflicted, and shall kill you: and ye shall be hated of all nations for my name's sake. And then shall many

be offended, and shall betray one another, and shall hate one another. And many false prophets shall rise, and shall deceive many. And because iniquity shall abound, the love of many shall wax cold. But he that shall endure unto the end, the same shall be saved. And this gospel of the kingdom shall be preached in all the world for a witness unto all nations; and then shall the end come. Matthew 24:3-14

The "beginning of sorrows" spoken of in Matthew 24 (e.g., wars and rumors of wars, ethnic conflicts, famines, and earthquakes) are sometimes called "birth pains", and just as in a woman's labor, these signs will become more frequent and intensify in strength as the end nears. This increasing escalation of signs is something that is taking place today.

There are many signs that indicate that the world is getting closer than ever to Christ's return. The fact that Israel has returned to the land of its ancestors as a nation after centuries is surely a fulfillment of prophecy, and in particular, Ezekiel 36-37. There are signs even in nature such as earthquakes, famine, pestilence, and signs in the heavens. These have always occurred, but like other birth pains are increasing in frequency and intensity.

And there shall be signs in the sun, and in the moon, and in the stars; and upon the earth distress of nations, with perplexity; the sea and the waves roaring; Men's hearts failing them for fear, and for looking after those things which are coming on the earth: for the powers of heaven shall be shaken. And then shall they see the Son of man coming in a cloud with power and great glory. And when these things begin to come to pass, then look up, and lift up your heads; for your redemption draweth nigh. Luke 21:25-28

Changes in society at the end times will include love of self; love of money with materialism; and love of evil with immorality. This is undoubtedly an accurate description of our modern age. This depravity can now be easily and quickly propagated in our daily lives through television, movies, the internet, and other media.

> This know also, that in the last days perilous times shall come. For men shall be lovers of their own selves, covetous, boasters, proud, blasphemers, disobedient to parents, unthankful, unholy, Without natural affection, trucebreakers, false accusers, incontinent, fierce, despisers of those that are good, Traitors, heady, highminded, lovers of pleasures more than lovers of God; Having a form of godliness, but denying the power thereof: from such turn away. 2 Timothy 3:1-5

Spiritual changes such as apostasy in the Church, persecution of believers, and the presence of many false Christs will become more apparent.

> Knowing this first, that there shall come in the last days scoffers, walking after their own lusts, And saying, Where is the promise of his coming? for since the fathers fell asleep, all things continue as they were from the beginning of the creation. 2 Peter 3:3-4

Increasing knowledge, travel, communications, and technology are signs that are definitely seen in our modern world and point to the nearness of the end times.

> But thou, O Daniel, shut up the words, and seal the book, even to the time of the end: many shall run to and fro, and knowledge shall be increased. Daniel 12:4

And finally, geopolitical changes, involving other nations as well as Israel, signal that we are getting closer to the latter days. The lining up of nations in the Middle East against Israel seems to indicate that the fulfillment of the War of Armageddon discussed in Ezekiel 38-39 is not that far away. In fact, the Bible predicts that there will be other wars as well as rumors of wars.[1]

> For nation shall rise against nation, and kingdom against kingdom: Matthew 24:7

The fact that these signs are apparent, but Christ has not returned yet, suggests that we may be close indeed to the prophetic end times.

In addition to these signs, Jesus said, "As it was in the days of Noah, so it will be at the coming of the Son of Man" (i.e., at the return of Jesus Christ). So, what were the days of Noah like?

> And as it was in the days of Noe, so shall it be also in the days of the Son of man. They did eat, they drank, they married wives, they were given in marriage, until the day that Noah entered into the ark, and the flood came, and destroyed them all. Likewise also as it was in the days of Lot; they did eat, they drank, they bought, they sold, they planted, they builded; But the same day that Lot went out of Sodom it rained fire and brimstone from heaven, and destroyed them all. Even thus shall it be in the day when the Son of man is revealed. Luke 17:26-30

"The days of Noah" were characterized by conditions such as: (a) unpreparedness, indifference, complacency, and apathy; (b) violence and lawlessness; (c) continually evil thoughts; and (d) demonic activity. These are all disorders that have been present throughout history but seem to be escalating in our present time. 1 Thessalonians 5:2-4 (written by Paul) and 2 Peter 3:10 (written by Peter) both speak of "the day of the Lord" as coming like "a thief in the night". As were the days of Noah and Lot, the words of Paul in 1 Thessalonians reflect the unpreparedness that will exist at the end times:

> For when they shall say, Peace and safety; then sudden destruction cometh upon them, as travail upon a woman with child; and they shall not escape. 1 Thessalonians 5:3

And, later in the same chapter, Paul explains that Christians need not be taken by surprise at our rescue from the coming destruction, reinforcing a prewrath viewpoint.

> For God hath not appointed us to wrath, but to obtain salvation by our Lord Jesus Christ, Who died for us, that, whether we wake or sleep, we should live together with him. 1 Thessalonians 5:9-10

Recall that neither Noah nor Abraham's nephew Lot experienced the wrath of God, but rather were spared from a time of destruction. Both were taken to a physical place of safety. These Old Testament examples again suggest a prewrath rapture. In the New Testament, the apostle Paul declared that the Church is delivered by rapture before the tribulation wrath (1Thess. 5:9-10; Rev. 3:10), and in Peter's symbolism the ark represents the Church (i.e., everyone who is joined to Christ by Spirit baptism). In this imagery the deliverance of Noah and his family in the ark (1 Peter 3:20) logically exemplify the prewrath rapture of the Church and deliverance from the coming wrath in the "latter days" of the Lord.[1]

The proposed timeline that will be outlined in the following chapters is, to be clear, just one theory on the timing and order of end time events. There are many well-known and respected Bible scholars with different views. So, one should not be dogmatic with so many controversial issues on this topic. Although this timeline does provide specific dates regarding the end times, it does not stipulate precise hours, which hopefully satisfies the verse that "of that day **and** hour knoweth no man". And, of course, no one can know the date for certain until events begin to unfold.

This timeline may have errors as so many attempted chronologies have in the past. However, this timeline is supported by scripture with no obvious or significant contradictions. Furthermore, it is built on the work of many respected eschatological experts including Tim Warner, Joel Richardson, David Rosenthal, Nelson Walters, Ed Knorr and many others. Much of the information that follows is simply a compilation of their work and found in their articles, books and videos. On the other hand, many of the conclusions of this book differ with their deductions, just as they disagree with each other on various points of prophecy. Although the following chapters provide a unique timeline and perspective to the end times, it is the groundwork of these scholars and their insights that have led to this new and different approach to the end time's order of events.

So, if these are indeed the latter days, as discussed in the remaining chapters, then the Church needs to be preparing itself for what the Bible states is coming. Our understanding of God's word should be improving and becoming clearer. Prophecy should be becoming sharper and more well-defined (and our understanding of it more perfect) as we study eschatology and come closer to those latter days.

God has known all things past, present, and future from the beginning of time.

> Declaring the end from the beginning, and from
> ancient times the things that are not yet done, saying,
> My counsel shall stand, and I will do all my pleasure.
> Isaiah 46:10

God not only knows the future and its timeline but has told us what that future will be in His word. It is up to you and me to study and learn what that future will be so that we will be prepared for the trials and deception that will occur in those "latter days". Hopefully, this study will encourage all of us to recognize the nearness of Christ's second return and to be watching, studying, and preparing as we wait for that return.

But before discussing a more specific future timeline, it is important to understand why that timeline will involve trials and tribulation for the Church. What exactly defines and is included in that tribulation period? And are tribulation and the wrath of God the same?

What Is the Tribulation?

When many Christians think of the Tribulation, they believe it is seven years in duration, the entire 70th week of Daniel. However, does the Bible actually say that the Tribulation is seven years? While in fact there is a final seven-year period that is often referred to as "the Tribulation", it is important in eschatology to properly define what that Tribulation is and when it occurs. This will also assist in determining when the Rapture (the taking away of the Church by Christ) takes place.

By calling the entire seven-year period "the Tribulation", it infers that "tribulation" and "wrath" are synonymous. And since God has not appointed His righteous to His wrath, the Rapture would consequently need to occur before the final seven years, which is consistent with the pretribulational view.

> For God hath not appointed us to wrath, but to obtain salvation by our Lord Jesus Christ, 1 Thess 5:9

Yet, the Bible refers to the tribulation that occurs in the second half of the seven-year period as "The **Great** Tribulation". Although there is a seven-year period in the end times, it denotes the entirety of "Daniel's 70th Week" and not necessarily the period referred to as "the Tribulation". The actual Great Tribulation does not begin until the midst or middle of the 70th week.

> And he shall confirm the covenant with many for one week: and in the **midst of the week** he shall cause the sacrifice and the oblation to cease, and for the overspreading of abominations he shall make it desolate, even until the consummation, and that determined shall be poured upon the desolate. Daniel 9:27

The Bible uses the term *great tribulation* in only three scriptures. In the first scripture, Jesus Himself stated that the "great tribulation" would not begin until after the abomination of desolation which will occur in the middle of the last seven years. Speaking to His disciples on the end times, Jesus referred to Daniel's prophecy where the Antichrist will defile the rebuilt Temple.

> When ye therefore shall see the abomination of desolation, spoken of by Daniel the prophet, stand in the holy place, (whoso readeth, let him understand:) Then let them which be in Judaea flee into the mountains: Let him which is on the housetop not come down to take any thing out of his house: Neither let him which is in the field return back to take his clothes. And woe unto them that are with child, and to them that give suck in those days! But pray ye that your flight be not in the winter, neither on the sabbath day: For then shall be great tribulation, such as was not since the beginning of the world to this time, no, nor ever shall be. Matt 24:15-21

The next two scripture references occur in Revelation:

> And I said unto him, Sir, thou knowest. And he said unto me, These are they which came out of great tribulation, and have washed their robes, and made them white in the blood of the Lamb. Rev. 7:14

> Behold, I will cast her into a bed, and them that commit adultery with her into great tribulation, except they repent of their deeds. Rev. 2:22

Since, according to Jesus, the Great Tribulation cannot start until sometime after the midpoint of the last seven years (when the abomination of desolation occurs), it is clear that the Rapture does not have to transpire before the start of the last seven years and indeed in all likelihood happens after the midpoint.

Does this imply then that Christians will undergo God's wrath? That would assume that tribulation (or persecution) and wrath are the same thing, and clearly, they are not.

Paul promised the early Christians that they would undergo persecution.

> All who will live godly in Christ Jesus shall suffer persecution. II Timothy 3:12

Of course, many Christians would rather overlook or ignore that promise. Yet, Paul also stated the purpose of that tribulation and how we should react to it.

> We glory in tribulations, knowing that tribulation teaches patience. Romans 5:3

The Bible adds that:

> Whoever the Lord loves he chastens, and he scourges every son whom he receives. If you endure chastening, then God is dealing with you as with sons; for what son is he whom the father does not chasten? But if you are without chastisement, of which all [children] are partakers, then you are bastards and not sons... Now no chastening for the present seems to be joyous, but [rather] grievous. Nevertheless, afterward it yields the peaceable fruit of righteousness to those who are exercised by it. Hebrews 12:6-11

God allows tribulation to enter the Christian's life because He loves them and is dealing with them as He would a son, producing righteousness in their lives. Still, some of the most heated arguments amongst Christians with regard to Bible prophecy is over whether or not Christians will be forced to go through the Great Tribulation. The teaching that Christians will not go through the Great Tribulation seems to be based more on wishful thinking than on a proper interpretation of scripture.

Christians clearly have undergone persecution throughout history. The Romans threw Christians to the lions. Hitler and Stalin persecuted and killed Jews and Christians (Stalin also killed non-Christians). And as a matter of fact, there are Christians today in third world countries who are still being persecuted and martyred for their faith in Jesus. So, it is intuitive that Christians will also suffer tribulation in the future.

However, if the Church will undergo persecution but is not to undergo God's wrath, then clearly there must be a difference between how the words *wrath* and *persecution* are used in the Bible. And, certainly there is an important difference. In fact, the word for *tribulation* is a totally different word than the word for *wrath*. The Greek word for tribulation is *thlipsis*. It means "affliction, anguish, burdened, persecution, tribulation, and trouble". When the Bible speaks of tribulation, it is referring to tribulation for Christians or the sufferings that Christians endure for Christ in this world.

> These things I have spoken unto you, that in me ye might have peace. In the world ye shall have tribulation *(thlipsis)*: but be of good cheer; I have overcome the world. John 16:33

Non-Christians, or unbelievers, do not experience the same tribulation the Bible describes. Though they can experience various degrees of difficulties, they are not necessarily ostracized or persecuted for their views and anti-Christian beliefs. The world has always been at enmity with Christians, who are persecuted for their faith. So, it is the **righteous** in Christ that have and will have tribulation, particularly in this last seven years.

On the other hand, the Greek word for wrath is *orge* (pronounced or-gay). It means "punishment, anger, indignation, vengeance, wrath". When the Bible speaks of wrath, it is referring to the Lord's vengeance and punishment that He executes against unbelievers. In other words, it is the **unrighteous** who experience the wrath of God.

God's wrath is seen not only in Old Testament passages but also in the New Testament.

> That day is a day of **wrath**, a day of trouble and distress, a day of wasteness and desolation, a day of darkness and gloominess, a day of clouds and thick darkness. A day of the trumpet and alarm against the fenced cities, and against the high towers. And I will bring distress upon men, that they shall walk like blind men, because they have sinned against the Lord: and their blood shall be poured out as dust, and their flesh as the dung. Neither their silver nor their gold shall be able to deliver them in the day of **the Lord's wrath**; but the whole land shall be devoured by the fire of his jealousy: for he shall make even a speedy riddance of all them that dwell in the land. Zephaniah 1:15-18

> Behold, the day of the Lord cometh, cruel both with **wrath** and fierce anger, to lay the land desolate: and he shall destroy the sinners thereof out of it. For the stars of heaven and the constellations thereof shall not give their light: the sun shall be darkened in his going forth, and the moon shall not cause her light to shine. And I will punish the world for their evil, and the wicked for their iniquity; and I will cause the arrogancy of the proud to cease, and will lay low the haughtiness of the terrible. Isaiah 13:9-11

> For the **wrath of God** is revealed from heaven against all ungodliness and unrighteousness of men, who hold the truth in unrighteousness; Romans 1:18

> For which things' sake the **wrath of God** cometh on the children of disobedience: Colossians 3:6

> And the kings of the earth, and the great men, and the rich men, and the chief captains, and the mighty men, and every bondman, and every free man, hid themselves in the dens and in the rocks of the mountains; And said to the mountains and rocks, Fall on us, and hide us from the face of him that sitteth on the throne, and from the **wrath of the Lamb**. For the great day of his wrath is come; and who shall be able to stand? Revelation 6:15-17

It is clear in scripture that God's wrath is reserved for the unrighteous, whereas tribulation is directed towards the righteous. Obviously, no one would want to be the object of God's wrath which would most certainly lead to destruction, and assuredly as His child, this could never happen. But to escape His wrath, one must be willing to endure His discipline through tribulation. Consequently, if Christians do not endure the wrath of God, they will have to be raptured prior to that wrath. In fact, the Lord Jesus Christ has, in essence through His resurrection, *already* delivered each Christian from the wrath to come!

> And to wait for his Son from heaven, whom he raised from the dead, even Jesus, which delivered us from the wrath to come. 1 Thessalonians 1:10

This verse does not say "will deliver". It says "delivered", which is past tense. The Bible states plainly what "the wrath to come" means. The wrath of God is directed toward those who refuse to repent and receive His mercy: the children of disobedience. The wrath of God is His punishment on **unbelievers**.

Although the righteous do not endure God's wrath, they do need to be prepared to go through tribulation. If they are not prepared to go through tribulation, then they run the risk of being deceived by Satan during this period. Christians need to understand and keep the difference between tribulation and wrath in their hearts and minds, so they will not be deceived in the end times. Often when one goes through tribulation, there is a tendency to blame God for those trials and turn away from Him. Turning from the Lord Jesus Christ, called the "apostasy" in the Bible, can lead to being spiritually set up to look for another Christ, a False Messiah. This is exactly what Satan is using and will use to condition Christians. Satan wants them to embrace a False Christ right now who will permit them to live ungodly in this present and future world but who they believe will still take them to heaven when they die.

If Satan fails to entice the Christian into following a counterfeit Christ now, he does not fret. He knows that most Christians have been thoroughly prepared to look for "another Christ" during the end times due to their belief in the false doctrine that the tribulation and the wrath of God are the same thing. As a result, they expect to be raptured prior to the beginning of the last seven years. So, when tribulation does come, they will look for a Messiah who will rescue them. But for many this will turn out to be a False Messiah, someone opposed to Christ called the Antichrist.

Carefully studying the difference between tribulation and wrath will prevent those undergoing tribulation from the spiritual fall for which the Antichrist's followers are hoping and planning. And although Christians are destined to undergo the Tribulation before being raptured, God promises to keep them from evil and to protect them during that period of trial. The Lord Jesus prayed to the Father:

> I pray not that thou shouldest take them out of the world, but that thou shouldest **keep them from the evil**. They are not of the world, even as I am not of the world. Sanctify them through thy truth: thy word is truth. John 17:15-17

God is quite able fulfill this promise to keep us from the evil during tribulation. But this promise is conditional. The condition or requirement to being protected in the times to come is being "not of the world" even as Jesus is not of the world. And the promise (if this condition is met) is "I pray not that thou shouldest take them out of the world, but that thou shouldest keep them from the evil."

In conclusion, for ease of understanding, whenever the term *the Tribulation* is used, it will be assumed to include the entire seven years of the 70th Week of Daniel. However, "the **Great** Tribulation" and the wrath of God do not begin until the second half of Daniel's 70th week. And as shown, the Church, made up of the righteous Christians, will experience the tribulation during these end times but not God's wrath.

Why Is There the Tribulation?

The Great Tribulation, a period that is also called Jacob's trouble, occurs during the last half of the 70th week of Daniel. It largely applies to Israel, but the whole world will learn lessons from it. And because of these lessons and trials, people all over the world will put their faith in Jesus Christ during these final years. However, its purposes are multifold. First, it will complete the punishment that God promised Israel and the Jews for their unbelief over the centuries, and especially for their rejection of the Messiah at His first coming. Through this discipline, it will also create a desire for the one true Messiah, and specifically push Israel to call upon the name of the Lord and plead for the return of Jesus.

> And it shall come to pass in that day, that I will seek to destroy all the nations that come against Jerusalem. And I will pour upon the house of David, and upon the inhabitants of Jerusalem, the spirit of grace and of supplications: and they shall look upon me whom they have pierced, and **they shall mourn for him**, as one mourneth for his only son, and shall be in bitterness for him, as one that is in bitterness for his firstborn. In that day shall there be a great mourning in Jerusalem, as the mourning of Hadadrimmon in the valley of Megiddon. And the land shall mourn, every family apart; the

family of the house of David apart, and their wives apart; the family of the house of Nathan apart, and their wives apart; The family of the house of Levi apart, and their wives apart; the family of Shimei apart, and their wives apart; All the families that remain, every family apart, and their wives apart. In that day there shall be a fountain opened to the house of David and to the inhabitants of Jerusalem for sin and for uncleanness. And it shall come to pass in that day, saith the LORD of hosts, that I will cut off the names of the idols out of the land, and they shall no more be remembered: and also I will cause the prophets and the unclean spirit to pass out of the land. Zechariah 12:9-13:2

The Tribulation will also bring an end to the "Times of the Gentiles" and deliver the Jewish people from Gentile domination (which will be explained in a later chapter entitled "Christians, Jews, and Gentiles"). It will cleanse the earth of wickedness, and prepare for the return of the Messiah and the Millennial Kingdom.

How Is the Tribulation Accomplished?[2]

In the book of Revelation chapters 4-5, these purposes of God's wrath and judgment are described being accomplished **legally** in a court room setting. The Great Tribulation will include God's judgment on Israel and the nations of the world. But as noted earlier, before He pronounces judgment, God always provides warnings. Before the Flood, He warned people for over 100 years. Before He destroyed Jerusalem and the Temple, He sent His prophets. And before the legal trial begins, He sends His warning in seven letters to the seven churches in Revelation 2-3. As will be seen in later chapters, these letters serve as a warning of God's coming wrath, not only to the churches that were present during the time that John wrote them but also to the Church in the end times. These letters function not only as a warning but as evidence of God's coming justified wrath. The seven seals of

Revelation 6-8 are then opened one by one announcing God's coming judgment.

R. Dean Davis in his dissertation *The Heavenly Court Scene of Revelation 4-5* outlines this legal interpretation for Revelation's judgements.[2] Revelation 4 sets the scene where the high court convenes. Similar court room settings found in other Bible passages demonstrate where and how God has passed judgment. For example, one place in scripture where God is seen passing judgment concerns Ahab. In this account, Ahab, king of Israel, was deciding with Jehoshaphat, the king of Judah, whether to attack the king of Assyria. Although many of the prophets promised victory in battle, they called one more prophet, Micaiah, who warned of defeat and the death of Ahab. 1Kings relates his vision of a heavenly court scene.

> And he said, Hear thou therefore the word of the Lord: I saw **the Lord sitting on his throne, and all the host of heaven standing by him on his right hand and on his left**. And the Lord said, Who shall persuade Ahab, that he may go up and fall at Ramothgilead? And one said on this manner, and another said on that manner. And there came forth a spirit, and stood before the Lord, and said, I will persuade him. And the Lord said unto him, Wherewith? And he said, I will go forth, and I will be a lying spirit in the mouth of all his prophets. And he said, Thou shalt persuade him, and prevail also: go forth, and do so. 1 Kings 22:19-22

Micaiah saw God sitting on His throne of judgment with Micaiah as a human witness and the "host of heaven" as heavenly witnesses. The defendant was Ahab, and the purpose of the court was to pass judgment on Ahab and to accomplish his sentencing of destruction. Despite the warnings provided by God, Ahab proceeded to attack the Assyrians and as a result was killed in battle as prophesied by Micaiah.

Another court room scene is seen in Isaiah 6.

In the year that king Uzziah died I saw also **the Lord sitting upon a throne**, high and lifted up, and his train filled the temple. Above it stood the **seraphims**: each one had six wings; with twain he covered his face, and with twain he covered his feet, and with twain he did fly. And one cried unto another, and said, Holy, holy, holy, is the Lord of hosts: the whole earth is full of his glory. And the posts of the door moved at the voice of him that cried, and the house was filled with smoke. Then said I, Woe is me! for I am undone; because I am a man of unclean lips, and I dwell in the midst of a people of unclean lips: for mine eyes have seen the King, the Lord of hosts. Then flew one of the seraphims unto me, having a live coal in his hand, which he had taken with the tongs from off the altar: And he laid it upon my mouth, and said, Lo, this hath touched thy lips; and thine iniquity is taken away, and thy sin purged. Also I heard the voice of the Lord, saying, Whom shall I send, and who will go for us? Then said I, Here am I; send me. And he said, Go, and tell this people, Hear ye indeed, but understand not; and see ye indeed, but perceive not. Make the heart of this people fat, and make their ears heavy, and shut their eyes; lest they see with their eyes, and hear with their ears, and understand with their heart, and convert, and be healed. Then said I, Lord, how long? And he answered, Until the cities be wasted without inhabitant, and the houses without man, and the land be utterly desolate, And the Lord have removed men far away, and there be a great forsaking in the midst of the land. But yet in it shall be a tenth, and it shall return, and shall be eaten: as a teil tree, and as an oak, whose substance is in them, when they cast their leaves: so the holy seed shall be the substance thereof. Isaiah 6:1-13

Again, in this narrative, God was sitting on His throne, this time in the Temple. The human witness at this trial was Isaiah, and the heavenly witnesses were the seraphim. The defendant was Judah who was judged for her iniquity. As with Ahab, Judah failed to observe God's warning and was judged guilty, resulting in the destruction of all of Judah except for a small remnant.

Ezekiel describes one more court room scene in chapters 1-11. God was sitting on His throne, this time in Jerusalem's First Temple. The throne was seen to be mobile. Ezekiel was the human witness, and the heavenly witnesses were four living creatures, later described as cherubim. On trial were Israel and Judah, yet again for their iniquity and abominations that they had committed. Judgment proceeded after the departure of God from the Temple, and all were destroyed except for the righteous who had been marked on their foreheads by a writer with an inkhorn. As demonstrated, God is always just before His punishment by always providing a warning and always sparing the righteous.

Finally, there is a passage in Daniel which is simply an earlier account of the same court room scene that is witnessed by John in Revelation.

> I beheld till the thrones were cast down, and **the Ancient of days did sit**, whose garment was white as snow, and the hair of his head like the pure wool: his throne was like the fiery flame, and his wheels as burning fire. A fiery stream issued and came forth from before him: **thousand thousands ministered unto him, and ten thousand times ten thousand stood before him**: the judgment was set, and **the books were opened**. I beheld then because of the voice of the great words which the horn spake: I beheld even till the beast was slain, and his body destroyed, and given to the burning flame. As concerning the rest of the beasts, they had their dominion taken away: yet their lives were prolonged for a season and time. I saw in the night visions, and, behold, one like the Son of man came with the clouds

of heaven, and came to the Ancient of days, and they brought him near before him. And there was given him dominion, and glory, and a kingdom, that all people, nations, and languages, should serve him: his dominion is an everlasting dominion, which shall not pass away, and his kingdom that which shall not be destroyed. Daniel 7:9-14

In this legal proceeding, the Ancient of Days, i.e., God, is sitting on His throne. Daniel is the human witness with the host of heaven (thousand thousands and ten thousand times ten thousand) acting as heavenly witnesses. As in Revelation, books are opened to determine who has the rightful authority over the earth, the beast or the Son of Man. The beast is slain and everlasting dominion given to the Son.

This same scenario in Daniel is replayed in Revelation 4 and 5.

4 After this I looked, and, behold, a door was opened in heaven: and the first voice which I heard was as it were of a trumpet talking with me; which said, Come up hither, and I will shew thee things which must be hereafter. And immediately I was in the spirit: and, behold, **a throne was set in heaven, and one sat on the throne**. And he that sat was to look upon like a jasper and a sardine stone: and there was a rainbow round about the throne, in sight like unto an emerald. And round about the throne were four and twenty seats: and upon the seats I saw **four and twenty elders** sitting, clothed in white raiment; and they had on their heads crowns of gold. And out of the throne proceeded lightnings and thunderings and voices: and there were seven lamps of fire burning before the throne, which are the seven Spirits of God. And before the throne there was a sea of glass like unto crystal: and in the midst of the throne, and round about the throne, were **four beasts** full of eyes before and behind. And the first

beast was like a lion, and the second beast like a calf, and the third beast had a face as a man, and the fourth beast was like a flying eagle. And the four beasts had each of them six wings about him; and they were full of eyes within: and they rest not day and night, saying, Holy, holy, holy, Lord God Almighty, which was, and is, and is to come. And when those beasts give glory and honour and thanks to him that sat on the throne, who liveth for ever and ever, The four and twenty elders fall down before him that sat on the throne, and worship him that liveth for ever and ever, and cast their crowns before the throne, saying, Thou art worthy, O Lord, to receive glory and honour and power: for thou hast created all things, and for thy pleasure they are and were created.

5 And I saw in the right hand of him that sat on **the throne** a book written within and on the backside, sealed with seven seals. And I saw a strong angel proclaiming with a loud voice, Who is worthy to open the book, and to loose the seals thereof? And no man in heaven, nor in earth, neither under the earth, was able to open the book, neither to look thereon. And I wept much, because no man was found worthy to open and to read the book, neither to look thereon. And one of **the elders** saith unto me, Weep not: behold, the Lion of the tribe of Judah, the Root of David, hath prevailed to open the book, and to loose the seven seals thereof. And I beheld, and, lo, in the midst of the throne and of the **four beasts**, and in the midst of the elders, stood a Lamb as it had been slain, having seven horns and seven eyes, which are the seven Spirits of God sent forth into all the earth. And he came and took the book out of the right hand of him that sat upon the throne. And when he had taken the book, the four beasts and four

and twenty elders fell down before the Lamb, having every one of them harps, and golden vials full of odours, which are the prayers of saints. And they sung a new song, saying, Thou art worthy to take the book, and to open the seals thereof: for thou wast slain, and hast redeemed us to God by thy blood out of every kindred, and tongue, and people, and nation; And hast made us unto our God kings and priests: and we shall reign on the earth. And I beheld, and I heard the voice of **many angels** round about the throne and the beasts and the elders: and the number of them was **ten thousand times ten thousand, and thousands of thousands**; Saying with a loud voice, Worthy is the Lamb that was slain to receive power, and riches, and wisdom, and strength, and honour, and glory, and blessing. And every creature which is in heaven, and on the earth, and under the earth, and such as are in the sea, and all that are in them, heard I saying, Blessing, and honour, and glory, and power, be unto him that sitteth upon the throne, and unto the Lamb for ever and ever. And the four beasts said, Amen. And the four and twenty elders fell down and worshipped him that liveth for ever and ever.

This time John is the human witness, but once again the Ancient of Days is seen sitting on His throne in heaven. The heavenly witnesses include four living creatures, twenty-four elders, and many angels (ten thousand times ten thousand and thousands of thousands). The rest of Revelation describes the legal proceedings to judge the unrighteous angels and people, while rewarding Jesus and the righteous. But before the sentence (seen in the trumpet and bowl judgments) is handed out, the seals are opened to reveal the contents of the scroll.

Some have described this scroll as a legal document, either a will or a real estate contract or even a marriage contract, brought before the court. Each of these have some validity. With Jesus' death on the cross, the scroll may represent his will, with a rightful and legal claim to His earthly kingdom. A real estate contract would give him legal ownership to the world and its kingdoms, and a marriage contract could demonstrate his renewed marriage covenant with Israel.

However, another way to interpret the scroll is to see it as legal evidence of man's iniquity, justifying and warning of God's coming wrath. The evidence increases as each seal is opened. The first seal demonstrates man's deception, and then, as the next seals are opened, man's proclivity for war, famine, death and killing the righteous is established. Whether the seals are seen as a legal document or as evidence against mankind, they demonstrate God's righteous and just judgment that is coming.

So, God's wrath, demonstrated in the trumpet and bowl judgments of Revelation, approaches.

> For the great day of his wrath is come; and who shall be
> able to stand? Revelation 6:17

Notably, in Revelation, there are 144,000 righteous who have been marked with the seal of the living God and are able to stand before the throne of God.

> And I saw another angel ascending from the east,
> **having the seal of the living God**: and he cried with a
> loud voice to the four angels, to whom it was given to
> hurt the earth and the sea, Saying, Hurt not the earth,
> neither the sea, nor the trees, till we have sealed the
> servants of our God in their foreheads. And I heard
> the number of them which were sealed: and there were
> sealed an hundred and forty and four thousand of all the
> tribes of the children of Israel. Revelation 7:2-4

> And I looked, and, lo, a Lamb stood on the mount Sion,
> and with him **an hundred forty and four thousand,**
> **having his Father's name written in their foreheads.**
> And I heard a voice from heaven, as the voice of many

waters, and as the voice of a great thunder: and I heard the voice of harpers harping with their harps: And they sung as it were a new song before the throne, and before the four beasts, and the elders: and no man could learn that song but the hundred and forty and four thousand, which were redeemed from the earth. These are they which were not defiled with women; for they are virgins. These are they which follow the Lamb whithersoever he goeth. These were redeemed from among men, being the firstfruits unto God and to the Lamb. And in their mouth was found no guile: for they are without fault before the throne of God. Revelation 14:1-5

This sealing of the 144,000 righteous with the "Father's name written in their forehead" in Revelation resembles the mark placed on the righteous in Ezekiel's court room (Eze 9:3-4). This "sealing" in Revelation like Ezekiel, helps confirm that this is a court room setting where God is justly pronouncing judgment on the wicked but sparing the righteous. (More about this 144,000 who are sealed will be discussed in the chapter on the "Christians, Jews and Gentiles.")

Finally, the court room setting ends with the opening of the seventh seal. With this seal there is a celestial silence that anticipates and precedes God's coming judgment.

And when he had opened the seventh seal, there was **silence in heaven** about the space of half an hour. Revelation 8:1

This silence is connected with the judgment that accompanies the coming of the "one like a son of man". In the context of the sixth seal, and the sequence of events that are about to occur, the silence in heaven must be imagery used for the divine wrath. In the Old Testament this same silence occurred when Yahweh in his temple was about to bring His judgments on the wicked.

Keep silence before me, O islands; and let the people renew their strength: let them come near; then let them speak: let us come near together to judgment. Isaiah 41:1

But the LORD is in his holy temple: let all the earth keep silence before him. Habakkuk 2:20

Be silent, O all flesh, before the LORD: for he is raised up out of his holy habitation. Zechariah 2:13

It is **only** after the evidence has been presented and warnings have been given that God, in His righteousness and holiness, sends judgment. This judgment is about to be displayed initially in the trumpet judgments, directed towards Israel, and the bowl judgments, directed toward the nations. The trial is now complete, and as the verdict is pronounced, there is an all-inclusive, reverential silence in heaven at what is about to unfold. Heaven together holds its breath at the seventh and final seal in anticipation of the imminent wrath of God.[2]

Now with a better understanding of what this seven-year period is and why it is necessary, a timeline of it and the various events happening within that framework will be presented. To reiterate and reemphasize, this is only one theory. One should not be too dogmatic with this subject, but a case will be made that this could be a timeline for the last seven years, Daniel's 70th Week. But as many say, "Time will tell."

CHAPTER 2

The Timeline

C hronology is the arrangement of events in the order of their occurrence. That is one of the primary objectives here- to present a possible timeline, ordering the events of the last seven years of the end times and then setting some possible dates for these events. This will include the timing for the beginning and end of Daniel's 70th Week, as well as notable events and people that occur during these final seven years. But before exploring any specific dates, the number "seven" is shown repeatedly to be of importance in Biblical time cycles. So, where does the number "seven" occur in Bible chronology? How is that important when it comes to eschatological timing? And finally, how does that relate to "the last **seven** years"?

A Seven Day Week[1]

Although a number of different systems over the course of history have been used to measure length and weight, the measurement of time has been far more uniform and standardized around the world. Historically, the large units of time were measured by movement of the earth in relation to the sun, moon, and stars. For example, the year is the time it takes for the earth to complete one full orbit around the sun. Then, there's the month which is based on how long it takes the moon to orbit the earth. And there's the day, which is the time it takes for the earth to rotate once on its own axis. The day is subdivided into twenty-four hours, an hour into sixty minutes, and finally a minute into sixty seconds. So, all of the major time measurements are related to the movement of the heavenly bodies, that is, all of them with one exception- the week.

The week is unique in that it is the only major time unit that is not connected to the movement of the heavenly bodies. Some may casually assume that the week is a division of the moon cycle. However, the lunar cycle is not a twenty-eight-day cycle, but approximately twenty-nine days, twelve hours, forty-four minutes and three seconds. Put in the decimal it is 29.5306 days, which cannot be divided evenly. The week is a period of exactly seven days, a unit of time that has no astronomical basis whatever. In fact, there are no known external rhythms in nature that could explain the near universal existence of a seven-day week. And yet, humans order their lives in a seven-day cycle.

How did this seven-day cycle become so popular, so universal, and come to occupy such an important place in the minds and calendars of people? How did it become such an important rhythm in human life? Where did it originate?

The origin of the week has long baffled anthropologists and scholars of ancient history, but now amazing new discoveries in the scientific world are shedding light on this mystery. The relatively new science of chronobiology has uncovered some totally unexpected facts about living things. Chronobiology is a field of biology that studies how our body's natural cycles (mental, physical, and emotional) are affected by solar and lunar rhythms.

It has been known for a long time that our bodies operate on a circadian or daily rhythm, as well as monthly and annual rhythms. But chronobiologists have only recently discovered seven-day cycles written into the very building blocks of plants and animals. And what is especially interesting is that this seven-day cycle is the central rhythm by which all other circadian rhythms in the body are tuned or orchestrated. For example, a normal menstrual cycle is twenty-eight days, and in fact, other body functions such as blood pressure, hormones, immune responses, and even mood operate on a seven-day cycle. The seven-day weekly cycle is embedded into genes.

But it is not only written into the biology of humans. The seven-day cycle is also found throughout nature in other animals, plants, and insects. Experiments conducted by leading scientists prove that seven-day cycles govern fundamental aspects in the lives of flies, rats, bees, and even primitive algae. In fact, the first genes that regulate biological rhythms, called "clock" genes, were discovered in the fruit fly. So, amazing as it may seem, it appears nearly everything was created with a seven-day biorhythmic cycle built into it, from complex humans down to simple bacteria and one-celled organisms. Science proves that the seven-day weekly cycle is etched deeply into our DNA and life on planet earth.

What explains these biological seven-day cycles or weekly rhythms? Simply this: the seven-day week was established by God Himself right back at the creation of the world, and that seven-day cycle was etched into mankind's DNA by God way back then. There God created everything in the world in six days and then rested on the seventh. This provided the model for cultures, societies, and civilizations all around the world. Here is what it says in Genesis:

> In the beginning God created the heaven and the earth... Thus the heavens and the earth were finished, and all the host of them. And on the seventh day God ended his work which he had made; and he rested on the seventh day from all his work which he had made. And God blessed the seventh day, and sanctified it: because that in it he had rested from all his work which God created and made. Genesis 1:1; 2:1-3

By the seventh day, God had finished the work that He had been doing. So, on the seventh day He rested from all His work. Then, God blessed the seventh day and made it holy, because on it He rested from all the work of creating that He had done. God makes it clear and simple. He is the one who created the seven-day cycle when He made the world, and He established it in the created order.

It is the cycle that humans were designed to function best on- work the first six days of the week and rest on the seventh. God placed the seven-day cycle in His creation, and that is the rhythm best for it. And to help man remember that, God placed this formula for optimum living right into the heart of the Ten Commandments, the ten principles He gave man to live by.

> Remember the sabbath day, to keep it holy. Six days shalt thou labour, and do all thy work: But the seventh day is the sabbath of the Lord thy God: in it thou shalt not do any work, thou, nor thy son, nor thy daughter, thy manservant, nor thy maidservant, nor thy cattle, nor thy stranger that is within thy gates: For in six days the Lord made heaven and earth, the sea, and all that in them is, and rested the seventh day: wherefore the Lord blessed the sabbath day, and hallowed it. Exodus 20:8-11

Scientists have noted that rhythm disruption due to circadian misalignment, e.g., shift work, jet lag, and even the daylight-saving time (DST) shift, may contribute to several human diseases including autoimmune diseases such as rheumatoid arthritis and multiple sclerosis.[2] So, God designed man to function best on certain daily patterns and in particular a seven-day cycle. Man is to work on the first six days and rest on the seventh day.

But down through history people have tried to change this God-given cycle. They have tried to break the seven-day pattern and change the length of the week with disastrous results. The French tried to change the seven-day cycle. In 1793 just after the French Revolution, France adopted a ten-day week in an attempt to increase productivity. During these years French society saw a stark increase in injuries, exhaustion, and illness. Work animals collapsed and died at astounding rates.

The Soviet Union and other societies have also tried similar changes to the seven-day weekly cycle, but like the French found that it did not work. They all soon reverted back to the original seven-day God-given model.

Another attempt will be made by the Antichrist in the end times to change God's natural times or seasons.

> And he shall speak great words against the most High, and shall wear out the saints of the most High, and **think to change times** and laws: and they shall be given into his hand until a time and times and the dividing of time. Daniel 7:25

But attempting to operate on a rhythm other than the one man was designed for, results in catastrophic results. Since that very first cycle of seven days, seven has delineated the number of days in a week, surviving throughout human history from Adam until the present.

Sabbatical Year

Two other Biblical time cycles that are important in establishing an end times timeline include the sabbatical year and the Jubilee year. Like the week they do not have an astronomical basis and have their origin in the number "seven".

The Sabbatical year is a group of seven years ending in the seventh or sabbatical year. It is sometimes called in Hebrew the *shmita*, meaning the "year of release". Just as the first five books of the Old Testament, the Torah, calls for Jews to work six days and rest on the seventh, it also calls for them to work the land six years and then to let it rest in the seventh year. This is where the term *sabbatical leave* in colleges and universities comes from, referring to a release from normal teaching duties granted to a professor for study or travel. The first reference about the sabbath year in the Bible occurs in Exodus:

> And six years thou shalt sow thy land, and shalt gather
> in the fruits thereof: But the **seventh** year thou shalt let
> it rest and lie still; that the poor of thy people may eat;
> and what they leave the beasts of the field shall eat. In
> like manner thou shalt deal with thy vineyard, and with
> thy oliveyard. Exodus 23:10-11

Unlike the weekly sabbath which was established from the beginning for all mankind, the sabbatical year and, as well as the jubilee year, were designated only for the Jews and were restricted to the land of Israel. This was God's commandment only to the Jews who were "released" from slavery in the land of Egypt.

Daniel's 70th Week involves a period of seven years (a week of years), and it seems likely that this is a sabbatical cycle with the last year corresponding to a sabbatical year on the proposed timeline.

Jubilee

The Jubilee year is the year at the end of seven cycles of *shmita* or sabbatical years. Since a sabbatical year is seven years, then seven sabbatical cycles are forty-nine years (seven times seven), and the next year is the fiftieth. Every fifty years, the Jews were to observe a Year of Jubilee. At that time, at least three things happened: (1) land was returned to its original owner, (2) slaves were freed, and (3) debts were cancelled. The Year of Jubilee represents restoration, freedom and renewal. It begins every fiftieth year on Yom Kippur, the 10th day of Tishri, which is the Day of Atonement.

> And thou shalt number seven sabbaths of years unto
> thee, seven times seven years; and the space of the seven
> sabbaths of years shall be unto thee forty and nine years.
> Then shalt thou cause the trumpet of the jubile to sound
> on the tenth day of the seventh month, in the day of
> atonement shall ye make the trumpet sound throughout
> all your land. And ye shall hallow the fiftieth year, and

proclaim liberty throughout all the land unto all the inhabitants thereof: it shall be a jubilee unto you; and ye shall return every man unto his possession an ye shall return every man unto his family. A jubilee shall that fiftieth year be unto you: ye shall not sow, neither reap that which growth of itself in it, nor gather the grapes in of thy vine undressed. For it is the jubilee; it shall be holy unto you: ye shall eat the increase thereof out of the field. In the year of the jubilee ye shall return every man unto possession. Leviticus 25:8-13

The Year of Jubilee with its accompanying redemption, therefore, has some interesting parallels with Bible prophecy and specifically Daniel's 70th Week. It is the time when the Earth itself will be returned to its rightful owner (Christ) and the land of Israel returned to the Jews, when slaves to sin (i.e., humans) are freed from their bondage, and when all debts are wiped out (and things start out new).

There is disagreement on whether the Jubilee cycle is a fifty-year period where the Jubilee year is added onto a forty-nine-year cycle (seven sabbatical cycles) or whether it is a forty-nine-year period where the Jubilee year is simply the first year of the next sabbatical cycle. Bible scholars, both Jewish and Christian, make cases for each position.

Another calendar that will be discussed shortly is the Millennial calendar of one thousand years. It is impossible to reconcile a Jubilee calendar of forty-nine years with a Millennial calendar of one thousand years, whereas, a Jubilee cycle of fifty years does divide evenly into a thousand-year Millennial calendar. Hence, for the purposes of this discussion and the timeline outlined here, it will be assumed that a Jubilee cycle is a period of fifty repeating years.

As will be seen, this is important when discussing the 70th week of Daniel. If a forty-nine-year Jubilee cycle is used, then seventy weeks of years would equal 490 years (70 x 7 = 490). However, in a fifty-year Jubilee cycle, an additional ten years would need to be added to account for the Jubilee years that occur after each forty-nine-year period. This would then mean that the seventy weeks of Daniel's prophecy is actually a total of five hundred years (490 + 10 = 500), not simply 490 years.

In either case, the Jubilee year was designed to give stability to the land by restoring the property to its original owner during that period. This may have implications regarding the last seven years where the events are primarily focused on the Jews and the land of Israel. As in the Jubilee year when the land was redeemed and restored to its original owner, the Jews and the land of Israel will be fully redeemed and restored to fellowship with God at the end of Daniel's 70th Week. Consequently, it would be logical to again conclude that God would design the last seven years to be a sabbatical set of years which is then followed by a Jubilee year at the start of the Millennium.

Daniel and the Last Seven Years

The prophecies of the Bible help to reveal God's grand design and His timeline. None do this more than the prophet Daniel who first introduced the concept of the last seven years in his Seventy Weeks prophecy.

> 24 **Seventy weeks** are determined upon thy people and upon thy holy city, to finish the transgression, and to make an end of sins, and to make reconciliation for iniquity, and to bring in everlasting righteousness, and to seal up the vision and prophecy, and to anoint the most Holy. 25 Know therefore and understand, that from the going forth of the commandment to restore and to build Jerusalem unto the Messiah the Prince shall be **seven weeks**, and **threescore and two weeks**: the street shall be built again, and the wall, even in troublous times. 26 And after threescore and two weeks shall Messiah be cut off, but not for himself: and the people of the prince that shall come shall destroy the city and the sanctuary; and the end thereof shall be with a flood and unto the end of the war desolations are determined. 27 And he

shall confirm the covenant with many for **one week**: and in the midst of the week he shall cause the sacrifice and the oblation to cease, and for the overspreading of abominations he shall make it desolate, even until the consummation, and that determined shall be poured upon the desolate. Daniel 9:24-27

The prophecy concerns a total of seventy weeks divided into three parts: seven weeks, sixty-two weeks, and a final one week. The word translated as *week* is the Hebrew word *sabua* which simply means "a group of seven". It could mean seven oranges or seven apples or seven anything. In this case, scholars have determined that a "week" equates to a group of seven years. This is concluded since the passage states that there is a total of sixty-nine (seven plus sixty-two) "weeks" from the commandment to rebuild Jerusalem (Cyrus' command in Ezra 1:2-4) until the Messiah is cut off (Jesus' crucifixion). It is known that this stretch of time was about five hundred years, and five hundred years divided by sixty-nine is approximately seven years. Therefore, the sixty-nine "weeks" must be "weeks of years" or groups of seven years. This leaves one group of seven years that has not yet been fulfilled, the final seven years or what is called Daniel's 70th Week.

There is a gap between the first sixty-nine weeks and that last week of seven years. In Scripture, there is evidence of a gap of several years between the start of a prophecy being fulfilled, and its ultimate fulfillment. Scriptural support for a gap between Jesus' first and second advent is found in verses such as the following.

The Spirit of the Sovereign LORD is on me, because the LORD has anointed me to preach good news to the poor. He has sent me to bind up the brokenhearted, to proclaim freedom for the captives and release from darkness for the prisoners, to proclaim the year of the LORD'S favor and the day of vengeance of our God ... Isaiah 61:1-2

For to us a child is born, to us a son is given, and the government will be on his shoulders. And he will be called Wonderful Counselor, Mighty God, Everlasting Father, Prince of Peace. Of the greatness of his government and peace there will be no end. He will reign on David's throne and over his kingdom, establishing and upholding it with justice and righteousness from that time on and forever. The zeal of the LORD Almighty will accomplish this. Isaiah 9:6-7

You will conceive and give birth to a son, and you are to call him Jesus. He will be great and will be called the Son of the Most High. The Lord God will give him the throne of his father David, and he will reign over Jacob's descendants forever; his kingdom will never end." Luke 1:31-33

She gave birth to a son, a male child, who will rule all the nations with an iron scepter. And her child was snatched up to God and to his throne. Revelation 12:5

They will fall by the sword and will be taken as prisoners to all the nations. Jerusalem will be trampled on by the Gentiles until the times of the Gentiles are fulfilled. Luke 21:24

The implication of these scriptures is that Jesus Christ's First Coming is separated from his Second Coming by an unspecified amount of time; but, after Christ's Second Coming He will be accepted as ruler and king—and He will rule forever.[3]

There is other evidence that there is a gap between the sixty-ninth and seventieth weeks. First, Daniel 9:26 itself states that the last week begins sometime "after" the sixty-nine weeks. Of course, it does not state how long after, i.e., whether it begins immediately or there is a gap. But the same verse states that the sanctuary would be destroyed, which occurred in 70 AD when the Jewish Temple was destroyed by the Romans. This happened forty years after Jesus' crucifixion. So, this did not transpire in a seven-year period immediately following the sixty-nine weeks. Finally, none of the events of Daniel 9:27 (e.g., the confirmation of a covenant) have yet occurred and confirms that there is a gap between the sixty-ninth and seventieth weeks. Hence, the seventieth week has not yet started and must begin sometime in the future.

Note that this prophecy refers only to Daniel's people, the Jews. The Church is not mentioned in the first sixty-nine weeks, and not even in the seventieth week. The Church fits into the large gap of time between weeks sixty-nine and seventy of Daniel's prophecy of the seventy weeks of years.

The concept of a final week or week of years is thus introduced, and this final week is divided in the middle (Daniel 9:27). Thus, there are two three and a half year periods in the final seven years. This is further substantiated by two separate scriptures in Revelation that describe a time period where the Antichrist is in power for forty-two months during the last part of Daniel's 70th Week. This forty-two-month period equates to three and a half years.

> But the court which is without the temple leave out, and measure it not; for it is given unto the Gentiles: and the holy city shall they tread under foot **forty and two months**. Revelation 11:2

> And there was given unto him a mouth speaking great things and blasphemies; and power was given unto him to continue **forty and two months**. Revelation 13:5

Furthermore, this last half of the final seven years (or three and a half years) is referred to as a "time, times, and the dividing of time" where a "time" is assumed by most to equal one year, a "times" is equal to two years, and "a dividing of time" or "half a time" is half a year.

Thus "a time and times and the dividing of time" is equal to three and a half years or forty-two months.

> And he shall speak great words against the most High, and shall wear out the saints of the most High, and think to change times and law: and they shall be given into his hand until **a time** *(iddan)* **and times and the dividing of time**. Daniel 7:25

> And one said to the man clothed in linen, which was upon the waters of the river, How long shall it be to the end of these wonders? And I heard the man clothed in linen, which was upon the waters of the river, when he held up his right hand and his left hand unto heaven, and sware by him that liveth for ever that it shall be for **a time** *(moed)***, times, and an half**: and when he shall have accomplished to scatter the power of the holy people, all these things shall be finished. Daniel 12:6-7

> And to the woman were given two wings of a great eagle, that she might fly into the wilderness, into her place, where she is nourished for **a time, and times, and half a time**, from the face of the serpent. Revelation 12:14

So, this last half of Daniel's 70th Week, which lasts forty-two months, is further divided into three parts: (1) a one-year period, (2) followed by a two-year period, and (3) finally a half year period. Daniel used different Hebrew words to define *time*, and in Daniel 7:25 he employed the word *iddan* which means "a set time or **a year**". However, in Daniel 12:6-7 the word *moed* was used and indicates "an appointed or fixed time". It is the word used when referring to Jewish Festivals.

Unlike our current Gregorian calendar which is a solar calendar, the Jewish calendar was a lunar calendar based on a monthly cycle. In addition, there were two separate Jewish calendars, a **civil** calendar which began on Tishri 1 (the Jewish festival of Rosh Hashanah which usually occurs in September or October) and a **sacred** calendar which began six months later in the month of Nisan with Passover on Nisan 14 (usually in March or April). By using two separate words for "time" Daniel is providing further information to explain that not only does a "time" last for one year but that it extends from one Jewish feast day until the same feast day one year later. But which feast day might that be?

The two most likely candidates are Rosh Hashanah and Passover. Daniel's use of the word *moed* indicates that the start of the last three and a half period, the middle of the final seven years, is linked to the sacred or festival calendar which again begins on Passover. And if the middle of the 70th Week of Daniel is indeed Passover, then the beginning and end of the final seven years would occur on Rosh Hashanah. The traditional day of creation is Rosh Hashanah, and that day, the start of the civil calendar, would be a likely match for the start of the final seven years. In this scenario, the first "time" beginning in the middle of the seven years would extend from one Passover to the next Passover. The following "times" would last for two years and again end on a Passover. Finally, the last "half a time" would continue from Passover until the following Rosh Hashanah, a period of six months or half a year. This would again conclude the final seven years on Rosh Hashanah.

Timelines in the Bible

Since the final seven years most likely start on Rosh Hashanah, the question is in what year specifically does that Rosh Hashanah start. In other words, when does the 70th Week of Daniel begin? There are several paths or timelines in the Bible that can be used to determine a likely date. Those dates are uncovered by Tim Warner in his book *The Time of the End* where he uses four different approaches to arrive at dates for the beginning and end of the 70th Week of Daniel.[4] By providing multiple avenues to arrive at dates, the accuracy of the timeline is increased. For as Paul stated in Corinthians:

> In the mouth of two or more witnesses shall every word
> be established. 2 Corinthians 13:1

The first timeline is the millennial timeline. A millennium is a thousand years. The early church fathers were chiliasts, another name for millennialists, and they believed that God had set a timeline for the world from the beginning.

> Declaring the end from the beginning, and from ancient times the things that are not yet done, saying, My counsel shall stand, and I will do all my pleasure. Isaiah 46:10

They also alleged that the six days of creation followed by a seventh day of rest were an image of the millennial timeline where there would be six thousand years from creation and then a thousand-year period of rest. This view was supported by verses comparing a day to a thousand years.

> For a thousand years in Your sight are like yesterday when it is past, And like a watch in the night. Ps 90:4

> But, beloved, do not forget this one thing, that with the Lord one day is as a thousand years, and a thousand years as one day. 2 Peter 3:8

More recently dispensationalists have made reference to a young earth model, with the Flood of Noah occurring around 2345 BC. Their Septa-Millennial Theory is a similar partitioning of the Biblical timeline, referring to the existence of seven blocks of one thousand years of time. In other words, it also represents a "one thousand years per day" view of history.

But, identifying the end of the six thousand years and the beginning of the Millennium requires knowing the year for the beginning of creation. Controversy has surrounded this topic, and many different Biblical chronologists have arrived at different conclusions as to the date of creation. Tim Warner in his book *The Time of the End* uses only Biblical data to arrive at a date, arguing that secular dating methods are inaccurate and flawed. A summary of his creation timeline, which again uses only scripture, is included in Appendix B. Using this creation timeline, along with the timeline for the genealogy from Adam to Abraham given in Appendix A, the date 3964 BC is calculated for the beginning of creation. This corresponds closely to many timelines that arrive at about 4000 BC for creation such as the year 4004 BC that was proposed by the well-known chronologist James Ussher.

Using 3964 BC as the date for creation and adding 6000 years arrives at the year 2036 AD as the start of the Millennium and the end of the 70th Week of Daniel. Although many would dispute this date, it nevertheless indicates that the end times could be fast approaching and the end of the first 6000 years is close.

The second method uses what is called the "Jubilee Calendar" to aid in identifying when the last seven years will start. As noted earlier, one of the earliest ways that the Bible broke up time was into fifty-year blocks of time called the Jubilee cycle. The Millennium also most likely begins with a year of Jubilee. Knowing in what year a previous Jubilee occurred would give the ability to date past as well as future Jubilee years. Unfortunately, there are no clear records of Israel keeping the Jubilee to help accurately determine other Jubilee years. However, scripture, as well as historical evidence, provides some useful clues. Beginning with Genesis:

> And the LORD said, "My Spirit shall not strive with man forever, for he is indeed flesh; yet his days shall be one hundred and twenty years." Genesis 6:3

The word for *years* in Hebrew is *saneh* which is simply a revolution or period of time. If that period of time in this Genesis passage is fifty years (and not one year as is commonly assumed), then one hundred and twenty periods of time would equal 6000 years (one hundred and twenty times fifty years). The next Jubilee will be the 40th Jubilee since the birth of Christ. If the calendar is rolled back to the time of Adam and Eve (circa 3964 BC), that would indicate the next Jubilee and the start of the Millennium would be the 120th in human history. It would also possibly be the 70th Jubilee since Moses received the Law in approximately 1464 BC or about 3484 years ago. This corresponds perfectly with the millennial timeline and again would result in the year 2036 AD at the beginning of the thousand-year Millennial jubilee.

One of the most cited indications for a recorded jubilee year occurs in Isaiah:

> And this shall be a sign unto thee, You shall eat this year such as groweth of itself; and the second year what springeth of the same: and in the third year sow ye, and reap, and plant vineyards, and eat the fruit thereof. And the remnant that is escaped of the house of Judah shall again take root downward, and bear fruit upward. For out of Jerusalem shall go forth a remnant, and they that escape out of Mount Zion: the zeal of the LORD of hosts shall do this. Isaiah 37:30-32

This was a message from Isaiah to King Hezekiah during the fifteenth and sixteenth year of his reign. The message stated that the Lord would answer Hezekiah's prayer when the kingdom of Judah was confronted with an invasion by the Assyrians. The answer to his prayer was nothing less than a promise from the Lord that He would feed the people of Judah for two years with whatever crops that grew all by themselves with no cultivation. It was essentially a proclamation of a Sabbath year followed by a Jubilee year, one right after the other. The difficulty occurs with dating exactly the fifteenth and sixteenth years of Hezekiah's reign. Using the creation timeline in Appendix B, Hezekiah's Jubilee year would have been in 534 B.C. This again would align with the next Jubilee occurring in 2036.

Another common conjecture as to when a year of jubilee occurred is the year of Jesus' announcement in the synagogue recorded in Luke 4. When Christ read the Isaiah 61 passage, He stopped and put down the scroll just before reading the words: "the day of vengeance of our

God"—implying that that part of the Scripture was still in the future, because it dealt with His Second Coming.

> The Spirit of the Lord God is upon me; because the Lord hath anointed me to preach good tidings unto the meek; he hath sent me to bind up the brokenhearted, to proclaim liberty to the captives, and the opening of the prison to them that are bound; To proclaim the acceptable year of the Lord, and the day of vengeance of our God; to comfort all that mourn; To appoint unto them that mourn in Zion, to give unto them beauty for ashes, the oil of joy for mourning, the garment of praise for the spirit of heaviness; that they might be called trees of righteousness, the planting of the Lord, that he might be glorified. Isaiah 61:1-3

> And he came to Nazareth, where He had been brought up: and, as his custom was, he went into the synagogue on the sabbath day, and stood up for to read. And there was delivered unto him the book of the prophet Isaias. And when He had opened the book, he found the place where it was written: The Spirit of the LORD is upon Me, because He hath anointed me to preach the gospel to the poor; He has sent Me to heal the brokenhearted, to preach deliverance to the captives, and recovering of sight to the blind, to set at liberty them that are bruised, to preach the acceptable year of the LORD. And he closed the book, and he gave it again to the minister, and sat down. And the eyes of all who were in the synagogue were fastened on him. And he began to say unto them, This day is this scripture fulfilled in your ears. Luke 4:16-21

According to Floyd Nolan Jones, this happened in AD 27 and was a Year of Jubilee, beginning on Tishri 10 (the Day of Atonement) on the

Jewish calendar. This would have been on Tuesday, September 28, 27 AD according to the Gregorian calendar and is the date when Christ started his public ministry according to Jones.[3] However, there is no hard evidence that this indeed was a Jubilee year other than assuming that Jesus' announcement concerned the Jubilee year. And if 27 AD was indeed a Jubilee year, it does not fit the timeline presented here. So, although this could relate to the year of jubilee, it cannot be used as conclusive evidence to determine an exact jubilee year.

On an historical note, Jewish sources (for example, Maimonides) state that Jubilees were last observed during the first temple period until the Babylonian exile (circa 586 BC). There is no evidence to suggest, however, that a Year of Jubilee was observed after this time.[3] So, while these scriptural and historical citations are interesting, they are not conclusive in establishing an accurate date for any Jubilee year much less the final Jubilee. Nevertheless, using 3964 BC as the creation year, a list of probable sabbath and jubilee years throughout history is outlined in Appendix C.

The third and fourth methods for determining the time of Christ's return also utilize the millennial and jubilee timeline. However, instead of using the time of creation as a starting point, these approaches use a period beginning during the first century AD. These dates are obviously more historically accurate due to their closer proximity to the present.

The third method's calculation begins dating from the year of Jesus' death and resurrection, which actually the first two methods also require to determine the year of creation. This stresses why it is so important to determine the year of Jesus' death in Bible chronology. Most Bible scholars date Jesus' crucifixion somewhere between AD 30 and 36, with the two most popular dates today being either 30 AD or 33 AD. If Jesus was crucified on April 3, 33 AD, as many assume, then the previous dating timelines as well as the following one are off by at least 3 years. However, for the following reasons, the year of 30 AD will be used and assumed to be the correct year for Jesus' death.

Nisan 10, 30 AD fell on Sunday, April 2, 30 AD, which would have been Palm Sunday. Christ would have died four days later on Nisan 14, 30 AD, which is Thursday, April 6, 30 AD. More specifically, he died at 3 PM, and that is also when the Passover lambs were sacrificed. Friday would have been a special Sabbath (the first day of the Feast of Unleavened Bread) and Saturday would have been a regular Sabbath. If Christ had died on Thursday afternoon and rose on Sunday morning, then he would have been in the grave for 3 days and 3 nights, fulfilling the biographical narrative of the prophet Jonah that Jesus referenced.

> But he answered and said unto them, An evil and adulterous generation seeketh after a sign; and there shall no sign be given to it, but the sign of the prophet Jonas: For as Jonas was three days and three nights in the whale's belly; so shall the Son of man be three days and three nights in the heart of the earth. Matt 12:39-40

Thus, Christ rose from the dead on Sunday, April 9, 30 AD. Obviously, as noted, if this assumption is wrong, then the rest of the dating process will be off by a corresponding number of years.

However, one of the most compelling reasons to use this year of 30 AD is related to the destruction of the Jewish temple which Jesus had predicted would occur within a "generation". In Matthew, Jesus stated:

> And Jesus said unto them, See ye not all these things? Verily I say unto you, There shall not be left here one stone upon another, that shall not be thrown down. Matthew 24:2

And then later in the chapter:

> Verily I say unto you, This generation shall not pass, till all these things be fulfilled. Matthew 24:34

The length of a generation has been debated with various number of years suggested including fifty, seventy, and one hundred. However, the books of Numbers and Hebrews imply that God calls forty years a generation.

And the LORD's anger was kindled against Israel, and he made them wander in the wilderness **forty years**, until all the generation, that had done evil in the sight of the LORD, was consumed. Numbers 32:13

Harden not your hearts, as in the provocation, in the day of temptation in the wilderness: When your fathers tempted me, proved me, and saw my works forty years. Wherefore I was grieved with that generation, and said, They do alway err in their heart; and they have not known my ways. Hebrews 3:8-10

Also, Matthew 1:17 states that from captivity in Babylon (534 BC according to our dating methods in Appendix B) until the birth of Christ is fourteen generations.

So all the generations from Abraham to David are fourteen generations; and from David until the carrying away into Babylon are fourteen generations; and from the carrying away into Babylon unto Christ are fourteen generations. Matthew 1:17

From 534 BC to Christ's birth in 4 BC is 530 years. When this is divided by 13 (the space between 14 generations), it arrives at 40.8 years per generation, which again suggests 40 years as the length of a generation. This is the average length of time from when a man is born until his first son is born, not the average age of a man, which according to Psalms is seventy to eighty years (Psalms 90:10). Since 70 AD was the year for destruction of the Temple, then forty years or one generation before this would have been 30 AD.

Non-scriptural support for a forty-year generation from Jesus' crucifixion until the destruction of the Temple occurs in the Jewish writings at that time. In the centuries following the destruction of the Temple in Jerusalem (70 AD), the Jewish people began writing two versions of Jewish thought, religious history and commentary. One was written in Palestine and became known as the Jerusalem Talmud. The other was written in Babylon and was known as the Babylonian Talmud. We read in the Jerusalem Talmud:

> Forty years before the destruction of the Temple, the western light went out, the crimson thread remained crimson, and the lot for the Lord always came up in the left hand. They would close the gates of the Temple by night and get up in the morning and find them wide open (Jacob Neusner, The Yerushalmi, p.156-157). [the Temple was destroyed in 70 CE]

A similar passage in the Babylonian Talmud states:

> Our rabbis taught: During the last forty years before the destruction of the Temple the lot ['For the Lord'] did not come up in the right hand; nor did the crimson-colored strap become white; nor did the western most light shine; and the doors of the Hekel [Temple] would open by themselves (Soncino version, Yoma 39b).

These writings stated that certain bad events began occurring regularly at the Temple forty years before its destruction and continued for the entire forty years between 30 AD and 70 AD. Since both Talmuds recount the same information, this indicates the knowledge of these events was accepted by the widespread Jewish community.[3] And since these things began to occur from the time Jesus was crucified, then 30 AD, i.e., forty years before the Temple destruction in 70 AD, is the most likely date for Jesus' crucifixion.

A number of other historical factors help to pinpoint the year of the death of Jesus. It is calculated that John the Baptist commenced his ministry c. AD 26, based on the historical note in the Book of Luke that John started preaching in the fifteenth year of Tiberius' reign.

> Now in the fifteenth year of the reign of Tiberius
> Caesar, Pontius Pilate being governor of Judaea, and
> Herod being tetrarch of Galilee, and his brother Philip
> tetrarch of Ituraea and of the region of Trachonitis, and
> Lysanias the tetrarch of Abilene, Luke 3:1

Tiberius was named emperor in AD 14, but he actually started reigning two years prior to that, AD 12, as co-regent with Augustus Caesar. Using the earlier date shows that John's ministry began c. AD 26–27. Jesus probably began His ministry soon after John began his and ministered for the next three and a half years, approximately. So, the end of Jesus' ministry would have been c. AD 29–30.

Pontius Pilate is known to have ruled Judea from AD 26–36. The crucifixion took place during a Passover (Mark 14:12) and that fact, plus astronomical data (the Jewish calendar was lunar-based), narrows the field again to two popular dates—April 7, AD 30, and April 3, AD 33. There are scholarly arguments supporting both dates; the later date (AD 33) would require Jesus to have had a longer ministry and to have begun it later. The earlier date (AD 30) would seem more in keeping with what can be deduced about the start of Jesus' ministry from Luke 3:1.

The importance of establishing the date of Jesus' crucifixion cannot be over emphasized. It is this date that is used to determine the year of creation and is fundamental in that calculation. So, that date is vital in both the Millennial and Jubilee timelines as well as this third timeline. Any error in the year of Christ's death and resurrection would necessarily create an error in these timelines.

But, assuming that the year 30 AD is correct for Christ's resurrection and applying it to the prophet Hosea's words, provides more confirmation and another time marker for the beginning of Daniel's 70th Week. Hosea states:

> After two days He will revive us; On the third day
> He will raise us up, That we may live in His sight.
> Hosea 6:2

Many Bible scholars conclude that the "two days" refers to a two millennia gap from Jesus' death to the start of the 70th Week, since "one day is with the Lord as a thousand years, and a thousand years as one day." (2 Peter 3:8) Two thousand years added to 30 AD arrives at the year 2030 AD which would be the year for the beginning of Daniel's 70th Week, the restart of God's prophetic timeline for the Jews.

There are other allusions in scripture that some have used to support a two-thousand-year gap between the two advents of Jesus. For example, Jesus stayed with the Samaritan woman, who was a prophetic type of the Church, for two days.

> So when the Samaritans were come unto him, they besought him that he would tarry with them: and he abode there two days. John 4:40

Also, Jesus deliberately remained two days before crossing the Jordan to raise Lazarus.

> When he had heard therefore that he was sick, he abode two days still in the same place where he was. John 11:6

Crossing the Jordan into Israel is a prophetic type of the Second Coming. And finally, the Good Samaritan, a prophetic type of Christ, gave the innkeeper two denarii to care for the wounded man, promising to return and settle the account. Two denarii equaled two day's wages or two day's stay at an inn and may be a prophetic type of the two "days" that would pass until the Lord returns.

The fourth and final method for establishing the timing of the 70th week of Daniel utilizes the date of the destruction of the **second** Jewish Temple. This year, as agreed by most historians, was almost certainly 70 AD and probably more specifically August 29, 70 AD as recorded by the notable Jewish historian Josephus.

But to understand the importance of this date requires examining the destruction of the **first** Jewish Temple. At that time, the Jews were exiled for seventy years, unable to perform their required daily sacrifices in Jerusalem. In Leviticus God had warned the Jews that:

> And after all this, if you do not obey Me, then I will punish you **seven times more** for your sins. Lev 26:18

This warning is repeated three more times in Leviticus 26. The question is "seven times" what. A logical conclusion is that it would be seven times the original punishment of seventy years as recorded in Jeremiah 25:

> And this whole land shall be a desolation, and an astonishment; and these nations shall serve the king of Babylon **seventy years**. And it shall come to pass, when seventy years are accomplished, that I will punish the king of Babylon, and that nation, saith the LORD, for their iniquity, and the land of the Chaldeans, and will make it perpetual desolations. Jeremiah 25:11-12

So, seven times seventy results in 490 years. However, as noted, the passage goes on to repeat this warning three more times, for a total of four warnings. If the punishment is repeated four times, then four times 490 years results in a total of 1960 years of punishment. Adding 1960 years to the destruction of the Second Jewish Temple in 70 AD again arrives at the year 2030 AD.

As noted earlier, the date for the destruction of the second Jewish Temple has been recorded as August 29, 70 AD. If this date is used as the date that the daily sacrifices ceased, and 1960 years is added to that date, then it can be concluded that the daily sacrifices might restart on August 29, 2030 AD.

Interestingly, this date corresponds to Elul 1 (August 29-30, 2030) on the Jewish calendar. The 1st of Elul or Rosh Chodesh Elul, a minor holiday marked by the birth of the new moon, signals the beginning of a 40-day spiritual preparation called the Season of Repentance or Teshuvah. The Season of Repentance culminates on the Day of

Atonement, forty days after Elul 1, which would be an appropriate date to restart the daily sacrifices at a rebuilt Jewish Temple.

Again, this analysis of the various timelines is outlined in much more detail in Tim Warner's book *Time of the End* and referring to that provides a much more in-depth explanation. Each of these methods on their own provide some evidence to arrive at a timing for Christ's second coming. However, taken together they provide a more compelling argument that the time of Christ's second return is fast approaching, a Christmas yet to come.

Below is a summary so far of the timeline that has been constructed. There is a seven-year final period that is divided into half with two three-and-a-half year stages separated by the abomination of desolation. This final seven years begins and ends on Rosh Hashanah. A probable year for the onset of the last seven years is 2029 with their conclusion in 2036. The second half, beginning at Passover, is further divided into three parts of a time, times, and a half time, ending again on Rosh Hashanah in 2036.

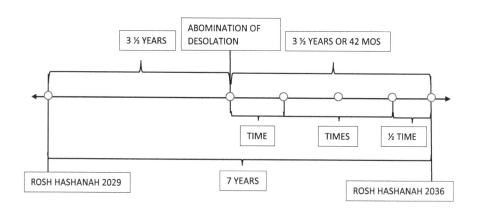

FEASTS[5]

As seen with the Jewish feasts or festivals of Rosh Hashanah and Passover, the feast days play a vital role in determining the order and timing of events in the last seven years. These festivals were not called

"**Jewish** feasts" in the Bible but were actually called "**God's** feasts" by the LORD himself.

> And the LORD spake unto Moses, saying, Speak unto the children of Israel and say unto them, Concerning the **feasts of the LORD**, which ye shall proclaim to be holy convocations, even these are **my** feasts. Leviticus 23:1-2

So, for both the Jews and non-Jews, it is important to know and to understand these feasts, not only when they occur, but also how they are celebrated, and what is the meaning and symbolism behind them. Some Christians believe that these feasts have been done away with since they are under grace and no longer under the law. However, Christians in the first century after Jesus' death continued to celebrate the festivals. As noted earlier, the Hebrew word for *festival* is *moed* which actually means "appointed time". God had the Jewish nation set aside certain dates or appointed times to commemorate events in the past as well as to signal events that would occur in the future, events that would impact not only Israel but the entire world. These feasts have ramifications especially for Christians who look forward to the return of their savior Jesus Christ. These feasts were and are representations of things to come both historical and future, and Paul makes it clear that the festivals are only "shadows" of things yet to come in the future.

> Let no man therefore judge you in meat, or in drink, or in respect of an holyday, or of the new moon, or of the sabbath days: Which are a shadow of things to come; but the body is of Christ. Colossians 2:16-17

They were clearly not completely fulfilled at the first coming of Jesus, since Jesus Himself states that He will celebrate Passover in the future when He returns.

> And he said unto them, With desire I have desired to this Passover with you before I suffer: For I say unto

you, I will not any more eat thereof, until it be fulfilled
in the kingdom of God. Luke 22:15-16

So, although these festivals have at least been partially fulfilled in
the past, they still have a significant part to play in the future, as well
as in the timing of end time events.

The feasts can also benefit us with our Christian walk by providing
a picture of God's plan of salvation through Jesus Christ and the
restoration of His fellowship with mankind.

There are seven festivals that were given to the Hebrew nation in
Leviticus 23:

1. Passover (Pesach)
2. Unleavened Bread (Hag HaMatzah)
3. First Fruits
4. Pentecost or Feast of Weeks (Shavuot)
5. Feast of Trumpets (Rosh Hashanah)
6. Day of Atonement (Yom Kippur)
7. Feast of Tabernacles (Sukkoth)

These festivals were associated with various harvest times of which
there were three main harvests in the land of Canaan: the barley, wheat,
and grape harvests. Each of these harvests correspond not only to the
festivals but also to a particular group of people that God deals with
throughout the Bible, and Paul in his letter to the Corinthians names
these distinctive groups.

But every man in his own order: **Christ the firstfruits**;
afterward **they that are Christ's** at his coming. Then
cometh the end, when he shall have delivered up the
kingdom to God, even the Father; when he shall have
put down all rule and all authority and power. For
he must reign, till he hath put **all enemies** under his
feet. The last enemy that shall be destroyed is death.
For he hath put all things under his feet. But when he

saith, all things are put under him, it is manifest that he is excepted, which did put all things under him. 1 Corinthians 15:23-27

The Feast of First Fruits occurred in the Spring at the barley harvest. Paul stated in 1Corinthians that the "firstfruits" is Christ. But John also goes on to call the 144,000 in Revelation the "firstfruits".

> And I looked, and, lo, a Lamb stood on the mount Sion, and with him an hundred forty and four thousand, having his father's name written in their foreheads. And I heard a voice from heaven, as the voice of many waters, and as the voice of a great thunder: and I heard the voice of harpers harping with their harps: And they sung as it were a new song before the throne, and before the four beasts, and the elders: and no man could learn that song but the hundred and forty and four thousand, which were redeemed from the earth. These are they which were not defiled with women; for they are virgins. These are they which follow the Lamb whithersoever he goeth. These were redeemed from among men, being the **firstfruits** unto God and to the Lamb. Revelation 14:1-4

These 144,000, who are called the "firstfruits", are made up of the twelve tribes of Israel.

> And I saw another angel ascending from the east, having the seal of the living God: and he cried with al loud voice to the four angels, to whom it was given to hurt the earth and the sea, Saying, Hurt not the earth, neither the sea, nor the trees till we have sealed the servants of our God in their foreheads. And I heard the number of them which were sealed: and there were

sealed and hundred and forty and four thousand of all the tribes of the children of Israel. Revelation 7:2-4

The 144,000, therefore, represent the children of Israel, the firstfruits of the land, the barley harvest.

1 Corinthians 15 then goes on to identify the next two groups. The second group is the Church, i.e., "they that are Christ's" (vs 23). The final remaining group is the bulk of mankind, the unrighteous nations who will be defeated when Jesus (at His second coming as a conquering king) will "put all enemies under his feet" (vs 25).

In addition to the Feast of Firstfruits, the feasts of Passover and Unleavened Bread always occur in the Spring, coinciding with the barley harvest, which represents the **first** part of God's harvest, the Jewish people.

> Israel was holiness unto the LORD, and the **firstfruits** of in increase: all that devour him shall offend; evil shall come upon them, saith the LORD. Jeremiah 2:3

> But glory, honour, and peace, to every man that worketh good, **to the Jew first**, and also to the Gentile. Romans 2:10

> For a certain woman, whose young daughter had an unclean spirit, heard of him, and came and fell at his feet: The woman was a Greek, a Syrophenician by nation; and she besought him that he would cast forth the devil out of her daughter. But Jesus said unto her, Let the children **first** be filled for it is not meet to take the children's bread, and to cast it unto the dogs. Mark 7:25-27

The Jewish people were clearly the focus of Jesus' ministry. They were the first of the first fruits of the gospel message and are represented by the first harvest, the barley harvest.

Although all of the Spring feasts had their fulfillment at least partially if not fully during Christ's first coming, they may still have a future fulfillment. Their completion at His first coming is demonstrated in Jesus who was the sacrificial lamb on Passover. The unleavened bread was a symbol of the Messiah who was without sin, and Jesus is the First Fruits of the harvest of the righteous souls who are dead in Christ, a harvest that will occur on the resurrection day of the Lord at the Rapture.

Pentecost occurred during the summer months at the time of the wheat harvest. The Feast of Pentecost is celebrated by observant Jews each year as a reminder that this is the day that the Law was given to Moses at Mount Sinai. Pentecost is likewise significant for believers as it is the day that the Holy Spirit was given and the Church was born. As it marked the beginning of the Church Age, it may also signal the day of Christ's return, ending the Church Age with the Rapture. Acts 1 and 2 record the beginning of the Church with the outpouring of the Holy Spirit on the Day of Pentecost:

> And when the day of Pentecost was fully come, they were all with one accord in one place. And suddenly there came a sound from heaven as of a rushing mighty wind, and it filled all the house where they were sitting. Acts 2:1-2

The first Pentecost occurred following the nation of Israel's exodus from Egypt. They came to the foot of Mount Sinai where God instructed Moses to consecrate the people and have them wash their clothes. Then at the sound of the trumpet they were to approach the mountain. This is significant because this is also the first time the word *trumpet* is mentioned in the Bible.

> There shall not an hand touch it, but he shall surely be stoned, or shot through; whether it be beast or man, it shall not live: when the trumpet soundeth long, they shall come up to the mount. And Moses went down

from the mount unto the people, and sanctified the people; and they washed their clothes. And he said unto the people, Be ready against the third day: come not at your wives. And it came to pass on the third day in the morning, that there were thunders and lightnings, and a thick cloud upon the mount, and the voice of the trumpet exceeding loud; so that all the people that was in the camp trembled. Exodus 19:13-16

This was the first divine trump heard by God's people as the trumpet was sounded by God Himself, causing them to gather nearby. Just as the first trump was sounded by God to call His people to Himself at Mount Sinai on the Day of Pentecost, the "last trump" mentioned by Paul to the Corinthians may indicated that God's people will be gathered or raptured to Himself also on the Day of Pentecost.

In a moment, in the twinkling of an eye, at the last trump: for the trumpet shall sound, and the dead shall be raised incorruptible, and we shall be changed. 1 Corinthians 15:52

Not only does the trumpet of Pentecost possibly signal the Rapture, but also the wheat harvest is a symbol of the gathering of God's people. In the Parable of the Wheat and Tares, Jesus uses the metaphor of "wheat" to describe the Church and its gathering at the harvest of righteous souls.

Another parable put he forth unto them, saying, The kingdom of heaven is likened unto a man which sowed good seed in his field: But while men slept, his enemy came and sowed tares among the wheat, and went his way. But when the blade was sprung up, and brought forth fruit, then appeared the tares also. So the servants of the householder came and said unto him, Sir didst not thou sow good seed in thy field? From whence then hath it tares? He said unto them, An enemy hath done this. The servants said unto him, Wilt thou then that we go and gather them up? But he said, Nay lest while ye gather up the tares, ye root up also the wheat with them. Let both grow together until the harvest: and in the time of harvest I will say to the reapers, Gather ye together first the tares, and bind them in bundles to burn them: but gather the wheat into my barn. Matthew 13:24-30

And I looked, and behold a white cloud, and upon the cloud one sat like unto the Son of man, having on his head a golden crown, and in his hand a sharp sickle. And another angel came out of the temple, crying with a loud voice to him that sat on the cloud, Thrust in thy sickle, and reap: for the time is come for thee to reap; for the harvest of the earth is ripe. Revelation 14:14-15

Both of these passages describe the harvesting of the righteous at the time of the end. Pentecost always occurs during the wheat harvest and by inference the harvesting of the wheat symbolizes the gathering or rapture of the Church at Jesus' second coming. So, Pentecost was at least partially fulfilled at Jesus' first coming and may have a further fulfillment at His second coming.

The final three Fall feasts have not yet been fulfilled but will in all likelihood be satisfied at the second coming of Jesus Christ just as the other feasts were fulfilled at his first coming. The Fall feasts all take place during the season of the grape harvest and, as has been noted, are an image of the unrighteous nations who are defeated and judged at the end.

And another angel came out of the temple which is in heaven, he also having a sharp sickle. And another angel came out from the altar, which had power over fire; and cried with a loud cry to him that had the sharp sickle, saying, Thrust in thy sharp sickle, and gather the clusters of the vine of the earth; for her grapes are fully ripe. And the angel thrust in his sickle into the earth, and gathered the vine of the earth, and cast it into the great winepress of the wrath of God. And the winepress was trodden without the city, and the blood came out of the winepress, even unto the horse bridles, by the space of a thousand and six hundred furlongs. Revelation 14:17-20

Let the heathen be wakened, and come up to the valley of Jehoshaphat: for there will I sit to judge all the heathen round about. Put ye in the sickle, for the harvest is ripe: come, get you down; for the press is full, the fats overflow; for their wickedness is great. Joel 3:12-13

Both of these passages describe God's wrath being poured out on the unrighteous nations who have persecuted His people, Israel. In summary, below is a table of the Feasts with their corresponding harvests and representative groups of people.

FEASTS	HARVEST	GROUP OF PEOPLE
Spring (Passover, Unleavened Bread, First Fruits)	Barley	Israel
Summer (Pentecost)	Wheat	Church
Fall (Trumpets, Day of Atonement, Tabernacles)	Grape	Unrighteous Nations

Just as these Spring feasts had their prophetic fulfillment on their exact day (for example, Christ the Lamb was sacrificed and died precisely on Passover), it can be assumed that the remaining Fall feasts will also be accomplished on their exact date in the future. Therefore, any timing of end time prophecy should account for events that fulfill those prophecies on the exact day of those specific feasts.

However, determining the precise date of future feast days is difficult. The Jewish calendar is a lunar calendar based on the appearance of a new moon to mark the beginning of a new month. Although today there is modern astronomy and computer programs to help calculate future new moons, in ancient times the new moon was not confirmed until two witnesses had confirmed its appearance and reported to Jewish leaders in Jerusalem. This is called Rosh Hodesh or the Day of the New Moon. The timing of Rosh Hodesh could differ depending on various factors such as weather conditions. Therefore, the verse in Matthew that states:

> But concerning that day and hour no one knows.
> Matthew 24:36

could imply the difficulty of determining future dates for not only any Day of the New Moon throughout the year but also any of the feast days which were based on the new moon cycle. Nevertheless, since these feast days have prophetic significance, a quick review along with their importance in timing of events is in order.

Passover

Passover is the first feast mentioned and marks the beginning of the festival or sacred calendar as opposed to the civil calendar which begins in the seventh month of Tishri on the Jewish calendar. Passover occurs on Nisan 14, usually in March or April. It was instituted for the Jews to remember their deliverance from Egyptian bondage. Passover was celebrated with an unblemished firstborn male lamb that was sacrificed and its blood poured on the altar. The lamb was selected and brought into the home four days before it was slain on Passover. Passover was also prophetic in that Jesus is the sacrificial lamb who died for our sins. He also had a four-day period of examination by the Jewish religious leaders and was similarly found without blemish. The part that Passover plays in the end times is uncertain. However, Jesus indicated that the Passover would not be completely fulfilled with His death and would play a part in the future.

> And he said unto them, With desire I have desired to
> eat this passover with you before I suffer: For I say unto
> you, I will not any more eat thereof, until it be fulfilled
> in the kingdom of God. Luke 22:15-16

Passover may be celebrated with Jesus at a future Second Exodus that he leads from Egypt during the last seven years. (See Chap. 8) Although Jesus came as a suffering sacrifice on Passover (30 AD), he will return as a conquering king to initiate His war against the unrighteous and to regain His kingdom on a Passover in 2036 according to the proposed timeline.

Also, since a Passover most likely occurs at the midpoint of the last seven years when the Antichrist commits the abomination of desolation, the Antichrist may use this feast day to present himself as The Messiah to the Jewish people and the world. This would be made believable by his resurrection from a deadly head wound, a deception that would undoubtedly cause many people to hail him as Christ. (See Appendix D)

Following the abomination of desolation in the middle of the last seven years, the Jews are instructed to flee from Judea.

> When ye therefore shall see the abomination of
> desolation, spoken of by Daniel the prophet, stand in the
> holy place, (whoso readeth, let him understand:) Then
> let them which be in Judaea flee into the mountains:
> Matthew 24:15-16

Just as the Jews fled Egypt into the wilderness on the first Passover, so, too, they may be forced to flee at the midpoint of the seven years on a Passover in 2033.

Unleavened Bread

The Feast of Unleavened Bread begins the day after Passover on Nisan 15. Leaven or yeast in bread is a symbol for sin, and unleavened bread is used to represent consecration and separation in order to live a sinless, holy life. The Jews were to cleanse all leaven from their homes and eat only unleavened bread called matzah for seven days, symbolizing a sinless, holy walk with God. During the preparation of the matzah, it is striped and pierced. The Feast of Unleavened Bread reminds us that Jesus is the sinless Bread of Life who was striped and pierced for our transgressions. This feast coincided with the day that Jesus was buried.

Feast of Firstfruits

Firstfruits begins on the day following the first Sabbath after Passover and consequently always occurs on Sunday, the first day of the week. It represents a theme of resurrection or new life. It is the same day on which Noah's Ark came to rest on Mount Ararat. It is the same day on which the Israelites passed through the Red Sea during their exodus from Egypt. It is the same day that the Israelites ate the firstfruits of the Promised Land (Israel) forty years later. And it is the same day that Jesus Christ rose from the dead.

On this date the first of the barley harvest was brought as an offering to the priest in the Tabernacle or Temple. The priest then offered the first of the harvest to God by waving it back and forth, reminding the Hebrews that God had given them the land and that He had provided the harvest. Jesus arose on Sunday, the day following the first Sabbath after Passover, and is the first of the firstfruits.

> But now is Christ risen from the dead, and become the firstfruits of them that slept. 1 Corinthians 15:20

Jesus arose on Firstfruits, and His resurrection marked the beginning of the harvest of souls.

Feast of Weeks (Pentecost)

Fifty days after the Feast of Firstfruits, the Feast of Weeks is celebrated. This, as noted earlier, occurred during the wheat harvest and commemorated the day that the Torah or Law was given to Moses on Mount Sinai. This was the day that God committed Himself in marriage to the Jews and was also the day that three thousand souls died due to their disobedience to God. At the Feast of Weeks, two loaves of bread with leaven were brought with seven male lambs, a young bull and two rams as a burnt offering. The sin offering was a male goat.

> And ye shall count unto you from the morrow after the sabbath, from the day that ye brought the sheath of the wave offering; seven sabbaths shall be complete: Even unto the morrow after the seventh sabbath shall ye number fifty days; and ye shall offer a new meat offering unto the LORD. Ye shall bring out of your habitations two wave loaves of two tenth deals: they shall be of fine flour; they shall be baken with leaven; they are the firstfruits unto the LORD. And ye shall offer with the bread seven lambs without blemish of the first year, and one young bullock, and two rams: they shall be for a burnt offering unto the LORD, with their meat offering, and their drink offerings, even an offering made by fire, of sweet savour unto the LORD. Then ye shall sacrifice one kid of the goats for a sin offering, and two lambs of the first year for a sacrifice of peace offerings. And the priest shall wave them with the bread of the firstfruits for a wave offering before the LORD, with the two rams: they shall be holy to the LORD for the priest. And ye shall proclaim on the selfsame day, that it may be an holy convocation unto you: ye shall do no servile work therein: it shall be a statute for ever in all your dwellings throughout your generations. Leviticus 23:15-21

Pentecost was one of the three mandatory festivals for all Jewish young men to appear before the Lord and was considered the closing feast of the Passover season. Whereas, Passover symbolized the physical freedom of God's people, Pentecost represented the spiritual redemption from bondage to idolatry and immorality. It marked the end of the barley season and the beginning of the wheat harvest. Pentecost is a celebration to reawaken and strengthen personal relationships with God by rededication to the observance and study of the Law. Fifty days after Jesus arose, the Holy Spirit was given to the Church, and God wrote the Law onto the hearts of the believers.

> But this shall be the covenant that I will make with the house of Israel; After those days, saith the LORD, I will put my law in their inward parts, and write it in their hearts; and will be their God, and they shall be my people. Jeremiah 31:33

While three thousand were killed at the first Pentecost (Exodus 32:28), three thousand souls were saved at this Pentecost (Acts 2:41), and Pentecost may be the day that the Church is saved from the wrath of God.

Feast of Trumpets

The Feast of Trumpets begins on the first day of the Jewish month of Tishri (corresponding to September or October). It marks the beginning of the Jewish civil New Year and as noted above probably designates the beginning of each of the last seven years. Although this festival was not given a specific name as the other feast days were, it is referred to as Yom Teruah (the day of the sounding of the shofar) and consequently became known as the Feast of Trumpets. It remembers the creation of the world which occurred on Tishri 1 and calls the people to rejoice in grateful recollection of God's benefits, imploring His blessing for the future year. It is also likely that Jesus actually was born physically into the world on Rosh Hashanah (September 22, 4 BC) and may figure in Jesus' coronation as king physically on the earth on the last Rosh Hashanah of the final seven years, possibly September 22, 2036. (This will be discussed more in the chapter on "The Second Coming of Christ.")

Day of Atonement

The Day of Atonement is the holiest and most solemn day of the Jewish year and is spent in prayer, fasting, and confession. It occurs ten days after the Feast of Trumpets.

> And the LORD spake unto Moses, saying, Also on the tenth day of this seventh month there shall be a day of atonement: it shall be an holy convocation unto you; and ye shall afflict your souls, and offer an offering made by fire unto the LORD. And ye shall do no work in that same day: for it is a day of Atonement, to make and atonement for you before the LORD your God. For whatsoever soul it be that shall not be afflicted in that same day, he shall be cut off from among his people. And whatsoever soul it be that doeth any work in that same day, the same soul will I destroy from among his people. Ye shall do no manner of work: it shall be a statute forever throughout your generations in all your dwellings. It shall be unto you a sabbath of rest, and ye shall afflict your souls: in the ninth day of the month at even, from even unto even, shall ye celebrate your sabbath. Leviticus 23:23-32

It is a day for judgment, but one where judgment was paused. Forgiveness for Israel was provided by the high priest who entered the Holy of Holies in the Temple or Tabernacle to make atonement for the nation. For one time during the year the whole of Israel ceased all worldly activities to stand before God. Their only hope lay in the blood sprinkled by the priest, their representative and mediator. This atonement was accomplished by sacrificing animals including two male goats. Although Christ the Messiah was our suffering, sacrificial offering at his first coming, at his second coming he will come with judgment that may occur on the Day of Atonement.

Feast of Tabernacles

To remind His people that they lived in booths when He brought them out of Egypt, God told the people they should live in booths for seven days. Every year at the Feast of Tabernacles, the Jews build temporary dwellings where they live and eat for seven days in joyful celebration. The Feast of Tabernacles begins five days after the Day of Atonement on the fifteenth of Tishri (September or October). Unlike the Day of Atonement which was the most solemn day of the year for the Jews, the Feast of Tabernacles was one of the most joyous times of the year. It reminds us that God is our tabernacle or dwelling place.

> For thou hast been a strength to the poor, a strength
> to the needy in his distress, a refuge from the storm,
> a shadow from the heat, when the blast of the terrible
> ones is as a storm against the wall. Isaiah 25:4

This holiday reminds us that this life is temporary and that we should not hold too tightly to the material things of this world. This feast speaks of a future time when men will again tabernacle with God, when He will dwell with them and they with Him.

> And I heard a great voice out of heaven saying, Behold,
> the tabernacle of God is with men, and he will dwell
> with them, and they shall be his people, and God himself
> shall be with them, and be their God. Revelation 21:3

Hanukkah

One other festival besides the original seven that must be mentioned is Hanukkah. Nearly two centuries before Christ, a Syrian tyrant named Antiochus Epiphanes ruled Judea. He worshipped the Greek gods and eventually refused the Jews the right to keep their holy traditions and worship their God. He even went so far as to desecrate their temple by sacrificing a forbidden and unclean pig on the Holy Altar and then set up an image of an idol in the Temple. Eventually a rebellion broke out led by Judah Maccabee, and the Syrians were driven out. The Temple was then cleansed and rededicated on Kislev 25 which occurs in the month of December. Hanukkah means "to dedicate" and it is sometimes called the Feast of Dedication. Since then, Hanukkah has been celebrated each year and was even observed by Jesus.

> And it was at Jerusalem the **feast of the dedication**, and it was winter. And Jesus walked in the temple in Solomon's porch. John 10:22-23

Many Christians do not believe that Jesus was actually born on Christmas day, the 25th of December. And many believe that Jesus' real birthday occurred during the Feast of Tabernacles.

> And the Word was made flesh, and dwelt (i.e., **tabernacled**) among us, (and we beheld his glory, the glory as of the only begotten of the Father,) full of grace and truth. John 1:14

But others conclude that his birthday was on another Fall feast, the Feast of Trumpets. Assuming Hanukkah was the time that Jesus was conceived and adding nine months for Mary's pregnancy, the approximate period for the birth of Jesus would be during the Fall feasts. So, many point to the Festival of Trumpets as well as the Feast of Tabernacles as the time of Jesus' birth. The Bible does not specifically give the date of Jesus' birth, but it was not during the winter months. Luke states that the shepherds were in the field watching the sheep (Luke 2:8), which was something that did not happen during the winter.

So, what about Jesus' conception? Was Jesus' conception prophesied in the Scriptures? And was this around what is called the Hanukkah and Christmas season? In the New Testament, a study of the time of the conception of John the Baptist reveals he was conceived about Sivan 30, the eleventh week (Luke 1:8-13, 24). Adding forty weeks for a normal pregnancy reveals that John the Baptist was born on or about Passover (Nisan 14). Six months after John's conception, Mary conceived Jesus

(Luke 1:26-33). Therefore, Jesus would have been conceived six months after Sivan 30 in the month of Kislev, around the time of Hanukkah. Consequently, many believe that the Messiah, the "light of the world", was conceived on the Festival of Lights—Hanukkah.

Also, there is evidence that Jesus' conception during Hanukkah was inferred by Jesus Himself in the Gospel of John.

> And it was at Jerusalem **the feast of the dedication**, and it was winter. And Jesus walked in the temple in Solomon's porch. Then came the Jews round about him, and said unto him, How long dost thou make us to doubt? If thou be the Christ, tell us plainly. Jesus answered them, I told you, and ye believed not: the works that I do in my Father's name, they bear witness of me. But ye believe not, because ye are not of my sheep, as I said unto you. My sheep hear my voice, and I know them, and they follow me: And I give unto them eternal life; and they shall never perish, neither shall any man pluck them out of my hand. My Father, which gave them me, is greater than all; and no man is able to pluck them out of my Father's hand. I and my Father are one. Then the Jews took up stones again to stone him. Jesus answered them, Many good works have I shewed you from my Father; for which of those works do ye stone me? The Jews answered him, saying, For a good work we stone thee not; but for blasphemy; and because that thou, being a man, makest thyself God. Jesus answered them, Is it not written in your law, I said, Ye are gods? If he called them gods, unto whom the word of God came, and the scripture cannot be broken; Say ye of him, whom the Father hath sanctified, and **sent into the world**, Thou blasphemest; because I said, I am the Son of God? If I do not the works of my Father, believe me not. But if I do, though ye believe not me, believe the

works: that ye may know, and believe, that the Father
is in me, and I in him. John 10:22-38

Jesus was telling them during this time of Hanukkah that His
Father had sent Him into the world. He was sent into the world by His
Father at conception nine months before His birth. And here, during
Hanukkah, was one of three times in the Gospels where Jesus spoke
about His Father sending Him into the world. Was He telling His
disciples about His day of conception?

The Old Testament as well prophesied of Jesus' conception.

> Therefore the Lord himself shall give you a sign; Behold,
> a virgin shall conceive, and bear a son, and shall call his
> name Immanuel. Isaiah 7:14

But did God disclose in scripture prior Jesus' birth what time of
year it was when this great event would happen, and could He also have
revealed to us in the Old Testament about the **specific** day? Suggestions
are found in the book of Haggai (written about 520 B.C.):

> Consider now from this day and upward, from **the four
> and twentieth day of the ninth month**, even from the
> day that the foundation of the Lord's temple was laid,
> consider it. Is the seed yet in the barn? yea, as yet the
> vine, and the fig tree, and the pomegranate, and the
> olive tree, hath not brought forth: from this day will I
> bless you. Haggai 2:18-19

Kislev is the ninth month in the Jewish calendar. Conception in
the virgin Mary was symbolically when the foundation of the LORD's
Temple was laid. So, this could imply that the date of Jesus' conception
was Kislev 24 or Hanukkah.

Hanukkah and the Christmas season are truly a most wonderful
time of year because this is when Love came into the world! This is
when God came into the world! This is when Jesus was likely conceived

in the womb of His beloved mother Mary! And, since life, according to the Bible, begins at conception, Christmas Day in December may in actuality be an appropriate day to celebrate Christ's first advent.

Yet, Hanukkah is important not just because of its historical consequence but because it is significant in future prophetic end time events. In the Book of Daniel, at the end of the last seven years, there is an additional period of seventy-five days that is appended. In this prophetic book, Daniel notes that:

> Blessed is he that waiteth, and cometh to the thousand three hundred and five and thirty days. Daniel 12:12

These 1335 days (1260 days + 75 days) add an additional seventy-five days to the end of the last half of the final seven years. Interestingly, there are seventy-five days between the Day of Atonement (Tishri 10) and Hanukkah (Kislev 25). It is, therefore, likely that this period of 1335 days comes to an end on Hanukkah.

Daniel also describes a period that lasts two thousand and three hundred days.

> Then I heard one saint speaking, and another saint said unto that certain saint which spake, How long shall be the vision concerning the daily sacrifice, and the transgression of desolation, to give both the sanctuary and the host to be trodden underfoot? And he said unto me, Unto two thousand and three hundred days; then shall the sanctuary shall be cleansed. Daniel 8:13-14

That 2300-day period begins with the daily sacrifices, followed by the transgression or abomination of desolation where the Temple is trodden underfoot and desecrated before finally being cleansed. This is similar to the original Hanukkah where the Temple was defiled and then eventually cleansed and rededicated on Kislev 25. Using the year 2036 as the last year of the 70th week of Daniel, Kislev 25 falls on December 15, 2036. Counting back 2300 days from that date arrives at August

29, 2030 as a date for the restarting of the daily sacrifices. Remarkably, this date corresponds exactly to 1960 years from the destruction of the second Jewish Temple by the Romans on August 29, 70 AD.

This date of 8/29/70 AD was given by the historian Josephus *(see www.josephus.org).* It is also the date given by Gary J. Goldberg and published in many scholastic Bible reference works. However, it is disputed by others such as Parker and Dubberstein who state that Av 9, 70 AD, the date of destruction of the Temple, occurred instead on 8/6/70 AD.

Nevertheless, August 29, 70 AD is a precise date that coincides exactly 1960 years before August 29, 2030 which again could be the date that the Temple sacrifices will be reinstituted. Also, as noted earlier, August 29-30, 2030 is Elul 1 on the Jewish calendar, the beginning of the Season of Repentance, which provides even more weight to the supposition that this date would be an appropriate day to restart the daily sacrifices.

In conclusion, it is clear that the original feasts as well as Hanukkah play an important part in understanding the timing of the events of the last seven years. Using this new information and adding the corresponding dates for the year 2036, the timeline of the last seven years takes on more detail.

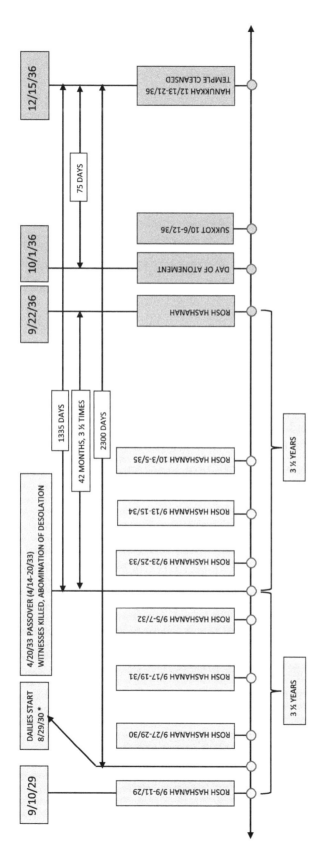

DANIEL'S LAST WEEK (7 YEARS) TIMELINE
2029-2036

*8/29/30 is exactly 1960 years from the destruction of the 2nd Temple when the daily sacrifices ceased on 8/30/70 AD

12/15/36

HANUKKAH 12/13-21/36
TEMPLE CLEANSED

75 DAYS

10/1/36

SUKKOT 10/6-12/36

DAY OF ATONEMENT

9/22/36

ROSH HASHANAH

1335 DAYS

42 MONTHS, 3 ½ TIMES

2300 DAYS

4/20/33 PASSOVER (4/14-20/33)
WITNESSES KILLED, ABOMINATION OF DESOLATION

ROSH HASHANAH 10/3-5/35

ROSH HASHANAH 9/13-15/34

ROSH HASHANAH 9/23-25/33

3 ½ YEARS

ROSH HASHANAH 9/5-7/32

ROSH HASHANAH 9/17-19/31

DAILIES START 8/29/30 *

ROSH HASHANAH 9/27-29/30

9/10/29

ROSH HASHANAH 9/9-11/29

3 ½ YEARS

SEALS, TRUMPETS, AND BOWLS

The book of Revelation further divides the last seven years into three parts that represent the final judgments of God that are poured out in the end times. The Seals on a scroll are specified in Revelation chapter 6, where they are opened and warn of God's coming judgment. Once the Seals are opened, the wrath of God is unleashed in the Trumpet judgments (chapters 8,9, and 11) and finally the Bowl judgments (chapter 16) where the full wrath of God is completed. Each of these divisions is broken up into seven distinct acts and judgments, resulting in three septet judgments: the seven seals, the seven trumpets, and the seven bowl judgments.

The Bible describes this last seven-year period as a woman travailing in pregnancy:

> For yourselves know perfectly that the day of the Lord so cometh as a thief in the night. For when they shall say, Peace and safety; then sudden destruction cometh upon them, as travail upon a woman with child; and they shall not escape. But ye, brethren, are not in darkness, that that day should overtake you as a thief. 1Thess 5:2-4

Just as a pregnancy is divided up into three trimesters, so the final seven years are divided up into three parts (the seals, trumpets, and bowls). And just as labor pains of pregnancy become more frequent and intense as the delivery approaches, advancing from the seals to the trumpets and then the bowls judgments demonstrate a progression in frequency (e.g., one year for each seal, one month for each trumpet and one week for each bowl). In addition, an increasing intensity and severity in the judgments occur as they advance.

There is considerable debate about the order of the septet judgments. Most believe that the events within each class of judgments are chronological, i.e., each of the seals occur one after the other, followed by the trumpets and then bowls. However, some scholars believe that the seals, trumpets, and bowls themselves happen concurrently or in parallel at the same time. This is easy to assume since there are similar judgments in each. For example, in both the second trumpet judgment and the second bowl judgment the seas are turned to blood. However, as seen before, the intensity of each increases from the one before. The trumpet judgments are limited to one third in scope, whereas the bowl judgments are a worldwide phenomenon. Also, prior to the seals, there are "lightnings, thunderings, and voices" (Revelation 4:5). After the seals there are "noises, thunderings, lightnings, and an **earthquake**" (Revelation 8:5). Following the trumpet judgments there are "lightnings, noises, thunderings, an earthquake, and **great hail**" (Revelation 11:19). And finally, at the seventh bowl:

> And there were **voices, and thunders, and lightnings; and there was a great earthquake**, such as was not since men were upon the earth, so mighty an earthquake, and so great. Revelation 16:18

> And there fell upon men a **great hail** out of heaven, every stone about the weight of a talent: and men blasphemed God because of the plague of the hail; for the plague thereof was exceeding great. Revelation 16:21

Although it is clear that there are similarities in the seals, trumpets and bowls, each period is distinctly different with each becoming more and more severe in intensity.

It seems, therefore, that the judgments occur sequentially in order just as it is presented in Revelation. And although most of Revelation is chronologically in order, there are several parenthetical interludes that summarize prior teaching before they are presented in more detail later on. For example, interruptions in the linear order of events appear in Revelation 12:1-15:5 which deals with Satan's opposition to God's plan of restoration through Christ, while Revelation 17 and 18 interrupts the sequence of events to discuss end time's Babylon. Nevertheless, despite these interludes, the judgments are plainly laid out in a sequential timeline.

The Seals

The judgments begin with the seven seals that are initially introduced in chapter 5 of Revelation:

> And I saw in the right hand of him that sat on the throne a book written within and on the backside, sealed with seven seals. And I saw a strong angel proclaiming with a loud voice, Who is worthy to open the book, and to loose **the seals** thereof? And no man in heaven, nor in earth, neither under the earth, was able to open the book, neither to look thereon. And I wept much, because no man was found worthy to open and to read the book, neither to look thereon. And one of the elders saith unto me, Weep not: behold, the Lion of the tribe of Juda, the Root of David, hath prevailed to open the book, and to loose the seven seals thereof. Revelation 5:1-5

As noted earlier, the opening of the book or scroll with seven seals occurs in heaven at a celestial court. It is clear that Jesus Christ, "the Lion of the tribe of Juda, the Root of David", is the only one legally approved to open the scroll. The purpose of this court and the contents of the scroll is to transfer the kingdoms of the world to the "Son of Man", property that had been previously usurped and stolen by Satan.

> I beheld till the thrones were cast down, and the Ancient of days did sit, whose garment was white as snow, and the hair of his head like the pure wool: his throne was like the fiery flame, and his wheels as burning fire. A fiery stream issued and came forth from before him: thousand thousands ministered unto him, and ten

CHRISTMAS YET TO COME

thousand times ten thousand stood before him: the judgment was set, and the books were opened. I beheld then because of the voice of the great words which the horn spake: I beheld even till the beast was slain, and his body destroyed, and given to the burning flame. As concerning the rest of the beasts, they had their dominion taken away: yet their lives were prolonged for a season and time. I saw in the night visions, and, behold, one like the Son of man came with the clouds of heaven, and came to the Ancient of days, and they brought him near before him. And there was given him dominion, and glory, and a kingdom, that all people, nations, and languages, should serve him: his dominion is an everlasting dominion, which shall not pass away, and his kingdom that which shall not be destroyed. Daniel 7:9-14

The first six seals are opened in Revelation chapter 6. The first four seals are commonly called "the Four Horsemen of the Apocalypse". The first seal (vs 1-2) marks the beginning of the last seven years which again likely begins on Rosh Hashanah. It involves a rider on a white horse going out conquering and to conquer, a picture of the Antichrist being let loose on the world. It is at this time that the Antichrist will confirm a covenant or agreement with Israel, possibly allowing them to rebuild the Temple and restart the daily sacrifices. This agreement will be broken in the middle of the seven years when the abomination of desolation occurs.

And he shall confirm the covenant with many for one week: and **in the midst of the week** he shall cause the sacrifice and the oblation to cease, and for the overspreading of abominations hew shall make it desolate, even until the consummation, and that determined shall be poured upon the desolate. Daniel 9:27

It is further proposed that there will be one year between the opening of each seal, so that each seal will be opened on a Rosh Hashanah. The time from the first seal to the seventh seal then is six years. The second, third, and fourth seals (vs 3-8) involve respectively wars, famine, and death. They are the riders of the red, black, and green horses. It is interesting that most Islamic countries particularly in the Middle East use a combination of these colors in their flags, and as will be seen, it is many of these same countries that will play a critical role in end times events.

The fifth seal (vs 9-11) displays the persecution of God's people, which brings more of God's vengeance on the world, but not until the world's evil has been filled up with the last martyr's death.

> And when he had opened the fifth seal, I saw under the altar the **souls of them that were slain** for the word of God, and for the testimony which they held: And they cried with a loud voice, saying, How long, O Lord, holy and true, dost thou not judge and avenge our blood on them that dwell on the earth? And white robes were given unto every one of them *(hekastos)*; and it was said unto them, that they should rest yet for a little season, until their fellowservants also and their brethren that should be killed as they were, should be fulfilled. Revelation 6:9-11

Most interpret the "souls of them that were slain" to include all those who have been martyred for "the word of God" in the past. However, if the fifth seal occurs just after the midpoint of the last seven years (according to the proposed timeline), then the "slain" may refer to the Two Witnesses who appear and have a ministry during the first half of the last seven years. After their ministry they are then killed at the midpoint of the 70th week of Daniel. The Greek word *hekastos* in Revelation 6:11 is usually translated as "each" or "every" which again could imply all of those who have been martyred in the past. However, *hekastos* can also be translated as "both" which would suggest that only two (as in the Two Witnesses) are given white robes at this time.

Also, the Greek word translated as "witness" in Revelation 11:3 is *martus*, which can certainly mean "witness" but can also just as well be translated as "martyr".

> And I will give power unto my two witnesses *(martus),* and they shall prophesy a thousand two hundred and threescore days, clothed in sackcloth. Revelation 11:3

So, again, these slain or martyrs, who are introduced at the 5th seal, may actually be the Two Witnesses described in Revelation 11. These two witnesses will be discussed in more detail in the next chapter.

When the sixth seal (vs 12-17) is opened there is a great earthquake along with other celestial disturbances. These are the heavenly wonders that announce the second coming of Jesus Christ and the imminent Day of the Lord.

> And I beheld when he had opened the sixth seal, and, lo, there was a great earthquake; and the sun became black as sackcloth of hair, and the moon became as blood; And the stars of heaven fell unto the earth, even as a fig tree casteth her untimely figs, when she is shaken of a mighty wind. And the heaven departed as a scroll when it is rolled together; and every mountain and island were moved out of their places. And the kings of the earth, and the great men, and the rich men, and the chief captains, and the mighty men, and every bondman, and every free man, hid themselves in the dens and in the rocks of the mountains; And said to the mountains and rocks, Fall on us, and hide us from the face of him that sitteth on the throne, and from the wrath of the Lamb: For the great day of his wrath is come; and who shall be able to stand? Revelation 6:12-17

These cosmic warnings are the same signs that the prophet Joel proclaimed would occur before the day of the LORD.

> And I will shew wonders in the heavens and in the earth, blood, and fire, and pillars of smoke. The sun shall be turned into darkness, and the moon into blood, before the great and the terrible day of the LORD come. Joel 2:30-31

Jesus himself also specified that these celestial signs would herald His second coming and would announce the coming rapture.

> Immediately after the tribulation of those days shall the sun be darkened, and the moon shall not give her light, and the stars shall fall from heaven and the powers of the heavens shall be shaken: And then shall appear he sign of the Son of man in heaven: and then shall all the tribes of the earth mourn, and they shall see the Son of man coming in the clouds of heaven with power and great glory. And he shall send his angels with a great sound of a trumpet, and they shall gather together his elect from the four winds, from one end of heaven to the other. Matthew 24:29-31

Sometime after the 6th seal and once these cosmic warnings happen before the 7th seal, the Rapture of the Church occurs. The Rapture is the first event in the Second Coming of Christ as will be discussed later. And as noted earlier, a likely date for the Rapture is on Pentecost, the Feast of Weeks. If the sixth and seventh seals are opened on Rosh Hashanah of 2034 and 2035 respectively, then the Rapture will possibly occur on Pentecost between these two dates, which would be on May 13, 2035.

After the Rapture, the 7th seal is opened which again likely happens on Rosh Hashanah, October 4, 2035. This day marks the beginning of the Day of the Lord and the start of the trumpet judgments. At the 7th seal, there is a short period of silence, "half an hour", which could represent the ten Days of Awe before the Day of Atonement. This period of silence demonstrates the gravity and solemnity of the occasion that portends the onset of God's wrath that begins with the trumpet judgments. As will be seen later in the chapter on "The Second Coming of Christ", the Day of the Lord is a one-year period of time that likely ends on the Day of Atonement, October 1, 2036 and marks the beginning of the Millennium as well as the start of a Jubilee year.

> And when he had opened the seventh seal, there was silence in heaven bout the space of half an hour. And I saw the seven angels which stood before God; and to them were given seven trumpets. Revelation 8:1-2

The Trumpets

The first six trumpets in Revelation 8 and 9 include the following judgments:

1. First trumpet (Rev 8:7) where one third of the earth, trees, grass is burned up
2. Second trumpet (Rev 8:8-9) where one third of the sea's creatures die and ships are destroyed
3. Third trumpet (Rev 8:10-11) where one third of the waters are polluted and many die
4. Fourth trumpet (Rev 8:12) where one third of the sun, moon, and stars are darkened
5. Fifth trumpet (Rev 9:1-11) where locusts/demons are released to torment people for five months
6. Sixth trumpet (Rev 9:13-19) where four bound demons are released to kill one third of humankind with an army

Although devastating, these trumpet judgments are limited in scope, affecting only one third of the earth, sea, and heaven. The restricted involvement of the trumpet judgments, as opposed to the bowl judgments (which, as will be seen, are more comprehensive and include the earth and all the nations) may imply a more regional effect of the trumpet judgments, involving primarily the Middle East.

There is a general theme throughout the Bible that God pours out His wrath first on the Jews and then on the Gentile nations who persecuted His people. This pattern may continue during the Day of Wrath where God's punishment is first directed towards His people the Jews in the trumpet judgments in order to purify His bride. This is then followed by the bowl judgments poured out on "the nations". This time of tribulation during the trumpet judgments on the Jews is sometimes referred to as the "day of Jacob's trouble".

> Alas! For that day is great, so that none is like it: it is even the time of Jacob's trouble; but he shall be saved out of it. Jeremiah 30:7

The sounding of the seventh trumpet (Rev 11:15) announces that Jesus Christ has begun his reign over the kingdoms of the world and the sovereignty of Satan is over.

> And the seventh angel sounded; and there were great voices in heaven, saying, **The kingdoms of this world are become the kingdoms of our Lord**, and of his Christ; and he shall reign for ever and ever. Rev 11:15

If it is assumed that each of the seal judgments lasts one year, then the seal judgments would last a total of six years. This would leave one last year in Daniel's 70th Week. Consequently, the trumpet judgments would need to occur within this last year. With the 7th seal, there is a short period of silence, "half an hour", which again could represent the ten Days of Awe before the Day of Atonement. The trumpet judgments would then begin on the Day of Atonement of the last year, October 13, 2035.

If the seals last six years, then how long do the trumpet judgments persist? The last three-and-one-half years begin on Passover and are

CHRISTMAS YET TO COME

broken up into three parts: a time, times and a half time. The first "time" would then begin and end on Passover in the middle of the last seven years. The second "times" would likewise begin and end two years later on a Passover in the middle of the last year. This would then leave six months for the "half time" from Passover to the last and seventh Rosh Hashanah. If the trumpet judgments begin on the Day of Atonement and end during the last year on Passover (which would be a likely day for the seventh trumpet where the kingdoms of this world "become the kingdoms of our Lord"), then this would be a period of six months, implying that the time between each trumpet judgment would be one month.

Supporting this idea is the fact that the effects of the fifth trumpet judgment last five months.

> And to them it was given that they should not kill them, but that they should be tormented five months: and their torment was as the torment of a scorpion, when he striketh a man. Revelation 9:5

So, any timeline of the last seven years needs to account for "five months" to complete the fifth trumpet. If the trumpet judgments do indeed start on the Day of Atonement of the last year and end six months later on Passover, then that would leave an additional six months or "half time" at the end of the seven years. If each trumpet judgment lasts one month, then the fifth judgment would start four months after the Day of Atonement which is in October 2035. The fifth trumpet would then occur in February 2036 which would leave enough time after the fifth trumpet (about seven months) for the five months of torment required for the fifth trumpet. This also would leave a five-month gap between the seventh trumpet and the end of the 70th week, providing adequate time for Christ to lead a second Exodus of Israel out from Egypt following Passover. This will be outlined and further explained in the chapter on "The Second Coming of Christ".

The Bowls

As noted earlier, during the progression of the 70ᵗʰ week, the events will most likely become more frequent just as a woman in labor experiences more frequent contractions the closer she gets to delivery. So, if the seals transpire over a six-year period and the trumpets over a span of six months, then one might postulate that the bowl judgments occur over a six-week period. A shortened period for the bowl judgments would also seem likely, since the severity of these judgments makes it unlikely that anyone or anything could survive a prolonged time for these harsh judgments.

Six weeks is about forty which is the number for testing and punishment in the Bible. Noah's flood lasted forty days. (Genesis 7:4, 12, 17 and Matthew 24:37-39) The Israelites wandered forty years in the wilderness for the forty days that the spies had spent scouting out the land. (Numbers 14:33-34, 32:13) No more than forty stripes were allowed for punishment. (Deuteronomy 25:3) Similarly, the wrath of God on the entire world during the bowl judgments may last about forty days. This forty-day period would fit within the seventy-five days that occur from the end of the seven years on Rosh Hashanah until the cleansing of the Temple at Hanukkah. Each of the seven bowl judgments in Revelation 16 would then occur about one week apart.

This would also be consistent with the length of the plagues in Egypt that may have lasted about one week each. The Book of Exodus states that the first plague where the waters became blood lasted seven days.

> And **seven days** were fulfilled, after that the Lord had smitten the river. Exodus 7:25

So, the following bowl judgments from Revelation 16, each lasting about seven days, are released onto the world:

1. First bowl (vs 2) where terrible sores appear on those with the mark of the beast
2. Second bowl (vs 3) where everything in the sea dies

3. Third bowl (vs 4-7) where all the waters are polluted
4. Fourth bowl (vs 8-9) where the sun burns and scorches people
5. Fifth bowl (vs 10-11) that brings complete darkness over the Antichrist's kingdom
6. Sixth bowl (vs 12-16) where the Euphrates River dries up, the kings of the East come, and the scene is set for the battle of Armageddon
7. Seventh bowl (17-21) where a great earthquake occurs, cities of nations fall, and a huge hailstorm ensues

The seals, trumpet judgments, and bowl judgments can then be summarized like this:

	SEALS	TRUMPETS	BOWLS
1ST	Rev 6:1-2 False Messiah (Antichrist)	Rev 8:7 Hailstones, fire & blood; 1/3 of Earth, trees, & green grass are burned up	Rev 16:2 Ugly and painful sores break out
2ND	Rev 6:3-4 War	Rev 8:8-9 A meteor(?) strikes the sea; 1/3 of sea turned to blood, 1/3 of sea creatures die, 1/3 of ships are destroyed	Rev 16:3 Everything in the sea dies
3RD	Rev 6:5-6 Inflation	Rev 8:10-11 Ball of fire (meteor? nuclear event?) goes into 1/3 of the springs and rivers; "Wormwood" event: many people die from the "bitter" waters	Rev 16:4 River and springs turn to blood
4TH	Rev 6:7-8 Sword, famine, plagues, & wild beasts	Rev 8:12 1/3 of the day and night are without light (i.e., sun, moon, and stars are affected; or perhaps light is filtered out)	Rev 16:8-9 Intense heat of the sun

	SEALS	TRUMPETS	BOWLS
5TH	Rev 6:9-10 Souls of the slain cry for justice	Rev 9:1-11 Locust-like creatures (demons) come from the Abyss	Rev 16:10-11 Darkness in the kingdom of the Beast
6TH	Rev 6:12-17 A great earthquake & signs in the heavens	Rev 9:14-19 Four fallen angels that were bound at the Euphrates River are released to kill 1/3 of mankind via an army of size 200 million (possibly demons)	Rev 16:12-16 Euphrates River is dried up to prepare the way for the kings from the East to enable them to come to Armageddon
7TH	Rev 8:1 Silence in heaven for ½ hour	Rev 11:15-19 Worship in heaven; thunder, rumblings, lightning, earthquake, and a great hailstorm	Rev 16:17-21 Thunder, lightning, etc.; the world's greatest earthquake; hailstones of 100 pounds each

The bowl judgments, as noted earlier, most likely occur during the seventy-five days after the seven-year period. So, when would the bowl judgments start? Daniel provides some helpful information:

> And from the time that the daily sacrifice shall be taken away and the abomination that maketh desolate set up, there shall be **a thousand two hundred and ninety days**. Daniel 12:11

So, the daily sacrifices are taken away and the abomination of desolation occur at Passover in 2033 (the midpoint between 2029 and 2036) according to the theory presented here. Passover of that year is April 20, 2033, and adding 1290 days to this date arrives at October 31, 2036 which is Cheshvan 10 on the Jewish calendar. The account of the Flood in Genesis indicates that the door to Noah's ark was closed on Cheshvan 10, removing any hope of salvation for the unrighteous not inside the ark. Once the door was closed, the rain and flood began, lasting forty days and forty nights. Similarly, this may be the date when

God effectively "closes the door" on the unrighteous and begins the bowl judgments that last forty days.

In conclusion, the seals, trumpets and bowl judgments occur sequentially and will result in the cleansing and purification of the earth before Christ's millennial reign. The seals deal primarily with the Church and conclude with its rapture. The trumpets are directed toward Israel, and the bowl judgments are aimed at the Gentile nations. How God deals with these different groups through the seals, trumpets, and bowls will be explained in more detail in the chapter on "The Second Coming of Christ". By adding this additional information related to the seals, trumpets, and bowls, the timeline takes on more elements, providing more specific dates for the 70th week of Daniel and the end times.

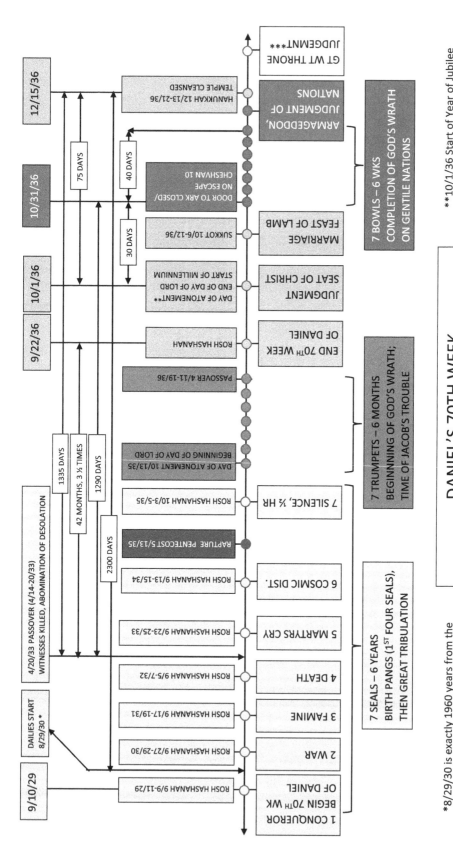

DANIEL'S 70TH WEEK

2029-2036

12/15/36

10/31/36

10/1/36

9/22/36

9/10/29

TEMPLE CLEANSED
HANUKKAH 12/13-21/36

GT WT THRONE
JUDGEMNT***

ARMAGEDDON,
JUDGMENT OF
NATIONS

7 BOWLS – 6 WKS
COMPLETION OF GOD'S WRATH
ON GENTILE NATIONS

75 DAYS

40 DAYS

30 DAYS

DOOR TO ARK CLOSED/
NO ESCAPE
CHESHVAN 10

SUKKOT 10/6-12/36

MARRIAGE
FEAST OF LAMB

START OF MILLENNIUM
END OF DAY OF LORD
DAY OF ATONEMENT**

JUDGMENT
SEAT OF CHRIST

ROSH HASHANAH

END 70TH WEEK
OF DANIEL

PASSOVER 4/11-19/36

1335 DAYS

42 MONTHS, 3 ½ TIMES

1290 DAYS

2300 DAYS

BEGINNNING OF DAY OF LORD
DAY OF ATONEMENT 10/13/35

7 TRUMPETS – 6 MONTHS
BEGINNNING OF GOD'S WRATH;
TIME OF JACOB'S TROUBLE

ROSH HASHANAH 10/3-5/35

7 SILENCE, ½ HR

RAPTURE PENTECOST 5/13/35

4/20/33 PASSOVER (4/14-20/33)
WITNESSES KILLED, ABOMINATION OF DESOLATION

ROSH HASHANAH 9/13-15/34

6 COSMIC DIST.

ROSH HASHANAH 9/23-25/33

5 MARTYRS CRY

ROSH HASHANAH 9/5-7/32

4 DEATH

ROSH HASHANAH 9/17-19/31

3 FAMINE

DAILIES START
8/29/30 *

ROSH HASHANAH 9/27-29/30

2 WAR

7 SEALS – 6 YEARS
BIRTH PANGS (1ST FOUR SEALS),
THEN GREAT TRIBULATION

ROSH HASHANAH 9/9-11/29

1 CONQUEROR
BEGIN 70TH WK
OF DANIEL

**10/1/36 Start of Year of Jubilee
***End of Millennium

*8/29/30 is exactly 1960 years from the
destruction of the 2ⁿᵈ Temple when the
daily sacrifices ceased on 8/30/70 AD

CHAPTER 3

Two Witnesses

The book of Revelation introduces Two Witnesses in chapter 11:

> And there was given me a reed like unto a rod: and the angel stood, saying, Rise, and measure the temple of God, and the altar, and them that worship therein. But the court which is without the temple leave out, and measure it not; for it is given unto the Gentiles: and the holy city shall they tread under foot forty and two months. And I will give power unto my **two witnesses**, and they shall prophesy a thousand two hundred and threescore days, clothed in sackcloth. These are the two olive trees, and the two candlesticks standing before the God of the earth. And if any man will hurt them, fire proceedeth out of their mouth, and devoureth their enemies: and if any man will hurt them, he must in this manner be killed. These have power to shut heaven, that it rain not in the days of their prophecy: and have power over waters to turn them to blood, and to smite the earth with all plagues, as often as they will. And when they shall have finished their testimony, the beast

that ascendeth out of the bottomless pit shall make war against them, and shall overcome them, and kill them. And their dead bodies shall lie in the street of the great city, which spiritually is called Sodom and Egypt, where also our Lord was crucified. And they of the people and kindreds and tongues and nations shall see their dead bodies three days and an half, and shall not suffer their dead bodies to be put in graves. And they that dwell upon the earth shall rejoice over them, and make merry, and shall send gifts one to another; because these two prophets tormented them that dwelt on the earth. And after three days and an half the Spirit of life from God entered into them, and they stood upon their feet; and great fear fell upon them which saw them. And they heard a great voice from heaven saying unto them, Come up hither. And they ascended up to heaven in a cloud; and their enemies beheld them. And the same hour was there a great earthquake, and the tenth part of the city fell, and in the earthquake were slain of men seven thousand: and the remnant were affrighted, and gave glory to the God of heaven. Revelation 11:1-13

A witness is a person who has seen an event, typically a crime or accident, take place and testifies about what they have seen. What is it that these two witnesses have seen, and why are there two?

There will be two witnesses, since scripture requires two or more witnesses to confirm a matter.

One witness shall not rise up against a man for any iniquity, or for any sin, in any sin that he sinneth: at the mouth of two witnesses, or at the mouth of three witnesses, shall the matter be established. Deuteronomy 19:15

Jesus quoted this passage in Matthew 18:16 when outlining the process of church discipline.

Also, the timing of the new moon on Yom Teruah or Rosh Hashanah required two witnesses in order to usher in the New Year. And Paul extended this principle to scripture.

> This is the third time I am coming to you. In the mouth of two or three witnesses shall every word be established. 2 Corinthians 13:1

So, difficult to understand prophecies and ideas are confirmed by two or more scriptures agreeing and emphasize why it is important that there are two witnesses.

But to what will the witnesses of Revelation 11 testify? They may witness to the essence of salvation that Paul outlines in the Book of Romans.

> That if thou shalt confess with thy mouth the Lord Jesus, and shalt believe in thine heart that God hath raised him from the dead, thou shalt be saved. Romans 10:9

Or possibly, these two persons were eye witnesses to Jesus' resurrection. That would be an appealing choice for the Two Witnesses. But, were there two witnesses who were eye witnesses and saw Jesus physically rise from the dead? Luke's account of the resurrection confirms that there actually were two witnesses to this event.

> And they (the women which came with him from Galilee) found the stone rolled away from the sepulchre. And they entered in, and found not the body of the Lord Jesus. And it came to pass, as they were much perplexed thereabout, behold, **two men** *(anayr)* stood by them in shining garments: And as they were afraid, and bowed down their faces to the earth, they said unto them, Why seek ye the living among the dead? Luke 24:2-5

Many assume that Luke meant angels when he wrote this. However, what was written is "two men" and is the same description of Moses and Elijah on the Mount of Transfiguration. The Greek word *anayr* is used which translates as "man" and not "angel". If an angel was implied then most likely the Greek word *angelos* would have been used. At the transfiguration, Moses and Elijah were discussing Jesus' departure. Was the transfiguration a last-minute briefing for Moses and Elijah so that they would be ready for what was to follow, the witnessing of the resurrection of Jesus?

The two men in dazzling garments were at the tomb ahead of the women, and look at what they said:

> And as they were afraid, and bowed down their faces to the earth, they said unto them, Why seek ye the living among the dead? He is not here, but is risen: remember how he spake unto you when he was yet in Galilee, Luke 24:5-6

It certainly looks like eye witness testimony. And later, at Jesus' ascension, Luke states:

> And while they looked stedfastly toward heaven as he went up, behold, **two men** *(anayr)* stood by them in white apparel; Acts 1:10

Again, Luke clearly says "men" and not "angels". And what two men might these have been? Again, possibly they were Moses and Elijah who are likely candidates for the Two Witnesses of Revelation, as will be seen later. So, they were quite possibly the witnesses of both the resurrection and ascension of Jesus. Not only are they two of the most respected Jewish leaders, but also, if this is correct, they were witnesses to the events that prove Jesus is the Son of God.

Alternatively, these "men" described in Luke's account of the resurrection could indeed have been angels. The Gospel of Mark (Mark 16:5) reports that the witness at the tomb was a young man and not an angel. However, Matthew tells us that an **angel** rolled away the stone (Matthew 28:2), and John reports that the two within the tomb were two **angels** (John 20:12). Both use the Greek word *aggelos* or *angelos* translated as "angel". This word simply means "messenger", either human or heavenly. Since the Gospel writers are evenly divided, it more likely refers to a human messenger in a glorified state.[1] Or perhaps, there were both human and angelic witnesses present which would explain the confusion.

Timing of the Two Witness' Ministry

These Two Witnesses described in Revelation are two prophets, whose ministry begins sometime during the Tribulation, lasts for 1260 days (Revelation 11:3), and ends when the beast or Antichrist ascends to power at the middle of the last seven years (Revelation 11:7) at which point they are killed. Many commentaries place the ministry of the Two Witnesses during the second half of the Tribulation [Dean, 2009].[2] However, this leaves some questions. Why would the ministry of the Two Witnesses take place in Jerusalem, if the Lord had told the Jews to flee (at the midpoint of the Tribulation)? When do the three-and-a-half days of partying by unbelievers following the two witness' death occur, if the witnesses minister to the end of the Tribulation (i.e., at Armageddon, and the return of Christ)? Since these questions are not easily explained with their ministry in the second half of the tribulation, other scholars believe that the Two Witnesses perform most, if not all, of their ministry in the first half of the Tribulation at a time when many Jews will be worshipping in the rebuilt temple.

If their ministry takes place in the first half of the final seven years, and if the conclusion of their time to minister occurs in the middle of those final seven years on Passover (April 20, 2033) as proposed earlier, then 1260 days (the length of the Two Witness' ministry) before this date would be November 7, 2029. This proposed starting date for the Two Witness' to begin their ministry occurs about two months after the start of the 70th week of Daniel on Rosh Hashanah September 10, 2029 and nearly nine months before the projected date for the restarting of the daily sacrifices on August 29, 2030. This could imply that part of the

Two Witnesses' ministry is to aid in building and preparing the Temple for worship and sacrifices during the first half of Daniel's 70th Week.

Identity of the Two Witnesses

While some consider the Two Witnesses to be allegorical characters, most believe that the Two Witnesses are actual people, either two new future prophets or more commonly two historical figures that reappear in the end times. The Two Witnesses' ministry is based in Jerusalem. They will minister in Jerusalem which is figuratively called "Sodom and Egypt" (Revelation 11:8), and this certainly characterizes and identifies Jerusalem because it is the city in which Christ was crucified. Consequently, their ministry will be directed to the Jews, since it is the nation of Israel that God has promised to save in the end times. Much of Israel's heart has been supernaturally hardened until the end times, and so, the mission of the Two Witnesses may be to witness primarily to the Jews. Because of this, it is likely that the Two Witnesses themselves are Jews, since a Jew would provide the most credibility to another Jew, i.e., someone who the Jews would be familiar with and trust.

In addition to the Jews, there is someone else to whom the Two Witnesses will testify. Revelation 11:4 states that the Two Witnesses will stand "before the God of the earth". So, who is the God or Lord of the earth? Most would assume that it is God the Father, the Lord of heaven and earth. But at the time of the Two Witnesses' testimony, who might be the "God of the earth"? This may actually not be referring to the Lord of heaven and earth but could likely be signifying the Antichrist who rules most of the earth. So, it appears that the Two Witnesses will likely witness to or against the Antichrist as well, standing before him just as Moses and Aaron stood before Pharaoh and testified to him to "let my people go". And just as God used Moses and Aaron to harden Pharaoh's heart, He will in all likelihood use the Two Witnesses to harden the Antichrist's heart, while performing signs and wonders.

> And the LORD said unto Moses, See, I have made thee
> a god to Pharaoh: and Aaron thy brother shall be thy

prophet. Thou shalt speak all that I command thee: and Aaron thy brother shall speak unto Pharaoh, that he send the children of Israel out of his land. And I will harden Pharaoh's heart, and multiply my signs and my wonders in the land of Egypt. Exodus 7:1-3

Note how much detail that Revelation 11:1-13 provides while describing the Two Witnesses and the events surrounding their lives. This is strong evidence suggesting that all the events, as well as the people and places, are real and literal. Some authors argue that the Two Witnesses are likely to be two new Jewish prophets chosen by God during the Tribulation, rather than two historical figures, especially since they are not mentioned by name in the book of Revelation [Walvoord, 1990; Fruchtenbaum, 2004]. However, most believe that they will be two historical figures who return to complete their ministry during the end times.[2]

Zechariah 4 is the Old Testament reference to Revelation 11.

And the angel that talked with me came again, and waked me, as a man that is wakened out of his sleep. And said unto me, What seest thou? And I said, I have looked, and behold a candlestick all of gold, with a bowl upon the top of it, and his seven lamps thereon, and seven pipes to the seven lamps, which are upon the top thereof: And two olive trees by it, one upon the right side of the bowl, and the other upon the left side thereof. So I answered and spake to the angel that talked with me, saying, What are these, my lord? Then the angel that talked with me answered and said unto me, Knowest thou not what these be? And I said, No, my lord. Then he answered and spake unto me, saying, This is the word of the LORD unto Zerubbabel, saying, Not by might, nor by power, but by my spirit, saith the LORD of hosts. Who art thou, O great mountain? before Zerubbabel thou shalt become a plain: and he shall bring forth the headstone thereof with shoutings, crying, Grace, grace unto it. Moreover the word of the LORD came unto me, saying, The hands of Zerubbabel have laid the foundation of this house; his hands shall also finish it; and thou shalt know that the LORD of hosts hath sent me unto you. For who hath despised the day of small things? for they shall rejoice, and shall see the plummet in the hand of Zerubbabel with those seven; they are the eyes of the LORD, which run to and fro through the whole earth. Then answered I, and said unto him, What are these two olive trees upon the right side of the candlestick and upon the left side thereof? And I answered again, and said unto him, What be these two olive branches which through the two golden pipes empty the golden oil out of themselves? And he answered me and said, Knowest thou not what these be? And I said, No, my lord. Then said he, These are the two anointed ones, that stand by the LORD of the whole earth. Zechariah 4:1-14

Like the Two Witnesses of Revelation, building and preparing the Temple for worship and sacrifices was part of the ministry of these two prophets in the Old Testament. Zechariah and Haggai, filled with God's Holy Spirit, gave messages from God to encourage and uplift the hands of Zerubbabel and Joshua the High Priest in their endeavor to rebuild the Temple. So, Zechariah and Haggai are likely the two olive trees mentioned in Zechariah 4.

Interestingly, there is only one candlestick or lampstand mentioned in this passage of Zechariah whereas there are two candlesticks or lampstands cited in Revelation 11. This may be because in the Old Testament there is only one covenant people, Israel, while in the New Testament there are two covenant people, Israel and the Church. This could provide a clue as to who the two olive trees or two witnesses are in Revelation 11. Most agree that one is Elijah, the prophet, since Malachi in the last book of the Old Testament actually names him.[3]

> Behold, I will send you Elijah the prophet before the
> coming of the great and dreadful day of the LORD:
> Malachi 4:5

Malachi actually makes reference to a "messenger", who would turn out to be John the Baptist.

> Behold, I will send my **messenger**, and he shall prepare
> the way before me: and the LORD, whom ye seek, shall
> suddenly come to his temple, even the **messenger** of the
> covenant, whom ye delight in: behold, he shall come,
> saith the LORD of hosts. Malachi 3:1

Isaiah 40:3-4 is a parallel passage about John the Baptist.

> The voice of him that crieth in the wilderness, Prepare
> ye the way of the LORD, make straight in the desert
> a highway for our God. Every valley shall be exalted,
> and every mountain and hill shall be made low: and the
> crooked shall be made straight, and the rough places
> plain: Isaiah 40:3-4

This passage provides the predicted role for John the Baptist to play as the one who would precede and prepare the way for Jesus at His first coming.

> In those days came John the Baptist, preaching in the
> wilderness of Judaea, And saying, Repent ye: for the
> kingdom of heaven is at hand. For this is he that was
> spoken of by the prophet Esaias, saying, The voice of
> one crying in the wilderness, Prepare ye the way of the
> Lord, make his paths straight. And the same John had
> his raiment of camel's hair, and a leathern girdle about
> his loins; and his meat was locusts and wild honey. Then
> went out to him Jerusalem, and all Judaea, and all the

region round about Jordan, And were baptized of him in Jordan, confessing their sins. Matthew 3:1-6

Elijah will prepare the way for Israel before Christ's second coming, since Israel rejected Jesus at His first coming. There are some who teach that the ministry of John the Baptist was a fulfillment of the prediction of the coming of Elijah from Malachi 4:5 at Christ's first coming. This is not the case. John the Baptist fulfilled a different prediction, that of Malachi 3:1 and Isaiah 40:3-5. Yet, John the Baptist was said to be "a forerunner" who would come first "in the spirit and power of Elijah" (Luke 1:17, Mark 9:12).

> And he shall go before him in the spirit and power of Elias, to turn the hearts of the fathers to the children, and the disobedient to the wisdom of the just; to make ready a people prepared for the Lord. Luke 1:17

> And he answered and told them, Elias verily cometh first, and restoreth all things; and how it is written of the Son of man, that he must suffer many things, and be set at nought. Mark 9:12

Christ told His disciples concerning John the Baptist:

> And if ye will receive it, this is Elias, which was for to come. Matthew 11:14

But Israel did not accept Jesus as their Messiah at His first coming and therefore, the kingdom did not arrive. In fact, when John the Baptist was asked directly, "Are you Elijah?" he clearly said, "I am not."

> And they asked him, What then? Art thou Elias? And he saith, I am not. Art thou that prophet? And he answered, No. John 1:21

This demonstrates that God can send additional representatives, such as John the Baptist, with a similar ministry and powers as the prophet Elijah. John the Baptist was a fulfillment of the prophecy in Luke 1, indicating that John the Baptist would do an Elijah-like work.

> And Jesus answered and said unto them, Elias truly shall first come, and restore all things. But I say unto you, That Elias is come already, and they knew him not, but have done unto him whatsoever they listed. Likewise shall also the Son of man suffer of them. Then the disciples understood that he spake unto them of John the Baptist. Matthew 17:11-13

Yet, Malachi 4:5 indicates another fulfillment of an Elijah-like work at the end of this age. Sometimes prophecies can have multiple fulfillments, and this prophecy regarding the work of Elijah seems to be one that falls into this category. John the Baptist was clearly a type of Elijah, and the account in Malachi 4 indicates that another "Elijah" will arise at the end of this age.

Since Zechariah speaks of a lampstand and an olive tree—two witnesses who were actual people (Zerubbabel, the civil leader, and Joshua, the religious leader) [Hitchcock, 2012][2], it is again reasonable to assume that the Two Witnesses in Revelation 11 are real people. In fact, we would be reading something into the text of Revelation 11 if we assume the opposite, given the connection to Zechariah 4. Because there are two lampstands representing Israel and the Church, some conclude that the first prophet is Elijah who characterizes Israel, and then infer that the second prophet comes from the Church age, identifying John the Apostle as the second witness. This is because John himself states:

> I John, who also am your brother and companion **in tribulation**, and in the kingdom and patience of Jesus Christ, was in the isle that is called Patmos, for the word of God, and for the testimony of Jesus Christ. Revelation 1:9

Since John states that he will be "in tribulation", it is argued that he will be present in those last seven years of tribulation and thus, must be one of the Two Witnesses along with Elijah. Although some dispensationalists do not think that the Two Witnesses will be people from the past, many believe that there are other historical pairs besides Elijah and John such as Moses and Elijah or Elijah and Enoch.

Moses (representing the Law) and Elijah (representing the Prophets) are the most popular candidates because they are Israel's greatest prophets in the Old Testament, and both appeared with Christ on the Mount of Transfiguration. Also, the miracles that the Two Witnesses perform are similar to the same miracles that Moses and Elijah performed in the Old Testament. In addition, Moses was buried by the Lord, and the place of burial was kept secret from all men.

> So Moses the servant of the LORD died there in the Land of Moab, according to the word of the LORD. And he buried him in a valley in the land of Moab, over against Bethpeor: but no man knoweth of his sepulchre unto this day. Deuteronomy 34:5-6

After the death of Moses, his body became the focus of a battle between Michael the archangel and the devil.

> Yet Michael the archangel, when contending with the devil he disputed about the body of Moses, durst not bring against him a railing accusation, but said, The Lord rebuke thee. Jude 1:9

Why would Michael fight Satan for the right to Moses' body? There are many theories, but one of the most convincing is that God planned to resurrect Moses and use him as one of the Two Witnesses.

It is also interesting to note that Moses and Elijah are mentioned together in the last book of the Old Testament, right before Elijah was named as one of the Two Witnesses.

Remember ye the law of Moses my servant, which I commanded unto him in Horeb for all Israel, with the statutes and judgments. Behold, I will send you Elijah the prophet before the coming of the great and dreadful day of the LORD: And he shall turn the heart of the fathers to the children, and the heart of the children to their fathers, lest I come and smite the earth with a curse. Malachi 4:4-6

Finally, if the Two Witnesses do appear on November 7, 2029 which is Cheshvan 29 on the Jewish calendar, then this would be fifty days after Yom Kippur and would occur on the Jewish holiday of Sigd. This could support the theory that Moses is the second witness, since *Sigd* is an Amharic word meaning "prostration" or "worship". According to Ethiopian Jewish tradition, Sigd is also the date that God first revealed Himself to Moses, lending credibility to Moses as the second olive tree.

Others believe that Elijah and Enoch are the Two Witnesses since these two did not die but were carried off rapture-like into heaven and will eventually come back in the Tribulation as the Two Witnesses. Although Enoch was not a Jew, which would seem to discount him as one of the Two Witnesses, the appeal of Enoch and Elijah as the Two Witnesses is that they are the only two people in the Bible who some say went to Heaven without dying. Also, they were favored by the early church fathers. Hippolytus (circa 200-235 BC) was the Bishop of Rome, and he wrote about the Antichrist and the Two Witnesses of Revelation 11 [Hitchcock, 2012]. Like Tertullian (also circa 200 BC), Hippolytus believed that the Two Witnesses would be Enoch and Elijah [Hedrick, 2020].[2] It appears that this is what much of the early church thought.

Again, some believe that scripture teaches that Enoch and Elijah never died but were raptured. If that is true, then it is also unclear whether they currently have resurrected bodies. Jesus was indeed the first to rise from the dead with a physically resurrected body. If Enoch and Elijah are the Two Witnesses in Revelation, then it would be consistent with the statement:

> And as it is appointed unto men once to die, but after this the judgment: Hebrews 9:27

According to Revelation 11, the Two Witnesses will die during the Tribulation. Moses has already died; therefore, he would die twice if he were to be one of the Two Witnesses. Thus, Enoch and Elijah deserve consideration as the Two Witnesses. Interestingly, if Enoch and Elijah already have resurrected bodies, then they cannot die [Hedrick, 2020].[2] That would rule both of them out as the Two Witnesses of Revelation 11; consequently, they must not have glorified bodies yet. Could they have gone to Heaven if they only have physical bodies? Conversely, if Enoch or Elijah is one of the Two Witnesses, that would imply he does not currently have a resurrected body, but rather some sort of an intermediate body.

A supporting Scripture for using Enoch as one of the Two Witnesses (Elijah the other) is:

> For as in Adam all die, even so in Christ shall all be made alive. 1 Corinthians 15:22

Some consider that Enoch and Elijah currently wait in heaven in their natural bodies. Enoch's message before the Flood is remarkably similar to what would be required in the end times:

> And Enoch also, the seventh from Adam, prophesied of these, saying, Behold, the Lord cometh with ten thousands of his saints, To execute judgment upon all, and to convince all that are ungodly among them of all their ungodly deeds which they have ungodly committed, and of all their hard speeches which ungodly sinners have spoken against him. Jude 1:14-15

Note that there appear to be exceptions to the "one death per person" rule; but these probably need to be viewed as exceptions perhaps as resuscitations rather than resurrections [Stewart, 2015b].² Examples include the following:

- Elijah raised a young boy to life (1 Kings 17:22).
- Elisha raised a young boy to life (2 Kings 4:32-33).
- When a body was thrown into Elisha's tomb, and it made contact with Elisha's bones, the person came to life (2 Kings 13:20-21).
- Christ raised Lazarus from the dead, after Lazarus had been dead for 4 days (Jhn 11:41-44).
- Jesus raised Jairus' daughter to life (Luke 8:52-55).
- Jesus raised the son of the widow from Nain to life (Luke 7:14-15).
- Peter raised Dorcas (Tabitha) to life (Acts 9:40-41).
- Paul raised Eutychus to life after the young man fell asleep and fell out of a window (Acts 20:9-11).²

Most believe that Christ was the very first person to rise from the dead with a perfected glorified body. Therefore, these examples may well be along the lines of resuscitation rather than translation to a perfected body, since a perfected body is not subject to death or decay. And we assume that these individuals eventually died some time after their "resuscitation". Some argue that Enoch and Elijah, who were raptured, each received a resurrected body, and this, of course, would be before Christ's resurrection. But it is still unclear whether they actually received a resurrected body or not. It seems unlikely that Enoch or Elijah would be "downgrading" from a perfected body to become one of the Two Witnesses in Revelation 11 just to die again.

Regardless of whom they are, the Two Witnesses appear to be real people who come to the earth to preach to the Jewish people (and ultimately to the world), turning many hearts to Christ.

Mission of the Two Witnesses

The mission of the Two Witnesses includes testifying to the Jews about the resurrection of Jesus and witnessing before the Antichrist. Also, it appears that part of their ministry will be to rebuild the Temple (if it has not already been rebuilt by the start of their ministry) and to restart the daily sacrifices. If this is the case, it begs the question as to why the daily sacrifices would even need to be resumed. If Jesus was the sacrificial offering for our sins once and for all, why would the sacrifices need to be recommenced? Many believe the false assumption that when Christ first came that he did away with the covenant that God made with Moses. However, Jesus himself declared:

> Think not that I am come to destroy the law, or the prophets: I am not come to destroy, but to fulfil. For verily I say unto you, Till heaven and earth pass, one jot or one tittle shall in no wise pass from the law, till all be fulfilled. Matthew 5:17-18

It is a incorrect supposition that when Christ came he ended the covenant that God made with Moses in Deuteronomy.

> And it shall come to pass, when all these things are come upon thee, the blessing and the curse, which I have set before thee, and thou shalt call them to mind among all the nations, whither the Lord thy God hath driven thee, And shalt return unto the Lord thy God, and shalt obey his voice according to all that I command thee this day, thou and thy children, with all thine heart, and with all thy soul; That then the Lord thy God will turn thy captivity, and have compassion upon thee, and will return and gather thee from all the nations, whither the Lord thy God hath scattered thee. If any of thine be driven out unto the outmost parts of heaven, from thence will the Lord thy God gather thee, and from thence will he fetch thee: And the Lord thy God will bring thee into the land which thy fathers possessed, and thou shalt possess it; and he will do thee good, and multiply thee above thy fathers. And the Lord thy God will circumcise thine heart, and the heart of thy seed, to

love the Lord thy God with all thine heart, and with all thy soul, that thou mayest live. And the Lord thy God will put all these curses upon thine enemies, and on them that hate thee, which persecuted thee. And thou shalt return and obey the voice of the Lord, and do all his commandments which I command thee this day. And the Lord thy God will make thee plenteous in every work of thine hand, in the fruit of thy body, and in the fruit of thy cattle, and in the fruit of thy land, for good: for the Lord will again rejoice over thee for good, as he rejoiced over thy fathers: If thou shalt hearken unto the voice of the Lord thy God, to keep his commandments and his statutes which are written in this book of the law, and if thou turn unto the Lord thy God with all thine heart, and with all thy soul. For this commandment which I command thee this day, it is not hidden from thee, neither is it far off. It is not in heaven, that thou shouldest say, Who shall go up for us to heaven, and bring it unto us, that we may hear it, and do it? Neither is it beyond the sea, that thou shouldest say, Who shall go over the sea for us, and bring it unto us, that we may hear it, and do it? But the word is very nigh unto thee, in thy mouth, and in thy heart, that thou mayest do it. See, I have set before thee this day life and good, and death and evil; In that I command thee this day to love the Lord thy God, to walk in his ways, and to keep his commandments and his statutes and his judgments, that thou mayest live and multiply: and the Lord thy God shall bless thee in the land whither thou goest to possess it. But if thine heart turn away, so that thou wilt not hear, but shalt be drawn away, and worship other gods, and serve them; I denounce unto you this day, that ye shall surely perish, and that ye shall not prolong your days upon the land, whither thou passest over Jordan to go to possess it. I call heaven and earth to record this day against you, that I have set before you life and death, blessing and cursing: therefore choose life, that both thou and thy seed may live: That thou mayest love the LORD thy God, and that thou mayest obey his voice, and that thou mayest cleave unto him: for he is thy life, and the length of thy days: that thou mayest dwell in the land which the LORD sware unto thy fathers, to Abraham, to Isaac, and to Jacob, to give them. Deuteronomy 30:1-20

The institution of the New Covenant allowed Jews who embraced the New Covenant to escape the curse of the Law and the curse on the people of Israel. This curse included the destruction of the Temple which occurred in AD 70, forty years after Jesus was crucified and ascended into heaven. God also said that He would drive the Jews out of the land if they did not walk according to His ordinance.

Paul stated that those who are under the law are under the curse.

For as many as are of the works of the law are under the curse: for it is written, Cursed is every one that continueth not in all things which are written in the book of the law to do them. Galatians 3:10

This implies that the Law was still in effect even after Christ had ascended back to heaven. The Romans, who came and destroyed the Temple, drove the Jews out of the land, which was a fulfillment of the Law. Therefore, the Law was not thrown out when the New Covenant was introduced. Otherwise, God would not have fulfilled the curse that He said He would bring if Israel turned away and did not obey His commandments.

But in the Law written in Deuteronomy 30, God said that He would do something even after He drove them out of the land. He said that He would bring them back to the land. If God had done away with the Law, then He would have been unable to fulfill this guarantee, even though He had promised to fulfill it.

Malachi promises the arrival of the Kingdom, but notice how it ends.

> But unto you that fear my name... Malachi 4:2

In other words, He is talking to the faithful remnant of Israel and says:

> **Remember ye the law of Moses** my servant, which I commanded unto him in Horeb for all Israel, with the statutes and judgments. Behold, I will send you Elijah the prophet before the coming of the great and dreadful day of the LORD: And he shall turn the heart of the fathers to the children, and the heart of the children to their fathers, lest I come and smite the earth with a curse. Malachi 4:4

If Elijah is not coming back until the end, then why would God tell His people to remember the law of Moses while at the same time having done away with the law of Moses? The Book of Daniel states:

> And **he shall confirm the covenant** with many for one week: and in the midst of the week he shall cause the sacrifice and the oblation to cease, and for the overspreading of abominations he shall make it desolate, even until the consummation, and that determined shall be poured upon the desolate. Daniel 9:27

He, that is the Antichrist, will renew and strengthen the covenant which has been set aside while Israel has been under the curse. During the last seven years, God will give Israel an opportunity for national repentance, which is what happens in Revelation 11 where God brings back Elijah as one of the Two Witnesses which He said He would do in Malachi 4. During the last seven years Israel will worship at the Temple. That is why the Temple itself is mentioned in Revelation 11. In order for Israel to repent according to the law of Moses, first of all they have to have a Temple, and second of all they have to worship at the Temple altar. God gives them the opportunity to do so during that seven-year window.

Yet, the whole earth will become corrupt prior to the return of Christ.

> But evil men and seducers shall wax worse and worse, deceiving, and being deceived. 2 Timothy 3:13

So, in addition to rebuilding the Temple and restarting the daily sacrifices, the mission of the Two Witnesses will be to encourage all people to repent and to turn their hearts to God.

To accomplish their mission the Two Witnesses are given power to perform miracles as well as divine protection from harm. However, after their mission is complete, the Two Witnesses are killed by the Antichrist. Their bodies are allowed to lay in the streets for three and a half days during which time the world rejoices. Most in the world will not like the Witness' message of repentance. People do not want to be told that what they are doing is wrong, that they are sinning and need to change. They will be angry because of the plagues being brought on them as punishments for not repenting of their sins, and they will blame the Two Witnesses for the torment so many will suffer. Yet, the rejoicing over their deaths will be short-lived. After the three and a half days, God will resurrect them from the dead, and their enemies will see them ascend to heaven.

One final mission of the Two Witnesses may be to prepare a place in the wilderness for the children of God to flee during the persecution by the Antichrist throughout the second half of the last seven weeks. In Revelation, John states:

> And the woman fled into the wilderness, where she hath a place prepared of God, that they should feed her there a thousand two hundred and threescore days. Revelation 12:6

Most take this to mean that the woman, that is Israel, will be in the wilderness for 1260 days after fleeing. This would require the 1260 days to equal the forty-two months or the "time, times and a half time" that occur in the second half of the last seven years. Many assume these time periods to be the same. However, although these time periods are close in number, they are not equal. For example, forty-two months equals 1239 days (29.5 days per month) not 1260 days. Since they are not equal, these time periods cannot be referencing the same periods of time. The only other place in scripture that specifically mentions 1260 days occurs in Revelation 11 where it also references the Two Witnesses.

> And I will give power unto my two witnesses, and they
> shall prophesy a thousand two hundred and threescore
> days, clothed in sackcloth. Revelation 11:3

So, if Revelation 12:6 also concerns the Two Witnesses, then the phrase "that they should feed her there a thousand two hundred and threescore days" most likely modifies the verb *prepare* and indicates the length of time that the Two Witnesses will be preparing a place in the wilderness rather than the length of time the woman (i.e., the children of God) will be in the wilderness. If this is the case, then one of the primary purposes of the Two Witnesses will be to make ready the place of safety in the wilderness to receive God's people after the Two Witnesses have been killed at the midpoint of the last seven years. This also is consistent with the Two Witnesses ministering in the first half of the last seven years and does not require them to be present during the forty-two months of the second half.[4]

Adding the additional information on the Two Witnesses, the timeline chart now becomes a little more detailed.

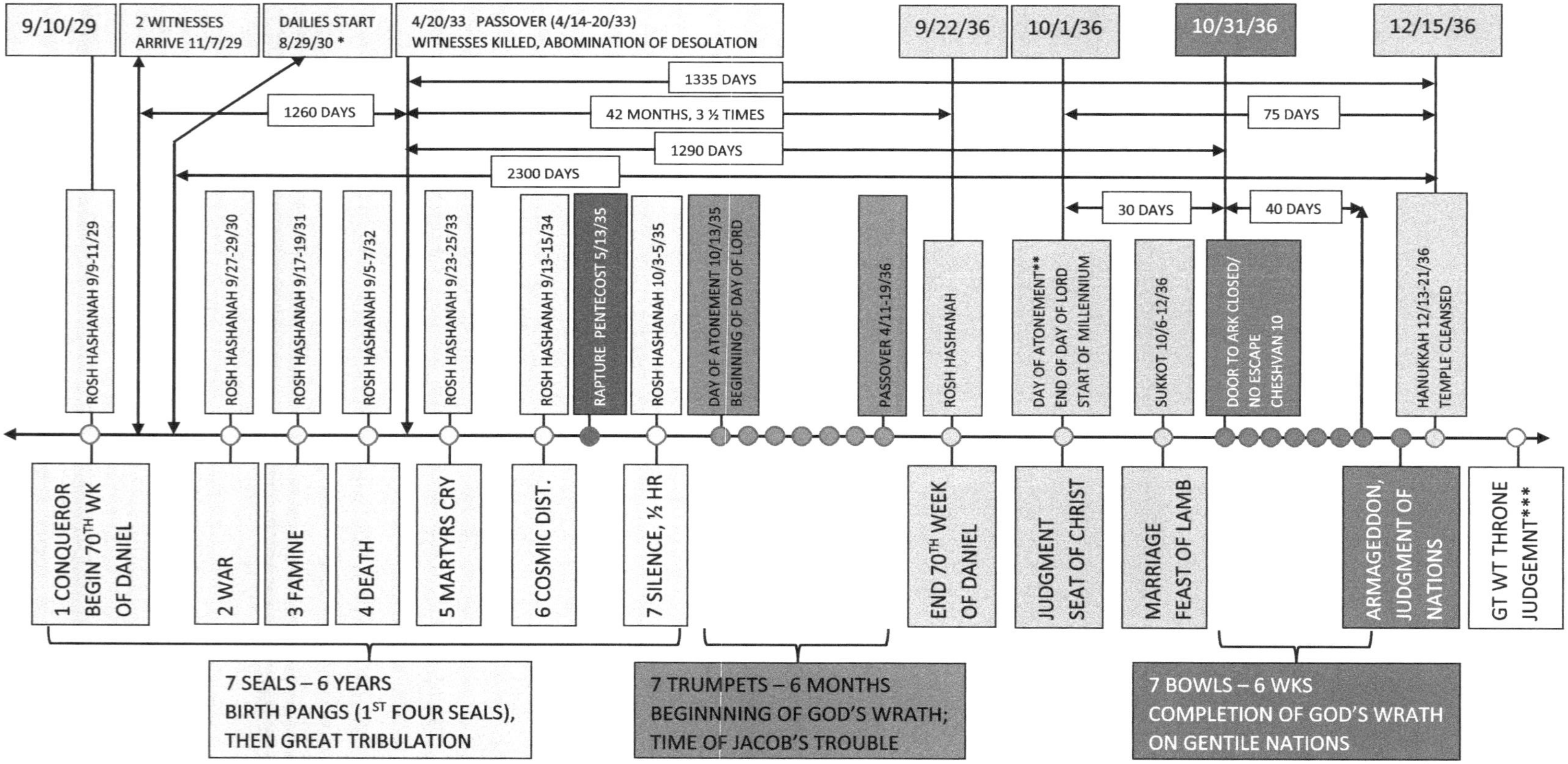
9/10/29
2 WITNESSES ARRIVE 11/7/29
DAILIES START 8/29/30 *
4/20/33 PASSOVER (4/14-20/33) WITNESSES KILLED, ABOMINATION OF DESOLATION
9/22/36
10/1/36
10/31/36
12/15/36
1335 DAYS
1260 DAYS
42 MONTHS, 3 ½ TIMES
75 DAYS
1290 DAYS
2300 DAYS
30 DAYS
40 DAYS
ROSH HASHANAH 9/9-11/29
ROSH HASHANAH 9/27-29/30
ROSH HASHANAH 9/17-19/31
ROSH HASHANAH 9/5-7/32
ROSH HASHANAH 9/23-25/33
ROSH HASHANAH 9/13-15/34
RAPTURE PENTECOST 5/13/35
ROSH HASHANAH 10/3-5/35
DAY OF ATONEMENT 10/13/35 BEGINNING OF DAY OF LORD
PASSOVER 4/11-19/36
ROSH HASHANAH
DAY OF ATONEMENT** END OF DAY OF LORD START OF MILLENNIUM
SUKKOT 10/6-12/36
DOOR TO ARK CLOSED/ NO ESCAPE CHESHVAN 10
HANUKKAH 12/13-21/36 TEMPLE CLEANSED
1 CONQUEROR BEGIN 70TH WK OF DANIEL
2 WAR
3 FAMINE
4 DEATH
5 MARTYRS CRY
6 COSMIC DIST.
7 SILENCE, ½ HR
END 70TH WEEK OF DANIEL
JUDGMENT SEAT OF CHRIST
MARRIAGE FEAST OF LAMB
ARMAGEDDON, JUDGMENT OF NATIONS
GT WT THRONE JUDGEMNT***
7 SEALS – 6 YEARS
BIRTH PANGS (1ST FOUR SEALS),
THEN GREAT TRIBULATION
7 TRUMPETS – 6 MONTHS
BEGINNNING OF GOD'S WRATH;
TIME OF JACOB'S TROUBLE
7 BOWLS – 6 WKS
COMPLETION OF GOD'S WRATH
ON GENTILE NATIONS

DANIEL'S 70TH WEEK

2029-2036

*8/29/30 is exactly 1960 years from the destruction of the 2nd Temple when the daily sacrifices ceased on 8/30/70 AD

**10/1/36 Start of Year of Jubilee

***End of Millennium

CHAPTER 4

The Beasts of Revelation

There are two beasts introduced in Revelation, and they are commonly referred to as the Antichrist and the False Prophet. In Christian eschatology, the Antichrist is a person prophesied in the Bible to oppose Christ and substitute himself in Christ's place before the Second Coming of Christ. Similar to the Two Witnesses, there are differing opinions on whether the Antichrist is a real person or just symbolic of forces that oppose Christ. The position taken here again is that the Bible, including Revelation, should be taken literally wherever possible and whenever the scripture is not clearly allegorical. Hence, the Antichrist discussed in the Bible should be considered to be a real human being who will appear on the world stage prior to the Second Coming of Jesus Christ.

The Beast Nature

Although the Antichrist is a real human being, the beast that appears in Revelation, can be seen to have three natures. First of all, the beast is a man, the Antichrist, and not just a symbol. There are many antichrists as noted in John's writings.

> Little children, it is the last time: and as ye have heard that antichrist shall come, even now are there many antichrists; whereby we know that it is the last time. 1 John 2:18

However, scripture is quite clear about this one specific antichrist who persecutes Israel and the Church in the end times, takes his seat in the Temple of God proclaiming himself to be God, and opposes the returning Lord Jesus Christ at the battle of Armageddon.

> Let no **man** deceive you by any means: for that day shall not come, except there come a falling away first, and that man of sin be revealed, the son of perdition; Who opposeth and exalteth himself above all that is called God, or that is worshipped; so that he as God sitteth in the temple of God, shewing himself that he is God. 2 Thessalonians 2:3-4

> They that see thee shall narrowly look upon thee, and consider thee, saying, Is this the **man** that made the earth to tremble, that did shake kingdoms; That made the world as a wilderness, and destroyed the cities thereof; that opened not the house of his prisoners? Isaiah 14:16-17

So, the beast is a man. However, the beast is not only a man but also at the same time refers to the kingdom or nation that is ruled by that man.

> Thus he said, The fourth beast shall be the fourth **kingdom** upon earth, which shall be diverse from all kingdoms, and shall devour the whole earth, and shall tread it down, and break it in pieces. Daniel 7:23

And finally, the beast has a demonic component who possesses the man, the Antichrist.

> The beast that thou sawest was, and is not; and shall
> ascend out of the bottomless pit, and go into perdition:
> and they that dwell on the earth shall wonder, whose
> names were not written in the book of life from the
> foundation of the world, when they behold the beast
> that was, and is not, and yet is. Revelation 17:8

The "bottomless pit" or "abyss" in scripture is known as a holding place for demons, and consequently the beast is also a demon. Daniel adds that the Antichrist, the man, will not act on his own but with the help of a foreign god.

> Thus shall he do in the most strong holds with a strange
> god, whom he shall acknowledge and increase with
> glory: and he shall cause them to rule over many, and
> shall divide the land for gain. Daniel 11:39

So, it is important to remember that in Daniel and Revelation when it refers to the "beast", it may be indicating the king (i.e., the man), or the kingdom, or the demon, or even all three natures of the beast.

In the book of Revelation, God reveals a prophecy concerning two individuals called "the beast" and "the false prophet", who will be opposed to the work of the Two Witnesses. The Antichrist, who manifests the man part of the beast, will be the civil or political leader who all people of the earth, except those faithful to God, will follow.

> And all that dwell upon the earth shall worship him, whose
> names are not written in the book of life of the Lamb slain
> from the foundation of the world. Revelation 13:8

The false prophet will be the head of the religious system supporting the political system headed by the beast. Satan will use the beast and the false prophet as counterfeits to the Two Witnesses. As a result, Satan will continue to deceive the whole world through signs, lying wonders and false religions.

Even him, whose coming is after the working of Satan with all power and signs and lying wonders, 2 Thess 2:9

For there shall arise false Christs, and false prophets, and shall shew great signs and wonders; insomuch that, if it were possible, they shall deceive the very elect. Matthew 24:24

Names and Examples of the Antichrist

The Antichrist has been called by many names throughout the Bible. The term *antichrist* is employed by the apostle John alone, and is defined by him in a manner which leaves no doubt as to its intrinsic meaning. With regard to its application there is less certainty. The first passage is:

Little children, it is the last time: and as ye have heard that antichrist shall come, even now are there many antichrists; whereby we know that it is the last time. 1 John 2:18

Here the apostle John makes direct reference to the false christs whose coming, it had been fore-told, should mark the last days. Following this, John adds:

Who is a liar but he that denieth that Jesus is the Christ? He is antichrist, that denieth the Father and the Son. 1 John 2:22

For many deceivers are entered into the world, who confess not that Jesus Christ is come in the flesh. This is a deceiver and an antichrist. 2 John 1:7

So, scripture defines antichrist as he "that denieth the Father and the Son;" and also that everyone that does not confess "that Jesus Christ is come in the flesh" is of antichrist.

Just as there are types of the Two Witnesses seen in the Bible who foreshadow the final two witnesses (e.g., Zerubbabel and Joshua in Zechariah 4, as well as John the Baptist in the New Testament) similarly, there have been many antichrists throughout the Bible who have foreshadowed the final Antichrist who appears in the last seven years. Scripture sometimes has double fulfillments. An example of this double fulfillment is Antiochus Epiphanes (short-term fulfillment) and the Antichrist (long-term fulfillment), both seen in Daniel. Antiochus Epiphanes desecrated the Second Temple (a short-term fulfillment of "the abomination that causes desolation") seen in Daniel 11:31, whereas the Antichrist desecrates the future, rebuilt temple (the long-term fulfillment) observed in Daniel 9:27 and Matthew 24:15-16.

Besides Antiochus Epiphanes, historically there have been other candidates mentioned as possible candidates for the end time's Antichrist, with Adolph Hitler cited frequently as a primary example. Yet, there have been other types or foreshadows of the Antichrist seen as early as Genesis in the Bible. Antichrist is the polar opposite of what Christ and the Two Witnesses stand for and represent, and his characteristics can be ascertained in these foreshadows.

The first indication in the Bible of the Antichrist is seen in Cain.

And Adam knew Eve his wife; and she conceived, and bare Cain, and said, I have gotten a man from the LORD. And she again bare his brother Abel. And Abel was a keeper of sheep, but Cain was a tiller of the ground. And in process of time it came to pass, that Cain brought of the fruit of the ground an offering unto the LORD. And Abel, he also brought of the firstlings of his flock and of the fat thereof. And the LORD had respect unto Abel and to his offering: But unto Cain and to his offering he had not respect. And Cain was very wroth, and his countenance fell. And the LORD said unto Cain, Why art thou wroth? and why is thy countenance fallen? If thou doest well, shalt thou not be accepted? and if thou doest not well, sin lieth at the door. And unto thee shall be his desire, and thou shalt rule over him. And Cain talked with Abel his brother: and it came to pass, when they were in the field, that Cain rose up against Abel his brother, and slew him. And the LORD said unto Cain, Where is Abel thy brother? And he said, I know not: Am I my brother's keeper? And he said, What hast thou done? the voice of thy brother's blood crieth unto me from the ground. And now art thou cursed from the earth, which hath opened her mouth to receive thy brother's blood from thy hand; When thou tillest the ground, it shall not henceforth yield unto thee her strength; a fugitive and a vagabond shalt thou be in the earth. And Cain said unto the LORD, My punishment is greater than I can bear. Behold, thou hast driven me out this day from the face of the earth; and from thy face shall I be hid; and I shall be a fugitive and a vagabond in the earth; and it shall come to pass, that every one that findeth me shall slay me. And the LORD said unto him, Therefore whosoever slayeth Cain, vengeance shall be taken on him sevenfold. And the LORD set a mark upon Cain, lest any finding him should kill him. And Cain went out from the presence of the LORD, and dwelt in the land of Nod, on the east of Eden. Genesis 4:1-16

Cain demonstrates the characteristic of false worship which is typical of the Antichrist. Cain is also the first indication of someone receiving a mark, which similarly is associated with the Antichrist as the "mark of the beast" in Revelation.

And the first went, and poured out his vial upon the earth; and there fell a noisome and grievous sore upon the men which had **the mark of the beast**, and upon them which worshipped his image. Revelation 16:2

The next prefigure of the Antichrist is revealed in Nimrod.

And Cush begat Nimrod: he began to be a mighty one in the earth. He was a mighty hunter before the LORD: wherefore it is said, Even as Nimrod the mighty hunter before the LORD. And the beginning of his kingdom was Babel, and Erech, and Accad, and Calneh, in the land of Shinar. Out of that land went forth Asshur, and builded Nineveh, and the city Rehoboth, and Calah, And Resen between Nineveh and Calah: the same is a great city. Genesis 10:8-12

And they said, Go to, let us build us a city and a tower, whose top **may reach unto heaven**; and let us make us a name, lest we be scattered abroad upon the face of the whole earth. Genesis 11:4

Nimrod exhibits disobedience to and rejection of God. In fact, he desired to "reach unto heaven" and to be God, which is another distinguishing characteristic of the Antichrist. Also, Nimrod is linked to "the Assyrian", which is another name used of the Antichrist.

And this man shall be the peace, when **the Assyrian** shall come into our land: and when he shall tread in our palaces, then shall we raise against him seven shepherds, and eight principal men. And they shall waste the land of Assyria with the sword, and the **land of Nimrod** in the entrances thereof: thus shall he deliver us from the Assyrian, when he cometh into our land, and when he treadeth within our borders. Micah 5:5-6

Isaiah likewise suggests that the Antichrist will be an Assyrian:

That I will break **the Assyrian** in my land, and upon my mountains tread him under foot: then shall his yoke depart from off them, and his burden depart from off their shoulders. This is the purpose that is purposed upon the whole earth: and this is the hand that is stretched out upon all the nations. Isaiah 14:25-26

A demonic aspect of the Antichrist and Nimrod is described in Isaiah also:

> Thy pomp is brought down to the grave, and the noise of thy viols: the worm is spread under thee, and the worms cover thee. How art thou fallen from heaven, O **Lucifer**, son of the morning! how art thou cut down to the ground, which didst weaken the nations! For thou hast said in thine heart, I will ascend into heaven, I will exalt my throne above the stars of God: I will sit also upon the mount of the congregation, in the sides of the north: I will ascend above the heights of the clouds; I will be like the most High. Yet thou shalt be brought down to hell, to the sides of the pit. They that see thee shall narrowly look upon thee, and consider thee, saying, Is this **the man** that made the earth to tremble, that did shake kingdoms; Isaiah 14:11-16

At the midpoint of the last seven years, it appears that the Antichrist is killed and is then resurrected.

> And I saw one of his heads as it were wounded to death; and his deadly wound was healed: and all the world wondered after the beast. Revelation 13:3

It is at this point that Satan is cast out of heaven and demonically empowers the Antichrist.

> And the great dragon was cast out, that old serpent, called the Devil, and Satan, which deceiveth the whole world: he was cast out into the earth, and his angels were cast out with him. Revelation 12:9

> And they worshipped the dragon which gave power
> unto the beast: and they worshipped the beast, saying,
> Who is like unto the beast? who is able to make war
> with him? Revelation 13:4

Another foreshadow of the Antichrist exemplified in the Bible is Pharaoh (Exodus 5-14), who enslaved and persecuted the people of God. Pharaoh had sorcerers who are similar to the False Prophet of the Antichrist. The plagues of Egypt parallel the trumpet and bowl judgments that occur during the reign of the Antichrist, and the hardness of Pharaoh's heart reflect the heart of antichrist. Finally, Pharaoh is destroyed in the Red Sea just as the Antichrist will ultimately be destroyed at the battle of Armageddon. So, Pharaoh is another type or prefigure of the Antichrist seen in the Bible.

Other examples or typologies of the Antichrist throughout the Bible can be cited. For example, Haman in the Book of Esther sought to exterminate the Jews, but just as he was defeated, so the Antichrist will be defeated in the end times.

Another example or name that is used for the Antichrist in the Bible is "Gog". Gog is the name of the person or his title that is used in Ezekiel to describe the leader of an army of a coalition of nations that come together "in the latter years" against the land of Israel but are supernaturally defeated.

> And the word of the LORD came unto me, saying, Son
> of man, set thy face against **Gog**, the land of Magog,
> the chief prince of Meshech and Tubal, and prophesy
> against him, And say, Thus saith the Lord GOD; Behold,
> I am against thee, O Gog, the chief prince of Meshech
> and Tubal: Ezekiel 38:1-3

This same name is used again in Revelation to designate one of the principles in a rebellion against the saints at the end of the Millennium

And shall go out to deceive the nations which are in the four quarters of the earth, **Gog**, and Magog, to gather them together to battle: the number of whom is as the sand of the sea. Revelation 20:8

Despite his initial deceptive appearance of one who is peace loving, both Ezekiel and Revelation indicate the hostile, combative nature of the Antichrist. More details about Gog and Magog, as well as another name for the Antichrist, the "little horn", will be discussed later in more detail on the chapter entitled "Wars".

Origin of the Antichrist

Some believe that the Antichrist is Jewish. Support for this comes from a description of the Antichrist in Daniel 11:37 which the King James Version translates as:

Neither shall he regard **the God of his fathers**, nor the desire of women, nor regard any god: for he shall magnify himself above all. Daniel 11:37

It is argued that "the God of his fathers" is the God of the Bible, and therefore, the Antichrist must be Jewish. However, almost all other English translations render this as "And he will show no regard for the **gods** of his fathers." The fact that "gods" is plural indicates that this refers to pagan deities and not the God of Israel. Thus, it implies that the Antichrist would more likely be Gentile and not Jewish.

Many contemporary eschatologists point to the Antichrist coming from a Revived Roman Empire. This idea was made popular by Hal Lindsey in his book *The Late Great Planet Earth* and further propagated in the Left Behind series by Tim LaHaye and Jerry B. Jenkins. The conclusion that the Antichrist is not Jewish but a Gentile who comes from a Revived Roman Empire can first be seen from biblical typology. Most commentators agree that Daniel 11 speaks of Antiochus Epiphanes, a Gentile, who typifies the future Antichrist. Nowhere is a Gentile ever seen as a type of Christ; and for good reason, too, since Christ Himself was to be a Jew. Since Antiochus is a Gentile, then it is inferred that the Antichrist will also be Gentile.

Additionally, biblical imagery supports a Gentile origin of the Antichrist. Scripture pictures the Antichrist as rising up out of the **sea**.

> And I stood upon the sand of the sea, and saw **a beast rise up out of the sea,** having seven heads and ten horns, and upon his horns ten crowns, and upon his heads the name of blasphemy. Revelation 13:1

In prophetic literature "the sea" is an image of the Gentile nations. Thus, the Antichrist here is seen as a Gentile progeny.

Furthermore, the nature of the "Times of the Gentiles" (Luke 21:24) supports a Gentile Antichrist. Fruchtenbaum notes:

> It is agreed by all premillennialists that the period known as the Times of the Gentiles does not end until the second coming of Christ. It is further agreed that the Antichrist is the final ruler of the Times of the Gentiles…. If this is so, how then can a Jew be the last ruler at a time when only Gentiles can have the preeminence? To say the Antichrist is to be a Jew would contradict the very nature of the Time of the Gentiles.[1]

Moreover, some believe that the Bible not only teaches the Antichrist will be Gentile, but it also implies that he will be of Roman descent. This is concluded from Daniel's 70th Week prophecy where the one cutting a covenant with Israel is said to represent the revived Roman Empire, since it was the Romans who destroyed Jerusalem and the Temple in A.D. 70.

> And after threescore and two weeks shall Messiah be cut off, but not for himself: and the **people of the prince** that shall come shall destroy the city and the sanctuary;

and the end thereof shall be with a flood, and unto the end of the war desolations are determined. And he shall confirm the covenant with many for one week: and in the midst of the week he shall cause the sacrifice and the oblation to cease, and for the overspreading of abominations he shall make it desolate, even until the consummation, and that determined shall be poured upon the desolate. Daniel 9:26-27

However, notice that it says "the people of the prince". Since it was the Romans under Titus who destroyed Jerusalem and the Temple in 70 AD, many Bible scholars believe that the Antichrist, the prince, will be of Roman origin and use this specific scripture to support that argument. Yet, although the people that destroyed Jerusalem were indeed Roman soldiers, these soldiers were made up of people from the surrounding area, primarily Syria. This was a common practice in the Roman army. After the Roman Empire had expanded too much for the army to be supplied by only Italian Romans, the conquered people themselves were used as Roman soldiers. The word *people* in Daniel 9:26 is the Hebrew word *am* which refers to ethnicity, and the ethnicity of the Roman soldiers who destroyed Jerusalem and the Temple was Syrian. So, this passage actually supports the idea that the Antichrist will be of Syrian descent and not Roman.

Finally, the idea that the Antichrist is a Gentile ruler is the thrust of Revelation 17:9–12. This passage says that the Beast (John's term in Revelation for the Antichrist) is one of "seven kings" (17:10), thus, a Gentile ruler. G. H. Lang notes:

This eight would be one of the former seven, and so in Revelation 13:3 one of his heads had been smitten unto death, and this death-stroke was healed, that is, a man formerly slain by violence is brought again to life. That he had been a former Gentile monarch seems to forbid that he is a Jew. There does not seem to be a word of Scripture that suggests this last notion.[1]

More recently, the theory of an Islamic (contrary to Roman) Antichrist has been promoted by Joel Richardson in his book *The Islamic Antichrist*.[2] Others, such as David Rosenthal[3], have also presented convincing arguments to support the Antichrist originating from an Islamic background. Rosenthal's argument will be outlined here, where the beast is identified as both a kingdom as well as the king who rules over that kingdom. This "beast" is described in both Daniel and Revelation.

Rosenthal begins his argument using Revelation chapter 17 to identify the possible candidates for the beast. To progressively narrow the possibilities of these candidates, he then moves to Daniel chapters 2, 7, and 8 before concluding back in Revelation chapter 13. A table, as shown below, will be used to itemize his conclusions, progressing from Revelation 17 and ending in Revelation 13. The table will be filled as progress is made through the scriptures, with the goal of ascertaining the identity of the Final Beast Kingdom of the Antichrist (i.e., whether the Final Beast Kingdom is Roman or is indeed Islamic).

REV 17	DANIEL 2	DANIEL 7	DANIEL 8	REV 13

Beginning with Revelation 17, the course of Gentile world powers through world history in relation to Israel is outlined.

> And the angel said unto me, Wherefore didst thou marvel? I will tell thee the mystery of the woman, and of the beast that carrieth her, which hath **the seven heads and ten horns**. The beast that thou sawest was, and is

> not; and shall ascend out of the bottomless pit, and go into perdition: and they that dwell on the earth shall wonder, whose names were not written in the book of life from the foundation of the world, when they behold the beast that was, and is not, and yet is. And here is the mind which hath wisdom. The seven heads are seven mountains, on which the woman sitteth. And there are **seven kings: five are fallen, and one is, and the other is not yet come**; and when he cometh, he must continue a short space. And **the beast that was, and is not, even he is the eighth, and is of the seven**, and goeth into perdition. Revelation 17:7-11

Seven heads with ten horns are described. Ten horns are a recurring theme in Biblical prophecy, where sometimes they are called ten toes and sometimes ten crowns. Revelation 17 also answers who or what these ten horns are.

> And **the ten horns which thou sawest are ten kings**, which have received no kingdom as yet; but receive power as kings one hour with the beast. These have one mind, and shall give their power and strength unto the beast. Revelation 17:12-13

So, the ten horns are a reference to ten kings who rule over ten geographic regions (which are not necessarily countries, since borders of countries have changed throughout history). The Antichrist will rule over these ten kings and geographic regions. These ten kings receive their authority all at one time, and consequently, this eliminates the possibility that these were ten Roman emperors or ten Muslim caliphs or any series of ten consecutive kings. They all reign at the same time and therefore are not in a series of consecutive rulers. Because no set of ten kings ruling all at the same time has occurred in history in this way, these ten kings must be future. They also all have one purpose or mind which is to give their power and strength to the beast. So, there will be ten future kings who rule the beast empire with the beast all at the same time. (Incidentally, the woman described in Revelation 17:7 is Mystery Babylon which will be discussed in the next chapter.)

The seven heads are representative of seven Gentile world powers that have occurred throughout human history. Unlike the ten horns that rule at the same time, these kingdoms ruled one after the other. Five of the seven heads or empires had fallen or come and gone as of the time that this was written by John in the first century. So, the five that had fallen were historic before John's time, and the empire described as "one that is" has to be Rome, since it was in power at the time that John wrote Revelation. Then, there will be two more future empires, a seventh and an eighth. A seventh empire will arise in the future from John's day. Following this seventh empire, there will be an eighth empire and king known as the Beast and Beast Empire that will ascend in the end time.

Again, the sixth empire existed in John's day, since it is described as "one is". This is clearly Rome since it was the empire that was in power at the writing of the Book of Revelation. Five empires preceded the Roman Empire and two will follow it. Because Greece, Medo-Persia, and Babylon are the three major empires that immediately came before Rome, they are identified as the third, fourth and fifth empires. In order to figure out the other kingdoms, it is important to note that Babylon, Medo-Persia, and Greece all had one thing in common, that is they were all large empires that persecuted the Hebrew people. Using that as a criterion for being a "head" or empire, the two powers that match this condition are Egypt, who was the first world power to persecute the Hebrews, and Assyria, who even took the ten northern tribes into captivity. So, Egypt is identified as the first empire and Assyria as the second.

The seventh kingdom is not specifically identified, but it is suggested that it is the Ottoman or Islamic empire, which was a series of caliphates through much of history. It is the only kingdom that conquered the Western Rome or the Byzantine Empire (which fell to the Muslim caliphate in 1453 AD) and also persecuted the Hebrew people. All seven of these kingdoms were Middle Eastern, including the Eastern or Byzantine Roman empire that was based in Turkey and Constantinople.

The eighth kingdom is described as "was, and is not". "Was" implies that the eighth kingdom is one of the previous seven empires (and therefore Middle Eastern) and "is not" indicates that it is not Rome, since that was the empire in power at the time that John wrote this. This also clearly rules out a Revived Roman Empire as the Final Beast Kingdom, which "is not yet come", and therefore, must be future. It also must be one of the first five empires that occurred before the time of John. Adding this information to the table, it identifies the seven kingdoms mentioned in Revelation 17 from which the final beast kingdom must come:

REV 17	DANIEL 2	DANIEL 7	DANIEL 8	REV 13
Egypt 1st king fallen				
Assyria 2nd king fallen				
Babylon 3rd king fallen				
Medo-Persia 4th king fallen				
Greece 5th king fallen				
Rome king that is				
Ottoman king not yet come				
Final Beast 7heads/ 7mountains & 10 horns; was & is not & yet is				

Now that the seven kingdoms have been established, Daniel 2 helps to narrow the choices for the eighth and Final Beast kingdom:

. [31] Thou, O king, sawest, and behold a great image. This great image, whose brightness was excellent, stood before thee; and the form thereof was terrible. [32] This image's head was of fine gold, his breast and his arms of silver, his belly and his thighs of brass, [33] His legs of iron, his feet part of iron and part of clay. [34] Thou sawest till that a stone was cut out without hands, which smote the image upon his feet that were of iron and clay, and brake them to pieces. [35] Then was the iron, the clay, the brass, the silver, and the gold, broken to pieces together, and became like the chaff of the summer threshing floors; and the wind carried them away, that no place was found for them: and the stone that smote the image became a great mountain, and filled the whole earth. [36] This is the dream; and we will tell the interpretation thereof before the king. [37] Thou, O king, art a king of kings: for the God of heaven hath given thee a kingdom, power, and strength, and glory. [38] And wheresoever the children of men dwell, the beasts of the field and the fowls of the heaven hath he given into thine hand, and hath made thee ruler over them all. Thou art this head of gold. [39] And after thee shall arise another kingdom inferior to thee, and another third kingdom of brass, which shall bear rule over all the earth. [40] And the fourth kingdom shall be strong as iron: forasmuch as iron breaketh in pieces and subdueth all things: and as iron that breaketh all these, shall it break in pieces and bruise. [41] And whereas thou sawest the feet and toes, part of potters' clay, and part of iron, the kingdom shall be divided; but there shall be in it of the strength of the iron, forasmuch as thou sawest the iron mixed with miry clay. [42] And as the toes of the feet were part of iron, and part of clay, so the kingdom shall be partly strong, and partly broken. [43] And whereas thou sawest iron mixed with miry clay, they shall mingle themselves with the seed of men: but they shall not cleave one to another, even as iron is not mixed with clay. [44] And in the days of these kings shall the God of heaven set up a kingdom, which shall never be destroyed: and the kingdom shall not be left to other people, but it shall break in pieces and consume all these kingdoms, and it shall stand for ever. [45] Forasmuch as thou sawest that the stone was cut out of the mountain without hands, and that it brake in pieces the iron, the brass, the clay, the silver, and the gold; the great God hath made known to the king what shall come to pass hereafter: and the dream is certain, and the interpretation thereof sure. [46] Then the king Nebuchadnezzar fell upon his face, and worshipped Daniel, and commanded that they should offer an oblation and sweet odours unto him. [47] The king answered unto Daniel, and said, Of a truth it is, that your God is a God of gods, and a Lord of kings, and a revealer of secrets, seeing thou couldest reveal this secret. [48] Then the king made Daniel a great man, and gave him many great gifts, and made him ruler over the whole province of Babylon, and chief of the governors over all the wise men of Babylon. [49] Then Daniel requested of the king, and he set Shadrach, Meshach, and Abednego, over the affairs of the province of Babylon: but Daniel sat in the gate of the king. Daniel 2:31-49

At the time of this prophecy Daniel is in captivity in Babylon, and Nebuchadnezzar the king has a dream of a colossus or statue. The statue is made up of a variety of metals that represent various kingdoms, which again symbolize the course of Gentile world kingdoms. The statue's head of gold represents Babylon. The chest and arms of silver represent Medo-Persia, and the belly and thighs of brass represent Greece. The fourth empire with legs of iron and toes of clay and iron is commonly interpreted as Rome, since it was historically the next kingdom to follow Greece. Consequently, it is naturally assumed that a Revived Roman

Empire will be the Final Beast Kingdom with ten toes or nations over which the Antichrist will rule. However, the text does not necessarily allude to an intermediate empire like Rome but actually jumps to a final empire at the end of world history. Clearly, the scripture states that a "stone", which is Jesus Christ will come at the end of history and will topple all the kingdoms of Babylon, Medo-Persia, and Greece **at the same time** and defeat the Final Beast empire. So, it appears that the colossus skips down from Greece, the belly and thighs of silver, to the Final Beast kingdom of iron comprised of ten nations (toes) of iron and clay. Daniel 2, then, narrows the candidates for the Final Beast empire to three kingdoms: Babylon, Medo-Persia, and Greece. Adding the information from Daniel 2, the table now looks like this:

REV 17	DANIEL 2	DANIEL 7	DANIEL 8	REV 13
Egypt 1st king fallen				
Assyria 2nd king fallen				
Babylon 3rd king fallen	**Babylon** head of gold			
Medo-Persia 4th king fallen	**Medo-Persia** chest & arms of silver			
Greece 5th king fallen	**Greece** thighs of brass			
Rome king that is				
Ottoman king not yet come				
Final Beast 7 heads/ 7 mountains & 10 horns; was & is not & yet is	**Final Beast** legs of iron & toes of clay & iron			

Next up on the table is Daniel 7:

In the first year of Belshazzar king of Babylon Daniel had a dream and visions of his head upon his bed: then he wrote the dream, and told the sum of the matters. [2] Daniel spake and said, I saw in my vision by night, and, behold, the four winds of the heaven strove upon the great sea. [3] And four great **beasts** came up from the sea, diverse one from another. [4] The first was like a lion, and had eagle's wings: I beheld till the wings thereof were plucked, and it was lifted up from the earth, and made stand upon the feet as a man, and a man's heart was given to it. [5] And behold another **beast**, a second, like to a bear, and it raised up itself on one side, and it had three ribs in the mouth of it between the teeth of it: and they said thus unto it, Arise, devour much flesh. [6] After this I beheld, and lo another, like a leopard, which had upon the back of it four wings of a fowl; the **beast** had also four heads; and dominion was given to it. [7] After this I saw in the night visions, and behold a fourth **beast**, dreadful and terrible, and strong exceedingly; and it had great iron teeth: it devoured and brake in pieces, and stamped the residue with the feet of it: and it was diverse from all the **beasts** that were before it; and it had ten horns. [8] I considered the horns, and, behold, there came up among them another little horn, before whom there were three of the first horns plucked up by the roots: and, behold, in this horn were eyes like the eyes of man, and a mouth speaking great things. [9] I beheld till the thrones were cast down, and the Ancient of days did sit, whose garment was white as snow, and the hair of his head like the pure wool: his throne was like the fiery flame, and his wheels as burning fire. [10] A fiery stream issued and came forth from before him: thousand thousands ministered unto him, and ten thousand times ten thousand stood before him: the judgment was set, and the books were opened. [11] I beheld then because of the voice of the great words which the horn spake: I beheld even till the **beast** was slain, and his body destroyed, and given to the burning flame. [12] As concerning the rest of the **beasts**, they had their dominion taken away: yet their lives were prolonged for a season and time. [13] I saw in the night visions, and, behold, one like the Son of man came with the clouds of heaven, and came to the Ancient of days, and they brought him near before him. [14] And there was given him dominion, and glory, and a kingdom, that all people, nations, and languages, should serve him: his dominion is an everlasting dominion, which shall not pass away, and his kingdom that which shall not be destroyed. [15] I Daniel was grieved in my spirit in the midst of my body, and the visions of my head troubled me. [16] I came near unto one of them that stood by, and asked him the truth of all this. So he told me, and made me know the interpretation of the things. [17] These great **beasts**, which are four, are four kings, which shall arise out of the earth. [18] But the saints of the most High shall take the kingdom, and possess the kingdom for ever, even for ever and ever. [19] Then I would know the truth of the fourth **beast**, which was diverse from all the others, exceeding dreadful, whose teeth were of iron, and his nails of brass; which devoured, brake in pieces, and stamped the residue with his feet; [20] And of the ten horns that were in his head, and of the other which came up, and before whom three fell; even of that horn that had eyes, and a mouth that spake very great things, whose look was more stout than his fellows. [21] I beheld, and the same horn made war with the saints, and prevailed against them; [22] Until the Ancient of days came, and judgment was given to the saints of the most

High; and the time came that the saints possessed the kingdom. [23] Thus he said, The fourth **beast** shall be the fourth kingdom upon earth, which shall be diverse from all kingdoms, and shall devour the whole earth, and shall tread it down, and break it in pieces. [24] And the ten horns out of this kingdom are ten kings that shall arise: and another shall rise after them; and he shall be diverse from the first, and he shall subdue three kings. [25] And he shall speak great words against the most High, and shall wear out the saints of the most High, and think to change times and laws: and they shall be given into his hand until a time and times and the dividing of time. [26] But the judgment shall sit, and they shall take away his dominion, to consume and to destroy it unto the end. [27] And the kingdom and dominion, and the greatness of the kingdom under the whole heaven, shall be given to the people of the saints of the most High, whose kingdom is an everlasting kingdom, and all dominions shall serve and obey him. [28] Hitherto is the end of the matter. As for me Daniel, my cogitations much troubled me, and my countenance changed in me: but I kept the matter in my heart. Daniel 7:1-28

Daniel chapters 2 and 7 are parallel passages that give similar information in different ways. So, a lot of the same information is the same. About fifty years passed between Daniel's interpretation of Nebuchadnezzar's dream in chapter 2 and his vision in chapter 7. In Daniel chapter 7, Daniel has a vision of four beasts. The first beast is like a lion; the second is like a bear; the third is like a leopard; and the fourth is distinct and unlike the previous three beasts. It is dreadful with strong iron teeth and ten horns. This is similar to the four kingdoms discussed in Daniel 2, with the ten horns in Daniel 7 corresponding to the ten toes of the colossus in Daniel 2. The first beast in Daniel 7, the lion, corresponds to Babylon of Daniel 2. The second beast, a bear, is Medo-Persia. The bear is raised up on one side, indicating the Medes who came first and were later followed by the stronger Persians. The third beast, a leopard, is Greece, and the fourth beast with ten horns is the Final Beast kingdom. Again, the prophecy in Daniel 7 jumps from the third beast to the end times, and just like the passage in Daniel 2, it focuses on only three of the seven empires: Babylon, Medo-Persia, and Greece.

REV 17	DANIEL 2	DANIEL 7	DANIEL 8	REV 13
Egypt 1st king fallen				
Assyria 2nd king fallen				
Babylon 3rd king fallen	**Babylon** head of gold	**Babylon** like a lion		
Medo-Persia 4th king fallen	**Medo-Persia** chest & arms of silver	**Medo-Persia** like a bear		
Greece 5th king fallen	**Greece** thighs of brass	**Greece** like a leopard		
Rome king that is				
Ottoman king not yet come				
Final Beast 7heads/ 7mountains & 10 horns; was & is not & yet is	**Final Beast** legs of iron & toes of clay & iron	**Final Beast** dreadful with strong iron teeth & 10 horns		

Continuing on to Daniel 8, things get a little more difficult. A vision of a ram and a he goat is described:

> In the third year of the reign of king Belshazzar a vision appeared unto me, even unto me Daniel, after that which appeared unto me at the first. [2] And I saw in a vision; and it came to pass, when I saw, that I was

at Shushan in the palace, which is in the province of Elam; and I saw in a vision, and I was by the river of Ulai. ³ Then I lifted up mine eyes, and saw, and, behold, there stood before the river a ram which had two horns: and the two horns were high; but one was higher than the other, and the higher came up last. ⁴ I saw the ram pushing westward, and northward, and southward; so that no beasts might stand before him, neither was there any that could deliver out of his hand; but he did according to his will, and became great. ⁵ And as I was considering, behold, an he goat came from the west on the face of the whole earth, and touched not the ground: and the goat had a notable horn between his eyes. ⁶ And he came to the ram that had two horns, which I had seen standing before the river, and ran unto him in the fury of his power. ⁷ And I saw him come close unto the ram, and he was moved with choler against him, and smote the ram, and brake his two horns: and there was no power in the ram to stand before him, but he cast him down to the ground, and stamped upon him: and there was none that could deliver the ram out of his hand. ⁸ Therefore the he goat waxed very great: and when he was strong, the great horn was broken; and for it came up four notable ones toward the four winds of heaven. ⁹ And out of one of them came forth a little horn, which waxed exceeding great, toward the south, and toward the east, and toward the pleasant land. ¹⁰ And it waxed great, even to the host of heaven; and it cast down some of the host and of the stars to the ground, and stamped upon them. ¹¹ Yea, he magnified himself even to the prince of the host, and by him the daily sacrifice was taken away, and the place of the sanctuary was cast down. ¹² And an host was given him against the daily sacrifice by reason of transgression, and it cast down the truth to the ground; and it practised, and prospered. ¹³

Then I heard one saint speaking, and another saint said unto that certain saint which spake, How long shall be the vision concerning the daily sacrifice, and the transgression of desolation, to give both the sanctuary and the host to be trodden under foot? [14] And he said unto me, Unto two thousand and three hundred days; then shall the sanctuary be cleansed. [15] And it came to pass, when I, even I Daniel, had seen the vision, and sought for the meaning, then, behold, there stood before me as the appearance of a man. [16] And I heard a man's voice between the banks of Ulai, which called, and said, Gabriel, make this man to understand the vision. [17] So he came near where I stood: and when he came, I was afraid, and fell upon my face: but he said unto me, Understand, O son of man: for at the **time of the end** shall be the vision. [18] Now as he was speaking with me, I was in a deep sleep on my face toward the ground: but he touched me, and set me upright. [19] And he said, Behold, I will make thee know what shall be **in the last end of the indignation: for at the time appointed the end shall be.** [20] The ram which thou sawest having two horns are the kings of Media and Persia. [21] And the rough goat is the king of Grecia: and the great horn that is between his eyes is the first king. [22] Now that being broken, whereas four stood up for it, four kingdoms shall stand up out of the nation, but not in his power. [23] And **in the latter time** of their kingdom, when the transgressors are come to the full, a king of fierce countenance, and understanding dark sentences, shall stand up. [24] And his power shall be mighty, but not by his own power: and he shall destroy wonderfully, and shall prosper, and practise, and shall destroy the mighty and the holy people. [25] And through his policy also he shall cause craft to prosper in his hand; and he shall magnify himself in his heart, and by peace shall destroy many: he shall also stand up against the Prince of princes; but he shall be broken without hand. [26] And the vision of the evening and the morning which was told is true: wherefore shut thou up the vision; for it shall be for many days. [27] And I Daniel fainted, and was sick certain days; afterward I rose up, and did the king's business; and I was astonished at the vision, but none understood it. Daniel 8:1-27

In verse 3, the ram had two horns, one higher than the other, and the higher came up later. This is the same concept in chapter 7 where the bear, which was raised up on one side, corresponded to the Medo-Persian empire, which in verse 20 is identified as the ram. Verse 4 describes the Persian empire that was pushing to the west, to the north, and to the south, and no one could stop them. Then, in verse 5, the he goat is introduced and "touched not the ground", indicating that it moved with great speed. The goat is clearly identified in verse 21 as Greece.

Many Bible scholars interpret Daniel 8 as historical. In other words, they believe that this is describing the Persian- Greek wars that began in 499 BC. This is historical to today, but to Daniel, who was writing this in about 600 BC, these wars were one hundred years in the future. So, most would consider this prophecy to be about something that occurred in the past. The he goat had a "notable horn between his eyes" which most consider to be a reference to Alexander the Great. History shows that the Persian empire was great, unstoppable, and moved to the west, where Alexander the Great smote the ram and broke his two horns.

In verse 8, the he goat, Alexander the Great, was broken: "the he goat waxed very great: and when he was strong, the great horn was broken." It is known that Alexander the Great died at a very early age of about thirty-three, and after he died, his empire was divided among his generals into four major kingdoms: "and for it came up four notable ones toward the four winds of heaven" vs 8. His empire was huge, including most of the Middle East. Interestingly, though his kingdom extended from Greece to the border of India and down to Egypt, Alexander never conquered Arabia because he died before he was able to conquer it. More about Arabia will be discussed in the next chapter on "Mystery Babylon".

There is some debate among scholars as to whether Alexander's kingdom was actually divided into four pieces or perhaps into more than four. Nevertheless, there were four major ones, including Cassander who took over the area of Greece and Macedonia; Lysimachus who ruled over northwest Turkey; Ptolemy who took over Egypt; and Seleucus who reigned over Turkey, Syria, and Persia or Iran, all the way to the border of India. The two main divisions were the Ptolemy empire in Egypt, the southern empire, and the Seleucid empire in Turkey, Iran and Syria, the northern empire.

Out of these four empires, specifically from one empire, the Seleucid or northern empire (which included areas of Turkey, Syria, and Iran), came a little ruler who historically became important and was called Antiochus Epiphanes.

> And out of one of them came forth a little horn, which waxed exceeding great, toward the south, and toward the east, and toward the pleasant land. And it waxed great, even to the host of heaven; and it cast down some of the host and of the stars to the ground, and stamped upon them. Yea, he magnified himself even to the prince of the host, and by him the daily sacrifice was taken away, and the place of the sanctuary was cast down. Daniel 8:9-11

> And it came to pass, when I, even I Daniel, had seen the vision, and sought for the meaning, then, behold, there stood before me as the appearance of a man. Daniel 8:15

As discussed earlier, Antiochus Epiphanes is a type or foreshadowing of the Antichrist. He is known for persecuting the Jewish people and eventually desecrating the Temple in Jerusalem by killing a pig on the altar and putting an image of his deity Zeus in the Temple. But the prophets often gave a near term fulfillment as well as a long term or last days fulfillment. Verse 19 indicates that this is a vision of the last days: "And he said, Behold, I will make thee know what shall be **in the last end** of the indignation: for at **the time appointed the end shall be**." And verse 23 adds: "And in **the latter time** of their kingdom". This implies that this vision is referring to the end times and not necessarily only to the time surrounding Alexander the Great. So, possibly this suggests that this is not simply historical to us but infers a future fulfillment of this prophecy, where this same scenario replays in the last days.

Certainly today, Iran, the ancient Persia, is moving to the west. Iran has done this in Iraq where it controls the capital of Babylon. Even further west in Syria, Iran controls the capital of Damascus and is putting military bases throughout Syria, which is one of the primary concerns of Israel. Iran also essentially controls the capital of Lebanon which is Beirut. So, that is west. Towards the south is Yemen. This skips over Saudi Arabia, which is a devout mortal enemy of Iran, since Saudi Arabia is Sunni Islam, and Iran is Shia Islam. In fact, Iran has threatened to destroy Saudi Arabia, which very well may happen in the last days. So, Iran is moving into Yemen to the south, essentially surrounding Saudi Arabia and controlling the entrance to the Red Sea. By controlling the choke point into the Red Sea, Iran can basically blackmail the world. Iran is also moving to the north into Azerbaijan which has lots of oil in the Caspian Sea, and Iran would like to control that oil. Thus, a case can be made that Iran now is moving to the west, south and north, which could possibly be the beginning of the end times fulfillment of Daniel's vision in chapter 8.

If this is true, then in the future a king from the west may be seen who will push back against Iran's move to dominate the region. Some speculated that this king from the west could be Turkey's President Recep Erdogan, who has made clear his desire to restore the Ottoman Empire and the Islamic caliphate. Iran and Turkey could come into conflict especially as they both attempt to move into and control Syria. If that were to happen and following Daniel 8 to its conclusion, then Erdogan would be killed and the region he controls would be divided up into four areas. It is certainly something that needs to be watched as well as other Turkish leaders that might arise.

So, in Daniel chapter 8, Babylon is eliminated as an option for the end times Beast Kingdom, which leaves Medo-Persia (the ram) and Greece (the he goat) as alternatives.

REV 17	DANIEL 2	DANIEL 7	DANIEL 8	REV 13
Egypt 1st king fallen				
Assyria 2nd king fallen				
Babylon 3rd king fallen	**Babylon** head of gold	**Babylon** like a lion		
Medo-Persia 4th king fallen	**Medo-Persia** chest & arms of silver	**Medo-Persia** like a bear	**Medo-Persia** ram with two horns	
Greece 5th king fallen	**Greece** thighs of brass	**Greece** like a leopard	**Greece** he goat with notable horn	
Rome king that is				
Ottoman king not yet come				
Final Beast 7heads/ 7mountains & 10 horns; was & is not & yet is	**Final Beast** legs of iron & toes of clay & iron	**Final Beast** dreadful with strong iron teeth & 10 horns	?	

Finally, looking at Revelation 13 now assists in identifying this Final Beast kingdom.

> And I stood upon the sand of the sea, and saw a beast
> rise up out of the sea, having seven heads and ten horns,

and upon his horns ten crowns, and upon his heads the name of blasphemy. And the beast which I saw was **like unto a leopard**, and his feet were as the feet of a bear, and his mouth as the mouth of a lion: and the dragon gave him his power, and his seat, and great authority. Revelation 13:1-2

Again, the seven heads or the seven Gentile world powers and the ten heads or ten regions that make up the Final Beast kingdom over which the Antichrist will rule are revealed. In verse 2, the beast is described as like a leopard, with feet like a bear, and a mouth like a lion. This is similar to Daniel 8 where the leopard is Greece, the bear is Medo-Persian and the lion is Babylon. However, the kingdoms are given in reverse order with Greece being listed first. The beast is again described as most like a leopard, with feet like a bear, and mouth like a lion. So, the beast is **most** like a leopard, and the focus in describing the Final Beast kingdom is on Greece.

Using a process of elimination, the "one that is" has to be Rome which consequently is removed as a candidate. The one that "is not" must be from before Rome, which would have to be either Egypt, Assyria, Babylon, Medo-Persia, or Greece. Yet, Daniel 2 and 7 narrows the options down to three empires with the emphasis over and over on Babylon, Medo-Persia, and Greece. Daniel chapter 8 removes Babylon as an option, leaving Medo-Persia and Greece as alternatives. Finally, Revelation 13 isolates the Final Beast kingdom to Greece.

Further support for an end time Grecian empire comes from the prophet Joel who foretelling the end time event of Armageddon stated:

For, behold, in those days, and in that time, when I shall bring again the captivity of Judah and Jerusalem, I will also gather all nations, and will bring them down into the valley of Jehoshaphat, and will plead with them there for my people and for my heritage Israel, whom they have scattered among the nations, and parted my land. And they have cast lots for my people; and have given a boy for an harlot, and sold a girl for wine, that they might drink. Yea, and what have ye to do with me, O Tyre, and Zidon, and all the coasts of Palestine? will ye render me a recompence? and if ye recompense me, swiftly and speedily will I return your recompence upon your own head; Because ye have taken my silver and my gold, and have carried into your temples my goodly pleasant things: The children also of Judah and the children of Jerusalem have ye sold unto the **Grecians**, that ye might remove them far from their border. Behold, I will raise them out of the place whither ye have sold them, and will return your recompence upon your own head: Joel 3:1-7

So, it appears from scripture that in the end times there will be a **Revived Grecian or Alexandrian Empire** (not a Revived Roman Empire) made up of ten regions over which the Antichrist will rule. This old Alexandrian Empire will be made up entirely of Islamic nations, who were (and many now are) persecutors of Israel. This empire will revive under the influence of Islam, and the Antichrist will come out of the region of the ancient Assyrian empire, which could mean the area of Turkey, Northern Iraq, or Northern Syria.

Interestingly, in Daniel 2, Nebuchadnezzar had the dream of a huge statue of five different materials: gold, silver, bronze, iron, and iron mixed with clay. The materials represented five different kingdoms that would rule over Israel, beginning with Nebuchadnezzar's Babylon and followed by Medo-Persia and Greece. There is then a break in time after which the Ottoman Empire rules. This is followed by a final kingdom represented by the feet and toes of the statue, consisting of iron mixed with clay.

And whereas thou sawest the feet and toes, part of potters' clay, and part of iron, the kingdom shall be divided; but there shall be in it of the strength of the iron, forasmuch as thou sawest the **iron mixed with miry clay**. Daniel 2:41

The "iron mixed with miry clay" indicates that some of the countries making up the final kingdom will be strong and some will be weak. Notice the phrase "iron mixed with clay". That is how Daniel described the final kingdom at the end of days. In this phrase, the word *mixed* is translated from the Hebrew word *arab*. An etymological study on this word shows that the root noun for this word means "desert", and as a proper noun it means "Arabia". Also, when Israel was delivered out of Egypt, scripture (Exodus 12:38) says that a "mixed multitude" came with them. The word used for *mixed* here again is the word *arab*. There are other words for *mix* in Hebrew that could have been used by Daniel such as the more common word *balal*. So, what Daniel may be indicating is that the Arab religion Islam will be the common denominator linking or binding the iron and clay together, which again supports the idea that the Final Kingdom is a Revived Grecian Kingdom made up of Arab Islamic states.

REV 17	DANIEL 2	DANIEL 7	DANIEL 8	REV 13
Egypt 1st king fallen				
Assyria 2nd king fallen				
Babylon 3rd king fallen	**Babylon** head of gold	**Babylon** like a lion		**Babylon (3)**
Medo-Persia 4th king fallen	**Medo-Persia** chest & arms of silver	**Medo-Persia** like a bear	**Medo-Persia** ram with two horns	**Medo-Persian (2)**
Greece 5th king fallen	**Greece** thighs of brass	**Greece** like a leopard	**Greece** he goat with notable horn	**Greece (1)**
Rome king that is				

REV 17	DANIEL 2	DANIEL 7	DANIEL 8	REV 13
Ottoman king not yet come				
Final Beast 7heads/ 7mountains & 10 horns; was & is not & yet is	**Final Beast** legs of iron & toes of clay & iron	**Final Beast** dreadful with strong iron teeth & 10 horns	?	**Revived Grecian Empire** 7 heads with 10 horns & 10 crowns on horns; like a leopard & feet as a bear & mouth of a lion

Despite recent actions in the Middle East that might support a Revived Grecian Empire made up of Islamic states, it is important not to base eschatology primarily on current events. Many people throughout history have been led astray by allowing the geopolitical events of their day to determine their view of Bible prophecy. One's view of prophecy should be defined by what the Bible has to say on that topic and not the newspaper. Nevertheless, it is still important to watch what is happening in current events to see if it does align with what the Bible says.

Therefore, it is noteworthy to observe that President Erdogan of Turkey has called for an Islamic worldwide army to come against Israel and recently in 2020 converted the Hagia Sophia from a museum to a mosque. Also, at the Hagia Sophia ceremony Erdogan vowed to liberate the al-Aqsa mosque on the Temple Mount in Jerusalem from Israel. He sees himself as the caliph or leader of a coming Islamic empire. Consequently, he is certainly one who bears watching as the latter days draw nearer.

God does not want His followers to be deceived by these counterfeits, but most people will be duped. To prevent this deception, those who study prophecy attempt to establish the identity of this coming leader or beast who is called "the Antichrist". However, despite these attempts to ascertain who he is or will be, his true identity will only be known for certain when he finally sets himself up in the Temple which he abominates at the midpoint of the 70th Week.

Career of the Antichrist[4]

In Daniel 8, the goat overcomes the ram. Afterwards, the goat's horn is broken and replaced by four beasts or four horns. The rising of the ten horns occurs at the same time followed by the rising of the little horn from among the ten horns. It is only after these events occur that the 70th Week will begin. Now, Jesus alluded to this in the Gospel of Luke in the parable of the fig tree.

> And he spake to them a parable; Behold the fig tree, and all the trees; When they now shoot forth, ye see and know of your own selves that summer is now nigh at hand. Luke 21:29-30

The "fig tree" represents Israel, and "all the trees" characterizes the surrounding Gentile nations. Israel began "sprouting leaves" in 1948 when it became a nation. But, in order to completely fulfill this prophecy, all the trees, i.e., Gentile nations, need to first be in place and undergo the activity detailed in Daniel 7 and 8. Then the 70th Week can begin.

At the beginning of the 70th Week, as seen earlier with the seal judgments, the Antichrist will confirm a covenant or agreement with Israel, possibly allowing them to rebuild the Temple and to restart the daily sacrifices. This agreement will be broken in the middle of the seven years when the abomination of desolation occurs.

> And he shall confirm the covenant with many for one week: and in the midst of the week he shall cause the sacrifice and the oblation to cease, and for the overspreading of abominations hew shall make it desolate, even until the consummation, and that determined shall be poured upon the desolate. Daniel 9:27

> And I saw, and behold a white horse: and he that sat on
> him had a bow; and a crown was given unto him: and he
> went forth conquering, and to conquer. Revelation 6:2

One of the first things the Antichrist does after the beginning of the 70th Week is to attempt to consolidate his kingdom. Daniel 11 speaks of an end time war between the King of the North and the King of the South. The particulars of the little horn's military campaign to unite his Kingdom are described in the following verses:

> And out of one of them came forth a little horn, which
> waxed exceeding great, toward the south, and toward
> the east, and toward the pleasant land. Daniel 8:9

> And in his estate shall stand up a vile person, to whom
> they shall not give the honour of the kingdom: but he
> shall come in peaceably, and obtain the kingdom by
> flatteries. Daniel 11:21

> And at the time of the end shall the king of the south
> push at him: and the king of the north shall come
> against him like a whirlwind, with chariots, and with
> horsemen, and with many ships; and he shall enter into
> the countries, and shall overflow and pass over. He shall
> enter also into the glorious land, and many countries
> shall be overthrown: but these shall escape out of his
> hand, even **Edom, and Moab, and the chief of the
> children of Ammon**. Daniel 11:40-41

By intrigue or flatteries, the little horn, i.e., the Antichrist, will acquire influence over the entire area that was the goat kingdom, similar to the ancient Seleucid empire that formed during the Wars of the Diadochi after Alexander the Great's death. In the Bible the rulers of this region were known as the Kings of the North. These Kings of the North were in opposition to the other major Kingdom that formed out of Alexander's realm, the Ptolemaic Kingdom or the Kings of the South. Daniel 11:40-41 tells us that these ancient wars will repeat in the end times, and that the Antichrist will ultimately triumph. These southern kings may act as one to oppose the aggression of the little horn and become the Kings of the South.

The text says that the King of the North will enter Israel, the beautiful or glorious land, and that many countries will fall. This text also shows who will not originally fall: Edom, Moab and Ammon, which collectively most scholars believe make up modern day Jordan. Continuing with scripture shows what happens next as a result of the Antichrist's actions:

> I considered the horns, and, behold, there came up among them another little horn, before whom there were **three of the first horns plucked up by the roots**: and, behold, in this horn were eyes like the eyes of man, and a mouth speaking great things. Daniel 7:8

> He shall stretch forth his hand also upon the countries: and the land of Egypt shall not escape. But he shall have power over the treasures of gold and of silver, and over all the precious things of Egypt: and the Libyans and the Ethiopians shall be at his steps. Daniel 11:42-43

The little horn will pluck out three of the four horns or kings and replaced them with puppet leaders under his control, but this is only four of the ten horns. He wants to consolidate all of them. So, he will gain control over the hidden treasures of gold and silver, over all the precious things of Egypt, and the Libyans and Ethiopians (although the correct Hebrew term here is *Cush*, which is Sudan) will follow at his heels. So, Egypt, then Libya, and then the Sudan, all fall to the Antichrist. Four of the five southern horns of the ten-kingdom confederacy were mentioned in just these couple of verses.

Interestingly, it also notes that for a period of time Jordan will remain outside of the Antichrist's control, and Saudi Arabia is not mentioned directly at all. However, at some point, which is probably the abomination of desolation that happens at the midpoint of the seven years, all ten horns will give their power to the Antichrist.

> And the ten horns which thou sawest are ten kings, which have received no kingdom as yet; but receive power as kings one hour with the beast. These have one mind, and shall give their power and strength unto the beast. Revelation 17:12-13

So, the Antichrist will consolidate and control all ten horns or kings of this region. Yet, the Middle East is only one portion of the world. Elsewhere he will destroy to an extraordinary degree. However, his power is not his own and will be supernatural or demonic in origin. Daniel 11 also notes that he will take action against the strongest fortresses, which could indicate other Western nations. This is accomplished with the help of a foreign god, who most likely is the demon beast that possesses him. People in Western nations may believe that they are safe and secure behind their military might, but these passages indicate that the Antichrist will be powerful because of the demonic power that possesses him, not due to his own ability or resources. Countries like Israel and the USA may think they are safe, but they are not. Supernatural power overcomes earthly power, and Western nations could be in for a rude shock.

The passage in Daniel 11 also shows that the Antichrist will hand out favors to those who help him, selling land that he acquires from victory and honoring those on his side. So, in addition to help from demons, he will have help from earthly forces, including the False Prophet who will be discussed shortly.

After the rise of the Antichrist, Jesus warns us about wars and disturbances which include rebellions and fighting in the streets. A portion of these disturbances might be the jihad that the False Prophet will be inciting. Jesus says not to be frightened by it. And the reason He warns us is that this indeed will be a frightening thing. Imagine one and a half billion Muslims worldwide, all rising as one in jihad.

These jihadists might be those that the little horn rewards. If they are, this is one way the little horn weakens the nations. Perhaps worldwide riots would all but shut down economic production and lead to famine just as the Bible also predicts. Conceivably, it is at this point, after the consolidating of his kingdom and the weakening of the nations, that the world reaches the midpoint of the 70th Week of Daniel.

Other events will concurrently be happening at the midpoint of the 70th Week of Daniel. First, Daniel 8 tells us that the stars of heaven (a frequent metaphor in the Bible for angels) fall to the earth, which may be the same event that John speaks of in Revelation.

> And the great dragon was cast out, that old serpent, called the Devil, and Satan, which deceiveth the whole world: he was cast out into the earth, and his angels were cast out with him. Revelation 12:9

Also, at the midpoint of the 70th Week, the Antichrist suffers a deadly head wound from which he is resurrected.

> And I saw one of his heads as it were wounded (*sfazo* in Greek) to death; and his deadly wound was healed: and all the world wondered after the beast. Revelation 13:3

> And he exerciseth all the power of the first beast before him, and causeth the earth and them which dwell therein to worship the first beast, whose deadly wound was healed. Revelation 13:12

One of the heads of the beast seemed to have had a fatal wound, but the fatal wound will be healed. The whole world will be astonished and as a result follow the beast. It is unclear whether the Antichrist himself will actually suffer a fatal wound, dies, and is raised to life again. Furthermore, where would the power source for the apparent resurrection come from? Because of the phrase "as it were wounded" or "seemed to have a fatal wound", some scholars think that the Antichrist will rise from the dead, and that he will use that as a mechanism to convince would-be followers that he is "the Christ". Others believe that the Antichrist cannot be resurrected at that time because the unsaved dead are resurrected at the Great White Throne judgment following the Millennium. Consequently, some believe that this is not an actual resurrection but a healing that will cause all the world to "wonder".

However, "one of his heads", referring to the Antichrist, is "wounded *(sfazo)* to death". The phrase "as it had been wounded to death" does not simply mean apparent death, for it is also used to describe the Messiah in Revelation.

> And I beheld, and, lo, in the midst of the throne and of the four beasts, and in the midst of the elders, stood a Lamb as it had been slain *(sfazo),* having seven horns and seven eyes, which are the seven Spirits of God sent forth into all the earth. Revelation 5:6

> And they sung a new song, saying, Thou art worthy to take the book, and to open the seals thereof: for thou wast slain *(sfazo)*, and hast redeemed us to God by thy blood out of every kindred, and tongue, and people, and nation; Revelation 5:9

In other words, the same word used of the wound received by the Lamb (wound or slain, *sfazo* in Greek) is used to describe the Beast's fatal head wound. So, if Christ actually died, then it appears that this ruler will also actually die. But his wound will be healed, which can only mean restoration to life.

Some argue that it is Satan that resurrects the Antichrist, while others contend that Satan cannot raise the dead, and conjecture that God may raise the Antichrist from the dead, perhaps to send people "a powerful delusion" (2 Thessalonians 2:11). Otherwise, this would be the first time that Satan has ever been able to raise the dead. His power and control of man is limited by God, but according to His wise providence God may permit Satan on this one occasion to have the power to raise the dead. When studied in the light of 2 Thessalonians 2, it may well be the tool he will use to deceive men. The coming of the lawless one will be in accordance with the work of Satan displayed in all kinds of counterfeit miracles, signs and wonders, and in every sort of evil that deceives those who are perishing.

> Even him, whose coming is after the working of Satan with all power and signs and lying wonders, And with all deceivableness of unrighteousness in them that perish; because they received not the love of the truth, that they might be saved. And for this cause God shall send them **strong delusion, that they should believe a lie**: 2 Thessalonians 2:9-11

It appears that "the lie" or delusion could be the resurrection of the Antichrist.

Contrary to the view that the "fatal wound" happens to the Antichrist the man, others conjecture that the fatal wound may be inflicted on an Islamic caliphate. This is in part because the words *head*, *mountains*, and even *beast* are sometimes used as metaphors for empires in the Bible. For example, the term *beast* in Daniel is used as a metaphor for the successive kingdoms or empires beginning with Nebuchadnezzar (see Daniel 7:5-7,11,19,23). Note also that the term *horn* is a metaphor for leader. So, it may be the revival of a previously great empire that will have suffered what the Bible calls a "fatal head wound", and is not the Antichrist as commonly understood by Western prophecy analysts. This empire could be the Islamic Ottoman Empire which replaced the Roman Empire after the fall of its remaining Eastern section and was one of the world's greatest empires. It was also the head of history's most anti-Christian empire. Ultimately it was dismantled and broken up by the Christian West in 1924. Islam is rising from the ashes of its past in order to claim its place as the most dominant world power. Islamists the world over are now seeking to return to the triumphant days when Muslims ruled the Middle East and non-Muslims were subservient. Besides the Ottoman Empire, some authors think that the "fatal wound" may symbolically refer to the Roman Empire which has long been dormant, and may someday come back to life.

It is likely after this miraculous recovery from a fatal head wound that the little horn takes over the Temple. In Daniel chapter 8 he exalts himself over Jesus the commander of the host and ends the sacrifice in the Temple.

> Yea, he magnified himself even to the prince of the host, and by him the daily sacrifice was taken away, and the place of the sanctuary was cast down. And an host was given him against the daily sacrifice by reason of transgression, and it cast down the truth to the ground; and it practised, and prospered. Daniel 8:11-12

This is of course the same event as seen in Daniel 9.

> And he shall confirm the covenant with many for one week: and in the midst of the week he shall cause the sacrifice and the oblation to cease, and for the overspreading of abominations he shall make it desolate, even until the consummation, and that determined shall be poured upon the desolate. Daniel 9:27

This same abomination or transgression of desolation is again mentioned later in Daniel 11.

> And arms shall stand on his part, and they shall pollute the sanctuary of strength, and shall take away the daily sacrifice, and they shall place the abomination that maketh desolate. Daniel 11:31

And Jesus mentions this abomination as well in Matthew.

> When ye therefore shall see the abomination of desolation, spoken of by Daniel the prophet, stand in

the holy place, (whoso readeth, let him understand:)
Matthew 24:15

Finally, Paul references this important sign in 2 Thessalonians.

> Let no man deceive you by any means: for that day shall
> not come, except there come a falling away first, and
> that man of sin be revealed, the son of perdition; Who
> opposeth and exalteth himself above all that is called
> God, or that is worshipped; so that he as God sitteth
> in the temple of God, shewing himself that he is God.
> 2 Thessalonians 2:3-4

The abomination of desolation is the single most significant sign of the end times. Paul is clear that this is the revealing of the man of sin. Although Daniel indicates a lot of signs about the little horn, it will be unclear that he actually is the beast until he sits in the Temple of God. Yet many ask: how can a Muslim receive worship. How can he exalt himself above all gods including his own? The Bible makes it clear that the little horn and the beast demon and Satan will only seek worship for themselves. So, it is likely that the Islamic religion is only a vehicle for the Antichrist and Isa, the Muslim Jesus, to get to this point. Once they are at this point, when the abomination of desolation happens, things may change. Islam actually allows a prophet to change the religion, and not only to change it but also to add to it. The problem with that is that Mohammed is the last of the prophets. Muslims call him the seal of the prophets, and they allow no more. But Isa supposedly was a prophet before Muhammad, and maybe he will he be allowed to declare the little horn to be God on earth or Allah on earth to the Muslims. In this way, he could fulfill Daniel 11:37.

> Neither shall he regard the God of his fathers, nor
> the desire of women, nor regard any god: for he shall
> magnify himself above all. Daniel 11:37

No longer will he worship Allah if he claims to be him in the flesh. So, that is a possible answer to the Muslim question. But what about the Jews? How will they accept him? The beast's and Satan's purpose is to receive worship that is intended for God and take it for themselves. The beast does not receive worship because he is deemed worthy to be the Messiah of Israel, as many claim. He receives worship out of deception and fear. In fact, Jesus said:

> I am come in my Father's name, and ye receive me not: if another shall come in his own name, him ye will receive. John 5:43

So, while Jesus came in His father's name Jehovah, as the Jewish Messiah, the Antichrist will come in his own name, not as a Jewish Messiah. Coming in the Father's name also means that Jesus fulfilled the Father's requirements for a Messiah. The Antichrist comes not fulfilling those things and not in the name of the God of Israel.

The Jews will worship the little horn, the Antichrist, (but not necessarily accept him) because of the four means he uses to receive worship. The first of the four means is by deception, using signs and wonders performed by the False Prophet.

> And he exerciseth all the power of the first beast before him, and causeth the earth and them which dwell therein to worship the first beast, whose deadly wound was healed. And he doeth great wonders, so that he maketh fire come down from heaven on the earth in the sight of men, Revelation 13:12-13

Jesus referred to these signs and states that they will be incredibly convincing.

> For there shall arise false Christs, and false prophets, and shall shew great signs and wonders; insomuch that,

if it were possible, they shall deceive the very elect.
Matthew 24:24

Those who see with their eyes only and not with faith will be completely overcome by these signs.

The second means that the Antichrist uses to gain worship is his ability to wage war.

> And they worshipped the dragon which gave power unto the beast: and they worshipped the beast, saying, Who is like unto the beast? who is able to make war with him? Revelation 13:4

Daniel tells us that the Antichrist is empowered by a demonic beast to wage war. The world will recognize the supernatural element in his victories. He will win when he should not, and then the world will worship him because of this supernatural aspect of his military exploits.

The third means by which the beast gains worship is economic. The False Prophet proposes the mark of the beast and demands that no one will be able to buy or sell except the one who has the mark.

> And that no man might buy or sell, save he had the mark, or the name of the beast, or the number of his name. Revelation 13:17

No one will be able to participate in the world system of commerce without taking the beast's mark. Those who are unprepared for this and are unwilling to go off the grid at that point will worship the beast to get what they need.

And the final means the Antichrist uses to receive worship will be the fear of death.

> And he had power to give life unto the image of the beast, that the image of the beast should both speak, and cause that as many as would not worship the image of the beast should be killed. Revelation 13:15

So, an evil image of the beast will be made, and it will be given breath. Then it will speak, and those who do not worship the image will be killed. The career of the little horn will center on receiving worship by these four means: by deception with false signs and wonders, by supernatural military victories, by economic control and by fear of death if people do not worship him. All people groups and religions are susceptible to these things, and the little horn's ethnic identity cannot be determined solely by his gaining worship from this group or that group. He will gain worship from all of them.

> And it was given unto him to make war with the saints, and to overcome them: and power was given him over all kindreds, and tongues, and nations. And all that dwell upon the earth shall worship him, whose names are not written in the book of life of the Lamb slain from the foundation of the world. Revelation 13:7-8

The Antichrist will receive worship from the world and persecute the saints. But finally, in Daniel 7 the court will sit and judgment will be passed in favor of the saints. As Daniel 8 relates:

> And through his policy also he shall cause craft to prosper in his hand; and he shall magnify himself in his heart, and by peace shall destroy many: he shall also stand up against the Prince of princes; but he shall be broken without hand. Daniel 8:25

Jesus will destroy the kingdom, kill the little horn, and throw the demon into the Lake of fire. The Antichrist's defeat will occur during Jesus' second coming. His overthrow by Jesus will transpire first at the Psalm 83 War and finally at the Gog Magog War of Armageddon at the end of the 70th Week. These wars are outlined in more detail on the chapter entitled "Wars". Following his defeat, he is cast into the lake of fire along with the False Prophet.

And I saw the beast, and the kings of the earth, and
their armies, gathered together to make war against
him that sat on the horse, and against his army. And
the beast was taken, and with him the false prophet
that wrought miracles before him, with which he
deceived them that had received the mark of the beast,
and them that worshipped his image. These both were
cast alive into a lake of fire burning with brimstone.
Revelation 19:19-20

Thus, ends the career of the Antichrist, beginning with his rise to
power after the Ram Goat War of Daniel 8 (again discussed later in the
chapter on "Wars") and prior to the start of the 70th Week. His peace
deal with Israel will allow them to build the Temple. His consolidation
of power with the ten-nation confederacy ensues, with the eventual
invasion of Israel where he suffers a fatal head wound from which he is
resurrected. Persecution of Jews and Christians and anyone who does
not worship the Antichrist follows. The second coming of Christ then
results in his defeat and death finally at the Battle of Armageddon.

FALSE PROPHET

In addition to the Antichrist, there is a second beast recorded in
Revelation who is just as powerful as the first beast.

And I beheld another beast coming up out of the earth;
and he had two horns like a lamb, and he spake as a
dragon. Revelation 13:11

Whereas the first beast is primarily political in nature and concerned
with ruling over a kingdom, this second beast is more of a religious
figure who uses his power to cause the world to worship the first beast,
the Antichrist. As a result, he is commonly referred to as the False
Prophet.

Jewish Origin of the False Prophet

As previously noted, the Antichrist will be a Middle Eastern Gentile man. The Antichrist is likely to be a Gentile for several reasons. First of all, the Old Testament type of the Antichrist was a Gentile, namely Antiochus Epiphanes. Secondly, he is identified as coming from the "sea" which is symbolic of the Gentile nations (while the "land" is symbolic of Israel).

> And I stood upon the sand of the sea, and saw **a beast rise up out of the sea**, having seven heads and ten horns, and upon his horns ten crowns, and upon his heads the name of blasphemy. Revelation 13:1

Thirdly, since he is part of the world's final Gentile world power, having a Jew lead this world power would not make sense.

And fourthly, the Antichrist will persecute the Jewish people that God "set apart" from the rest of the nations. The intent was to use Israel as an example of how God blesses the nations that proclaim Him as the one true God. However, much of Israel has disobeyed God throughout the centuries. Nevertheless, God has promised to bless the descendants of Abraham, Isaac, and Jacob. He is not through with Israel yet.

So, while the Antichrist is likely a Gentile, coming from the "sea", the second beast of Revelation, the False Prophet, probably is of Jewish background. Unlike the Antichrist, he comes out of the "earth", which again is symbolic of Israel.

> And I beheld **another beast coming up out of the earth**; and he had two horns like a lamb, and he spake as a dragon. Revelation 13:11

Islamic writings also show that they expect a man to arise in the end times named Isa. Muslims believe that he will say that he is the historic Jesus returned to earth. He will announce that Judgment Day has come, and he will call all Muslims, both radical and moderate, to rise up in worldwide jihad. Eerily, Jesus speaks of something very similar.

> And he said, Take heed that ye be not deceived: for many shall come in my name, saying, I am Christ; and the time draweth near: go ye not therefore after them. But when ye shall hear of wars and commotions, be not terrified: for these things must first come to pass; but the end is not by and by. Luke 21:8-9

Jesus warns that false prophets will come, claiming to be him, the historic Jesus, and that they will say the end time is near. The Bible's predictions are very similar to the Muslim writings. Isa will likely claim to be the real Jesus, but obviously he will not be. He will in all probability be a Muslim and will deny that Jesus ever was divine and ever died on a cross. He will claim to only be a prophet, not the son of God. If he does arise, he will likely be the False Prophet. Satan, the great deceiver, has concocted a similar but false narrative where just as Christian end times prophecy contains three main individuals (Jesus, the Antichrist, and the False Prophet), Islamic eschatology has similar corresponding characters called the Mahdi (their messiah and political leader), Isa (their Jesus and spiritual leader who again may be the Christian False Prophet), and the ad-Dijjal (their false messiah who may be the true Christian Jesus).

	Messiah	End Times Prophet	False Messiah
Christian	Jesus	False Prophet	Antichrist
Islamic	Mahdi or Twelfth Imam	Isa (Muslim Jesus)	Ad-Dijjal

Persian Origin of the False Prophet

Besides describing the second beast as "coming out of the earth", Revelation also states that "he had two horns like a lamb". The "two horns" could be the two divisions of Israel, Judah and Israel, indicating again that the False Prophet is Jewish. Interestingly, the only other reference in the Bible that depicts a sheep with two horns is in Daniel 8 where Daniel is given a vision of a ram and a goat. The ram or male sheep is described with two horns and is later specifically identified as Persia or modern-day Iran.

> And he came to the ram that had two horns, which I had seen standing before the river, and ran unto him in the fury of his power. Daniel 8:6

> The ram which thou sawest having two horns are the kings of Media and Persia. Daniel 8:20

This could be a hint that the false prophet is of Persian as well as of Jewish descent. Today, the largest concentration of Israeli Persians is located in the city of Holon, just outside of Tel Aviv, Israel where 250,000 Jews of Iranian descent live. Holon is a city on the central coastal strip of Israel, south of Tel Aviv. It is part of the metropolitan Gush Dan area in what was the territory originally given to the tribe of Dan.

Danite Origin of the False Prophet

Although some have indicated that the Antichrist might come from the tribe of Dan, it could actually be the False Prophet who is a descendant from the tribe of Dan. Of course, this is speculation, but the tribe of Dan does have an interesting history throughout the Bible as well as historical texts. According to the book of Genesis, Dan (which in Hebrew means "judgment" or "he judged"), was the fifth son of Jacob and the first son of Bilhah. He was the founder of the Israelite tribe of Dan. In the biblical account, Dan's mother Bilhah is described as Rachel's handmaid, who eventually becomes one of Jacob's wives.

> And when Rachel saw that she bare Jacob no children, Rachel envied her sister; and said unto Jacob, Give me children, or else I die. And Jacob's anger was kindled

against Rachel: and he said, Am I in God's stead, who hath withheld from thee the fruit of the womb? And she said, Behold my maid Bilhah, go in unto her; and she shall bear upon my knees, that I may also have children by her. And she gave him Bilhah her handmaid to wife: and Jacob went in unto her. And Bilhah conceived, and bare Jacob a son. And Rachel said, God hath judged me, and hath also heard my voice, and hath given me a son: therefore called she his name Dan. Genesis 30:1-6

Dan was the father of Hushim, according to Gen 46:23, and Samson was a descendant of Dan. Dan was given a blessing by his father, Jacob, just before he died. The blessing is recorded in Genesis.

Dan shall judge his people, as one of the tribes of Israel. Dan shall be a serpent by the way, an adder in the path, that biteth the horse heels, so that his rider shall fall backward. I have waited for thy salvation, O LORD. Genesis 49:16-18

Here, prophecy asserts that Dan's descendants would judge his people at some future time. At least part of the blessing was fulfilled by Samson who judged Israel for twenty years (Judges 15:16, 20). This ancestral information is provided in Judges 16:31 where it states that Samson's father was Manoah who was a Danite (Judges 13:2). Thus, Samson was a Danite who judged Israel, fulfilling the prophecy.[5] However, this judging from Dan may come from a future Danite False Prophet.

The next part of the blessing reveals that Dan would be like the serpent in the Garden of Eden, which seems to have been interpreted as connecting Dan to Belial, a connection made, for example, in the apocryphal Testament of Dan. *Belial* is a term occurring in the Hebrew Bible and used to characterize the wicked or worthless. It later became personified as the Devil in Jewish and Christian texts.

Also, there is a link between Dan, the serpent, and the horse and his rider. This rider associated with Dan in Genesis could be a reference to the same rider who sits on a white horse described in the first seal of Revelation 6. It is a common theme in the Old Testament that the Lord triumphs over the horse and his rider (Exodus 15:1,21; Jeremiah 51:21; Zechariah 12:4). This rider in the first seal is commonly assumed to be the Antichrist. So, a connection between Danite False Prophet and the Antichrist may be implied in this prophecy of Jacob.

Before entering the Promised Land, Moses, just as Jacob had done before his death, pronounced a final blessing on Israel's twelve tribes. In regards to the tribe of Dan, he stated:

> And of Dan he said, Dan is a lion's whelp: he shall leap
> from Bashan. Deuteronomy 33:22

Jacob, as seen earlier, compared Dan to a serpent and an adder or horned serpent. So, the lion of the tribe of Dan should not be confused with the lion of the tribe of Judah. Satan deceptively tries to mimic God, as seen above in his attempt to imitate Christ, the rider of the white horse in Revelation 19. Here, again, Satan's attempted deception continues with his comparison to a lion, a common metaphor for Christ. In fact, Psalms connects these descriptions of Dan as a young lion with the dragon, which is a reference to Satan and the Antichrist.

> Thou shalt tread upon the lion and adder: the **young
> lion** and the dragon shalt thou trample under feet.
> Psalm 91:13

A different link between the "young lion", (a possible reference to the False Prophet) and the "Assyrian" or Antichrist, occurs in Hosea.

> Ephraim is oppressed and broken in judgment, because he
> willingly walked after the commandment. Therefore will
> I be unto Ephraim as a moth, and to the house of Judah
> as rottenness. When Ephraim saw his sickness, and Judah

saw his wound, then went Ephraim to the **Assyrian**, and sent to king Jareb: yet could he not heal you, nor cure you of your wound. For I will be unto Ephraim as a lion, and as a **young lion** to the house of Judah: I, even I, will tear and go away; I will take away, and none shall rescue him. I will go and return to my place, till they acknowledge their offence, and seek my face: in their affliction they will seek me early. Hosea 5:11-15

Interestingly, in a chapter that begins by describing Jesus as coming from Bethlehem (Micah 5:2), the prophet Micah also associates the Assyrian or Antichrist with a young lion.

And this man shall be the peace, when **the Assyrian** shall come into our land: and when he shall tread in our palaces, then shall we raise against him seven shepherds, and eight principal men. And they shall waste the land of Assyria with the sword, and the land of Nimrod in the entrances thereof: thus shall he deliver us from the Assyrian, when he cometh into our land, and when he treadeth within our borders. And the remnant of Jacob shall be in the midst of many people as a dew from the LORD, as the showers upon the grass, that tarrieth not for man, nor waiteth for the sons of men. And the remnant of Jacob shall be among the Gentiles in the midst of many people as a lion among the beasts of the forest, as a **young lion** among the flocks of sheep: who, if he go through, both treadeth down, and teareth in pieces, and none can deliver. Micah 5:5-8

Dan is also prophesied to "leap from Bashan" in Deuteronomy 33:32. Scholars are uncertain why this should be, since the tribe did not live in the Bashan plain, east of the Jordan River. Elliot's Commentary for English Readers notes that the taking of Laish by Dan is probably referred to. It was a sudden, treacherous surprise, like the spring of a lion on his prey.

And they took the things which Micah had made, and the priest which he had, and came unto Laish, unto a people that were at quiet and secure: and they smote them with the edge of the sword, and burnt the city with fire. And there was no deliverer, because it was far from Zidon, and they had no business with any man; and it was in the valley that lieth by Bethrehob. And they built a city, and dwelt therein. Jdg 18:27-28

Throughout scripture Bashan represents opposition to God. For example, in Psalms the "hill of Bashan" is opposed to God's hill.

The hill of God is as the hill of Bashan; an high hill as the hill of Bashan. Psalm 68:15

Also, the "king of Bashan" is reproved by Amos.

Hear this word, ye kine of Bashan, that are in the mountain of Samaria, which oppress the poor, which crush the needy, which say to their masters, Bring, and let us drink. Amos 4:1

And finally, the "bulls of Bashan" represent the enemies of Christ in Psalms.

Many bulls have compassed me: strong bulls of Bashan have beset me round. Psalm 22:12

So, Dan was like a lion cub - a lion in its fierceness of attacking whatever might threaten, but a cub in being second in importance to the ones it defends, much like the False Prophet.

Throughout the Old Testament, Dan is not faithful to the God of Abraham, Jacob and Isaac. When the Israelites entered the Promised Land, the tribe of Dan was given the seventh opportunity to select their territory.

And the seventh lot came out for the tribe of the children of Dan according to their families. And the coast of their inheritance was Zorah, and Eshtaol, and Irshemesh, And Shaalabbin, and Ajalon, and Jethlah, And Elon, and Thimnathah, and Ekron, And Eltekeh, and Gibbethon, and Baalath, And Jehud, and Beneberak, and Gathrimmon, And Mejarkon, and Rakkon, with the border before Japho. And the coast of the children of Dan went out too little for them: therefore the children of Dan went up to fight against Leshem, and took it, and smote it with the edge of the sword, and possessed it, and dwelt therein, and called Leshem, Dan, after the name of Dan their father. This is the inheritance of the tribe of the children of Dan according to their families, these cities with their villages. When they had made an end of dividing the land for inheritance by their coasts, the children of Israel gave an inheritance to Joshua the son of Nun among them: According to the word of the LORD they gave him the city which he asked, even Timnathserah in mount Ephraim: and he built the city, and dwelt therein. These are the inheritances, which Eleazar the priest, and Joshua the son of Nun, and the heads of the fathers of the tribes of the children of Israel, divided for an inheritance by lot in Shiloh before the LORD, at the door of the tabernacle of the congregation. So they made an end of dividing the country. Joshua 19:40-51

However, they were not able to occupy their selected territory due to a lack of faith. As a result, they later moved north and in the process of moving north, the Danites stole Micah's idols (a story relayed in Judges 18:1-31).

Then answered the five men that went to spy out the country of Laish, and said unto their brethren, Do ye know that there is in these houses an ephod, and teraphim, and a graven image, and a molten image? now therefore consider what ye have to do. And they turned thitherward, and came to the house of the young man the Levite, even unto the house of Micah, and saluted him. And the six hundred men appointed with their weapons of war, which were of the children of Dan, stood by the entering of the gate. And the five men that went to spy out the land went up, and came in thither, and took the graven image, and the ephod, and the teraphim, and the molten image: and the priest stood in the entering of the gate with the six hundred men that were appointed with weapons of war. And these went into Micah's house, and fetched the carved image, the ephod, and the teraphim, and the molten image. Then said the priest unto them, What do ye? And they said unto him, Hold thy peace, lay thine hand upon thy mouth, and go with us, and be to us a father and a priest: is it better for thee to be a priest unto the house of one man, or that thou be a priest unto a tribe and a family in Israel? Judges 18:14-19

Consequently, Micah's priest agreed to be the priest for the Danites.

And the priest's heart was glad, and he took the ephod, and the teraphim, and the graven image, and went in the midst of the people. Judges 18:20

And they took the things which Micah had made, and the priest which he had, and came unto Laish, unto a people that were at quiet and secure: and they smote them with the edge of the sword, and burnt the city with fire. Judges 18:27

Judges 18:30 gives a final sad report on Dan.

> And the children of Dan set up the graven image: and
> Jonathan, the son of Gershom, the son of Manasseh, he
> and his sons were priests to the tribe of Dan until the
> day of the captivity of the land. Judges 18:30

The sad report is that the Danites continued in apostasy and idolatrous worship until the Assyrian Empire took them captive in 722 B.C. (1 Kings 12:28-30; 2 Kings 10:29).

Because the Book of Judges, in the account of Micah's Idol, describes the tribe of Dan as having used the ephod and the teraphim in worship, and pictures Samson (a member of the tribe of Dan) as failing to adhere to the rules of a Nazarite, classical rabbinical writers conclude that Dan was very much a black sheep in Israel. In the Book of Jeremiah, the area north of Canaan is associated with darkness and evil. Consequently, rabbinical sources have typically treated Dan as the archetype of wickedness.

In the apocryphal Testament of the Patriarchs, Dan is portrayed as having hated Joseph, and having been the one that invented the idea of deceiving Jacob by the smearing of Joseph's coat with the blood of a kid. In the apocryphal Prayer of Asenath, Dan is portrayed as plotting with the Egyptian crown prince, against Joseph and Asenath.[6]

In the New Testament, John the Apostle omits the tribe of Dan when mentioning the twelve tribes of the sons of Israel while describing the 144,000 sealed Israelites.

> And I heard the number of them which were sealed:
> and there were sealed an hundred and forty and four
> thousand of all the tribes of the children of Israel.Of
> the tribe of Juda were sealed twelve thousand. Of the
> tribe of Reuben were sealed twelve thousand. Of the
> tribe of Gad were sealed twelve thousand. Of the tribe
> of Aser were sealed twelve thousand. Of the tribe of
> Nephthalim were sealed twelve thousand. Of the tribe
> of Manasses were sealed twelve thousand. Of the tribe
> of Simeon were sealed twelve thousand. Of the tribe

of Levi were sealed twelve thousand. Of the tribe of Issachar were sealed twelve thousand. Of the tribe of Zabulon were sealed twelve thousand. Of the tribe of Joseph were sealed twelve thousand. Of the tribe of Benjamin were sealed twelve thousand. Revelation 7:4-8

Instead of Dan, the tribe of Joseph appears twice (represented also by Manasseh). Although the selection of the twelve tribes does not include the names of Ephraim and Dan, their names were used for the twelve tribes that settled in the Promised Land. It has been suggested that this could be because of their pagan practices. This led early church fathers such as Irenaeus, Hippolytus of Rome and some Millennialists to propose that the Antichrist would come from the tribe of Dan, drawing the belief from a verse in the Book of Jeremiah.

The snorting of his horses was heard from Dan: the whole land trembled at the sound of the neighing of his strong ones; for they are come, and have devoured the land, and all that is in it; the city, and those that dwell therein. Jeremiah 8:16

Although Samson was the most famous Danite, there was another man most likely from the tribe of Dan. His name was Simon Magus, but he was also known as Simon the Sorcerer and Simon the Magician. His confrontation with Peter is recorded in Acts 8:9-24. He came from the village of Gitta in Samaria. This was a site settled by the tribe of Dan according to the Jewish historian Josephus. Justin Martyr, who was himself a 2nd-century native of Samaria, wrote that nearly all the Samaritans in his time were adherents of Simon. Surviving orthodox texts, such as those of Irenaeus, Justin Martyr, Hippolytus, and Epiphanius, regarded Simon as the source of all heresies, including Gnosticism.

So, although the evidence is circumstantial at best, a case can be made that the False Prophet will be Jewish in origin (possibly a Persian Jew) and may come from the tribe of Dan with their history of apostasy.

Despite this apostasy and even though the tribe of Dan is missing from the list of tribes making up the 144,000 during the 70th Week of Daniel, they do appear in Ezekiel's end time's narrative.

> Now these are the names of the tribes. From the north end to the coast of the way of Hethlon, as one goeth to Hamath, Hazarenan, the border of Damascus northward, to the coast of Hamath; for these are his sides east and west; a portion for Dan. And by the border of Dan, from the east side unto the west side, a portion for Asher. Ezekiel 48:1-2

> And at the east side four thousand and five hundred: and three gates; and one gate of Joseph, one gate of Benjamin, one gate of Dan. Ezekiel 48:32

These passages reveal that the tribe of Dan will have land apportioned to them during the Millennial Kingdom. This provides a great spiritual illustration using the tribe of Dan. The tribe of Dan rejected their God and their rejection continues to this day. They will continue to reject God in the tribulation of the last seven years, but they will turn to God at the end because our God will draw them to Christ.

> For I would not, brethren, that ye should be ignorant of this mystery, lest ye should be wise in your own conceits; that blindness in part is happened to Israel, until the fulness of the Gentiles be come in. And so **all Israel** shall be saved: as it is written, There shall come out of Sion the Deliverer, and shall turn away ungodliness from Jacob: Romans 11:25-26

The Danites will come to the Lord in saving faith, demonstrating God's mercy and grace once again and His faithfulness to keep His promises.

False Elijah

The False Prophet has the same power as the Antichrist and uses that power to cause the world to worship the Antichrist.

> And he exerciseth all the power of the first beast before him, and causeth the earth and them which dwell therein to worship the first beast, whose deadly wound was healed. Revelation 13:12

The use of the term *earth* which is often a metaphor for Israel may imply that it is Israel and the Jews that the False Prophet causes to worship the Antichrist. Perhaps this is because the False Prophet may be Jewish himself. This power is manifested by the performance of miracles, including the ability to call down fire from heaven.

> And he doeth great wonders, so that he maketh fire come down from heaven on the earth in the sight of men, Revelation 13:13

This is similar to Elijah's miracle of calling down fire in his confrontation with the false prophets of Baal.

> Then the fire of the LORD fell, and consumed the burnt sacrifice, and the wood, and the stones, and the dust, and licked up the water that was in the trench. 1 Kings 18:38

Jewish tradition spoke often of the future return of Elijah. For example, a written collection of Jewish oral tradition called the Mishnah (*Edduyot* 8:7) states that Elijah will come to settle all disputes and reconcile all discrepancies in the holy books. At the end of the passage, "The Sages say, Elijah will come … to make peace in the world, as it is said…" This is followed by quoting Malachi's mention of Elijah coming before the day of the LORD.

> Behold, I will send you Elijah the prophet before the
> coming of the great and dreadful day of the LORD: And
> he shall turn the heart of the fathers to the children, and
> the heart of the children to their fathers, lest I come and
> smite the earth with a curse. Malachi 4:5-6

Just as the False Prophet in Revelation is associated with healing the deadly wound of the Antichrist (Rev 13:12), he is also involved with the resurrection of the dead in the Mishnah where it states in *Sotah 9:15*: "The resurrection of the dead shall come through Elijah of blessed memory." The resurrection was expected to happen at the end of history, and Elijah here is definitely associated with the end of time.

Although the timeline presented earlier uses Cheshvan 29 as a likely date for the return of Elijah, the Jews again are expecting Elijah on Passover (Nisan 14). So, might a false Elijah come on Passover? Imagine two thousand years of the Jews waiting for Elijah every year, pouring a cup of wine for him and opening the door on Passover. Then a man appears claiming to be Elijah, doing demonically empowered signs and wonders, perhaps even calling down fire from heaven. One can imagine how overwhelmingly deceptive this would be for the Jews. And as noted, many Christians will easily be deceived by him as well, because Christians also know that Elijah is to come. Signs and wonders will be awfully hard to discount.

So, how is it that Jews will be deceived into worshipping anyone except the one true Jewish Messiah who fulfills all the requirements found in scripture? If their very Jewish but false Elijah claims that someone is the Messiah, even if that Messiah is not Jewish, many will go along with it because that is what their Elijah said. Even though he is a false Elijah, he would be a very convincing Pied Piper, leading others to receive and follow a false messiah. This is exactly what Jesus prophesied to the Jewish leaders.

> I am come in my Father's name, and ye receive me not:
> if another shall come in his own name, him ye will
> receive. John 5:43

Jesus came fulfilling all the requirements of Messiah. He came in the name of Jehovah. But someone in the future will come in a different name, in his own name. He will claim to be a god, and that is the one that some of the Jews will accept, possibly because a miracle working Elijah will say so. This deception may also work on Christians taken in by a false Elijah, and that is why it is important to be able to discern whether or not he is the real deal.

One of the very first things a false Elijah may undertake is a Passover sacrifice. When the real Elijah took on the prophets of Baal in 1 Kings, a holy fire consumed the sacrifice.

> Then the fire of the LORD fell, and consumed the burnt sacrifice, and the wood, and the stones, and the dust, and licked up the water that was in the trench. 1 Kings 18:38

So, a false Elijah may call down fire on Passover on a sacrifice. But it would be a demonic fire from the sky. In the Torah, Aaron's two sons brought incense before the Lord termed "strange fire", and they were consumed immediately. But in this circumstance, it may take a while before God consumes this false Elijah. Yet, a miracle like that certainly would convince almost everyone that this is the true Elijah.

That might additionally include Muslims who also believe that Elijah is expected to come back along with the mysterious figure known as the Khadr during the last judgment or day of the Lord. So, a miracle working Elijah would catch their attention as well and possibly convince many. Again, it is hard to discount a real miracle, even a demonic one. Perhaps this is how Elijah might accomplish what no one else has permission to have sacrifices performed on the Temple Mount.

Maybe enough Muslims will believe that this is the true Elijah, too, so that they go along with his plan. This plan might include the sacrifice of a Passover lamb on the Temple Mount within a Tabernacle which could easily be set up in a matter of days. This would also explain how a one world religion might begin. Jews, Muslims, and Christians all revere Elijah and are looking for his return, and this might be a common bond that links the three faiths together.

One might surmise that if he arrives, a false Elijah just might be the False Prophet, the second beast of Revelation. He evidently shares a lot of the same qualities, including perhaps the ability to call down fire from heaven. Yet, what about Isa, the Muslim Jesus? Of course, there will be many false messiahs and prophets, possibly a Messiah Ben Joseph and a Messiah Ben David, both of whom the Jews are expecting. Perhaps a false messiah could be one that the Muslims are waiting for, since both the Sunni Muslims and Shia Muslims each assert a Messiah of their own, called the Mahdi or the Twelfth Imam. And then, there might be the Muslim Jesus claiming to be Jesus himself or others that have not been considered.

It may be, and most likely will be, deceptively confusing during the end times, and extreme caution should be taken in trying to sort out who these characters are too soon. Clearly, though, the man who will sit in the Temple of God and will desecrate it is the Antichrist. It is good that God gave us such a definitive sign because it will be very confusing to sort out who is who without a sign like that. Correspondingly, at some point, the Jew's sacrificial system will begin again. So, while determining who these characters are during these end times may be confusing, these are two reliable events on which to base where we are at on the timeline.

666

Finally, in one of Revelation's most famous prophecies (still future), the False Prophet will cause all of mankind to receive a mark on (or in) their right hand or their forehead in order to buy or sell.

> And he causeth all, both small and great, rich and poor,
> free and bond, to receive a mark in their right hand, or
> in their foreheads: And that no man might buy or sell,
> save he that had the mark, or the name of the beast, or
> the number of his name. Here is wisdom. Let him that
> hath understanding count the number of the beast: for it

is the number of a man; and his number is **Six hundred threescore and six**. Rev 13:16-18

Note that "666" is the "number of a man", so the question naturally arises as to who that man will be. As it is written it could refer either to the first or the second beast. Also, it may either imply a number associated with the beast's name, or that the name itself has the numerical value of six-hundred, sixty, six (since all Greek letters also correspond to numbers). Using this method of converting letters to numbers which is called *gematria*, various names have been proposed for the number 666, including the Roman Caesar Nero as well as many popes and other world leaders. This method is not only confusing but also leads to all sorts of speculation, and in all reality, gematria most likely plays no part at all in determining the number of the Beast - 666.

Scripture itself offers both a simple and viable alternate solution to gematria. God told his people in the Book of Numbers to number their households according to their names (name equates to number).

> Take ye the sum of all the congregation of the children of Israel, after their families, by the house of their fathers, with the **number of their names**, every male by their polls; Numbers 1:2

This Greek word *arithmos*, translated as, "number" in the KJV, et.al., is used some ten times in the New Testament (Acts 4:4; 5:36; 6:7; 11:21; Rom. 9:27; Rev. 5:11; 9:16; 13:18 twice; and Rev. 20:8) in exactly the same identical grammatical case/tense (noun/nominative/singular/masculine) as that of Revelation 13:18. Thus, it is used in each and every passage as a calculated number, intended to signify a total of counted persons in a group/family/etc.

Therefore, this word is implied to be the basis and the manner of the taking of a census of people or a simple counting of heads. It does not involve the computing of a number by means of converting letters into number values and then searching for someone to fit into the gematric mathematical formula. Neither does it utilize some symbolic numerological value to be transposed by assumption onto an idea of one's own making. It simply refers to a counted number of persons - hence, a household.

The Bible records only one other man, besides the beast in Revelation, associated with the number 666 when Ezra recorded in a census the captives and their families who returned to Jerusalem from the Babylonian captivity.

> Now these are the children of the province that went up out of the captivity, of those which had been carried away, whom Nebuchadnezzar the king of Babylon had carried away unto Babylon, and came again unto Jerusalem and Judah, every one unto his city; Ezra 2:1

The children of Adonikam, six hundred sixty and six. Ezra 2:13

Adonikam, which in Hebrew means "risen master" could indicate a pledge of loyalty to the Antichrist who is resurrected after his fatal head wound and could possibly be used as the name of the False Prophet.

The only other place in the Bible that references the number 666 is in regards to Solomon in two passages describing the same events, one in Chronicles and one in Kings.

> Now the weight of gold that came to Solomon in one year was six hundred and threescore and six talents of gold; Beside that which chapmen and merchants brought. And all the kings of Arabia and governors of the country brought gold and silver to Solomon. 2 Chronicles 9:13-14

> Now the weight of gold that came to Solomon in one year was six hundred threescore and six talents of gold, Beside that he had of the merchantmen, and of the traffick of the spice merchants, and of all the kings of Arabia, and of the governors of the country. 1 Kings 10:14-15

These verses refer to a monetary system rather than to a man. The Book of Revelation actually appears to describe a cashless society. This is not at all surprising in today's world, with the emphasis on electronic commerce, credit cards, online banking, digital currency etc.; and especially so, given the amount of financial fraud that goes on, including counterfeiting, identity theft, and other forms of financial crime. In many nations today, there are few effective deterrents or penalties for financial crimes. Furthermore, many financial payments and transactions today go through computers (e.g., online transactions in a store, or even transactions from home, over the Web) and do not involve the physical transfer of cash.[7]

The Books of Chronicles and Kings go on to describe how Solomon, in addition to accumulating great wealth, increased in military might, inter-married with rulers of other countries, and honored other gods from countries around him rather than exclusively honoring the Creator. These are things that world rulers like the Antichrist or False Prophet would do to gain power and maintain peace. It serves as an example and implies that a set of world leaders will arise that will seem to be as wise and respected as Solomon. They will work to bring peace and prosperity to the world. Of necessity, they will amass wealth, build a strong military, and promote inter-religious cooperation. They will also, at some point, limit the ability to buy or sell as yet another means of necessary power and control. In the end they will end up killing those who do not honor the laws of their government above conflicting laws given by the creator.

In summary, the False Prophet could appear at the same time as or just before the Antichrist. His name may be similar to "Adonikam" or "Solomon" or possibly a derivative of "Solomon" such as "Suleiman". These are names that should at least be kept in mind as the end times are approached. Also, the False Prophet will likely be Jewish and possibly of Persian descent as well as from the tribe of Dan. He may be considered to be Elijah, and like Elijah will exercise great power that will deceive many in the end times, convincing them to worship the Antichrist.

CHAPTER 5

Mystery Babylon[1,2,3,4]

A future, proud, boastful, evil, blood-thirsty harlot named as Babylon the Great, mother of harlots, is described in Revelation 17 and 18. It goes on to portray what she does, where she lives, and what she is like. This woman is representative of a city, and for the last 2000 years, since John wrote Revelation, people have sought to understand the identity of who this Mystery Babylon is. Joel Richardson in his book Mystery Babylon outlines the characteristics of this city that help to identify it, using geopolitical, economic, and religious elements that make up its attributes.

First of all, it is a literal city. Revelation repeatedly refers to it as a "city".

> And the woman which thou sawest is **that great city**, which reigneth over the kings of the earth. Rev 17:18

> Standing afar off for the fear of her torment, saying, Alas, alas **that great city** Babylon, that mighty city! for in one hour is thy judgment come. Revelation 18:10

In addition to being a "great" city (Rev. 17:18), it is a "port" city (Rev. 17:1; 18:17-19) even though it is located in the wilderness or desert (Rev. 17:3).

> And there came one of the seven angels which had the seven vials, and talked with me, saying unto me, Come hither; I will shew unto thee the judgment of the great whore that **sitteth upon many waters**: Revelation 17:1

> For in one hour so great riches is come to nought. And every shipmaster, and all the company in ships, and sailors, and as many as trade **by sea**, stood afar off, And cried when they saw the smoke of her burning, saying, What city is like unto this **great** city! And they cast dust on their heads, and cried, weeping and wailing, saying, Alas, alas that great city, wherein were made rich all that had ships in the sea by reason of her costliness! for in one hour is she made desolate. Revelation 18:17-19

> So he carried me away in the spirit into **the wilderness**: and I saw a woman sit upon a scarlet coloured beast, full of names of blasphemy, having seven heads and ten horns. Revelation 17:3

Economically, it is a financial hub that is a consumer (not a producer) city (Rev 18:11-13) with one of its imports involving human trafficking and slavery. It is a city of excess luxury (Rev 18:7) that is portrayed as representing royalty (Rev 17:4). It is an economic seducer that amplifies its influence to the world (Rev 18:3, 17).

> And the merchants of the earth shall weep and mourn over her; for no man buyeth their merchandise any more: The merchandise of gold, and silver, and precious stones, and of pearls, and fine linen, and purple, and silk, and scarlet, and all thyine wood, and all manner vessels

of ivory, and all manner vessels of most precious wood, and of brass, and iron, and marble, And cinnamon, and odours, and ointments, and frankincense, and wine, and oil, and fine flour, and wheat, and beasts, and sheep, and horses, and chariots, and slaves, and souls of men. Revelation 18:11-13

How much she hath glorified herself, and lived deliciously, so much torment and sorrow give her: for she saith in her heart, I sit a queen, and am no widow, and shall see no sorrow. Revelation 18:7

And the woman was arrayed in purple and scarlet colour, and decked with gold and precious stones and pearls, having a golden cup in her hand full of abominations and filthiness of her fornication: Rev 17:4

For all nations have drunk of the wine of the wrath of her fornication, and the kings of the earth have committed fornication with her, and the merchants of the earth are waxed rich through the abundance of her delicacies. Revelation 18:3

Despite its economic importance, it is its religion that it exports to the world and gives it the name harlot (Rev 17:5). It is a city of idolatry, a religious capital and missionary center, spreading her false religion (Rev 17:2, 15) and promoting the murder of both Christians and Jews (Rev 17:6).

And upon her forehead was a name written, Mystery, Babylon The Great, The Mother Of Harlots And Abominations Of The Earth. Revelation 17:5

With whom the kings of the earth have committed fornication, and the inhabitants of the earth have been made drunk with the wine of her fornication. Revelation 17:2

And he saith unto me, The waters which thou sawest, where the whore sitteth, are peoples, and multitudes, and nations, and tongues. Revelation 17:15

And I saw the woman drunken with the blood of the saints, and with the blood of the martyrs of Jesus: and when I saw her, I wondered with great admiration. Revelation 17:6

Notwithstanding all its splendor, this woman or city will finally be decimated by the God of heaven at the end of the age at which heaven rejoices (Rev 18:19-21).

And they cast dust on their heads, and cried, weeping and wailing, saying, Alas, alas that great city, wherein were made rich all that had ships in the sea by reason of her costliness! for in one hour is she made desolate. Rejoice over her, thou heaven, and ye holy apostles and prophets; for God hath avenged you on her. And a mighty angel took up a stone like a great millstone, and cast it into the sea, saying, Thus with violence shall that great city Babylon be thrown down, and shall be found no more at all. Rev 18:19-21

Many alternatives throughout history have been offered as to the identity of who this woman, this city Mystery Babylon, is. Suggestions have included Rome and the Catholic Church, New York City, Jerusalem, and even the actual city of Babylon itself. If one takes the position that the Final Beast Kingdom is a Revived Roman Empire, then Rome or the Catholic Church or even possibly New York City would logically be a choice for Mystery Babylon. However, as outlined previously, the Final Beast Kingdom is in all likelihood a Revived

Grecian Empire made up of Islamic nations, making each of these cities doubtful candidates for Mystery Babylon. Also, each of these has additional flaws matching the description of Mystery Babylon that was just outlined. These shortcomings, that are outlined in more detail by Joel Richardson, once more make them an improbable match for Mystery Babylon.

Jerusalem is another widely suggested candidate for Mystery Babylon. Proponents cite Revelation 18:24 where Mystery Babylon is condemned for killing the prophets.

> And in her was found the blood of prophets, and of saints, and of all that were slain upon the earth. Revelation 18:24

They link this with Jesus' accusation in Matthew:

> Wherefore ye be witnesses unto yourselves, that ye are the children of them which killed the prophets. Fill ye up then the measure of your fathers. Ye serpents, ye generation of vipers, how can ye escape the damnation of hell? Wherefore, behold, I send unto you prophets, and wise men, and scribes: and some of them ye shall kill and crucify; and some of them shall ye scourge in your synagogues, and persecute them from city to city: That upon you may come all the righteous blood shed upon the earth, from the blood of righteous Abel unto the blood of Zacharias son of Barachias, whom ye slew between the temple and the altar. Verily I say unto you, All these things shall come upon this generation. **O Jerusalem, Jerusalem, thou that killest the prophets**, and stonest them which are sent unto thee, how often would I have gathered thy children together, even as a hen gathereth her chickens under her wings, and ye would not! Matthew 23:31-37

Yet, obviously, many saints have been killed in other cities, such as Paul's death in Rome. And today Christians are killed daily throughout the Middle East and North Africa. So, Jesus' charge is more likely an indictment of Old Testament and first century Jerusalem.

Also, in Revelation, heaven is reported to rejoice at the destruction of Mystery Babylon.

> And after these things I heard a great voice of much people in heaven, saying, Alleluia; Salvation, and glory, and honour, and power, unto the Lord our God: For true and righteous are his judgments: for he hath judged the great whore, which did corrupt the earth with her fornication, and hath avenged the blood of his servants at her hand. And again they said, Alleluia And her smoke rose up for ever and ever. And the four and twenty elders and the four beasts fell down and worshipped God that sat on the throne, saying, Amen; Alleluia. And a voice came out of the throne, saying, Praise our God, all ye his servants, and ye that fear him, both small and great. And I heard as it were the voice of a great multitude, and as the voice of many waters, and as the voice of mighty thunderings, saying, Alleluia: for the Lord God omnipotent reigneth. Revelation 19:1-6

This is completely contrary to and inconsistent with the weeping by Jeremiah (Lam 2:11) and even Jesus himself (Luke 19:41) at the destruction of Jerusalem.

> Mine eyes do fail with tears, my bowels are troubled, my liver is poured upon the earth, for the destruction of the daughter of my people; because the children and the sucklings swoon in the streets of the city. Lamentations 2:11

And when he was come near, he beheld the city, and wept over it, Luke 19:41

In addition, Babylon is eventually destroyed forever (Rev 18:21), whereas Jerusalem is prophesied to last forever (Jer 17:25) and is clearly present in the Millennium (Isaiah 2:3).

> And a mighty angel took up a stone like a great millstone, and cast it into the sea, saying, Thus with violence shall that **great city Babylon** be thrown down, and **shall be found no more at all**. Rev 18:21

> Then shall there enter into the gates of this city kings and princes sitting upon the throne of David, riding in chariots and on horses, they, and their princes, the men of Judah, and the inhabitants of **Jerusalem: and this city shall remain for ever**. Jeremiah 17:25

> And many people shall go and say, Come ye, and let us go up to the mountain of the Lord, to the house of the God of Jacob; and he will teach us of his ways, and we will walk in his paths: for out of Zion shall go forth the law, and the word of the Lord from **Jerusalem**. Isaiah 2:3

For all these reasons, Jerusalem is not a good fit as the city of Mystery Babylon, and although the literal city of Babylon would be a possible match, it currently lies in ruins and currently exists only in the minds of its planners. It is also important to recognize that understanding of Bible prophecy and deciphering who that great city is cannot come simply from current events and from only reading a few New Testament books that describe Mystery Babylon. Although these are helpful, in order to understand current times, as well as historical New Testament events, comprehension of the Old Testament which gives the foundation for the prophecy located in the New Testament is essential. There is a tendency, especially in the United States, to see the Bible from a Western centered point of view. Yet, the Bible actually has an Israel, Jerusalem, and Middle Eastern centered vantage point. So, while studying Bible prophecy, it is important to be grounded in Old Testament scripture and to view it from the position of those who wrote it at a particular place and time.

Accordingly, a review and background of the book of Daniel is essential to understanding Revelation's Mystery Babylon. In chapter nine Daniel the Prophet is in captivity in the literal city of Babylon, where he has been for about seventy years. He is reading the book of Jeremiah the prophet, who had prophesied about the captivity of the Jewish people in Babylon. Specifically, Daniel is reading about how long Jeremiah had said the captivity would last, that is seventy years. Daniel then realizes that they are at the end of their captivity and cries out to the Lord in a prayer (Daniel 9:4-19). He confesses the sins of the Jewish people and pleads for forgiveness and their restoration to Jerusalem. As he cries out, he receives an answer from Gabriel, an angel:

> Seventy weeks are determined upon thy people and upon thy holy city, to finish the transgression, and to make an end of sins, and to make reconciliation for iniquity, and to bring in everlasting righteousness, and to seal up the vision and prophecy, and to anoint the most Holy. Daniel 9:24

In other words, seventy sevens of weeks or about five hundred years are determined on Daniel's people the Jews, for the Lord to put an end to sin and for Jesus Christ to return as King of Kings and to consummate the ages, exactly as God had said it would happen all along. As noted, before, the seventy weeks prophesied in Daniel are broken up into sections. The first sixty-nine weeks began at the time that the command was given to restore Jerusalem and ended at the crucifixion of Jesus Christ. Then, there is a gap between the end of the first sixty-nine weeks and the beginning of the last week of seven years. That gap has been the last two thousand years called the Church Age.

After this gap, there is the final seven years at the end known as "The 70th Week of Daniel"

GEOPOLITCAL ASPECTS OF MYSTERY BABYLON

Knowing that the end on God's timeline is nearing, let's look again at that final seven years to see who are the primary characters and what is going to happen. To help understand that, let's summarize Daniel chapters 2 and 7. In Daniel chapter 2, Nebuchadnezzar, the king of Babylon, has a vision of a colossus. That colossus depicts the course of Gentile world powers through human history. Daniel interprets the vision, identifying the gold head as representing Babylon. The silver chest and arms depict Medo-Persia. The brass belly and thighs portray Greece (actually Turkey and Syria), and the iron and clay legs and feet illustrate the Final Beast Kingdom, a Revived Grecian Empire, which was shown earlier to most likely consist of an Islamic coalition headed by the Antichrist.

Also, as seen previously, Daniel 7 is a parallel prophecy to Daniel 2. In this vision there are four beasts: a lion, a bear, a leopard, and a dreadful fourth beast with iron teeth and ten horns. These again correspond to Babylon, Medo-Persia, Greece, and the Final Beast Kingdom, respectively. This final empire will rule over the world, and when it says "world", it is speaking from an Israel-Middle Eastern point of view. At the point in time when this was written, the "world" was much more confined. So, what is being described in Daniel 2 and 7 is a ten-nation confederation that will come together during the end of days. This will be Satan's one last attempt to push his agenda on the world, but the Lord eventually destroys those final empires, the final colossus, along with the beast.

> Thou sawest till that a stone (i.e. Jesus Christ) was cut out without hands, which smote the image upon his feet that were of iron and clay, and brake them to pieces. Then was the iron, the clay, the brass, the silver,

CHRISTMAS YET TO COME

and the gold, broken to pieces together, and became like the chaff of the summer threshingfloors; and the wind carried them away, that no place was found for them: and the stone that smote the image became a great mountain, and filled the whole earth. Daniel 2:34-35

This coalition of ten nations just described in the Old Testament book of Daniel is again illustrated in Revelation 17:[5]

> And the ten horns which thou sawest are ten kings, which have received no kingdom as yet; but receive power as kings one hour with the beast. These have one mind, and shall give their power and strength unto the beast. These shall make war with the Lamb, and the Lamb shall overcome them: for he is Lord of lords, and King of kings: and they that are with him are called, and chosen, and faithful. Rev 17:12-14

Revelation 17, however, for the most part describes a woman, and this woman is in partnership with the beast. She rides the beast who "carrieth her".

> And the angel said unto me, Wherefore didst thou marvel? I will tell thee the mystery of the woman, and of the beast that **carrieth her**, which hath the seven heads and ten horns. Revelation 17:7

The woman is arrayed in scarlet and purple (Revelation 17:4), and the beast is scarlet colored (Revelation 17:3).

> So he carried me away in the spirit into the wilderness: and I saw a woman sit upon a scarlet coloured beast, full of names of blasphemy, having seven heads and ten horns. And the woman was arrayed in purple and scarlet colour, and decked with gold and precious stones and pearls, having a golden cup in her hand

189

full of abominations and filthiness of her fornication:
Revelation 17:3-4

In other words, they match each other. They are part of a team, and they cooperate with each other. The woman is identified as a city, a geographic region that has power over the beast confederation. Now, since the beast has been identified as an alliance of Islamic nations located in the Middle East, and the woman rules over this beast, that should provide a very strong indicator as to the identity of the woman. Since the beast is a group of Middle Eastern Islamic nations ruled by the Antichrist, and the woman works synergistically with them, they must have some sort of important connection. With that in mind, a likely candidate for Mystery Babylon is the Islamic country of Saudi Arabia and specifically the city of Mecca.

RELIGIOUS NATURE OF MYSTERY BABYLON AND MECCA

The description of Mystery Babylon in Revelation 17 and 18 uses many symbols from Old Testament prophecy. Understanding those prophecies in their historical setting and fulfillment is necessary to grasp the meaning of these symbols. Earlier John states in Revelation that:

> And there followed another angel, saying, Babylon is fallen, is fallen, that great city, because she made all nations drink of the wine of the wrath of her fornication. Revelation 14:8

Fornication and prostitution are consistent metaphors in scripture for worship of idols and gods other than the one true God and His Son. Fornication and prostitution of God's covenant people under the Old Covenant, whom God temporarily divorced, is seen throughout the book of Ezekiel.

But thou didst trust in thine own beauty, and playedst the harlot because of thy renown, and pouredst out thy fornications on every one that passed by; his it was. Ezekiel 16:15

And in all thine abominations and thy whoredoms thou hast not remembered the days of thy youth, when thou wast naked and bare, and wast polluted in thy blood. Ezekiel 16:22

Wherefore say unto the house of Israel, Thus saith the Lord GOD; Are ye polluted after the manner of your fathers? and commit ye whoredom after their abominations? For when ye offer your gifts, when ye make your sons to pass through the fire, ye pollute yourselves with all your idols, even unto this day: and shall I be enquired of by you, O house of Israel? As I live, saith the Lord GOD, I will not be enquired of by you. Ezekiel 20:30-31

Although Israel and Jerusalem were described here as committing fornication with idols and other gods, Mecca and Saudi Arabia have been the fountainhead or source of the greatest perpetration of false religion on humanity that perhaps the world has ever seen. What is described in Revelation 17 is a religious system (and as will later be seen an economic system) that has worldwide influence especially over the nations making up the beast empire during the time of Daniel's 70th Week.

Islam is one of the world's major religions, along with Hinduism, Judaism, Buddhism and Christianity. Since its birth in Arabia more than 1,400 years ago it has grown rapidly, making a profound impact on philosophy, literature, the arts, science and medicine. It is one of the largest religions in the world, and today it is estimated that there are over one billion Muslims worldwide.

The Islamic traditions they follow are as varied as the nations where they live. The two main branches of Islam are Sunnism and Shi'ism. However, Islam's central teaching is that there is one all-powerful, all-knowing God, who is referred to by the Arabic name, Allah. In Arabic, Islam means "surrender" or "submission" to the will of God. Islam was founded by the prophet Mohammed, who was born in Mecca around 570 AD and settled in Medina around 622 AD. Muslims believe Mohammed was the last and most important in a series of prophets that include Abraham, Moses and Jesus.

The holy book of Islam is the *Qur'an*, which means "the timeless words of God". The core practices are known as the Five Pillars—daily prayer, faith, fasting, alms giving and pilgrimage. Performing this pilgrimage, called the *hajj*, is the fifth pillar of Islam. Hajj means "to set out for a place" and for Muslims that place is Mecca. It is mandatory for every Muslim to make the journey at least once in a lifetime. Over 2 million Muslims made the pilgrimage in 2015.

The Kaaba is in the central part of Mecca and is the center, focal point of Islam worldwide. It is a black building that looks like a box, sixty feet square and sixty feet high. This is the location to which millions of Muslims throughout the world pray daily and perform the hajj, directing worship, that should be given to the one true God, to a false, counterfeit deity and to idols that are in an ultimate sense, worship to Satan. Saudi Arabia has been the source of this false religion which they have spread to the world.

> For all nations have drunk of the wine of the wrath of her fornication, and the kings of the earth have committed fornication with her, and the merchants of the earth are waxed rich through the abundance of her delicacies. Revelation 18:3

While Mecca is the center of Islam, Jerusalem and the Temple Mount are the focal point of Judaism. Yet, Islam has spread even there, and for Muslims the Temple Mount is their third holiest site, the location of the Dome of the Rock and the Al-Aqsa Mosque. Today, the Temple Mount is controlled by an Islamic Waqf, an organization run by Jordan. But control of that Waqf has been subtly altered just recently in 2020. Jordan's control of the Temple Mount has been under pressure by Turkey, and in order to counter balance this pressure, Jordan has turned its attention to Saudi Arabia. It is reported that Mohammed bin Salman, the crown prince of Saudi Arabia, could be added to a special position on the Islamic Waqf Council that controls the Temple Mount. Saudi Arabia already has control of Medina and Mecca, the two holiest sites in the Muslim world, and control of the Temple Mount in Jerusalem would give them control of the three holiest sites in Islam. Saudi Arabia, which is Sunni, views Shiite controlled Iran as their greatest threat in the Middle East. So, forming an alliance with Israel, who is viewed as the Great Satan to Iran, could make political sense. It could also help Mohammed bin Salman to be looked upon favorably by the world community and give him and Saudi Arabia power and clout within the Sunni world. In addition, if Mohammed bin Salman lent support to a treaty with Israel, this could potentially qualify him as a candidate to be the Antichrist.

> And he shall confirm the covenant with many for one week: and in the midst of the week he shall cause the sacrifice and the oblation to cease, and for the overspreading of abominations he shall make it desolate, even until the consummation, and that determined shall be poured upon the desolate. Daniel 9:27

Yet, that is not probable since the Antichrist will be expected to come from the area of Turkey (as noted earlier). It is more likely that Mohammed bin Salman being from Saudi Arabia could be the King of the South who fights against the King of the North, the Antichrist, and loses.

> And at the time of the end shall the king of the south push at him: and the king of the north shall come against him like a whirlwind, with chariots, and with

horsemen, and with many ships; and he shall enter
into the countries, and shall overflow and pass over.
Daniel 11:40

In any case, Mohammed bin Salman is someone who bears watching
in the future. How he will affect the politics and prophetic events,
especially those related to the Temple predicted for the end times, is
something that will need to be observed closely.

Not only has Saudi Arabia promoted and spread worship of Islam,
a false religion, but it has also been one of the worst, if not the worst,
persecutor of those who direct their worship to the one true God. In
the end times John describes the woman:

> And I saw the woman drunken with the blood of the
> saints, and with the blood of the martyrs of Jesus: and
> when I saw her, I wondered with great admiration.
> Revelation 17:6

Throughout their history, both Jews and Christians have been
oppressed, mistreated, and slain for their faith. Early Christians were
persecuted for their faith not only by the Romans who controlled many
of the lands across which early Christianity was spread in the Roman
Empire but also by the Jews from whose religion Christianity arose.
Later schisms in the Church led to various Christian denominations
themselves frequently persecuting one another. More recently, in the
20th century, Christian populations have been persecuted by various
states including the Islamic Ottoman Empire, which committed the
Armenian genocide during World War I. Other atheist states such as the
Soviet Union, Communist Albania, and North Korea have committed
equally severe mass exterminations. Then there was the attempted
Jewish genocide by the Nazis of Germany. But currently, some of the
most severe persecution of Christians occur in Islamic states such as
Iran, Iraq and Indonesia, as well as by Islamic terrorist organizations
like ISIL (Islamic State of Iraq and the Levant). So, Islamic Saudi

Arabia certainly today meets the criteria of spreading this false religion to the world while persecuting the true saints of God.

GEOECONOMIC CHARACTERISTICS OF MYSTERY BABYLON & MECCA

As noted earlier, Revelation 17 clearly portrays Babylon the Great as a prosperous, affluent woman.

> And the woman was arrayed in purple and scarlet colour, and decked with gold and precious stones and pearls, having a golden cup in her hand full of abominations and filthiness of her fornication: Rev 17:4

Revelation 18 adds to this description and further elaborates on the wealth and abundance of that great city, and its destruction which makes the merchants of the world wail because of the loss of the riches that they had accumulated by her.

> And after these things I saw another angel come down from heaven, having great power; and the earth was lightened with his glory. And he cried mightily with a strong voice, saying, Babylon the great is fallen, is fallen, and is become the habitation of devils, and the hold of every foul spirit, and a cage of every unclean and hateful bird. For all nations have drunk of the wine of the wrath of her fornication, and the kings of the earth have committed fornication with her, and the merchants of the earth are waxed rich through the abundance of her delicacies. And I heard another voice from heaven, saying, Come out of her, my people, that ye be not partakers of her sins, and that ye receive not of her plagues. For her sins have reached unto heaven, and God hath remembered her iniquities. Reward her even as she rewarded you, and double unto her double according to

her works: in the cup which she hath filled fill to her double. How much she hath glorified herself, and lived deliciously, so much torment and sorrow give her: for she saith in her heart, I sit a queen, and am no widow, and shall see no sorrow. Therefore shall her plagues come in one day, death, and mourning, and famine; and she shall be utterly burned with fire: for strong is the Lord God who judgeth her. And the kings of the earth, who have committed fornication and lived deliciously with her, shall bewail her, and lament for her, when they shall see the smoke of her burning, Standing afar off for the fear of her torment, saying, Alas, alas that great city Babylon, that mighty city! for in one hour is thy judgment come. And the merchants of the earth shall weep and mourn over her; for no man buyeth their merchandise any more: The merchandise of gold, and silver, and precious stones, and of pearls, and fine linen, and purple, and silk, and scarlet, and all thyine wood, and all manner vessels of ivory, and all manner vessels of most precious wood, and of brass, and iron, and marble, And cinnamon, and odours, and ointments, and frankincense, and wine, and oil, and fine flour, and wheat, and beasts, and sheep, and horses, and chariots, and slaves, and souls of men. And the fruits that thy soul lusted after are departed from thee, and all things which were dainty and goodly are departed from thee, and thou shalt find them no more at all. The merchants of these things, which were made rich by her, shall stand afar off for the fear of her torment, weeping and wailing, And saying, Alas, alas that great city, that was clothed in fine linen, and purple, and scarlet, and decked with gold, and precious stones, and pearls! For in one hour so great riches is come to nought. And every shipmaster, and all the company in ships, and sailors, and as many as trade by sea, stood afar off, And cried when they saw the smoke of her burning, saying, What city is like unto this great city! And they cast dust on their heads, and cried, weeping and wailing, saying, Alas, alas that great city, wherein were made rich all that had ships in the sea by reason of her costliness! for in one hour is she made desolate. Rejoice over her, thou heaven, and ye holy apostles and prophets; for God hath avenged you on her. And a mighty angel took up a stone like a great millstone, and cast it into the sea, saying, Thus with violence shall that great city Babylon be thrown down, and shall be found no more at all. And the voice of harpers, and musicians, and of pipers, and trumpeters, shall be heard no more at all in thee; and no craftsman, of whatsoever craft he be, shall be found any more in thee; and the sound of a millstone shall be heard no more at all in thee; And the light of a candle shall shine no more at all in thee; and the voice of the bridegroom and of the bride shall be heard no more at all in thee: for thy merchants were the great men of the earth; for by thy sorceries were all nations deceived. And in her was found the blood of prophets, and of saints, and of all that were slain upon the earth. Revelation 18:1-24

Not only is Mecca and Saudi Arabia a religious center for Muslims but it is also being turned into an unbelievable financial center. Although it is a giant sandbox, what is amazing is that in the 1930's oil was discovered there. This completely transformed what looked like a waste land into an amazing economic powerhouse.

With the billions of dollars from oil revenue, Mecca is being completely changed so that many, many more people can come to worship. They have essentially bulldozed most of central Mecca to make way for the fourth largest tower on planet earth, a clock tower, called The Mecca Royal Clock Tower, dedicated to Allah with a moon observatory at the top. It is actually made up of seven towers with the clock tower being the largest. By square footage it is the largest building on planet earth. Around this they are building skyscrapers for very wealthy Muslims around the world to buy a piece of Mecca. Within the clock tower are multiple hotels as well as four thousand shops as part of the complex. The monarchy of Saudi Arabia is planning on completely transforming Mecca and are using the religious system of Islam to build something economically that has never been seen before.

Other major cities in Saudi Arabia include Medina and the capital city of Riyadh. In Riyadh they are building what is called The King Abdullah Financial Center. Concerned that their oil-based economy will not last forever, the Saudis are transitioning to an economy based on other things including industry, finance, entertainment, and shipping. Just south of Riyadh they are planning a city the size of Las Vegas, an entertainment center to provide a place in their home state to go without leaving their own country. This includes a Six Flags, costing three quarters of a billion dollars. Also, on the Arabian Peninsula is Dubai, a financial center for the world, that has the tallest building in the world called the Burj Khalifa.

Of course, Mecca is an inland city, about forty miles from the Red Sea. As noted, Saudi Arabia is a giant sand box. This fits the description of Babylon the Great in Revelation 17.

> So he carried me away in the spirit into the **wilderness:** and I saw a woman sit upon a scarlet coloured beast, full of names of blasphemy, having seven heads and ten horns. Revelation 17:3

This word "wilderness" also means "desert", and Isaiah likewise describes it as a desert or wasteland, applying it to Arabia.

> The burden of **Dumah** *(name of the fourth son of Ishmael and the tribe descended from him; and hence also the region in Arabia which they inhabited).* He calleth to me out of Seir, Watchman, what of the night? Watchman, what of the night? Isaiah 21:11

The burden upon **Arabia**. In the forest in **Arabia** shall ye lodge, O ye travelling companies of Dedanim. Isaiah 21:13

For thus hath the LORD said unto me, Within a year, according to the years of an hireling, and all the glory of **Kedar** *(a son of Ishmael and also a North Arabian tribe)* shall fail: Isaiah 21:16

Let the wilderness and the cities thereof lift up their voice, the villages that Kedar doth inhabit: let the inhabitants of the rock sing, let them shout from the top of the mountains. Isaiah 42:11

Despite its description as a desert, Babylon the Great in Revelation 17:1 is also pictured as a city that "sitteth on many waters". It appears to be a seaport from the description in Revelation 18 as well as a desert wasteland. So, does Mecca fit that description? Actually, Arabia is sometimes called the "Desert of the Seas".

The burden of the **desert of the sea**. As whirlwinds in the south pass through; so it cometh from the desert, from a terrible land. Isaiah 21:1

This certainly does not describe New York City, Rome or even Babylon. Saudi Arabia is surrounded by the Red Sea, Arabian Sea and the Persian Gulf. And in fact, Jeremiah defines Babylon the Great's destruction as occurring specifically on the Red Sea.

The earth is moved at the noise of their fall, at the cry the noise thereof was heard in the Red sea. Jer 49:21

So, Saudi Arabia is uniquely positioned in the world. The nearest city to Mecca on the Red Sea is the seaport of Jeddah. In Jeddah plans are being made to build the tallest building in the world, a skyscraper that will be nearly twice as tall as the Mecca clock tower. What is interesting though is just north of Jeddah they are planning on building a new port city called the KAEC, the King Abdullah Economic City that will be based on shipping. In a report by the King Abdullah Port, it is quoted that:

> With its strategic location and state-of-the-art technologies, all managed by national and global experts who strive to offer the best possible services, King Abdullah Port has earned its place at the heart of the world's major shipping lines, all within a solid plan that will bring to reality its vision of becoming one of the largest ports in the world.

> "There are plenty of aspects that set King Abdullah Port apart from others in the region, on top which is its strategic location," says Abdullah Hameedadin, Managing Director of the Ports Development company. "Some 20% to 25% of the world's non-petroleum trade passes through the Red Sea which translates into about 730 million tonnes of freight on more than 11,000 vessels having passed through the Suez Canal in 2015."

> Given these astounding figures, King Abdullah Port's strategic location in the Red Sea is bound to make it the premier gateway for goods into Saudi Arabia and the emerging markets of neighboring countries, and a hub for the transshipment industry in Middle Eastern ports and beyond.

In Revelation 18, the merchants, who see the devastation and smoke of Babylon the Great's burning, are far off in their ships, wailing and wondering who is going to buy their merchandise anymore. This could very much be a description of what will happen to the KAEC. It is Saudi Arabia's attempt to bring the world's banking system to itself, perfectly positioned on the Red Sea next to the city of Jeddah and the Islamic religious center in Mecca. All three of these cities (Mecca,

Jeddah, and KAEC) will be linked by the world's fastest train system, taking only twenty to thirty minutes to get to any one of the cities.

So, Mystery Babylon will be a religious and economic world center for the world's largest false religious system that has duped the nations. This will not only include the nations of the Middle East but also countries throughout the world. And Saudi Arabia has the financial resources to accomplish it. There are about nineteen million citizens in Saudi Arabia, but there are nine million expatriates from other countries who live in Saudi Arabia servicing the country. Many of these expatriates, especially women, have no rights. In many instances these people become slaves, trapped and unable to leave because their passports are held by their employers. This is how Saudi Arabia is funding their excesses, with cheap labor coming in from other places.

In addition, through the years, Saudi Arabia has bribed and paid off countries throughout the world, including the United States. They have funded many universities, including Harvard and Georgetown, as well as others, to set up Islamic Studies programs. There have been many well documented books written, outlining where the Clintons, Jimmy Carter, as well as the Bushes, were given hundreds of millions of dollars by the Saudis. So, the Saudis have been the biggest sponsor of Islam worldwide of any country in the world and are the fountainhead of this false religion, spreading it with billions of dollars around the world and certainly meeting the geographic, religious, and economic criteria for Mystery Babylon outlined in Revelation.

THE DESTRUCTION OF BABYLON

Babylon the Great is eventually destroyed in the end as chronicled in Revelation.

> And he cried mightily with a strong voice, saying, Babylon the great is fallen, is fallen, and is become the habitation of devils, and the hold of every foul spirit, and a cage of every unclean and hateful bird. Revelation 18:2

This had previously been foretold by Isaiah.

> And, behold, here cometh a chariot of men, with a
> couple of horsemen. And he answered and said, Babylon
> is fallen, is fallen; and all the graven images of her gods
> he hath broken unto the ground. Isaiah 21:9

The timing for the destruction of the woman, Babylon the Great, is difficult to pinpoint exactly. However, it most likely occurs after the Rapture, and is associated with the Day of the Lord, when God's wrath is poured out on the earth. (More about the Day of the Lord will be discussed in the chapter on "The Second Coming of Christ".) Isaiah links the Day of the Lord and the destruction of Babylon.

> The burden of Babylon, which Isaiah the son of Amoz
> did see... Howl ye; for the day of the Lord is at hand;
> it shall come as a destruction from the Almighty.
> Isaiah 13:1;6

It is during the Day of the Lord that Mystery Babylon, the mother of all harlots, will be judged by the Lord and destroyed. Surprisingly, although it is the Lord who is responsible for its destruction, he uses the beast to accomplish that annihilation. As noted earlier, the beast is a group of Middle Eastern Islamic nations ruled by the Antichrist, and the woman works synergistically with them. Despite their partnership, the beast hates the woman (Rev 17:16), and the woman, Mystery Babylon, is eventually destroyed by its own partner, the beast (Rev 17:16-17).

> And the ten horns which thou sawest upon the beast,
> these shall hate the whore, and shall make her desolate
> and naked, and shall eat her flesh, and burn her with
> fire. For God hath put in their hearts to fulfil his will,
> and to agree, and give their kingdom unto the beast,
> until the words of God shall be fulfilled. Rev 17:16-17

All will be judged, but there is a special judgment that is reserved for Mystery Babylon, because she is the one that the kings of the earth have committed fornication with, the one that has duped the nations, and the one that has perpetrated this hoax on humanity. This hoax, a false religion that has pulled people away from the one true God to a deceptive, misleading religious system, will end during the day of the Lord, an ending that will come suddenly and quickly, with results that last forever.

A TALE OF TWO CITIES AND TWO WOMEN

Ultimately, the story that is written in the Bible and concluded in Revelation is a tale of two cities and two women. There is a contrast between Babylon (the wicked prostitute of Revelation 18-19) and Jerusalem (the woman of Revelation 12 which represents God's chosen people Israel). Babylon, the mother of harlots and the greatest culprit that the world has ever seen in spreading a false religious system, is Mecca, Saudi Arabia. It is a counterfeit of everything that Satan knows God will ultimately accomplish in Jerusalem, God's holy city.

> And I saw a new heaven and a new earth: for the first heaven and the first earth were passed away; and there was no more sea. And I John saw **the holy city, new Jerusalem**, coming down from God out of heaven, prepared as a bride adorned for her husband. Revelation 21:1-2

> And there came unto me one of the seven angels which had the seven vials full of the seven last plagues, and talked with me, saying, Come hither, I will shew thee the bride, the Lamb's wife. And he carried me away in the spirit to a great and high mountain, and shewed me that great city, **the holy Jerusalem**, descending out of heaven from God, Revelation 21:9-10

These two women in Revelation are foreshadowed as early as Genesis with the story of Abraham and his wife Sarai and her servant Hagar. Hagar was Abraham's concubine and was purchased in Egypt. She served as a maid to Abraham's childless wife, Sarai, who gave Hagar to Abraham to conceive an heir. When Hagar became pregnant, her meek manner changed to arrogance. With Abraham's reluctant permission, Sarai treated Hagar so harshly that she fled into the wilderness. There, by a spring of water, she was found by an angel of the Lord, who told her to return home. She was promised that she would have many descendants through a son, Ishmael, who would grow up to be a "wild man" in constant struggle with all other men. Hagar then returned home to bear this child.

16 Now Sarai Abram's wife bare him no children: and she had an handmaid, an Egyptian, whose name was Hagar. [2] And Sarai said unto Abram, Behold now, the Lord hath restrained me from bearing: I pray thee, go in unto my m aid; it may be that I may obtain children by her. And Abram hearkened to the voice of Sarai. [3] And Sarai Abram's wife took Hagar her maid the Egyptian, after Abram had dwelt ten years in the land of Canaan, and gave her to her husband Abram to be his wife. [4] And he went in unto Hagar, and she conceived: and when she saw that she had conceived, her mistress was despised in her eyes. [5] And Sarai said unto Abram, My wrong be upon thee: I have given my maid into thy bosom; and when she saw that she had conceived, I was despised in her eyes: the Lord judge between me and thee. [6] But Abram said unto Sarai, Behold, thy maid is in thine hand; do to her as it pleaseth thee. And when Sarai dealt hardly with her, she fled from her face. [7] And the angel of the Lord found her by a fountain of water in the wilderness, by the fountain in the way to Shur. [8] And he said, Hagar, Sarai's maid, whence camest thou? and whither wilt thou go? And she said, I flee from

the face of my mistress Sarai. ⁹ And the angel of the Lord said unto her, Return to thy mistress, and submit thyself under her hands. ¹⁰ And the angel of the Lord said unto her, I will multiply thy seed exceedingly, that it shall not be numbered for multitude. ¹¹ And the angel of the Lord said unto her, Behold, thou art with child and shalt bear a son, and shalt call his name Ishmael; because the Lord hath heard thy affliction. ¹² And he will be a wild man; his hand will be against every man, and every man's hand against him; and he shall dwell in the presence of all his brethren. ¹³ And she called the name of the Lord that spake unto her, Thou God seest me: for she said, Have I also here looked after him that seeth me? ¹⁴ Wherefore the well was called Beerlahairoi; behold, it is between Kadesh and Bered. ¹⁵ And Hagar bare Abram a son: and Abram called his son's name, which Hagar bare, Ishmael. ¹⁶ And Abram was fourscore and six years old, when Hagar bare Ishmael to Abram. Genesis 16:1-16

About fourteen years after the birth of Ishmael, Isaac (Abraham's son with whom God had promised to make a covenant) was born to Sarai. One day Sarai saw Isaac and Ishmael playing together and fearing that Ishmael would also become an heir, sent the son and mother into the desert. There God sustained them and was with Ishmael until he grew up. Ishmael became the progenitor of the Ishmaelites, generally thought to be the Arabians or Arabs. There are also legends stating that Ishmael was an ancestor of Muhammad.

And the child grew, and was weaned: and Abraham made a great feast the same day that Isaac was weaned. And Sarah saw the son of Hagar the Egyptian, which she had born unto Abraham, mocking. Wherefore she said unto Abraham, Cast out this bondwoman and her son: for the son of this bondwoman shall not be heir with my son, even with Isaac. And the thing was very grievous in Abraham's sight because of his son. And God said unto Abraham, Let it not be grievous in thy sight because of the lad, and because of thy bondwoman; in all that Sarah hath said unto thee, hearken unto her voice; for in Isaac shall thy seed be called. And also of the son of the bondwoman will I make a nation, because he is thy seed. And Abraham rose up early in the morning, and took bread, and a bottle of water, and gave it unto Hagar, putting it on her shoulder, and the child, and sent her away: and she departed, and wandered in the wilderness of Beersheba. And the water was spent in the bottle, and she cast the child under one of the shrubs. And she went, and sat her down over against him a good way off, as it were a bow shot: for she said, Let me not see the death of the child. And she sat over against him, and lift up her voice, and wept. And God heard the voice of the lad; and the angel of God called to Hagar out of heaven, and said unto her, What aileth thee, Hagar? fear not; for God hath heard the voice of the lad where he is. Arise, lift up the lad, and hold him in thine hand; for I will make him a great nation. And God opened her eyes, and she saw a well of water; and she went, and filled the bottle with water, and gave the lad drink. And God was with the lad; and he grew, and dwelt in the wilderness, and became an archer. And he dwelt in the wilderness of Paran: and his mother took him a wife out of the land of Egypt. Genesis 21:8-21

As a result of this early family struggle, the Middle East conflict has become the longest-running battle in history. Just as Arab-Israeli tensions began in Genesis (with Sarah, Hagar and Ishmael) they have persisted throughout history. However, they will eventually conclude in the end times, as seen in the Book of Revelation, with the climactic battle of Armageddon.

In the New Testament, Paul uses this conflict between Sarah and Hagar to support his argument that justification is by faith in Christ Jesus and not by doing the law.

> Tell me, ye that desire to be under the law, do ye not hear the law? For it is written, that Abraham had two sons, the one by a bondmaid, the other by a freewoman. But he who was of the bondwoman was born after the flesh; but he of the freewoman was by promise. Which things are an allegory: for these are the two covenants; the one from the mount Sinai, which gendereth to bondage, which is Agar. For this Agar is **mount Sinai in Arabia**, and answereth to **Jerusalem** which now is, and is in bondage with her children. But Jerusalem which is above is free, which is the mother of us all. For it is written, Rejoice, thou barren that bearest not; break forth and cry, thou that travailest not: for the desolate hath many more children than she which hath an husband. Now we, brethren, as Isaac was, are the children of promise. But as then he that was born after the flesh persecuted him that was born after the Spirit, even so it is now. Nevertheless what saith the scripture? Cast out the bondwoman and her son: for the son of the bondwoman shall not be heir with the son of the freewoman. So then, brethren, we are not children of the bondwoman, but of the free. Galatians 4:21-31

Paul strings together multiple pictures in these short eleven verses to compare two women. Hagar and her son Ishmael correspond to Mount Sinai in Arabia and represent the law. Whereas, Sarah and Isaac are symbolic of the gospel and relate to Jerusalem located on Mount Zion. Paul also describes Jerusalem, as a mother of us all who are "the children of promise". This is in contrast to Hagar who was a bondwoman and "not an heir with the son of the freewoman".

Although the location of Mount Zion is well established and refers to a hill on the south side of Jerusalem's Armenian Quarter, the location of Mount Sinai is widely debated. Traditionally it has been located between the Gulf of Suez and the Gulf of Aqaba in the Sinai Desert. But Paul locates Mount Sinai in Arabia (Gal 4:25), and a more recent discovery and theory places it across the Red Sea situated in the mountain range of Jabal al-Laws also in Saudi Arabia.

The ancient Mount Zion encompassed all of Jerusalem, including the Temple Mount. Upon this hilly range of sacred land, scripture shows a rich heritage of God's redemptive work even before the name Zion surfaced. There, Abraham agreed to do the unthinkable; he bound his only son and prepared to sacrifice him, having faith that God would instead, "provide Himself a lamb for a burnt offering" (Genesis 22:1-24). Also, on this mountain, Jacob had his dream that allowed him to climb to heaven (Genesis 28:11-19). David purchased the threshing floor of Ornan the Jebusite and sacrificed oxen to atone for his sin on this mountain (1 Chronicles 21:14-18). It is there that Solomon built the magnificent temple of the Lord (2 Chron 3:1), and finally it is there that the future Third Temple will be built.

In contrast to Mount Zion, it was at Mount Sinai that Moses received the Ten Commandment and consequently, represents enslavement to the Law. Just as the Israelites were unable to keep the Law and thought they could create a god in the form of a golden calf at Mount Sinai, sin and the inability to keep God's commandments is reflected by Mount Sinai. Interestingly, Moses was already familiar with Mount Sinai since it is there that he had seen the burning bush. It is also to Mount Sinai that Jesus at His Second Coming may lead a second exodus of Jews, just as Moses led the first exodus of the Israelites. (This second exodus will be discussed further in the chapter on "The Second Coming of Christ".) So, the part that Mount Sinai plays in end time's prophecy emphasizes the importance of knowing its location.

The differences in these women, who are linked with different cities and mountains, demonstrates the contrast between Satan (Babylon and

Mount Sinai) and the one true God, illustrated by Mount Zion and the holy city Jerusalem. It exemplifies Satan and his counterfeit system trying to usurp what rightfully belongs to the one true God. It is also a picture of slaves and freemen: Ishmael is the son of a slave, but Isaac is freeborn. The freeborn son, not the slave son, will inherit the family estate. Paul speaks about their births: Ishmael was born in the ordinary way, but Isaac was born of God's promise. And finally, there is a picture of persecution: the son born as a product of human will (Ishmael) persecuted the son born as a result of a promise (Isaac). It is Ishmael, represented by Mount Sinai located in Arabia, who persecuted Isaac, the father of the Israelites, and it is likely from the Arabs and Saudi Arabia that Babylon the Great will arise as the mother of all harlots and the greatest of all persecutors.

CHAPTER 6

Christians, Jews and Gentiles

I n order to understand the 70th week of Daniel, it is important to recognize the different groups of people with whom God is dealing during this timeframe. In fact, there are three distinct groups that God has dealt with throughout history and will continue to deal with in the 70th Week and beyond. Comprehending who these groups are and how God has and will interact with them is critical in understanding the timing and sequence of events that unfold during the last 70th Week. These groups include Israel, the Church, and the nations of Gentiles.

Israel refers to the Jewish people and in scripture is understood to mean both the ancient and modern land of Israel as well as the descendants of Jacob (i.e., the ancestral line of Abraham, Isaac, and Jacob). Recall that Jacob's name was changed to "Israel" in Genesis 32:28. The word *Israel* is found seventy-three times in the New Testament and always refers to the physical descendants of Abraham, Isaac, and Jacob. Sometimes the term *Israel* in the New Testament refers to Jews in faith and sometimes it refers to Jews in unbelief. However, the term *Israel* in the New Testament always refers to those who are physical Jews. This word never refers to Gentiles, the Church, or even a group that is a mixture of both Jews and Gentiles.

In a similar manner, the New Testament also never designates the Church as "Israel". The Church is the Body of Christ, that is, all believers in Jesus Christ. It is one body, without differentiation. The Gentiles are those who are neither Jews nor the Church. It is, however, possible for Gentiles (in their pre-saved condition) to become part of the Church, and for Jewish people to become part of the Church, as well. In fact, the Church is made up of people who were formerly Jews or Gentiles. However, the Church, a group of individuals defined by their spiritual beliefs, cannot become Israel, a physical nation of Jews.

Some general differences between each group are outlined in the table below.

ISRAEL	CHURCH	GENTILES
Physical entity of one nation & its people who are Jewish	Spiritual entity of individual Jewish and Gentile believers in Christ	Physical entity of many nations and people who are non-Jewish
Israel gave birth to Christ	Christ gave birth to Church	Seek death of Israel and the Church
Vehicle of God's redemption	Recipient of God's redemption	Reject God's redemption
All nations blessed/saved through them	Restore Israel by making them jealous	Restore/purify Israel & the Church by persecution
Under the Law of Moses	Under the Law of Christ	Without law
Atonement under the Law (Old Covenant)	Righteousness/salvation by grace through faith in Christ (New Covenant)	Unrighteous/unsaved
Has priesthood for one true God	Is the priesthood	No priesthood for one true God; Priesthood for false gods
Bride of Christ, wife of God	Body of Christ (In Christ)	Apart from Christ/God

ISRAEL	CHURCH	GENTILES
Resurrected at the start of the Millennium	Resurrected at the Rapture	Resurrected at the end of the Millennium
Occupy physical earthly Israel during Millennium	Occupy New Jerusalem during Millennium	Occupy the earth except for Israel during Millennium
Gates of the New Jerusalem are named after 12 tribes of Israel	Foundations of the New Jerusalem are named after the 12 apostles	Not named in New Jerusalem

God has dealt differently and separately with each of these groups throughout history and will likewise deal distinctly with each group in the future, particularly during the 70th Week of Daniel. Theologians have suggested various ways that God has dealt with each group, and these can be divided roughly into primarily three different systems: Covenant Theology, Classic Dispensationalism, and Progressive Dispensationalism. Although these provide major ways to look at these groups, there are many other views that fall between these systems.

The chart below summarizes some of the answers that these major approaches take regarding questions concerning how God has dealt with these different groups throughout history and will deal with them in the future.

	Classic Dispensationalism	Covenant Theology	Progressive Dispensationalism
Bible Interpretation	OT- Literal NT- Allegorical	Allegorical	Literal
God's People	2 distinct people- Israel and the Church	1 people- Old and New Testament saints not distinct	Non-distinct, i.e., no separation of Israel and the Church
God's Plan	2 plans- an earthly plan for Israel and heavenly plan for the Church	1 plan- heavenly for Church	1 plan- earthly for Israel and the Church

	Classic Dispensationalism	Covenant Theology	Progressive Dispensationalism
Salvation	By the Law (Old Covenant) in OT, by grace (New Covenant) in NT	1 plan by grace through faith	1 plan by grace through faith
Church	NT saints	OT and NT saints	OT and NT saints
God's Dealing with Israel	Interrupted by the Church	Replaced by the Church	Continuous and fulfilled by the Church
Millennium	Pre-millennial literal 1000-year future manifestation of God's kingdom	Amillennial-God's kingdom is already present (spiritual) or Post-millennial-kingdom is being established on earth with culmination at Christ's coming	Pre-millennial literal 1000-year future manifestation of God's kingdom

The Covenant Theology or Amillennial system approaches the scripture from an allegorical or symbolic viewpoint, where God's kingdom is not in the future but is already present or is being established now on earth with the culmination at Christ's coming. It views the Church as consisting of both Old and New Testament saints with one plan of salvation for both, which is by grace through faith in Christ.

The dispensationalists divide history into seven periods or "dispensations" where God has dealt with mankind differently. The idea of dispensation is introduced by Paul.

> That in the **dispensation** of the fulness of times he might gather together in one all things in Christ, both which are in heaven, and which are on earth; even in him: Ephesians 1:10

The word *dispensation* comes from the Greek word *oikonomia* which is a compound word meaning "house rules". It essentially means the way that a man deals with those in his household. In other words, dispensation refers to a period of time in which God deals with the human race in a distinct way, and as circumstances change, the way God rules also changes. For example, before the fall of man, man did not know what sin was and lived in the Dispensation of Innocence. However, once man sinned, the rules changed, and he entered the Dispensation of Conscience where God dealt differently with man. These dispensations are outlined in the table below.

Dispensation	Covenant	Begins With	Ends With	Covenant Type	Covenant Applies to whom?	Covenant Continues Today?	Scripture
1 Innocence	Edenic	Creation	Fall of Man	Conditional	All mankind	No	Gen 1:26-30 Gen 2:15-17
2 Conscience	Adamic	Fall	Flood	Unconditional	All mankind	Yes	Gen 3:14-19
3 Human Government	Noahic	Flood	Call of Abraham	Unconditional	All mankind	Yes	Gen 8:20-9:17
4 Promise	Abrahamic	Call of Abraham	Mosaic Law	Unconditional	Abraham and his seed	Yes, everlasting	Gen 12:1-3
5 Law	Mosaic	Mosaic Law	Death of Christ	Conditional	Israel	No	Exodus 20-40
6 Grace	New Covenant	Death of Christ	Second Coming	Unconditional	All mankind	Present Age, everlasting	Jer 31:31-35 Luke 22:20 Heb 8:4-13
7 Kingdom	Davidic; Palestinian; New Covenant	Second Coming	End of Millennium	Unconditional	David, Israel	Future, everlasting	2 Sam 7:5-19 Deut 30:1-10

Classic Dispensationalism takes a more literal approach regarding the Old Testament but an allegorical slant in interpreting the New Testament. It views the Church and Israel as distinct groups, where God has an earthly plan for Israel but a heavenly plan for the Church.

In this approach, God has allowed the Church to temporarily interrupt His treatment of Israel.

In order to take a more literal approach to both the Old and New Testament, Progressive Dispensationalism was proposed where there is no distinction between Israel and the Church. In this progressive methodology, there is one plan of salvation, grace through faith, that has been God's plan all along and was fulfilled by the Church. It is important to understand these viewpoints, since each system of looking at these groups affects one's view of the end times.

Yet, more important than placing oneself in a particular viewpoint is understanding the questions that they attempt to answer: Do you take a completely literal approach to the Bible? What is God's plan, particularly in regards to salvation? Who make up God's people? And, in fact, some of the confusion in determining which of these approaches is correct, or whether they are all flawed, arises from how each method defines what or who Israel is and who is included in the Church. In each approach, clearly, Israel is a nation that consists of individuals who may or may not be part of the Church. Throughout scripture God has dealt corporately with Israel as a **nation**, whereas the Church is made up of **individuals** who God deals with as separate persons according to their faith. This obviously includes New Testament saints, and in the Covenant Theology and Progressive Dispensationalism viewpoint, incorporates the Old Testament saints as well. This viewpoint uses Paul's listing in Hebrews 11 of people of faith, who are declared righteous according to that faith.

> By faith Noah, being warned of God of things not seen as yet, moved with fear, prepared an ark to the saving of his house; by the which he condemned the world, and became heir of the **righteousness which is by faith**. Hebrews 11:7

Also, it is clear in scripture that Christ first took his gospel message to the Jews, who as a nation rejected it, and then has offered it to the Gentiles for a period of time.

For a small moment have I forsaken thee; but with great mercies will I gather thee. In a little wrath I hid my face from thee for a moment; but with everlasting kindness will I have mercy on thee, saith the LORD thy Redeemer. Isaiah 54:7-8

For I would not, brethren, that ye should be ignorant of this mystery, lest ye should be wise in your own conceits; that blindness in part is happened to Israel, until the fulness of the Gentiles be come in. And so **all** Israel shall be saved: as it is written, There shall come out of Sion the Deliverer, and shall turn away ungodliness from Jacob: For this is my covenant unto them, when I shall take away their sins. Romans 11:25-27

Although, for a short while God has hidden Himself from Israel, He has promised to eventually save **all** Israel, both the house of Israel and the house of Judah, i.e., **all** twelve tribes.

Behold, the days come, saith the LORD, that I will make a new covenant with the house of Israel, and with the house of Judah: Not according to the covenant that I made with their fathers in the day that I took them by the hand to bring them out of the land of Egypt; which my covenant they brake, although I was an husband unto them, saith the LORD: But this shall be the covenant that I will make with the house of Israel; After those days, saith the LORD, I will put my law in their inward parts, and write it in their hearts; and will be their God, and they shall be my people. And they shall teach no more every man his neighbour, and every man his brother, saying, Know the LORD: for they shall all know me, from the least of them unto the greatest of them, saith the LORD: for I will forgive

their iniquity, and I will remember their sin no more.
Jeremiah 31:31-34

However, Classic Dispensationalism defines the Church as consisting of only New Testament saints, and as will be seen in the chapter on "Judgments", the Old Testament saints are more likely to be resurrected at the end of the 70th Week of Daniel, rather than with the Church before that. So, while it is difficult to be dogmatic about the status of the Old Testament saints in regards to the Church, it is my opinion that the Church began after Christ's death and resurrection, and consequently, the Old Testament saints fall into a different category, more consistent with Classic Dispensationalism.

ISRAEL, THE BRIDE

God has always had a special and separate relationship with Israel. The entire story of the Hebrew Bible (the Old Testament) tells the story of God's interaction with one particular nation, Israel. The Hebrew Scriptures are full of language about Israel's special status as God's chosen nation. For example, as the Israelites are about to enter the land, Moses declares to them:

> For thou art an holy people unto the LORD thy God: the LORD thy God hath chosen thee to be a special people unto himself, above all people that are upon the face of the earth. Deuteronomy 7:6

Throughout the Bible, scripture uses the imagery of a marriage between God and Israel, who He considers His wife. As seen above in Jeremiah 31:32, God considered Himself the husband of Israel. Joel Richardson in his book *Sinai to Zion* describes in detail how God joined Himself to Israel with a marriage covenant, referred to as the Old Covenant, at Mount Sinai. However, after repeated violations of the covenant, God divorced Israel.

> Thus saith the LORD, Where is the bill of your mother's divorcement, whom I have put away? or which of my creditors is it to whom I have sold you? Behold, for your iniquities have ye sold yourselves, and for your transgressions is your mother put away. Isaiah 50:1

The entire Book of Deuteronomy is that of an ancient marriage contract, where Moses took all the various facets of the three earlier books (Exodus, Leviticus, and Numbers) and presented them in the form of an ancient marriage contract. However, the Book of Hosea was God's bill of divorcement of the Northern Kingdom of Israel, and the Book of Jeremiah is the bill of divorcement of the Southern Kingdom of Judah.

Even after nearly one hundred years of separation, during which time the blessings of Deuteronomy continued to be withheld, Israel still failed to return to God her husband. Because she worshiped the gods of the Egyptians, the Egyptians would destroy her. Because she worshiped the deities of Assyria, the Assyrians would devastate her. Because she worshiped the idols of Babylon, the Babylonians would make her desolate. The nations who worshiped the very gods Israel committed adultery with would be the ones who would invade and destroy the nation of Israel. The aim of this punishment was not so God could be vengeful and get His revenge upon Israel, but rather to cause her to stop sinning, to stop her adulteries, and to return to Him. [Fruchtenbaum, 2004, pp. 576-579][1]

> And yet for all that, when they be in the land of their enemies, I will not cast them away, neither will I abhor them, to destroy them utterly, and to break my covenant with them: for I am the LORD their God. But I will for their sakes remember the covenant of their ancestors, whom I brought forth out of the land of Egypt in the sight of the heathen, that I might be their God: I am the LORD. Leviticus 26:44-45

Several major prophets in the Old Testament wrote about this situation where God had cast Israel away. However, they did not leave things in a state of hopelessness but spoke of a coming day when Israel would again become the restored Wife of Jehovah. Of course, this will require a brand-new marriage contract, and this marriage contract is found in Jeremiah 31:31-34 as seen above. Also, according to Ezekiel, God will enter into an everlasting covenant with Israel in the future.

> Nevertheless I will remember my covenant with thee in the days of thy youth, and I will establish unto thee an everlasting covenant. Then thou shalt remember thy ways, and be ashamed, when thou shalt receive thy sisters, thine elder and thy younger: and I will give them unto thee for daughters, but not by thy covenant. And I will establish my covenant with thee; and thou shalt know that I am the LORD: That thou mayest remember, and be confounded, and never open thy mouth any more because of thy shame, when I am pacified toward thee for all that thou hast done, saith the Lord GOD. Ezekiel 16:60-63

This everlasting covenant is the same as the New Covenant in Jeremiah 31:31-34. The restoration of Israel as Jehovah's wife is also described in Isaiah. [Fruchtenbaum, 2004, pp. 581-582][1]

> Sing, O barren, thou that didst not bear; break forth into singing, and cry aloud, thou that didst not travail with child: for more are the children of the desolate than the children of the married wife, saith the LORD. Enlarge the place of thy tent, and let them stretch forth the curtains of thine habitations: spare not, lengthen thy cords, and strengthen thy stakes; For thou shalt break forth on the right hand and on the left; and thy seed shall inherit the Gentiles, and make the desolate cities to be inhabited. Fear not; for thou shalt not be ashamed:

> neither be thou confounded; for thou shalt not be put
> to shame: for thou shalt forget the shame of thy youth,
> and shalt not remember the reproach of thy widowhood
> any more. For thy Maker is thine husband; the LORD of
> hosts is his name; and thy Redeemer the Holy One of
> Israel; The God of the whole earth shall he be called.
> For the LORD hath called thee as a woman forsaken
> and grieved in spirit, and a wife of youth, when thou
> wast refused, saith thy God. For a small moment have I
> forsaken thee; but with great mercies will I gather thee.
> In a little wrath I hid my face from thee for a moment;
> but with everlasting kindness will I have mercy on thee,
> saith the LORD thy Redeemer. Isaiah 54:1-8

Yet, the process of restoration will require a period of discipline called the Great Tribulation or the time of Jacob's Trouble, which will occur in the second half of the 70th Week. Israel will be attacked, invaded, and defeated by the Antichrist and will flee into the wilderness as described by Hosea.

> Therefore, behold, I will allure her, and bring her into
> the wilderness, and speak comfortably unto her. And I
> will give her her vineyards from thence, and the valley of
> Achor for a door of hope: and she shall sing there, as in
> the days of her youth, and as in the day when she came
> up out of the land of Egypt. And it shall be at that day,
> saith the LORD, that thou shalt call me Ishi; and shalt
> call me no more Baali. For I will take away the names
> of Baalim out of her mouth, and they shall no more be
> remembered by their name. And in that day will I make
> a covenant for them with the beasts of the field and with
> the fowls of heaven, and with the creeping things of the
> ground: and I will break the bow and the sword and
> the battle out of the earth, and will make them to lie
> down safely. And I will betroth thee unto me for ever;

yea, I will betroth thee unto me in righteousness, and in judgment, and in lovingkindness, and in mercies. I will even betroth thee unto me in faithfulness: and thou shalt know the LORD. And it shall come to pass in that day, I will hear, saith the LORD, I will hear the heavens, and they shall hear the earth; And the earth shall hear the corn, and the wine, and the oil; and they shall hear Jezreel. And I will sow her unto me in the earth; and I will have mercy upon her that had not obtained mercy; and I will say to them which were not my people, Thou art my people; and they shall say, Thou art my God. Hosea 2:14-23

Zechariah states that two-thirds of the Jews will be killed at this time and that one-third will survive. Of that one-third, half will flee into the wilderness and half will remain in the city. But after a great earthquake, that half will also take flight.

And it shall come to pass, that in all the land, saith the LORD, two parts therein shall be cut off and die; but the third shall be left therein. And I will bring the third part through the fire, and will refine them as silver is refined, and will try them as gold is tried: they shall call on my name, and I will hear them: I will say, It is my people: and they shall say, The LORD is my God. Zechariah 13:8-9

For I will gather all nations against Jerusalem to battle; and the city shall be taken, and the houses rifled, and the women ravished; and half of the city shall go forth into captivity, and the residue of the people shall not be cut off from the city. Zechariah 14:2

But just as God bore Israel up on eagles' wings during the first exodus (Exodus 19:4), He will bear them up on the wings of an eagle during this flight (Revelation 12:14).

> Ye have seen what I did unto the Egyptians, and how I bare you on eagles' wings, and brought you unto myself. Exodus 19:4

> And to the woman were given two wings of a great eagle, that she might fly into the wilderness, into her place, where she is nourished for a time, and times, and half a time, from the face of the serpent. Rev 12:14

It is after this "time, times, and half a time" or about three and a half years that God restores Israel to the land and remarries them at the marriage supper of the Lamb.

> Let us be glad and rejoice, and give honour to him: for the marriage of the Lamb is come, and his wife hath made herself ready. Revelation 19:7

Some mistakenly assume that the Church is the bride of Christ. Yet, nowhere does scripture refer to the Church as the bride of Christ. In fact, Paul calls the Church the "body of Christ".

> Now ye are the body of Christ, and members in particular. 1 Corinthians 12:27

> So we, being many, are one body in Christ, and every one members one of another. Romans 12:5

If the Church is the body of Christ and is already "in Christ", then there would be no need to marry Christ, since the Church is already joined to Him. The Book of Revelations also identifies the bride as Israel.

And I John saw the holy city, new Jerusalem, coming down from God out of heaven, prepared as a bride adorned for her husband. Revelation 21:2

Jerusalem is often used in scripture to refer to Israel as a whole. Remember Jesus' words as he looked back over the city:

O Jerusalem, Jerusalem, which killest the prophets, and stonest them that are sent unto thee; how often would I have gathered thy children together, as a hen doth gather her brood under her wings, and ye would not! Behold, your house is left unto you desolate: and verily I say unto you, Ye shall not see me, **until the time** come when ye shall say, Blessed is he that cometh in the name of the Lord. Luke 13:34-35

Jesus is speaking of the people Israel, and the term *until the time come* seems to speak of a time of preparation before they finally receive Jesus and the Messiah at some date in the future. That future date and its completion can be found in Revelation.

Let us be glad and rejoice, and give honour to him: for the marriage of the Lamb is come, and his wife hath made herself ready. Revelation 19:7

When Jesus returns for His bride, where will He go?

And his feet shall stand in that day upon **the mount of Olives, which is before Jerusalem** on the east, and the mount of Olives shall cleave in the midst thereof toward the east and toward the west, and there shall be a very great valley; and half of the mountain shall remove toward the north, and half of it toward the south. Zechariah 14:4

The groom goes to **Jerusalem** for His bride. He does not go to Rome or to the U.S. but to Jerusalem, implying that Israel is His bride. Also, if the bride is being prepared for Jesus' return at this time, does that not fit better as a reference to Israel, who is not ready for His return, rather than to the *ekklesia*, the Church, who is already justified, washed, and in Him?

Israel, divorced from God long ago, can now give herself into marriage, prepared as she has been through years of affliction. Israel is also repeatedly referred to as the "daughter of Zion" especially in this verse describing Jesus' Palm Sunday ride into Jerusalem, the city that again symbolizes Israel.

> Rejoice greatly, O **daughter of Zion**; shout, O daughter of Jerusalem: behold, thy King cometh unto thee: he is just, and having salvation; lowly, and riding upon an ass, and upon a colt the foal of an ass. Zech 9:9

The Bride of Christ is the daughter of Zion, Israel, but the wedding or marriage feast will be the final union of two groups into one people, the daughter of Zion with Jesus and his Body of called ones, the Church.

So, to summarize using Ariel Canada's Statement of Faith at the web site http://arielcanada.com: God called a people to Himself who are the physical descendants of Abraham, Isaac, and Jacob. Israel is the Wife of Jehovah, unfaithful in the past, divorced in the present, and to be reunited in the future. God has made four unconditional covenants with this elect nation that have remained unfulfilled (the Mosaic Covenant, the Palestinian or Land Covenant, the New Covenant, and the Davidic Covenant). God intends to fulfill all His promises to Israel in a literal way just as His warnings and judgments were fulfilled in a literal way. In Israel's history of unbelief there has always been a believing remnant according to the election of grace. There will be a national regeneration of Israel at which time all of the provisions of the unconditional covenants will be fulfilled, including the seed, land, and blessing aspects.

The life and times of the Wife of Jehovah can be outlined in six stages:

1. the marriage contract (Deut. 5:1-3; 6:10-15; 7:6-11; Ezek. 16:8),
2. the great adultery (Jer. 3:1-5; 31:32; Ezek. 16:15-34; Hosea 2:2-5
3. the separation (Deut. 24:1; Isa. 50:1),
4. the divorce (Jer. 3:6-10),
5. the punishment (Jer. 3:11-18; Ezek. 16:35-43, 58-59; Hosea 2:6-13),
6. the remarriage with restored blessings (Isa. 54:1-8; 62:4-5; Jer. 31:31-34;
   Ezek. 16:60-63; Hosea 2:14-23). [Hitchcock & Ice, 2007, p. 37]

It is the last two stages that have yet to be completed and will see their fulfillment at the marriage supper of the Lamb in the last 70th Week. Romans 11:25–32 wraps up a long section about God's plans for His Israelite people.

> For I would not, brethren, that ye should be ignorant of this mystery, lest ye should be wise in your own conceits; that blindness in part is happened to Israel, until the fulness of the Gentiles be come in. And so all Israel shall be saved: as it is written, There shall come out of Sion the Deliverer, and shall turn away ungodliness from Jacob: For this is my covenant unto them, when I shall take away their sins. As concerning the gospel, they are enemies for your sakes: but as touching the election, they are beloved for the father's sakes. For the gifts and calling of God are without repentance. For as ye in times past have not believed God, yet have now obtained mercy through their unbelief: Even so have these also now not believed, that through your mercy they also may obtain mercy. For God hath concluded them all in unbelief, that he might have mercy upon all. Romans 11:25-32

In short, He plans to remove the hardening of Israel's unbelief and renew His covenant with them. This will occur as many Jewish people come to faith in Christ at some future time. Israel remains deeply loved by God because of His irrevocable promises and calling for the patriarchs.

The Law

Yet, because of their unbelief in Jesus as their Messiah, most of Israel has elected to remain under the Law. But after Jesus' resurrection at his first coming, is the Law still necessary and in effect? Or are just parts of the Law to be kept? And finally, will it remain in effect after Jesus' second return and into the Millennium?

At the first marriage on Mount Sinai, the Law was the marriage contract that bound Israel to Christ. Parts of it were intended only for the Jews, while other sections were guidelines for all mankind. In the Old Testament, the Law can be understood to have three parts: ceremonial, civil, and moral. The *ceremonial law* related specifically to Israel's worship. It was the way the Jew actually took care of sin. If they were unrighteous, they could be made righteous again with a sin offering and a burnt or peace offering. For example:

> Speak unto the children of Israel, and say unto them, If any man of you bring an offering unto the LORD, ye shall bring your offering of the cattle, even of the herd, and of the flock. If his offering be a burnt sacrifice of the herd, let him offer a male without blemish: he shall offer it of his own voluntary will at the door of the tabernacle of the congregation before the LORD. Leviticus 1:2-3

God's purpose through the Law, and specifically the ceremonial law, was to continue His plan that He has had from the beginning, to restore fellowship between a fallen, sinful man and a holy God. Its primary purpose was to be completed in and by Jesus Christ, who fulfilled the ceremonial law by becoming our sin offering, our burnt offering, our peace offering. So, these ceremonial laws, therefore, were no longer necessary after Jesus' death and resurrection. While we are no longer bound by ceremonial law, the principles behind them—to worship and love a holy God—still apply. Jesus was often accused by the Pharisees of violating the ceremonial law.

The *civil law* applied to daily living in Israel and pertained only to Israel. For example:

> When thou dost lend thy brother any thing, thou shalt not go into his house to fetch his pledge. Thou shalt stand abroad, and the man to whom thou dost lend shall bring out the pledge abroad unto thee. Deuteronomy 24:10-11

The Jubilee was also part of the civil law. Some believe that the Jubilee applies to Christians, but, in fact, it related only to Jewish families. The land that had originally been assigned to them was returned to them in the Year of Jubilee. So, this is part of the civil law and pertained only to Israel. Because modern society and culture are so radically different from that time and setting, all of these guidelines cannot be followed specifically. But again, the principles behind the commands are timeless and should help guide one's conduct.

The *moral law* (such as the Ten Commandments) is the direct command of God, and it requires strict obedience. It is the law that informs what is right and what is wrong and applies to everyone. For example:

Thou shalt not kill. Exodus 20:13

It was wrong to murder before Jesus' death, burial, and resurrection, and it is still wrong to murder after Jesus' death, burial, and resurrection. And it will still be wrong when Jesus returns and into the Millennium. The moral law reveals the nature and will of God, and it still applies today. Jesus obeyed the moral law completely.

The Mosaic Law of the Old Testament was written for the chosen people of Israel. As a result, there is a distinction between how the Law relates to the Jews compared to Christians. This directly relates to the purpose of the Law and how it is applied today and will be applied in the future.

Israel was chosen for a specific purpose as stated in Genesis.

> Now the LORD had said unto Abram, Get thee out of thy country, and from thy kindred, and from thy father's house, unto a land that I will shew thee: And I will make of thee a great nation, and I will bless thee, and make thy name great; and thou shalt be a blessing: And I will bless them that bless thee, and curse him that curseth thee: and in thee shall all families of the earth be blessed. Genesis 12:1-3

They were God's instruments to accomplish a plan of rescue for the world, where God would become a man as a member of the Jewish race and die on the cross for man's crimes against God. They were not chosen just to be saved themselves but rather were chosen to be used to accomplish God's plan of salvation for **all** of mankind. And by maintaining the Law, Israel was able to come into the presence of God.

However, there were several shortcomings associated with the Law. First, although there was a high priest who would regularly offer an animal sacrifice for their sins, such sacrifices could never fully and finally secure their forgiveness.

> For it is not possible that the blood of bulls and of goats should take away sins. Hebrews 10:4

Second, the law of the Old Covenant that came through Moses was unable to give people the ability to fully keep and obey it. The Law of Moses was very clear in stating, "Thou shalt not…" or "Do this and live" or "Be ye holy." However, there was nothing in the law itself that could empower the people to obey it. The Law of Moses told the people of Israel what they should and should not do, but it was never capable of supplying them with the ability or the spiritual power to keep it.

Third, the Old or Mosaic Covenant was temporary. It was designed by God with a built-in obsolescence. God never intended for the Old Covenant to last forever. He never intended for it to be the final revelation of his will for mankind. This is known because Hebrews 8:5 explains that everything Moses did in constructing the Old Covenant tabernacle, together with its rituals and sacrifices, was only "a copy and shadow of the heavenly things". Also, the Old Covenant was plainly temporary according to what is taught in Jeremiah 31:31-34, a passage that is cited in Hebrews 8:8-12. There it explains that God always intended to establish a new covenant with His people that would be different from the one He made with Moses and Israel following the exodus from Egypt. To this can be added:

> In that he saith, A new covenant, he hath made the first old. Now that which decayeth and waxeth old is ready to vanish away. Hebrews 8:13[2]

The solution to these problems with the Old Covenant was manifested through Christ's death and resurrection, which offered a permanent and complete plan for man to fellowship once again with God. Many Jews took advantage of the mercy offered through that plan, but most did not. The fact that Israel was chosen to accomplish God's salvation did not actually secure their salvation. It secured a salvation plan for the world, and whether they individually participated in it or not was another question. Yet, Christians, according to Galatians, i.e., those who believe in Jesus Christ, are now the "seed" of Abraham and thus heirs according to the promise.

> Now to Abraham and his seed were the promises made. He saith not, And to seeds, as of many; but as of one, And to thy seed, which is Christ. Galatians 3:16

> There is neither Jew nor Greek, there is neither bond nor free, there is neither male nor female: for ye are all one in Christ Jesus. And if ye be Christ's, then are ye

Abraham's seed, and heirs according to the promise.
Galatians 3:28-29

In other words, the Church of Jesus Christ is the **true** Israel of God in a spiritual sense.

That does not mean believing Jews are excluded or replaced as heirs of the promise made to Abraham. All ethnic Jews who believe in Jesus are members of the New Covenant. But so too are ethnic Gentiles who believe in Jesus. The blood in your veins no longer matters for anything. The only thing that matters is the faith in your heart: if you trust in Jesus, whether you are male or female, slave or free, Jew or Gentile, you are the seed of Abraham, the true Israel of God, and thus members of the New Covenant.

However, that also does not mean that the Law as a way for Israel to fellowship with God was ended by the New Covenant. As Jesus stated in Matthew:

> Think not that I am come to destroy the law, or the prophets: I am not come to destroy, but to fulfil. For verily I say unto you, Till heaven and earth pass, one jot or one tittle shall in no wise pass from the law, till all be fulfilled. Whosoever therefore shall break one of these least commandments, and shall teach men so, he shall be called the least in the kingdom of heaven: but whosoever shall do and teach them, the same shall be called great in the kingdom of heaven. For I say unto you, That except your righteousness shall exceed the righteousness of the scribes and Pharisees, ye shall in no case enter into the kingdom of heaven. Matthew 5:17-20

Jews, as individuals, can choose to remain under the Old Covenant of the Law or can accept the New Covenant that Jesus brought through His blood sacrifice. The problem with keeping the Law now is that the sacrifices required by the Law have been unable to be performed since the destruction of the Temple in 70 AD by the Romans. In addition, there has been no red heifer, as required by the Law, available now for nearly two thousand years (more about this will be discussed in the chapter on "The Temple"). However, during the 70th Week, God will permit Israel to rebuild the Temple and to once again begin the Temple sacrifices, allowing them another opportunity for repentance nationally. As happened with the Second Temple, this Third Temple will be desecrated and the Jews will be dispersed. Jesus will return to save His people, and Israel will corporately as a nation "look upon" Him, acknowledging Him as the Christ, their Messiah. All Israel will repent and place their hope and trust in God forever.

> And it shall come to pass in that day, that I will seek to destroy all the nations that come against Jerusalem. And I will pour upon the house of David, and upon the inhabitants of Jerusalem, the spirit of grace and of supplications: and they shall look upon me whom they have pierced, and they shall mourn for him, as one mourneth for his only son, and shall be in bitterness for him, as one that is in bitterness for his firstborn. In that day shall there be a great mourning in Jerusalem, as the mourning of Hadadrimmon in the valley of Megiddon. And the land shall mourn, every family apart; the family of the house of David apart, and their wives apart; the family of the house of Nathan apart, and their wives apart; Zechariah 12:9-12

Surprisingly, just as the celebration of Jewish feasts (like the Feast of Tabernacles) will continue in the Millennium, there will also be sacrificial offerings at this time. Though it may sound strange, the Bible does indicate that animal sacrifices will take place during the Millennial Kingdom. Ezekiel 43-46 outlines these sacrificial practices as it describes the Jewish temple that will exist during the Millennial Kingdom and what takes place in it. Specifically, the ancestral line of Zadok will offer sacrifices (Ezekiel 44:15), and detailed animal sacrifices are described in chapters 45 and 46 which include the sacrifice of rams, lambs, and bulls.

In addition to Ezekiel, Isaiah discusses sacrifices in the future Millennial Kingdom, stating: "their burnt offerings and their sacrifices will be accepted on my altar" (Isaiah 56:7). Zechariah adds:

> And it shall come to pass, that every one that is left of all the nations which came against Jerusalem shall even go up from year to year to worship the King, the Lord of hosts, and to keep the feast of tabernacles. Zechariah 14:16

This celebration will also include animal sacrifices. Jeremiah notes that during this time period:[3]

> Neither shall the priests the Levites want a man before me to offer burnt offerings, and to kindle meat offerings, and to do sacrifice continually. Jeremiah 33:18

However, if Jesus' sacrifice was the only efficacious, once-for-all sacrifice to expiate sin (Heb. 9:12), why should animal sacrifices, which could never take away sin (Heb 10:4), be offered in the Millennial Temple during the Millennium?[4]

It is true that the sacrifices in the Millennial Temple will not expiate sin, just as the Mosaic offerings could not take away sin (Heb 10:4). Many conservative commentators believe these offerings will simply be memorials, similar to communion that Christians take in remembrance of Christ's sacrifice on the cross. They believe the offerings will serve as visible reminders of Christ's efficacious work.[4]

Although this is true, it seems that these sacrifices also will have an additional function. Scripture says they will be offered "to make atonement for the house of Israel" (Ezek. 45:17; cf. vv. 15, 20). This sacrificial system will not constitute a return to the Old Testament Mosaic Covenant or Law but will be a new system set up by the Lord with a dispensational distinctive applicable to the Millennial Kingdom.

The Hebrew word for *atonement* means "covering". The blood sacrifices that made atonement never removed sin; they simply covered it, staving off God's divine anger and punishment by providing a ransom. Christ's death on the cross (not the Levitical sacrificial system) made it possible for people's sins to be taken away.[4]

The animal sacrifices during the Millennium will ceremonially cover uncleanness and prevent human defilement of the Millennial Temple. This system will be needed because God's glorious presence will again dwell on Earth in the midst of sinners. This purging act propitiates God, i.e., satisfies God's wrath, enabling Him to dwell among His people. The atonement-cleansing was necessary in Leviticus because God's shekinah glory dwelt in the Tabernacle (Ex. 40:34). God resided in the midst of sinful, unclean people. Similarly, Ezekiel predicted the return of God's glory to the Millennial Temple. Thus, people worshiping at the Temple will need to atone for their uncleanness, so it will not cause defilement.[4]

As part of God's plan to restore man to fellowship with Him, the future animal sacrifices will not deal with eternal salvation but, rather, with finite cleansing of impurities from everyone who survived the Great Tribulation (they will have mortal bodies) and the children born to them during Christ's thousand-year reign. Those mortals will still have to trust Christ by faith to become saved, but the Law has not and will not pass until heaven and earth pass and **all** is fulfilled as Jesus stated (Matthew 5:18).[4]

The 144,000

As God's conduit to accomplish His restoration plan for man, the Jewish people have been consistently attacked by Satan in his attempt to utterly destroy them. God has also had to purge the wicked from His people in order to purify them. Yet, throughout the course of history, God has always kept a remnant of His faithful and righteous servants. When God destroyed the earth with the Great Flood, He preserved a remnant in Noah and his family. In the days of the Prophet Elijah, God let it be known that He had left a remnant. According to 1 Kings 19,

Elijah thought the nation of Israel had totally departed from God. But God informed Elijah that He had left for Himself seven thousand people who would serve and honor Him. Those seven thousand were God's remnant.

> Yet I have left me seven thousand in Israel, all the knees which have not bowed unto Baal, and every mouth which hath not kissed him. 1 Kings 19:18

During the days of the Prophet Isaiah, God gave Isaiah a vision of Israel.

> The vision of Isaiah the son of Amoz, which he saw concerning Judah and Jerusalem in the days of Uzziah, Jotham, Ahaz, and Hezekiah, kings of Judah. Hear, O heavens, and give ear, O earth: for the LORD hath spoken, I have nourished and brought up children, and they have rebelled against me. The ox knoweth his owner, and the ass his master's crib: but Israel doth not know, my people doth not consider. Ah sinful nation, a people laden with iniquity, a seed of evildoers, children that are corrupters: they have forsaken the LORD, they have provoked the Holy One of Israel unto anger, they are gone away backward. Why should ye be stricken any more? ye will revolt more and more: the whole head is sick, and the whole heart faint. From the sole of the foot even unto the head there is no soundness in it; but wounds, and bruises, and putrifying sores: they have not been closed, neither bound up, neither mollified with ointment. Your country is desolate, your cities are burned with fire: your land, strangers devour it in your presence, and it is desolate, as overthrown by strangers. And the daughter of Zion is left as a cottage in a vineyard, as a lodge in a garden of cucumbers, as a besieged city Except the LORD of hosts had left

unto us a very small **remnant**, we should have been as Sodom, and we should have been like unto Gomorrah. Isaiah 1:1-9

Isaiah said that the nation had become a "sinful nation, a people laden with iniquity, a seed of evildoers, children that are corrupters: they have forsaken the LORD, they have provoked the Holy One of Israel unto anger, they are gone away backward". Isaiah went onto say in verse 9, "Except the LORD of hosts had left unto us a very small remnant, we should have been as Sodom, and we should have been like unto Gomorrah."

The New Testament adds in Romans:

Even so then at this present time also there is a **remnant** according to the election of grace. Romans 11:5

Paul's point is that just as the Lord did in the time of Elijah, He continued to preserve a remnant of ethnic Israelites in the first century, as exemplified by Paul and many other Jewish Christians. Today, God continues to preserve a remnant of ethnic Israelites, Jews who have trusted in Christ alone for salvation. When the Church, including Christian Jews, is raptured after the 6th seal, God will preserve a remnant of 144,000 Jews as described in Revelation.

And after these things I saw four angels standing on the four corners of the earth, holding the four winds of the earth, that the wind should not blow on the earth, nor on the sea, nor on any tree. And I saw another angel ascending from the east, having the seal of the living God: and he cried with a loud voice to the four angels, to whom it was given to hurt the earth and the sea, Saying, Hurt not the earth, neither the sea, nor the trees, till we have sealed the servants of our God in their foreheads. And I heard the number of them which were sealed: and there were sealed an hundred and forty and four thousand of all the tribes of the children of Israel. Of the tribe of Juda were sealed twelve thousand. Of the tribe of Reuben were sealed twelve thousand. Of the tribe of Gad were sealed twelve thousand. Of the tribe of Aser were sealed twelve thousand. Of the tribe of Nephthalim were sealed twelve thousand. Of the tribe of Manasses were sealed twelve thousand. Of the tribe of Simeon were sealed twelve thousand. Of the tribe of Levi were sealed twelve thousand. Of the tribe of Issachar were sealed twelve thousand. Of the tribe of Zabulon were sealed twelve thousand. Of the tribe of Joseph were sealed twelve thousand. Of the tribe of Benjamin were sealed twelve thousand. Revelation 7:1-8

The 144,000 appear again in Revelation in chapter 14:

And I looked, and, lo, a Lamb stood on the mount Sion, and with him an hundred forty and four thousand, having his Father's name written in their foreheads. And I heard a voice from heaven, as the voice of many waters, and as the voice of a great thunder: and I heard the voice of harpers harping with their harps: And they sung as it were a new song before the throne, and before the four beasts, and the elders: and no man could learn that song but the hundred and forty and four thousand, which were redeemed from the earth. These are they which were not defiled with women; for they are virgins. These are they which follow the Lamb whithersoever he goeth. These were redeemed from among men, being the firstfruits unto God and to the Lamb. And in their mouth was found no guile: for they are without fault before the throne of God. Revelation 14:1-5

The 144,000 are made up of twelve thousand from each of the twelve tribes of Israel and will be sealed by God. This will guarantee their safety from God's wrath which soon follows their sealing. Scripture repeatedly speaks of the children of God as being sealed. For example, in the story of the Passover, the children of Israel were sealed by the blood on the lintel and on the two doorposts, protecting their firstborn from death.

> For I will pass through the land of Egypt this night, and will smite all the firstborn in the land of Egypt, both man and beast; and against all the gods of Egypt I will execute judgment: I am the LORD. And the blood shall be to you for a token upon the houses where ye are: and when I see the blood, I will pass over you, and the plague shall not be upon you to destroy you, when I smite the land of Egypt. Exodus 12:12-13

Also, similar to the sealing of the 144,000 is Ezekiel's account of the marking of a faithful remnant prior to the outpouring of God's wrath on the wicked.

> He cried also in mine ears with a loud voice, saying, Cause them that have charge over the city to draw near, even every man with his destroying weapon in his hand. And, behold, six men came from the way of the higher gate, which lieth toward the north, and every man a slaughter weapon in his hand; and one man among them was clothed with linen, with a writer's inkhorn by his side: and they went in, and stood beside the brasen altar. And the glory of the God of Israel was gone up from the cherub, whereupon he was, to the threshold of the house. And he called to the man clothed with linen, which had the writer's inkhorn by his side; And the LORD said unto him, Go through the midst of the city, through the midst of Jerusalem, and **set a mark upon the foreheads of the men** that sigh and that cry for all the abominations that be done in the midst thereof.

And to the others he said in mine hearing, Go ye after him through the city, and smite: let not your eye spare, neither have ye pity: Slay utterly old and young, both maids, and little children, and women: but come not near any man upon whom is the mark; and begin at my sanctuary. Then they began at the ancient men which were before the house. And he said unto them, Defile the house, and fill the courts with the slain: go ye forth. And they went forth, and slew in the city. And it came to pass, while they were slaying them, and I was left, that I fell upon my face, and cried, and said, Ah Lord GOD! wilt thou destroy all the residue of Israel in thy pouring out of thy fury upon Jerusalem? Then said he unto me, The iniquity of the house of Israel and Judah is exceeding great, and the land is full of blood, and the city full of perverseness: for they say, The LORD hath forsaken the earth, and the LORD seeth not. And as for me also, mine eye shall not spare, neither will I have pity, but I will recompense their way upon their head. And, behold, the man clothed with linen, which had the inkhorn by his side, reported the matter, saying, I have done as thou hast commanded me. Ezekiel 9:1-11

In the New Testament, several references are given that concern the sealing of the Church.

In whom ye also trusted, after that ye heard the word of truth, the gospel of your salvation: in whom also after that ye believed, ye were **sealed** with that holy Spirit of promise, Ephesians 1:13

Now he which stablisheth us with you in Christ, and hath anointed us, is God; Who hath also **sealed** us, and given the earnest of the Spirit in our hearts. 2 Corinthians 1:21-22

> And grieve not the holy Spirit of God, whereby ye are
> **sealed** unto the day of redemption. Ephesians 4:30

When God through the Holy Spirit seals a person, He designates that that person belongs to Him and is sealed by the blood of Jesus Christ. Their mark is really the blood of the atonement similar to what was manifest in the Old Testament when Israel stroked the blood-mark upon the doorpost. God sealed His own with blood, and the mark of the sealing is essentially the verification of being purchased by the blood of Jesus Christ. Likewise, when the 144,000 are sealed, they will be marked by God as belonging to Him with His name written on their foreheads (Rev 14:1). Consequently, they will be guaranteed God's protection from His coming wrath during the time of Jacob's trouble.

At least part of the 144,000 do not initially have saving faith in Jesus Christ, but God does use certain criteria in choosing those He will seal. Some consider the 144,000 to be only symbolic of a spiritual Israel, i.e., the Church, while a literal reading of scripture identifies the 144,000 as Jews, who are physical descendants of Abraham (Revelation 7:5-8). Revelation also characterizes them as truthful with no lie or falsehood found in their mouths (Revelation 14:5). This is consistent with those sealed or marked in Ezekiel where God chooses those who are distressed by the wickedness that is occurring among His people.

> And the LORD said unto him, Go through the midst
> of the city, through the midst of Jerusalem, and set a
> mark upon the foreheads of the **men that sigh and that
> cry for all the abominations that be done in the midst
> thereof**. Ezekiel 9:4

So, although they may have not recognized Jesus as their Messiah initially, they are Jews seeking to remain faithful and true to the God of their fathers. Once the Church is raptured, it is these 144,000 that God selects to be His remnant. They will eventually be redeemed and become followers of the Lamb, Jesus Christ (Revelation 14:4). They will be presented to God and to the Lamb as the *firstfruits*

(Revelation 14:4) of the Great Tribulation, appearing with Jesus on Mount Zion (Revelation 14:1) where Christ will reign with them in His kingdom.

> Then the moon shall be confounded, and the sun ashamed, when the LORD of hosts shall reign in mount Zion, and in Jerusalem, and before his ancients gloriously. Isaiah 24:23

Some, especially those among the pretribulation camp, believe that the 144,000 will act as evangelists to the unbelieving world once the Church is raptured. However, there is no specific scripture to support this idea. We do know that they will be God's servants (Revelation 7:3), and they will sing a song that no one else can sing (Revelation 14:3). They will be a kingdom of priests in the Millennium along with the twelve apostles who will rule over the twelve tribes of Israel as promised by Jesus.

> Ye are they which have continued with me in my temptations. And I appoint unto you a kingdom, as my Father hath appointed unto me; That ye may eat and drink at my table in my kingdom, and sit on thrones judging the twelve tribes of Israel. Luke 22:28-30

Interestingly, the population of Jerusalem in 2020 was 931,756 of which Jews make up 75%. According to *populationreview.com*, it is projected that in 2035 the population will increase to 1,143,645. That would project out to a Jewish population in Jerusalem of 857,734. Assuming that half of these are males, then there would be approximately 428, 867 Jewish males in Jerusalem at that time. As noted earlier, Zechariah states that two-thirds of the Jews will be killed at this time and that one-third will survive.

> And it shall come to pass, that in all the land, saith the LORD, two parts therein shall be cut off and die; but the

third shall be left therein. And I will bring the third part through the fire, and will refine them as silver is refined, and will try them as gold is tried: they shall call on my name, and I will hear them: I will say, It is my people: and they shall say, The LORD is my God. Zechariah 13:8-9

One third of the Jewish males in Jerusalem at that time would be about 142,956 which is remarkably close to the number of 144,000, within less than a 1% error. So, the "third part" referred to in Zechariah may be a reference to the 144,000.

Another approach, looking at whether the population statistics of Israel support the number of 144,000 seen in Revelation, would be to look not at just Jerusalem but the entire land of Israel and to assume that the 144,000 would most likely be made up of ultra-orthodox Jews who do seek to remain faithful and true to the God of their fathers. The population of Israel in 2020 was 8,655,535 of which again about 75% are Jewish. So, the Israeli Jewish population in 2020 is 6,491,651. Since ultra-orthodox Jews make up 8% of the Jewish population, this calculates out to 519,332 ultra-orthodox Jews in Israel as of 2020. The rate of growth of the ultra-orthodox population is estimated to be 4.2%. Therefore, the ultra-orthodox population would grow by 63% in 15 years to the year 2035, resulting in about 846,511 ultra-orthodox Jews in Israel by the year 2035 and 423,256 male ultra-orthodox Jews. Again, assuming that two-thirds of the Jews will be killed at this time, one-third of this number is 141,085 which again is close (within 2%) to the number 144,000. Even though it is speculation, it does confirm that the number 144,000 is a realistic number considering the current population of Israel.

THE CHURCH

Besides Israel and the Gentiles, there is now a new people group, the Church, made up of both Jews and Gentiles. In the book of Acts, both

Israel and the Church are mentioned and exist simultaneously. The term *Israel* is used twenty times and *ekklesia* (Church) nineteen times, yet the two groups are always kept distinct. [Woods, 2016a, pp. 149-150] The Church is made up of citizens of the Kingdom and is called to be a governing assembly. It is often and clearly referred to as the **body** of Christ.[1]

> And he gave some, apostles; and some, prophets; and some, evangelists; and some, pastors and teachers; For the perfecting of the saints, for the work of the ministry, for the edifying of the **body of Christ**: Ephesians 4:11-12

> That the Gentiles should be fellowheirs, and of the same **body**, and partakers of his promise in Christ by the gospel: Ephesians 3:6

Nowhere in scripture is the Church, which represents the body of Christ and already joined with or in Him, called the **bride** of Christ. Although God chose Israel as His bride for a unique role and relationship with Him, it does not mean that He favors one group over another. In fact, it results in the exact opposite. Instead, God works out His plan to extend His love to all the world through Israel's seed, Jesus. His love for all people, even for the Gentile nations, is displayed in the ministry of Jesus and his disciples. For example, one of Jesus' early followers was a non-Jewish, Samaritan woman who was not from the chosen nation of Israel.[6,7]

> And many of the Samaritans of that city believed on him for the saying of the woman, which testified, He told me all that ever I did. So when the Samaritans were come unto him, they besought him that he would tarry with them: and he abode there two days. And many more believed because of his own word; And said unto the woman, Now we believe, not because of thy saying: for we have heard him ourselves, and know

that this is indeed the Christ, the Saviour of the world.
John 4:39-42

Jesus invited her into a conversation and revealed to her that he is the Messiah that she and her people had been waiting for. This woman then went on to invite many others into the story of Jesus.

The New Testament contains many other stories of Jesus and his followers extending this invitation to all people.

> The centurion answered and said, Lord, I am not worthy that thou shouldest come under my roof: but speak the word only, and my servant shall be healed. For I am a man under authority, having soldiers under me: and I say to this man, Go, and he goeth; and to another, Come, and he cometh; and to my servant, Do this, and he doeth it. When Jesus heard it, he marvelled, and said to them that followed, Verily I say unto you, I have not found so great faith, no, not in Israel. And I say unto you, That many shall come from the east and west, and shall sit down with Abraham, and Isaac, and Jacob, in the kingdom of heaven. But the children of the kingdom shall be cast out into outer darkness: there shall be weeping and gnashing of teeth. Matthew 8:8-12

> And it came to pass, as he went to Jerusalem, that he passed through the midst of Samaria and Galilee. And as he entered into a certain village, there met him ten men that were lepers, which stood afar off: And they lifted up their voices, and said, Jesus, Master, have mercy on us. And when he saw them, he said unto them, Go shew yourselves unto the priests. And it came to pass, that, as they went, they were cleansed. And one of them, when he saw that he was healed, turned back, and with a loud voice glorified God, And fell down on his face at his feet, giving him thanks: and he was

a Samaritan. And Jesus answering said, Were there not ten cleansed? but where are the nine? There are not found that returned to give glory to God, save this stranger. And he said unto him, Arise, go thy way: thy faith hath made thee whole. Luke 17:11-19

These stories of the Gentile centurion and the Samaritan leper demonstrate God's love for all people, not only the Jews. Also, the Book of Acts relates the story of God directing Peter to take the gospel to the Gentiles and concludes with:

For they heard them speak with tongues, and magnify God. Then answered Peter, Can any man forbid water, that these should not be baptized, which have received the Holy Ghost as well as we? And he commanded them to be baptized in the name of the Lord. Then prayed they him to tarry certain days. Acts 10:46-48

Later in Acts, the story of the Gentiles hearing and receiving the Good News after the rejection by the Jews continues.

Then Paul and Barnabas waxed bold, and said, It was necessary that the word of God should first have been spoken to you: but seeing ye put it from you, and judge yourselves unworthy of everlasting life, lo, we turn to the Gentiles. For so hath the Lord commanded us, saying, I have set thee to be a light of the Gentiles, that thou shouldest be for salvation unto the ends of the earth. And when the Gentiles heard this, they were glad, and glorified the word of the Lord: and as many as were ordained to eternal life believed. Acts 13:46-48

Israel holds a special place with God. Yet, following their rejection of His son, the gospel of salvation was then offered to the Gentiles, who have been grafted into the olive tree of God's chosen people Israel. This was God's plan from the beginning to rescue all nations and to restore them back into fellowship with Him.

> For God so loved **the world**, that he gave his only begotten Son, that whosoever believeth in him should not perish, but have everlasting life. John 3:16

God is using the Church to take His message of salvation to the world that does include Israel as well. He is working through the Church to make Israel jealous and thereby once again bring them back to God as a holy and separate nation, a kingdom of priests to Him. So, although there is and always has been only one plan of salvation for all mankind, God has had a unique purpose for different groups in order to accomplish that plan.

Did the Church replace Israel?[8,9]

It is clear that the Church and Israel are separate and distinct groups. They have separate and distinct purposes but one goal – to reestablish fellowship with God. Some have taught in the past and still believe that Israel has completed its purpose and that God is now finished with them. They conclude that the Church has now replaced Israel. Those who believe that the Church has superseded or replaced Israel argue that God chose the Jewish people after the fall of Adam in order to prepare the world for the coming of Jesus Christ, the Savior. They then presume that after Christ came, the special role of the Jewish people came to an end, and its place was taken by the Church, the new Israel.

Replacement theologians believe that God turned from the Jews (after they rejected Christ) and transferred His covenant promises from Israel to the Church. In other words, any Old Testament promises made to Israel now belong to the "true Israel", that is, to all believers of Jesus Christ. Jewish people who accept Jesus Christ become part of "true Israel" which does not discriminate between Jews and Gentiles, male and female, free and bond, etc. When defending their position, scholars embracing replacement theology sometimes emphasize that God is not "racist" or "sexist". They argue that the nation of Israel is not given "special treatment" by God, and there is no final restoration of (physical) Israel in the Middle East.

There is little doubt that many theologians of the early church promoted Replacement Theology. Irenaeus (130-200 AD) wrote, "For inasmuch as the former [the Jews] have rejected the Son of God, and cast Him out of the vineyard when they slew Him, God has justly rejected them, and given to the Gentiles outside the vineyard the fruits of its cultivation." Clement of Alexandria (c. 195) claimed that Israel "denied the Lord" and thus "forfeited the place of the true Israel." [Vlach, 2010] Replacement theology has been the dominant view of the Church from the third century until the middle of the nineteenth century. The Roman Catholic church has been supersessionist, i.e., supporters of replacement theology, as were the first-generation Reformers, including, unfortunately, Martin Luther and John Calvin [Vlach, 2010]. Despite the good that Martin Luther did in advancing Protestantism, later in life, tragically, he became anti-Semitic, which unfortunately is generally the end conclusion of replacement theology.[1]

Those who are in favor of this replacement theological interpretation often refer to the Book of Jeremiah.

> Behold, the days come, saith the LORD, that I will make a new covenant with the house of Israel, and with the house of Judah: Not according to the covenant that I made with their fathers in the day that I took them by the hand to bring them out of the land of Egypt; which my covenant they brake, **although I was an husband** unto them, saith the LORD: Jeremiah 31:31-32

This same passage is quoted in the New Testament in Hebrews.

> For finding fault with them, he saith, Behold, the days come, saith the Lord, when I will make a new covenant with the house of Israel and with the house of Judah:

> Not according to the covenant that I made with their
> fathers in the day when I took them by the hand to lead
> them out of the land of Egypt; because they continued
> not in my covenant, and **I regarded them not**, saith the
> Lord. Hebrews 8:8-9

However, the Book of Hebrews contains a remarkable difference from Jeremiah. Instead of the phrase "although I was an husband", it reads, "I regarded them not." These words in Hebrews are a cornerstone of Christian supersessionist theology which believes that the people of Israel no longer find favor with the God of Israel because God has made a new declaration of love to the Christian church.

Hebrews differs significantly from Jeremiah because it quotes a translation of the Hebrew Bible into Greek. This translation, known as the Septuagint, describes a relationship that has been terminated: God seeks a divorce. However, in the Hebrew text, God wants to continue the relationship. Both the Septuagint and Hebrews use the Greek verb *ameleo*, meaning "to ignore, not to care about, to abandon" which is similar in meaning to the Hebrew word *ga'al*. Yet, in the Hebrew Bible, the verb is *ba'al*, which can be translated as "to be a husband, to be faithful, to be the Lord".

The best explanation of the difference between the Hebrew and Greek texts is that either the translators of the Septuagint were translating from a Hebrew manuscript that contained a different word or that the translators misread the manuscript that they were reading. The translator might have misread *ba'al* ("to be a husband, to be faithful") as the word *ga'al* ("not to care about, to despise, to abandon"). [9]

If the book of Hebrews uses the word *ga'al* in its translation, then those who employ Hebrews 8:9 as a cornerstone of their theology are silently claiming that the Hebrew text in Jeremiah 31:31-32 is inferior to the text of the Septuagint. It is not a question of being "biblical" or "unbiblical" but rather a choice between two biblical manuscript traditions. Hence, readers should ask themselves whether *ba'al* ("to be faithful") or *ga'al* ("to despise") best represents how the God of Israel is described in the biblical texts in general and in Jeremiah in particular.[9]

Since the mid-nineteenth century, replacement theology "has received serious criticism and widespread rejection" thanks to dispensationalism and a more literal understanding of the Old Testament, especially with respect to Israel and the promises made to it. Vlach adds that the Holocaust and the re-establishment of the state of Israel have been significant factors, as well. Paul's letter to the Romans demonstrates the error of replacement theology. Romans 9 and 10 may suggest that God has replaced Israel with the Church, but Romans 11 argues that Israel—i.e., physical Israel and the Jews—is still in God's plan for the future. After all, if God could break His covenant with the Jews, would not that mean that He could do so with Christians, too? God has made many declarations about his unconditional promises to Israel. God has not (permanently) rejected Israel. Even Israel's rejection of Christ could not break the "everlasting covenant" that God made with Israel, because it was an unconditional covenant; therefore, there were no conditions that Israel had to fulfill. Ownership of the land is unconditional; but, enjoyment of the land is conditional [Fruchtenbaum, 2013b].[1]

A common argument is that God has only ever had one people who worship Him, namely, the set of all believers in the God of the Bible. In the days before Jesus Christ's ministry on Earth, this obviously included those who believed in the writings and God of the Old Testament (since the New Testament was not written until the years following Christ's ministry). Although this is true, the problem occurs when people also demand that the Christian Church has replaced Israel with respect to the promises made by God. Dispensationalists would argue that there is no difference between Jew and Gentile today: that God accepts all people who believe in Jesus Christ, and in fact, they become part of one body of believers.

However, at some point in the future, at the Rapture, God will remove the Church and once again deal primarily with the Jews. The hope is that many Jews will come to faith in Jesus Christ. Some Jews, at least 144,000, will accept Jesus as their Messiah. But for now, Romans 11:25-26 teaches that Israel has experienced a hardening in part until the full number of the Gentiles (Christian Church) has come in—and so all Israel will be saved. Unfortunately, it will take the last seven-year period of Daniel, and especially the last half, for Israel to cry out to the Lord for deliverance. Then they will long for the return of the Messiah, and He will deliver all of them that remain at His Second Coming.

In the Book of Matthew, Jesus said:

> And I say also unto thee, That thou art Peter, and upon this rock I will build my church; and the gates of hell shall not prevail against it. Matthew 16:18

The Church had not existed before he said this. It was born on the Day of Pentecost (following Christ's ascension), when the Holy Spirit was poured out on three thousand people. So, the Church did not replaced Israel; rather, it has in a sense temporarily interrupted (but not replaced) God's dealings with Israel as a nation. When the 70th Week of Daniel starts, God's primary attention on Israel and her restoration will once again begin. That focus will intensify when the Church is raptured after the sixth seal and the trumpet judgments commence.

> After this I beheld, and, lo, a great multitude, which no man could number, of all nations, and kindreds, and people, and tongues, stood before the throne, and before the Lamb, clothed with white robes, and palms in their hands; And cried with a loud voice, saying, Salvation to our God which sitteth upon the throne, and unto the Lamb. And all the angels stood round about the throne, and about the elders and the four beasts, and fell before the throne on their faces, and worshipped God, Saying, Amen: Blessing, and glory, and wisdom, and thanksgiving, and honour, and power, and might, be unto our God for ever and ever. Amen. And one of the elders answered, saying unto me, What are these which are arrayed in white robes? and whence came they? And I said unto him, Sir, thou knowest. And he said to me, These are they which came out of great tribulation, and

have washed their robes, and made them white in the blood of the Lamb. Therefore are they before the throne of God, and serve him day and night in his temple: and he that sitteth on the throne shall dwell among them. They shall hunger no more, neither thirst any more; neither shall the sun light on them, nor any heat. For the Lamb which is in the midst of the throne shall feed them, and shall lead them unto living fountains of waters: and God shall wipe away all tears from their eyes. Rev 7:9-17

So, God raptures His Church, but to where does He take His faithful?

Destination of the Church

God has promised that His righteous will not endure His wrath.

For God hath not appointed us to wrath, but to obtain salvation by our Lord Jesus Christ, 1 Thess 5:9

As seen above in Revelation 7:9-17 the Church is removed or "raptured" before God begins to pour out His wrath, and the Church then appears in **heaven** right after the sealing of the 144,000. This scene, of the Church being removed before God's wrath, is repeated later in Revelation 14.

And I looked, and behold a white cloud, and upon the cloud one sat like unto the Son of man, having on his head a golden crown, and in his hand a sharp sickle. And another angel came out of the temple, crying with a loud voice to him that sat on the cloud, Thrust in thy sickle, and reap: for the time is come for thee to reap; for the harvest of the earth is ripe. And he that sat on the cloud thrust in his sickle on the earth; and the earth was reaped. Revelation 14:14-16

No reference to the Church is seen in Revelation again until they return with Christ to fight the battle of Armageddon.

> And the armies which were in heaven followed him upon white horses, clothed in fine linen, white and clean. Revelation 19:14

More about the rapture will be discussed in the chapter on "The Second Coming of Christ", but it is unequivocal that initially believers will meet Jesus in the clouds. That is clear since Paul teaches it in 1 Thessalonians.

> Then we which are alive and remain shall be caught up together with them in the clouds, to meet the Lord in the air: and so shall we ever be with the Lord. 1 Thessalonians 4:17

So, the saints meet Jesus in the air and then what? Do they then come down immediately to earth, escorting Christ to His kingdom on the physical earth? Or do they just remain in the air? Or are they taken to heaven before the throne of the Father while His wrath is poured out on the earth? The answers to these questions, regarding the destination of the saints after the rapture, is given in several scriptures. In 2 Corinthians:

> Knowing that he which raised up the Lord Jesus shall raise up us also by Jesus, and shall present us with you. For all things are for your sakes, that the abundant grace might through the thanksgiving of many redound to the glory of God. 2 Corinthians 4:14-15

This states that Jesus raises us up, which is the resurrection, and soon after this we are taken up to meet Jesus in the air, i.e., the rapture. He then presents us to the glory of God, which, of course, is in heaven. Also, before his final departure, Jesus promised:

In my Father's house are many mansions: if it were not so, I would have told you. I go to prepare a place for you. And if I go and prepare a place for you, I will come again, and receive you unto myself; that where I am, there ye may be also. John 14:2-3

This again is speaking within the context of the rapture, and Jesus promises to take us to where He is, that is to heaven. Another passage of scripture that supports heaven as a destination, is again Revelation 7.

And one of the elders answered, saying unto me, What are these which are arrayed in white robes? and whence came they? And I said unto him, Sir, thou knowest. And he said to me, These are they which came out of great tribulation, and have washed their robes, and made them white in the blood of the Lamb. Therefore are they **before the throne of God**, and serve him day and night in his temple: and he that sitteth on the throne shall dwell among them. Revelation 7:13-15

Clearly, the saints are before the throne of God in heaven. Finally, even the Old Testament supports the view that heaven is the destination of the saints after the rapture.

Thy dead men shall live, together with my dead body shall they arise. Awake and sing, ye that dwell in dust: for thy dew is as the dew of herbs, and the earth shall cast out the dead. Come, my people, enter thou into thy chambers, and shut thy doors about thee: hide thyself as it were for a little moment, until the indignation be overpast. For, behold, the LORD cometh out of his place to punish the inhabitants of the earth for their iniquity: the earth also shall disclose her blood, and shall no more cover her slain. Isaiah 26:19-21

Notice the undeniably explicit resurrection language here, and as seen, the rapture follows the resurrection. Isaiah states here that the resurrection of God's people happens before the wrath of God. Then, after the resurrection, they enter into chambers which are in heaven. These chambers or rooms are most likely within the mansions in heaven described by Jesus in the Gospel of John.[10]

As Revelation teaches, after the wrath of God is completed, the saints descend from heaven to New Jerusalem, which with some speculation may very well contain the same rooms or chambers in which the saints were hidden from God's wrath. They will then reign with Christ for one thousand years during the Millennium as "kings and priests" or as some Bible translations state, a "kingdom of priests".

> Blessed and holy is he that hath part in the first resurrection: on such the second death hath no power, but they shall be priests of God and of Christ, and shall reign with him a thousand years. Revelation 20:6

> And hath made us kings and priests unto God and his Father; to him be glory and dominion for ever and ever. Amen. Revelation 1:6

Persecution of the Church and the Great Apostasy

The Church is raptured between the sixth and seventh seals about five and a half years after the beginning of the 70th Week of Daniel. Although it is spared God's wrath, it will still endure about two years of severe persecution during the Great Tribulation which begins at the midpoint of the 70th week. It is during this persecution that the Church will be purified and many will fall away from their faith. The Bible indicates that the Church will experience a great apostasy or falling away during the end times.

> Let no man deceive you by any means: for that day shall not come, except there come a falling away *(apostasia)*

first, and that man of sin be revealed, the son of perdition; 2 Thessalonians 2:3

The KJV calls it the "falling away", while the NIV and ESV call it "the rebellion". And that is what an apostasy is: a rebellion, an abandonment of the truth. The end times will include a wholesale rejection of God's revelation, a further "falling away" of an already fallen world.

The Greek word translated "rebellion" or "falling away" in 2 Thessalonians 2:3 is *apostasia*, from which we get the English word *apostasy*. It refers to a general defection from the true God, the Bible, and the Christian faith. Every age has its defectors, but the falling away at the end times will be complete and worldwide. The whole world will be in rebellion against God and His Son. In the Book of Matthew, Jesus warned the disciples concerning the final days.

> Then shall they deliver you up to be afflicted, and shall kill you: and ye shall be hated of all nations for my name's sake. And then shall many be offended, and shall betray one another, and shall hate one another. And many false prophets shall rise, and shall deceive many. And because iniquity shall abound, the love of many shall wax cold. Matthew 24:9-12

As can be seen, there will be several reasons for the great apostasy of the end times. Fear of being afflicted or suffering as well as being killed for their faith is given as one of the chief explanations for the falling away. Also, amazing signs and wonders will be performed by false prophets, chiefly the False Prophet, which will deceive Christians into abandoning their faith. Finally, "iniquity shall abound" and for Christians who are not strong in their faith, this massive, persistent assault on their principles and beliefs will cause their love to "wax cold".

How much of the Church will fall away? How "great" will be the Great Apostasy? In His Olivet Discourse, Jesus relates the Parable of the Wise and Foolish Virgins.

Then shall the kingdom of heaven be likened unto ten virgins, which took their lamps, and went forth to meet the bridegroom. And five of them were wise, and **five were foolish**. They that were foolish took their lamps, and took no oil with them: But the wise took oil in their vessels with their lamps. While the bridegroom tarried, they all slumbered and slept. And at midnight there was a cry made, Behold, the bridegroom cometh; go ye out to meet him. Then all those virgins arose, and trimmed their lamps. And the foolish said unto the wise, Give us of your oil; for our lamps are gone out. But the wise answered, saying, Not so; lest there be not enough for us and you: but go ye rather to them that sell, and buy for yourselves. And while they went to buy, the bridegroom came; and they that were ready went in with him to the marriage: and the door was shut. Afterward came also the other virgins, saying, Lord, Lord, open to us. But he answered and said, Verily I say unto you, I know you not. Watch therefore, for ye know neither the day nor the hour wherein the Son of man cometh. Matthew 25:1-13

There are five wise virgins (the faithful church) and five foolish virgins (the part of the Church that abandons its faith). This indicates that perhaps up to half or fifty percent of the Church could fall away during this time. Of course, this is speculation, but it underscores why it is vitally important to know and be prepared for what will happen during this tumultuous period in history.

THE GENTILES- "FULLNESS OF" AND "TIMES OF" THE GENTILES

Gentiles are all non-Jews who may or may not be part of the Church. Throughout history God has used them as a rod of chastening upon Israel, to further God's purpose concerning them. It began with Israel's first oppression by the Gentiles in Egypt and has continued with various

Gentile empires since then, including the Assyrian, Babylonian, Medo-Persian, Grecian, Roman, and more recently the Ottoman/Islamic empire. As seen earlier, a Gentile kingdom, most likely a Revived Grecian Empire ruled by the Antichrist, will again be used by God to correct and humble Israel in the 70th Week. This will eventually result in the restoration of God's chosen nation which will occur at the end of the 70th Week with the return of the Messiah in glory. At this time Jesus will deliver Israel from the Gentiles and exalt them as the head of all nations in the Millennium and forever (Luke 21:24; Romans 11:25-32; Revelation 19:11-20:10).

Recent events in the Middle East have focused attention on the political and prophetic significance of Israel's possession of their ancient capital of Jerusalem. For the first time since 70 AD Israel is in complete possession of the city of Jerusalem and its surrounding territory. Yet, administration of the Temple Mount was given back to the Waqf, an Islamic religious trust under Jordanian custodianship, although Israel does maintain control of security of the Temple Mount. Under these circumstances, it is only natural that attention should be focused upon the prophecy recorded in Luke.

> And they shall fall by the edge of the sword, and shall be led away captive into all nations: and Jerusalem shall be trodden down of the Gentiles, until the **times of the Gentiles** be fulfilled. Luke 21:24

Does the present occupation of Jerusalem signify, in keeping with this prophecy, that the "times of the Gentiles" have come to an end? A superficial study of this passage would seem to indicate that this is the case, and that now Israel is moving into a new phase of its long history. Careful students, acquainted with the history of the interpretation of this verse, however, sense the danger of reaching too hasty a conclusion. As a matter of fact, there are a number of important considerations which affect the interpretation of this passage.[11]

Definition of Terms

Expositors, pondering the meaning of Luke 21:24, soon become aware of the fact that this term, "the times of the Gentiles", is found only here in the Bible. The problem of definition of terms, therefore, becomes an acute one, inasmuch as in this passage there is only the description that Jerusalem "shall be trodden down by the Gentiles" as indicating the character of this period. Under these circumstances, a variety of definitions can be made depending upon the theological presuppositions of the interpreter. Some consider the times of the Gentiles as the end of the Gentile dispensation. Others believe that it is the physical possession of Jerusalem that becomes of central importance. The fact that Israel was dispossessed of their ancient city in 70 AD, and has today repossessed the city, therefore, becomes a matter of physical and prophetic significance.[11]

Relation of "Times of the Gentiles" to "The Fullness of the Gentiles"[12]

In attempting to define the expression "the **times** of the Gentiles", it becomes exegetically (the process of interpreting scripture) important to determine what relation, if any, there is between this term and that found in Romans ("the **fullness** of the Gentiles") where it is stated:

> For I would not, brethren, that ye should be ignorant of this mystery, lest ye should be wise in your own conceits; that blindness in part is happened to Israel, until **the fulness of the Gentiles** be come in. And so all Israel shall be saved: as it is written, There shall come out of Sion the Deliverer, and shall turn away ungodliness from Jacob: For this is my covenant unto them, when I shall take away their sins. As concerning the gospel, they are enemies for your sakes: but as touching the election, they are beloved for the father's sakes. For the gifts and calling of God are without repentance. For as

ye in times past have not believed God, yet have now obtained mercy through their unbelief: Even so have these also now not believed, that through your mercy they also may obtain mercy. For God hath concluded them all in unbelief, that he might have mercy upon all. Romans 11:25-32

The tendency on the part of many postmillennial and amillennial writers is to equate "the fulness of the Gentiles" with the "times of the Gentiles", making them both refer to the same period of time.

The determination of the meaning of the phrase "the fullness of the Gentiles" is, in itself, an exegetical problem of no small moment. There are just as many divergent views of this term as there is of the expression "the times of the Gentiles". Because of their interrelationship, however, it is impossible to clarify one without defining the other.

The eleventh chapter of Romans deals with the subject of Israel's future. The chapter is introduced with the question, "Hath God cast away his people?" The point of view is taken that Israel, for the moment, has been set aside and that Gentiles are in the place of primary blessing. The theme of the chapter, however, is that the time will come when the Gentile blessing will cease and Israel again will be blessed of God. The argument is summarized by Paul in Romans:

Now if the fall of them (Israel) be the riches of the world, and the diminishing of them the riches of the Gentiles; how much more their **fulness**? Romans 11:12

In other words, the present "fullness" of the Gentiles is contrasted with the future "fullness" of Israel.

It is with this background that we come to Romans 11:25, where it is stated,

For I would not, brethren, that ye should be ignorant of this mystery, lest ye should be wise in your own conceits;

that blindness in part is happened to Israel, until **the fulness of the Gentiles** be come in. Romans 11:25

It is clear from the passage that the future condition of Israel (removal of their spiritual blindness) is dependent on the culmination of the present state of the Gentiles.

The time element is clearly indicated by the word *until*. This definitely introduces a time factor, contrasting the present situation to that which will follow when the fullness of the Gentiles comes in.

When the two concepts, "the times of the Gentiles" and "the fullness of the Gentiles" are compared, it becomes evident that "the times of the Gentiles" is primarily a **political** term and has to do with the political overlordship of Jerusalem. By contrast, the term "the fullness of the Gentiles" refers to the present age in which Gentiles predominate in the Church. It becomes clear, therefore, that, while the two concepts may be contemporaneous at least for much of their fulfillment, the end point of the two periods are somewhat different. The times of the Gentiles will end only when Israel will permanently gain **political,** as well as physical, control of Jerusalem on earth at the second advent of Christ, whereas the fullness of the Gentiles will be completed when God's present **spiritual** task of winning Jew and Gentile to Christ is completed. The "fullness of the Gentiles" then applies mainly to Christian Gentiles leading in the Church, whereas "times of the Gentiles" refers primarily to Gentiles dominating Israel and Jerusalem politically.

Therefore, the timeline that has been presented would bring the period of **the fullness of the Gentiles to a close at the Rapture of the Church**. The close of the period between Christ's first and second coming will bring terrible judgment upon the Gentile world. It is, therefore, reasonable to assume that the period of Gentile **blessing** will end before the period of Gentile **judgment** comes. In any event, it is safe to say that the two terms do not mean precisely the same thing and do not have the same characteristics, and it is better to interpret the two terms in the light of their context.

End of the Times of the Gentiles

Generally speaking, most Bible scholars bring "the times of the Gentiles" to a close with the second coming of Christ, and the variety of opinions concentrate more upon the time of its beginning. Because the expression is cast in the context of a future time when Jerusalem will be surrounded by armies and destroyed, a prophecy fulfilled in 70 AD, many have concluded that the times of the Gentiles began at that time. A close examination of the passage in Luke 21, however, does not indicate that the times of the Gentiles began with the destruction of Jerusalem. The passage deals only with the time of conclusion of the times of the Gentiles, not its beginning. For this reason, a sound judgment in the matter must be based upon the total teaching of the Bible concerning the relationship between Gentiles and the people of Israel.

Here, many scholars find the answer in the prophecies of the book of Daniel which trace the course of Gentile power from Nebuchadnezzar, 600 B.C., to the coming of the Son of Man from heaven which is fulfilled by the second coming of Jesus Christ to the earth to reign. In both the prophecies of Daniel and the New Testament, however, it is clear that Gentile dominion does not end until the second coming of Jesus Christ **to the earth and specifically to reign in Jerusalem**. The tensions between Israel and the Gentile world cannot be finally resolved until Jesus Christ Himself returns physically to the earth in Jerusalem to reign.

With this as a background, the question now can fairly be faced. Is the present occupation of Jerusalem by Israel the ending point indicated in Luke 21:24? Has, as a matter of fact, the predicted sway of Gentiles over Israel ceased? A careful survey of the Scriptures indicates that the present occupation of Jerusalem must necessarily be temporary. Gentiles are still in a dominant position in world politics and the fullness of the Gentiles has not yet been brought in, since the Rapture of the Church has not taken place. There is a period still ahead, anticipated in Daniel in which a future ruler in the Middle Eastern area will make a covenant with the people of Israel for seven years.

> And he shall confirm the covenant with many for one week: and in the midst of the week he shall cause the sacrifice and the oblation to cease, and for the overspreading of abominations he shall make it desolate, even until the consummation, and that determined shall be poured upon the desolate. Daniel 9:27

If this futuristic interpretation is correct, Israel, in the nature of this covenant, will still be under Gentile supervision in the broad sense of the term. As commonly interpreted, the period of peace introduced by the covenant will terminate after it has run half its course and the period of great tribulation will follow. According to the predictions of Christ Himself, Israel will then be forced to flee to the mountains (Matthew 24:16) and Jerusalem will again come under the tramp of Gentile feet. It is also clear from Zechariah 14 that Jerusalem will become the bone of contention and the source of a great battle at the second coming of Christ.

In view of these prophecies, it can hardly be said today that Jerusalem is delivered forever from the overlordship of Gentile political power. The fact is that the entire Holy Land will be overrun by Gentile forces in the final great world conflict. Under these circumstances, it may be concluded that it is too hasty to assume that the times of the Gentiles have been completed. If the term itself refers to the entire period of Gentile overlordship over Israel, it can scarcely be construed as being completed in contemporary events.

The study of the Scriptures, however, does support the idea that the present reoccupation of Jerusalem by Israel is a matter of tremendous Biblical and prophetic importance. This is not that the times of political overlordship are ended, but it does provide the necessary interlude of Jewish possession to make possible the situation described at the end of the age where Israel, for a time at least, is at peace under a covenant relationship with her Gentile neighbors and able to have a temple in which sacrifices once again are offered as indicated in Daniel 9:27. The presence of the Jews in Jerusalem, their ancient city, may be the last preparatory step prior to the important sequence of events that lead to the second coming of Jesus Christ.

CONCLUSION

I n conclusion, there are three distinct groups that are dealt with throughout the Bible: Israel, the Church, and the Gentiles. God has been orchestrating His plan to redeem each of these groups, and although He has used them for different purposes throughout history, there has always been one and only one plan of salvation for all mankind, that of grace through faith in Jesus Christ, His son.

After undergoing persecution and a "falling away", the Church will be raptured after the 6th seal, protected from God's wrath in heaven. The Church will then return with Christ at the end of the 70th Week to fight the Battle of Armageddon and will rule with Him throughout the Millennium.

Also, during the last half of the 70th Week, Israel will undergo a great tribulation called the "time of Jacob's Trouble" when two thirds of them will be killed. After the 6th seal, this remnant of 144,000 Jews will be sealed and will flee into the wilderness where they will be under God's protection. They will then become followers of Christ and servants of God in the Millennium.

The "fullness of the Gentiles", a period of spiritual blessing for the Gentiles, will end at the Rapture, whereas the "times of the Gentiles" will conclude at the second coming of Christ to the earth when the Gentiles no longer have political control of Jerusalem. A chart of what happens with the Church and Israel, specifically the 144,000, during the 70th Week of Daniel is shown below.

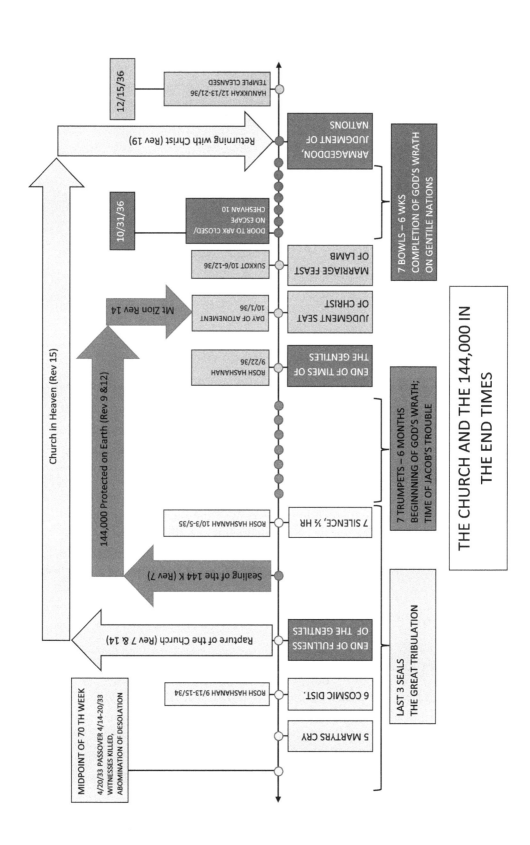

THE CHURCH AND THE 144,000 IN
THE END TIMES

CHAPTER 7

The Temple

The most important event to confirm the timing of the end times is the abomination of desolation by the Antichrist in the middle of the 70th Week of Daniel. But in order for this to occur, a Jewish temple, the Third Temple, must be rebuilt. That has not happened since the Second Temple was destroyed by the Romans two thousand years ago. So, who might rebuild it and where? How could it be accomplished and what is required to make it acceptable for worship? And finally, when would the rebuilding occur on a timeline for the 70th Week?

Since the fall of man, God's desire has been to restore fellowship and dwell with man. To that purpose, His plan through Israel initially included the construction of a mobile, transportable Tabernacle, which was a copy of the Tabernacle in heaven.

> A minister of the sanctuary, and of the true tabernacle, which the Lord pitched, and not man. For every high priest is ordained to offer gifts and sacrifices: wherefore it is of necessity that this man have somewhat also to offer. For if he were on earth, he should not be a priest, seeing that there are priests that offer gifts according to the law: Who serve unto the example and **shadow**

of heavenly things, as Moses was admonished of God when he was about to make the tabernacle: for, See, saith he, that thou make all things according to the pattern shewed to thee in the mount. Hebrews 8:2-5

The Tabernacle was then replaced centuries later by a Temple that was in a permanent, fixed location in Jerusalem. This first Jewish temple was eventually destroyed in 534 BC according to the timeline in Appendix B (or 586 BC using secular data). A second temple was then built about 120 years later. This second temple, also, was eventually demolished nearly two thousand years ago in 70 AD.

Today, many look forward to the building of a third Jewish temple as a fulfillment of end times Bible prophecy. But if the sanctuary was a copy and a shadow of what is in Heaven (Hebrews 8:5) and Jesus now serves in the sanctuary which is the true tabernacle set up by the Lord (Hebrews 8:2), why should anyone contemplate building a third temple? It is because the Holy Temple in Jerusalem was never simply a building or structure but an earthly dwelling place for the Divine Presence of God.

> And let them make me a sanctuary; that I may dwell *(shakan)*among them. Exodus 25:8

> So that the priests could not stand to minister because of the cloud: for the glory of the LORD had filled the house of the LORD. 1 Kings 8:11

This dwelling (*shakan*) forms the related word *shekhinah*, which is not found in the original Hebrew Bible, but it is used in rabbinic literature and Bible translations to describe the Lord's Divine Presence.

The Prophet Ezekiel witnessed the departure of this Divine Presence from the Temple.

> Then the glory of the LORD departed from off the threshold of the house, and stood over the cherubims.

> And the cherubims lifted up their wings, and mounted up from the earth in my sight: when they went out, the wheels also were beside them, and every one stood at the door of the east gate of the LORD's house; and the glory of the God of Israel was over them above. Ezekiel 10:18-19

But Ezekiel also saw the rebuilding of an eternal and permanent dwelling place of God on the Temple Mount in the Holy City of Jerusalem.

> And the glory of the LORD came into the house by the way of the gate whose prospect is toward the east. So the spirit took me up, and brought me into the inner court; and, behold, the glory of the LORD filled the house. And I heard him speaking unto me out of the house; and the man stood by me. And he said unto me, Son of man, the place of my throne, and the place of the soles of my feet, where I will dwell in the midst of the children of Israel for ever, and my holy name, shall the house of Israel no more defile, neither they, nor their kings, by their whoredom, nor by the carcases of their kings in their high places. Eze 43:4-7

Rabbi Moses Maimonides, a medieval Jewish philosopher and Torah scholar, said that the Temple had two primary purposes:

1. To reveal to mankind the Divine Presence of God, which dwelt above the mercy seat of the Ark of the Covenant. (i.e., providing a place for God to dwell with man)

> And there I will meet with thee, and I will commune with thee from above the mercy seat, from between the two cherubims which are upon the ark of the testimony,

of all things which I will give thee in commandment unto the children of Israel. Exodus 25:22

2. To facilitate the offering of the required sacrifices. (i.e., providing a way to purify the Israelites in order to allow them to be in the presence of a Holy God)[1]

These purposes also applied to the Tabernacle which was a portable sanctuary constructed by Moses as a place of worship for the Hebrew tribes during the period of wandering that preceded their arrival in the Promised Land. The Jewish word for tabernacle means "to dwell" or "to pitch one's tent among". God's desire is to "tabernacle" or dwell among man, and after the tabernacle was constructed, God came to dwell with man.

> Then a cloud covered the tent of the congregation, and the glory of the LORD filled the tabernacle. And Moses was not able to enter into the tent of the congregation, because the cloud abode thereon, and the glory of the LORD filled the tabernacle. Exodus 40:34-35

This dwelling place moved to a variety of locations until finally under David the Kingdom of Israel was unified. The main content of the Tabernacle was the Ark of the Covenant, which carried the tablets of the covenant.

After God settled the Children of Israel in the land promised to Abraham, there was no more reason for a tent which was pitched and moved. So, King David planned to build a temple for God which would house His Ark and His Glory (2 Samuel 7). But God wanted it built by Solomon, the son of David (2 Samuel 7:12,13).

It is clear that the Tabernacle, even though it was not a permanent structure, was also known as the House of God (Exodus 23:19, 34:26, Deuteronomy 23:18, Judges 18:31, 20:18, 21:2). Nevertheless, there were differences between the Tabernacle and the Temple other than their mobility. The tabernacle of Moses was built only by Jews and was intended for Jews alone. However, King Solomon's Temple was built by Jews as well as pagan Sidonians and Tyrenians. Moreover, King Solomon's Temple was built to be a "house of prayer for **all** people", not just the Jews.

> Even them will I bring to my holy mountain, and make them joyful in my house of prayer: their burnt offerings and their sacrifices shall be accepted upon mine altar; for mine house shall be called an house of prayer for **all** people. Isaiah 56:7

The Temple revealed to the Jews that God's scope of salvation included **all** of mankind.

The First Temple in Jerusalem

After Solomon came to power, he began working on the Temple according to God's command (1 Kings 5:3-5). After its completion, he moved the Ark from the Tabernacle to the Temple (1 Kings 8:3-9). And similar to the Tabernacle where Moses could not enter because of the Glory of God, the cloud filled the Temple so that the priest could not stand to minister (1 Kings 8:10,11). Furthermore, God appeared to Solomon and told him that He had consecrated the Temple to Himself by putting His name there, and His eyes and heart would be there perpetually. But He also warned Solomon, that if he or his children should turn away from God, that the Temple would be destroyed (1 Kings 9:2-9).

Inevitably, Solomon did sin, and because of his sins, God decided to separate the unified nation of Israel (1 Kings 11:9-13). Ten tribes, known as the House of Israel, were handed over to Jeroboam, while the rest, known as the House of Judah, were left in the hands of Rehoboam, the son of Solomon (1 Kings 11:29-36). These were the two houses of Israel revealed in Jeremiah and Hebrews, where the New Covenant is mentioned. Both of these kingdoms would eventually fall, according to the warnings of the Prophets, due to their disobedience. First the

Kingdom of Israel fell to Assyria and then the Kingdom of Judah to Babylonia, at which time the Temple built by Solomon was also razed to the ground (2 Chronicles 36:19, Ezra 5:12) around 586 BC according to secular dating methods.

The Second Temple in Jerusalem

The Temple was eventually rebuilt under the leadership of Ezra and Nehemiah (Ezra 5:13, 6:14) and under the patronage of King Cyrus of the Persian Empire. It was then added onto by Herod the Great and was known as Herod's Temple. This is the Temple that occurs in the Gospel accounts. This same temple was also destroyed, according to the words of Jesus, in 70 AD by the Romans under Titus. It is believed that all the disciples of Jesus, except for John but including Paul, would have been killed off by Rome before the destruction of the Second Temple in 70 AD.

God let the house that was built for Himself be destroyed twice in history because of the transgressions of the people. Yet, as per the Prophet Micah:

> But in the last days it shall come to pass, that the mountain of the house of the LORD shall be established in the top of the mountains, and it shall be exalted above the hills; and people shall flow unto it. And many nations shall come, and say, Come, and let us go up to the mountain of the LORD, and to the house of the God of Jacob; and he will teach us of his ways, and we will walk in his paths: for the law shall go forth of Zion, and the word of the LORD from Jerusalem. And he shall judge among many people, and rebuke strong nations afar off; and they shall beat their swords into plowshares, and their spears into pruninghooks: nation shall not lift up a sword against nation, neither shall they learn war any more. Micah 4:1-3

The Third Temple in Jerusalem

Today many are anticipating the rebuilding of a third Jewish temple. Despite end time events unfolding before our very eyes almost daily, many skeptics around the globe like to proclaim that God has rejected the people of Israel and that the nation of Israel has been rebirthed by man alone. Yet, scripture is clear that God never intended to reject His People forever.

> Thou whom I have taken from the ends of the earth, and called thee from the chief men thereof, and said unto thee, Thou art my servant; I have chosen thee, and not cast thee away. Isaiah 41:9

God always planned to bring the Jewish people back to the land on His terms, not man's. And just as the prophets foretold, the Jewish people are returning to the Holy Land from the four corners of the earth after nineteen centuries of global exile.

Fear not: for I am with thee: I will bring thy seed from the east, and gather thee from the west; I will say to the north, Give up; and to the south, Keep not back: bring my sons from far, and my daughters from the ends of the earth; Isaiah 43:5-6

Just as some mistakenly believe that the Church has replaced Israel, many believe that the Church is now the Temple of God and that there is no need for a rebuilt Jewish temple. In fact, some call today's church buildings the House of God. While our bodies are called the "house of God" in several places in the New Testament, nowhere in scripture has another building ever been called the House of God other than the Temple that stood in Jerusalem.

Even though the Temple in Jerusalem was known to be a place of high importance in the scriptures, there are many who believe that the Temple was purposeless after the resurrection of Messiah. Yet, even after the resurrection, the early church spent most of their time in the Temple.

And they, continuing daily with one accord in the temple, and breaking bread from house to house, did eat their meat with gladness and singleness of heart, Acts 2:46

The Apostle Paul also offered sacrifices of purification at the Temple.

Then Paul took the men, and the next day purifying himself with them entered into the temple, to signify the accomplishment of the days of purification, until that an offering should be offered for every one of them. And when the seven days were almost ended, the Jews which were of Asia, when they saw him in the temple, stirred up all the people, and laid hands on him, Acts 21:26-27

Whereupon certain Jews from Asia found me purified in the temple, neither with multitude, nor with tumult. Acts 24:18

This clearly shows that the importance of the Temple never dwindled in the eyes of the early church. However, many question the necessity of the Temple because of verses such as:

Howbeit the most High dwelleth not in temples made with hands; as saith the prophet, Heaven is my throne, and earth is my footstool: what house will ye build me? saith the Lord: or what is the place of my rest? Hath not my hand made all these things? Act 7:48-50

God that made the world and all things therein, seeing that he is Lord of heaven and earth, dwelleth not in temples made with hands; Act 17:24

The fact is that the thoughts conveyed above by Stephen and Paul are nothing new but originate from the Old Testament Scriptures. The Temple was not a place made for God to live in, as even the Heavens cannot contain Him. These thoughts are not new ideas revealed after Christ but are what was always apparent to everyone even before Christ.

> But will God indeed dwell on the earth? behold, the heaven and heaven of heavens cannot contain thee; how much less this house that I have builded? 1 Kings 8:27

> But who is able to build him an house, seeing the heaven and heaven of heavens cannot contain him? who am I then, that I should build him an house, save only to burn sacrifice before him? 2 Chronicles 2:6

> But will God in very deed dwell with men on the earth? behold, heaven and the heaven of heavens cannot contain thee; how much less this house which I have built! 2 Chronicles 6:18

> Thus saith the LORD, The heaven is my throne, and the earth is my footstool: where is the house that ye build unto me? and where is the place of my rest? Isaiah 66:1

Also, Paul even uses Greek philosophy in Acts to emphasize that God cannot be contained in a manmade structure:

> God that made the world and all things therein, seeing that he is Lord of heaven and earth, dwelleth not in temples made with hands; Acts 17:24

The Temple was never built to contain God, but as a place that was specially chosen to host His Holy presence, His shekinah glory, on Earth. It is very unlikely that the significance of the Temple ever changed after the Messiah's resurrection because of this reason.

Another reason many do not see a purpose for a physical Temple in Jerusalem is because of the belief that Christ replaced it. This conviction comes from Jesus' own statement recorded in John.

> Jesus answered and said unto them, Destroy this temple, and in three days I will raise it up. Then said the Jews, Forty and six years was this temple in building, and wilt thou rear it up in three days? But he spake of the temple of his body. John 2:19-21

It is true that Jesus equaled Himself to the Temple. Rightly so, as God's glory resided in Christ just as in the Temple. Verses such as these have led people to believe that Christ has done away with the Temple of God.

> Jesus saith unto her, Woman, believe me, the hour cometh, when ye shall neither in this mountain, nor yet at Jerusalem, worship the Father. John 4:21

> And Jesus cried with a loud voice, and gave up the ghost. And the veil of the temple was rent in twain from the top to the bottom. Mark 15:37-38

John 4:21 could be most likely speaking of the destruction about to fall on Jerusalem, which Jesus spoke of many times in His ministry.

> And shall lay thee even with the ground, and thy children within thee; and they shall not leave in thee one stone upon another; because thou knewest not the time of thy visitation. Luke 19:44

> As for these things which ye behold, the days will come, in the which there shall not be left one stone upon another, that shall not be thrown down. Luke 21:6

Yet, the idea of the Temple veil (which separated the Holiest of Holies where the Ark of the Covenant resided with God's presence from the rest of the Temple) being torn has become one if not the main reason that many believe in the futility of a new, rebuilt third Temple. In the Gospels, Christ's death leads to the veil of the Temple being torn in two. Many interpret this as a sign that the **separation** between God and Man was removed through this act and that we can now freely go into the Holiest of Holies and God's presence. However, others actually see the torn veil as symbolic of the **departure** of God's blessing and the impending destruction that will come upon the Temple.

Those scholars who believe this rending of the Temple veil is indicative of the new access that all believers have to God through Christ are more inclined to believe that our bodies have wholly replaced the Temple in Jerusalem. There are many verses in the New Testament writings that compare our bodies to the Temple of God, such as:

> Know ye not that ye are the temple of God, and that the Spirit of God dwelleth in you? 1 Corinthians 3:16

> What? know ye not that your body is the temple of the Holy Ghost which is in you, which ye have of God, and ye are not your own? 1 Corinthians 6:19

> And what agreement hath the temple of God with idols? for ye are the temple of the living God; as God hath said, I will dwell in them, and walk in them; and I will be their God, and they shall be my people. 2 Corinthians 6:16

> In whom all the building fitly framed together groweth unto an holy temple in the Lord: Ephesians 2:21

> Ye also, as lively stones, are built up a spiritual house, an holy priesthood, to offer up spiritual sacrifices, acceptable to God by Jesus Christ. 1 Peter 2:5

So, what is to be made of this? Have our bodies replaced any remnant of a physical Temple in Jerusalem? Indeed, our bodies are a dwelling place for God, as Paul himself writes to the Corinthians.

> And what agreement hath the temple of God with idols? for ye are the temple of the living God; as God hath said, **I will dwell in them, and walk in them**; and I will be their God, and they shall be my people. 2 Corinthians 6:16

He is quoting "I will dwell in them, and walk in them" from the Old Testament Scriptures.

> And I will dwell among the children of Israel, and will be their God. Exodus 29:45

> And I will walk among you, and will be your God, and ye shall be my people. Leviticus 26:12

> And he said unto me, Son of man, the place of my throne, and the place of the soles of my feet, where I will dwell in the midst of the children of Israel for ever, and my holy name, shall the house of Israel no more defile, neither they, nor their kings, by their whoredom, nor by the carcases of their kings in their high places. Ezekiel 43:7

So, it is not a new thought to think of one's body as a dwelling place for God. The physical Temple in Jerusalem on the other hand is, and always has been, a central part of both God's Word and prophecy.

> And it shall come to pass in the last days, that the mountain of the LORD'S house shall be established in the top of the mountains, and shall be exalted above the hills; and all nations shall flow unto it. And many people shall go and say, Come ye, and let us go up to

the mountain of the LORD, to the house of the God of Jacob; and he will teach us of his ways, and we will walk in his paths: for out of Zion shall go forth the law, and the word of the LORD from Jerusalem. Isaiah 2:2-3

Also the sons of the stranger, that join themselves to the LORD, to serve him, and to love the name of the LORD, to be his servants, every one that keepeth the sabbath from polluting it, and taketh hold of my covenant; Even them will I bring to my holy mountain, and make them joyful in my house of prayer: their burnt offerings and their sacrifices shall be accepted upon mine altar; for mine house shall be called an house of prayer for all people. Isaiah 56:6-7

Also see Ezekiel chapters 40 to 48

God instituted a material Tabernacle and later a Temple in Jerusalem, whereas, the synagogue and the Church both stood for bodies of people and not physical structures. While God is not contained in a man-made house, it was His choice to create such a place for His glory to reside and for the people to come to Him with the designated sacrifices. While not all assemblies or buildings can be called "The House of God" in a Biblical sense, the Temple of God is far from an abolished precept. Neither Jesus, His disciples, nor Paul ever directly said anything about the Temple being anything other than the House of God. In fact, the interaction between the Temple and the first century believers was a close one, as we even see with Paul. The tearing of the veil at Christ's death or the fact that our bodies are called a dwelling place of God, does not mean that the Temple in Jerusalem was any less important in the Bible we hold in our hands today.

Even though there is a fair amount of debate among Christian denominations about whether a Third Temple will ever be built, prophetic verses in the Bible would have us believe that a main sign of the end of days is that the Antichrist will set himself up in the Temple of God, and then stop the Jewish daily sacrifices at that temple. Daniel and Jesus, as well as John and Paul, all refer to a temple that will exist during the tribulation period or the 70th Week of Daniel. None of these mentioned the actual building of the edifice, only that one will exist.

First of all, Daniel states:

> And arms shall stand on his part, and they shall pollute the sanctuary of strength, and shall take away the daily sacrifice, and they shall place the abomination that maketh desolate. Daniel 11:31

This obviously is talking about a physical temple. Daniel also refers to this again in Daniel 9:

> And he will confirm a covenant with the many for one week, but in the middle of the week he will put a stop to sacrifice and grain offering; and on the **wing of abominations** will come the one who makes desolate, until a complete destruction, one that is decreed, gushes forth on the one who makes desolate. Daniel 9:27 (NASB)

Although it is not apparent in this passage that there is a physical building, it speaks of a wing of abominations like a wing of the Temple, and it is clear that sacrifice and grain offerings are being eliminated. So, this is not something that is just spiritual. In the Septuagint version of Daniel 9:27 with slightly different wording, the Temple is mentioned in that verse and that the abomination of desolation is placed on the Temple.

> And one week shall establish the covenant with many: and in the midst of the week my sacrifice and drink offering shall be taken away: **and on the temple the abomination of desolations**; and at the end of time an end shall be put to the desolation. Daniel 9:27 (LXX)

And in Daniel 8:

> Yea, he magnified himself even to the prince of the
> host, and by him the daily sacrifice was taken away, and
> the place of the sanctuary was cast down. Daniel 8:11

Again, this is clearly a physical location. So, in three places
Daniel refers to the three things that occur at the midpoint: (1) the
desecration of the Temple, implying a physical temple; (2) the end of the
regular sacrifices, i.e., physical sacrifices; and (3) the setting up of the
abomination of desolation. Jesus, of course, refers to this abomination
of desolation, also.

> When ye therefore shall see the abomination of
> desolation, spoken of by Daniel the prophet, **stand in the
> holy place**, (whoso readeth, let him understand:) Then
> let them which be in Judaea flee into the mountains:
> Matthew 24:15-16

Note that the abomination of desolation is to stand in the Holy
Place, indicating the existence of a temple. And, if the Temple is to be
desecrated, there must be one present. For sacrifices and grain offerings
to end, they must be actual, physical sacrifices and offerings, and they
must be taking place at the time of the Antichrist. This is simple logic,
logic that is reinforced by the Apostle Paul.

> Let no man deceive you by any means: for that day shall
> not come, except there come a falling away first, and
> that man of sin be revealed, the son of perdition; Who
> opposeth and exalteth himself above all that is called
> God, or that is worshipped; so that he as God **sitteth
> in the temple of God**, shewing himself that he is God.
> 2 Thessalonians 2:3-4

Now, only a physical person can take a seat in the Temple of God.
This cannot be something that happens within the heart of an individual

believer. It has to be a physical temple. The Apostle John also supports the idea that there will be a physical temple in Jerusalem as well.

> And there was given me a reed like unto a rod: and the angel stood, saying, Rise, and **measure the temple of God**, and the altar, and them that worship therein. Revelation 11:1

You can only measure a physical thing, not the heart of a man. It is clear, therefore, that there will be a literal, physical temple during the 70th Week of Daniel. This temple will also, as confirmed by scripture, be located in Jerusalem.

First of all, consider that sacrifices can only be offered in the Temple of Jerusalem.

> But unto **the place which the LORD your God shall choose** out of all your tribes to put his name there, even unto his habitation shall ye seek, and thither thou shalt come: And thither ye shall bring your burnt offerings, and your sacrifices, and your tithes, and heave offerings of your hand, and your vows, and your freewill offerings, and the firstlings of your herds and of your flocks: Deuteronomy 12:5-6

> For **the LORD hath chosen Zion**; he hath desired it for his habitation. This is my rest for ever: here will I dwell; for I have desired it. Psalm 132:13-14

> That thine eyes may be open toward this house night and day, even toward the place of which thou hast said, **My name shall be there**: that thou mayest hearken unto the prayer which thy servant shall make toward this place. 1 Kings 8:29

And, secondly, the place in which God chose to put His name was Jerusalem.

> But **I have chosen Jerusalem**, that my name might be there; and have chosen David to be over my people Israel. 2 Chronicles 6:6

> And unto his son will I give one tribe, that David my servant may have a light alway before me in **Jerusalem, the city which I have chosen me to put my name there**. 1 Kings 11:36

From this, one can deduce that the Temple of God where sacrifices will be offered in these prophetic verses is none other than a real, physical temple in Jerusalem. However, since the destruction of the Second Temple in AD 70, the Jewish people have no longer been able to offer these sacrifices. In fact, many of the commandments in the Torah cannot be performed without a Temple. And without a Temple, the people of Israel have remained ceremonially unclean since its destruction. So, with no Temple in Jerusalem, the Jewish people now worship the God of Israel in their local community synagogues and in the study of Torah.

In conclusion, if the prophecies regarding the abomination of desolation by the Antichrist are to come to fruition, there must be a Third Temple built in the future. Although in mainstream Orthodox Judaism the rebuilding of the Temple is generally left to the coming of the Jewish Messiah and to divine providence, a number of organizations, generally representing a small minority of Orthodox Jews, have been formed with the objective of realizing the immediate construction of a Third Temple in present times. The Temple Institute and the Temple Mount and Eretz Yisrael Faithful Movement each state that its goal is to build the Third Temple on the Temple Mount (Mount Moriah), and the Temple Institute has already made several items to be used in the Third Temple. Yet, if the Third Temple is a physical structure in the end times, who actually will build it?

WHO WILL BUILD THE THIRD TEMPLE?[5]

The Bible does not say directly who constructs the Temple. So, to figure out who is going to build it, it is important to first consider their motive for building it. For one, certainly the Jews have motivation. Prayer for the building of the Temple is a formal part of the Jewish tradition of the three times daily Amidah prayer. Orthodox Jews in particular realize that the Temple is associated with the return of the Messiah. Also, a temple is required for the sacrifices for the remission of sins. So, for all these reasons, a temple is highly desired by the Jews.

However, the Jews do not realize there will be both the Third Temple built by human hands and a Fourth Temple, sometimes referred to as Ezekiel's Temple, built in the Millennial Kingdom by the Messiah himself. As a result, they have extreme difficulty reconciling conflicting verses like this:

> Behold, I will send my messenger, and he shall prepare the way before me: and the LORD, whom ye seek, shall suddenly come to his temple, even the messenger of the covenant, whom ye delight in: behold, he shall come, saith the LORD of hosts. Malachi 3:1

Malachi certainly implies that this Temple is built prior to the coming of the Messiah. This, of course, is going to be the Third Temple. However, Zechariah describes a different temple that relates to the Millennial Kingdom and will be built by Jesus himself.

> And speak unto him, saying, Thus speaketh the LORD of hosts, saying, Behold the man whose name is The BRANCH; and he shall grow up out of his place, and he shall build the temple of the LORD: Even he shall build the temple of the LORD; and he shall bear the glory, and shall sit and rule upon his throne; and he shall be a priest upon his throne: and the counsel of peace shall be between them both. Zechariah 6:12-13

Zechariah is telling us that Jesus will be both priest and king in this coming Fourth Temple during the Millennial Kingdom. Unfortunately, the unsaved Jews do not realize there will be a Tribulation period followed by a Millennial Kingdom and that there are actually different temples in both periods. Orthodox Jewish scholars generally believe that the latter verse, the one about the Millennial Temple, is the true one and that the Temple should be built in accord with the Messiah.

The Temple Institute, however, which is the group preparing implements and clothing to be worn and used by priests in the coming temple, believes that the Third Temple could be rebuilt today in Jerusalem even before the Messiah arrives. They accept that this concurs precisely with the opinion of the sages of Israel recorded in the Talmud, the authoritative body of Jewish tradition, containing the full account of the civil and religious laws of the Jews. Consequently, they believe that the holy temple will be built in the future and will be reestablished before the institution of the Kingdom of David.

So, the unsaved Jews within Jerusalem, although they are divided, are certainly motivated to see a temple built. But who else could be stirred to construct a temple? Who else would derive a benefit from a temple? The Arabs might be motivated, but only if there was a negotiated peace in a trade involving a temple for some of the Israeli land. But the Arabs really have little or no interest in a Jewish temple in and of itself.

Might the Western powers want a temple? Again, they will only if including it is part of a peace deal that leads to what they think would be lasting peace in the region. And what about Christians? A lot of Christians are motivated to help. Many even contribute to see this Third Temple built because they know it precedes the coming of Jesus. Yet, they do not really have the political muscle to get a temple built.

What about the Antichrist? Will he have a vested interest in the Temple? Of course, he could, for the Temple is a means to establishing himself as worthy to be worshipped as a god. In explanation of this, there is difficulty in Judaism deciding whether the Messiah builds the Temple or human hands build it. So, if the Antichrist helps in the construction of the Temple and the opening of a path to building it, he may likely claim Zechariah 6:12 for himself and declare himself to be the man called the Branch, the Messiah who builds the Temple. What is very interesting about this passage in Zechariah 6 is the aspect about the type of crown that is worn.

> Then take silver and gold, and make **crowns** *(stephanos)*, and set them upon the head of Joshua the son of Josedech, the high priest; And the **crowns** *(stephanos)* shall be to Helem, and to Tobijah, and to Jedaiah, and to Hen the son of Zephaniah, for a memorial in the temple of the LORD. And they that are far off shall come and build in the temple of the LORD, and **ye shall know that the LORD of hosts hath sent me unto you**. And this shall come to pass, if ye will diligently obey the voice of the LORD your God. Zechariah 6:11,14-15

These crowns in Zechariah are *stephanos* crowns as translated in the Greek Septuagint. *Stephanos* is the same type of crown seen worn on the head of the rider of the white horse in Revelation 6.

> And I saw, and behold a white horse: and he that sat on him had a bow; and a crown *(stephanos)* was given unto him: and he went forth conquering, and to conquer. Revelation 6:2

However, Jesus, when he later returns to the earth on a White Horse, wears "diadem" crowns.

> His eyes were as a flame of fire, and on his head were many crowns *(diadema)*; and he had a name written, that no man knew, but he himself. Revelation 19:12

This differentiates the rider of the white horse in Revelation 6 from Jesus. This rider is many times associated with the Antichrist. So, one can definitely see the Antichrist quoting this verse, which is meant to be about Jesus, and usurping it for himself, especially the part that says, "and ye shall know that the LORD of hosts hath sent me unto you".

How will the Jews accept the Antichrist, especially if he is Islamic? Part of the answer may be that he accomplishes something no one else can, the building of the Third Temple. One of the main signs, if not the main sign, in Judaism to identify who the Messiah will be, is that he will rebuild the Temple. So, just imagine if a man claiming to be the Messiah actually gets this accomplished. It will give him great credibility to be the Messiah or at least suspected to be the Messiah, in the minds of many people. You can see what an important point this might be in the end times. And do not forget that part of the verse from Zechariah 6:14 states that the crown will become a memorial or reminder in the Temple of the Lord. There is the possibility of the Antichrist receiving such a crown and then putting it on display in the Temple to remind the Jewish people that he is the one that got this done.

The idea of the Antichrist building the Temple is not at all new. Bishop Hippolytus of Rome was the first to introduce that idea back in the third century. Several medieval holy men also proposed this including Scorpiace, Severus, Robanus Maurus, and also Adso the Monk. So, the idea has been around for quite some time.

It has been theorized that the name of the Antichrist may be "Solomon" or an ethnically equivalent name like Suleiman or Salman, because this name is biblically linked to the number 666 (1 Kings 10:14, 2 Chronicle 9:14). Solomon's greatest personal achievement was building the First Temple. And the Antichrist, who has some of Solomon's characteristics, may have as one of his greatest achievements the building of the Third Temple.

Many Jews and Muslims do agree that there is not much difference between the Islamic Mahdi and the Jewish Messiah. As a result, many Arabs realize it is likely that it is the Mahdi who may build the Temple and by means of this, Jews may come to worship the Islamic Mahdi.

Of course, it is all just speculation because there is no verse in the Bible that says the Temple will be built by the Antichrist. And there is no verse in the Bible that says that it will be built by the Jews, either, or by anyone else. We simply do not know who builds it. We only know that at some point the Antichrist desecrates it.

The Temple and the Two Witnesses[6]

The Two Witnesses in Revelation 11 may also likely play a role in the building of the future Third Temple and in its sacrifices. Rabbi Chaim Richman, head of the Temple Institute, confirmed in a lecture in 2018 that the Institute assumes that the process to building the Temple likely will be a gradual step by step progression that could include an interim Tabernacle. But who is it that will grant authority to build the Temple, when that authority can only come from God? Although Israel's parliament, the Knesset, and the ruling Muslim Waqf can grant political authorization, that does not include God's authority. The Sanhedrin of seventy Orthodox Jewish leaders would like to think that they have that authority, but deep inside they know that it is not the same as God granting them that authority. King David after all wanted to build the first temple, but God denied him the right to do it and gave that privilege to his son Solomon. So, the Sanhedrin and the Temple Institute, who have prepared all the implements for the Temple, might want to build a temple, but they are waiting for one important ingredient, permission from God.

Who is it that could grant them that permission today? It would have to be someone who has that authority from God, either the Messiah, who most Jews believe should be the one to build the Temple, or Elijah the Prophet who goes ahead of the Messiah. They are the only two with the biblical right to authorize a construction project like that in the mind of religious Jews. On every Passover observant Jews set a place for Elijah the Prophet at their table in hopes that he might join them, and at the end of the meal they open their doors to see if he has arrived. They expect Elijah, despite the fact that they are missing Jesus, the one who actually is standing at that same door and knocking, the one who is their Passover lamb. They expect Elijah because the Prophet Malachi prophesied that Elijah would come prior to the Messiah.

> Behold, I will send my messenger, and he shall prepare
> the way before me: and the LORD, whom ye seek, shall
> suddenly come to his temple, even the messenger of the

covenant, whom ye delight in: behold, he shall come, saith the LORD of hosts. Malachi 3:1

Note carefully that the messenger comes first and only then does the Lord come suddenly to his Temple. This is not lost upon the Jewish rabbis trying to understand what is required to build the Temple. They have reasoned that this messenger must give the permission in order for the Messiah to come suddenly to the Temple. In other words, the Temple already has to be present if the Messiah is going to come to it suddenly. In the next chapter of Malachi, he identifies the messenger.

> Behold, I will send you Elijah the prophet before the coming of the great and dreadful day of the LORD: And he shall turn the heart of the fathers to the children, and the heart of the children to their fathers, lest I come and smite the earth with a curse. Malachi 4:5-6

So, the rabbis believe that Elijah may be the one to give permission to build a new temple. And since the Passover seder dinner not only commemorates the Jew's historical redemption from Egypt but also calls to mind their future redemption when Elijah and the Messiah appear, they link Elijah's coming to Passover. However, Elijah's return on Passover is simply tradition, and as outlined previously, another likely return date for Elijah as one of the Two Witnesses is 1260 days before Passover, which is on Cheshvan 29 or November 7 in the year 2029. Since, according to the timeline outlined earlier, the daily sacrifices will not start until August 29, 2030, this would provide over nine months to build a temple. This is more than adequate time with all the preparations that have already been made by the Temple Institute.

So, what are Christians to think, if and when a man claiming to be Elijah happens to appear, especially if he does miracles by calling down fire from heaven like the historic Elijah, and then calling for the building of the Temple? Would this possibly be the Elijah prophesied by Jesus himself to come, the one of whom Jesus said:

> And his disciples asked him, saying, Why then say the scribes that Elias must first come? And Jesus answered and said unto them, Elias truly shall first come, and restore all things. Matthew 17:10-11

Jesus said this after the death of John the Baptist. How can Christians decide if this is the real Elijah, one of the Two Witnesses, since it is possible that someone claiming to be Elijah the Prophet and or someone claiming to be the Jewish Messiah will come on the scene before the Temple is built? The Jews want permission from God to build it, and maybe a demonic witness, a false Elijah or false Messiah, will give them that go-ahead from Satan to build it. This fits perfectly with Jesus' statement in the Olivet Discourse. Interestingly the disciples were asking about the Temple and its destruction when Jesus answered this way:

> And Jesus answered and said unto them, Take heed that no man deceive you. For many shall come in my name, saying, I am Christ; and shall deceive many. Matthew 24:4-5

So, the end time's signs seem to begin with the arrival of false messiahs, not one but several, in fact. Jesus said many would come in his name. Jesus also said false prophets would accompany the false messiahs.

> For there shall arise false Christs, and false prophets, and shall shew great signs and wonders; insomuch that, if it were possible, they shall deceive the very elect. Matthew 24:24

This will be such a great deception that Jesus felt the need to emphasize it.

> Behold, I have told you before. Wherefore if they shall say unto you, Behold, he is in the desert; go not forth:

behold, he is in the **secret chambers**; believe it not.
Matthew 24:25-26

So, what are these secret chambers or inner rooms? Might they be the inner rooms of the Temple? Jesus might have been referring to the Holy of Holies in the Holy Place, the two inner rooms of the Temple. Remember Jesus said that the abomination of desolation would be seen standing in the Holy Place (Matthew 24:15) which is one of the two inner rooms. Jesus said the deceptions of these false prophets and messiahs are so carefully planned and so skillfully carried out that even God's chosen ones would be deceived if that were possible. And the only reason it is impossible is that Jesus told us that he will not come that way.

> For as the lightning cometh out of the east, and shineth even unto the west; so shall also the coming of the Son of man be. Matthew 24:27

Anyone appearing in the Temple claiming to be the Messiah but does not come on the clouds in great glory, so that every eye sees, is a false Messiah. No matter how slick his presentation is or how convincing his signs and wonders are, he is not the true Messiah. And any Elijah that proclaims this false messiah as the true Messiah is likewise false.

LOCATION, LOCATION, LOCATION

But before the sacrifices can be restarted and the Antichrist can desecrate the Temple, it must be rebuilt. What is stopping the Temple from being built right now? There are two major obstacles to the reconstruction of the Third Temple. The biggest one pertains to its location. Most scholars believe the first two temples stood where the Dome of the Rock, an Islamic shrine on the Temple Mount in the Old City of Jerusalem, currently stands. If the Third Temple is to be built where the Dome of the Rock is now, that Muslim structure would have to be removed either by man or by an act of God. And if it was removed by man, World War III would probably erupt overnight. So, this is a major obstacle.

The second obstacle is the attitude of the Jewish people and their leaders. The average Israeli is very secular and irreligious, and they know that any attempt to build a Third Temple would result in an immediate war with the Muslims. Something would have to happen to create a surge of nationalistic pride that would demand a third temple. This catalytic event could, for example, be the discovery of the Ark of the Covenant. If the Ark of the Covenant is discovered, it could instantly spark nationalistic pride and religious fervor, stirring Israel to build a temple to hold the Ark.

Returning to the first problem of location, the Temple Mount is the third most holy site in all of Islam, the site of the Dome of the Rock and the Al-Aqsa Mosque. Unlike the Al-Aqsa Mosque on the southern side of the Temple Mount, the Dome of the Rock is actually a shrine and not a mosque. The Al-Aqsa Mosque was originally built in 705 AD and was then rebuilt in 754 AD, 780 AD, and 1035 AD [Wikipedia, 2019]. The Dome of the Rock was originally built in 691-692 AD and was rebuilt in 1022-1023 AD. Muslims believe that the dome is built over the spot where Mohammad ascended into heaven, making it a very holy site in Islam. It would be a huge problem to build the Third Temple on a Muslim holy site.

Additionally, it is unclear precisely where the Third Temple should be located, because it is not known precisely where the first and second temples were built. Recall that the second temple was completely destroyed in accordance with Jesus Christ's prophecy about the Temple in Matthew.

> And Jesus went out, and departed from the temple: and his disciples came to him for to shew him the buildings of the temple. And Jesus said unto them, See ye not all these things? verily I say unto you, There shall not be left here one stone upon another, that shall not be thrown down. Matthew 24:1-2

The Romans leveled the whole city of Jerusalem around 135 AD and built a Roman city on top of it. Thus, it is not easy to determine the precise location of the Temple. For Israel to unilaterally attempt to build a temple on the Temple Mount would again very likely start World War III. It would have to be negotiated, but it is hard to imagine though that anyone could sell such an idea. There would be such resistance from all sections of Islam that even the Antichrist, even if he were Islamic, would have difficulty being able to promote that. As a result, some believe that a better solution would be to convince the Jews that the Temple actually existed somewhere else in the past and that that would be a more accurate site for their coming Third Temple.

But what exactly was located on the Temple Mount in the time of Jesus? Was it the Jewish Temple or was it a Roman Fort known as the Antonia Fortress? If it was the Roman fort, we can expect a very different set of end time events and timetables than if it was the Jewish Temple. Who built the Antonia Fortress, why was it built, and how many Roman soldiers were housed there? These are just some of the questions that need to be answered to determine the location of the Fort Antonia with precision. Because if it can be determined where the fort was located, it will also help fix where the location of the Temple was.

There are two main theories regarding the location of the ancient Jewish Temples. One theory assumes that the current Temple Mount was the Antonia Fortress, a Roman fort during the times of Jesus. In this theory the Temple was located south of the Temple Mount in the City of David, and Jesus' trial took place on the rock currently housed and protected under the Dome of the Rock. Several major books like *The Temples that Jerusalem Forgot* and *The Temple* as well as hundreds of YouTube videos have explored this theory. This is probably the main theory accepted in America.

The second theory is that the Temple Mount was where the actual Jewish Temple in biblical times was located, and the Antonia Fortress was a much smaller four tower structure located directly north of the Mount. This is the most popular theory in the Middle East and Israel.

As noted in the first theory, many, especially Westerners, believe that the Temple was located in the City of David, and what it is called the Temple Mount today was actually the Antonia Fortress. The late Bible scholar Ernest Martin had suggested that Israel's first two temples were not built on the Temple Mount but slightly south of it in the ancient city of David. If this turns out to be an accurate site, it would be a revolutionary finding that would all but eliminate the issues of contesting the Temple Mount with the Muslims. Rather than build the Temple on the Temple Mount, it could be built on a site south of the Dome of the Rock and Al-Aqsa Mosque without all the political and religious complications.

So, although many believe the Temple Mount is where the original temple was, Josephus tells us that if someone came upon the city of Jerusalem after its destruction in AD 70, they would not even know it had been a city. That is how extreme the damage was. And then, the Jews were taken into exile for nearly 2000 years. As a result, it is difficult for anyone to know exactly where the Temple was after all that time.

The earliest mention of the Temple Mount as the site of the Temples was in 325 AD by the emperor Constantine. This was 250 years after the destruction of the Temple, and Constantine assumed this site was the Temple location because it was the highest ground. So, frankly calling it the "Temple Mount" was pure conjecture. Today, it is simply tradition but not absolute fact.

Also remember that in Matthew 24 Jesus stated that not one stone of the Temple would remain on another. But as can obviously be seen, the Western Wall or Wailing Wall, which many consider part of the Temple has many stones upon one another, thousands of Herodian stones. Was Jesus mistaken or is the Temple Mount something other than the site of the original Temple? Obviously, Jesus was not mistaken.

So, what might the current Temple Mount area have been? A number of scholars think it may have been the site of the former Roman fort, the Antonio Fortress and not the Temple. They also surmise that the famous rock within the Dome of the Rock was the stone pavement where Jesus was tried by Pilate, not the sight of the Holy of Holies. They come to this conclusion since the Temple Mount is the exact size and shape of Roman forts of that era. Additionally, the rock within the Dome of the Rock is rough and not at all smooth. It is, therefore, a very inappropriate place for the Temple since the site was biblically and originally a threshing floor for wheat.

In stark contrast to this theory, most current models of the Antonio Fortress show it is dwarfed by the massive Temple area. In this example a tiny little Roman fort next to a massive Hebrew temple would not have demonstrated the proper relationship of power in the first century. Also, this fort supposedly housed 10,000 soldiers of the Roman Legion and their support staff, almost like a small city unto itself. Yet, this tiny fort would have only supported one hundred to two hundred people. So, using these assumptions it would make more sense that the massive Temple Mount area was the ancient fort and that the Temple was somewhere else.

Also, notice in this model that the Western Wall would then be part of the fort, a fort that was not torn down in 70 AD as was the Temple. Josephus and other eyewitnesses tell us that the fort was the only thing left standing in the city. And the fact that the Western Wall has survived would contradict Jesus' prophecy about the stones of the Temple, if it had been part of the Temple.

Another major scriptural support for Martin's theory that the Temple was elsewhere and not on the Temple Mount is that there is no fresh water supply necessary to wash away the blood of the sacrifices on what is currently called the Temple Mount. There are only storage systems there for water. The only spring of fresh water in Jerusalem, the Gihon Spring, is right below the site that Martin suggests, six hundred feet south of the so-called Temple Mount. Joel 3:18 and additionally Psalm 87 both testify to a spring of water within the Temple. This seemingly would not apply to what is currently called the Temple Mount. The ancient Pool of Siloam, which has just recently been located, was found at the same alternative site and was fed by the same Gihon Spring. This famous pool near where Jesus healed the man born blind from birth was known as the world's largest *mikvah* or baptismal. It seems unlikely that worshippers would have bathed there to purify themselves and then had to climb the quarter mile to what is now the Temple Mount. It would make much more sense if the *mikvah* in the City of David and the Temple were next to each other.

Despite this evidence, there are also compelling data to show that the Temple Mount was indeed the site of the Jewish temples. First, there is the history of Fort Antonio itself. The Hasmonean kings built the fort about 150 BC to protect the Temple, and this took place prior to the Roman occupation in 63 BC. So, the Romans did not actually build the fort. Herod updated it and named it for his superior and patron Marc Anthony. This argues against the Temple Mount being the Antonia Fortress, since a common assumption is that the Temple Mount is the size and shape of a typical Roman fort. This is true but is only a coincidence, since Fort Antonia was not built by or for the Romans. It was built by the Jews prior to the Romans in order to protect the Temple. It was never intended to house Romans. So, using the size of the Temple Mount as evidence is not a valid claim.

Next, the description that the most famous Jewish historian Josephus gives us of the fort is not of some sprawling, multi-acre, open plaza but rather that of a tower that loomed above the Temple Mount. Josephus repeatedly refers to it as the Tower Antonia and states that it had been built by John Hyrcanus. Josephus says:

> The general appearance of the whole *(Fort Antonia)* was that of a tower, with other towers at each of the four corners; three of these turrets were fifty cubits high, while the south-east angle rose to seventy cubits and so commanded a view of the whole area of the temple. The Jewish War, Book V, 238

Again, this disputes the claim that the Antonia Fortress was the entire Temple Mount. Obviously, that does not match Josephus' description of being a tower and still occupying the entire Mount.

The fortress housed some of the Roman garrison of Jerusalem, and the Jews also stored the priceless vestments of the high priest there as well. But contrary to popular Christian tradition, it was not the headquarters of the Roman governor or prefect. Pontius Pilate did not have his offices there. Both of the major Jewish historians of this era, Philo and Josephus, wrote that the Roman governors stayed in Herod's

Palace while they were in Jerusalem and not at the fort. In Josephus' Jewish Wars 214:8 he stated that the governors held their trials on the pavement in front of this palace that is Herod's Palace on the other side of town.

This has enormous implications for where Pilate's trial of Jesus took place. Josephus stated that Herod's Palace was located on the Western Hill of Jerusalem on the other side of town from the Temple Mount (Jewish Wars 5:2). In support of this, twenty years ago archaeological remains of that Palace were found right where Josephus said on the Western Hill. Pilate's trial of Jesus is recorded in John.

> Then led they Jesus from Caiaphas unto **the hall of judgment**: and it was early; and they themselves went not into the judgment hall, lest they should be defiled; but that they might eat the passover. John 18:28

The trial took place at the Hall of Judgment or the Praetorium, which is now known was not in Fort Antonia but rather was in Herod's Palace. Pilate then pronounced judgment on "the Pavement".

> When Pilate therefore heard that saying, he brought Jesus forth, and sat down in the judgment seat in a place that is called **the Pavement**, but in the Hebrew, Gabbatha. John 19:13

If the Praetorium was not in the Fort, then neither was the Pavement. These pavements were usually beautiful marble mosaics. Julius Caesar was known to even carry his marble floor around with him wherever he went. So, this also argues against the Antonia Fortress being on the Temple Mount. A big part of that theory is that the rock under the Dome of the Rock was the Pavement. It is now known that it was not. It is also unlikely that a Roman governor would have sat on a very uneven foundation stone such as that under the Dome but would have desired an opulent floor that was even and level.

A fourth important issue is to consider how large a garrison of Roman troops were housed in the Antonia Fortress. A common theory held is that the entire Tenth Legion of six thousand troops was housed there at the time of Jesus. The scholars who support this theory claim that only the thirty-five acres of the Temple Mount could adequately house them.

The Tenth Legion definitely fought in the siege of Jerusalem in AD 70 and was stationed there after the siege. So, they were outside the city at that time trying to get in and were actually based in Syria prior to the Jewish rule. A single Roman cohort of about six hundred soldiers was based in Jerusalem on an ongoing basis, and this cohort was reinforced during the times of the pilgrim feasts. At these Jewish feasts Jerusalem did have to house many, if not most, of the six thousand men of the Tenth Legion, who were brought in to keep order. What many fail to consider, however, is that in addition to these six thousand soldiers, Josephus related that there were 2.7 million pilgrims in town for the feasts, and one thousand priests alone worked on the Temple Mount. The space needed for the Temple services was massively bigger than the space needed to house the soldiers.

Consequently, with those types of numbers they were probably not that worried about housing a few thousand soldiers. Some of those Tenth Legionnaires stayed at the Antonio, but many, if not most, stayed at Herod's Palace on the other side of town. So, the Antonia was not the primary residence of all the men when the Tenth Legion was in town, and forty-nine weeks out of the year, only six hundred soldiers lived at the Antonia near the Praetorium and at other locations around town.

This explains a mystery to those who believe that the entire Tenth Legion was staying in town in AD 66 when the Jewish revolt began. When the Jews began their revolt against the Romans, they easily overran the fort and stayed in control of it throughout the entire four-year war. The fortress was one of the last Jewish strongholds in the city that the Romans conquered during the siege of Jerusalem. So, if a few zealots were able to hold off the Romans for four years in this court, why was not the entire Tenth Legion able to protect it initially? If a legion had been stationed in the fort at the time of the beginning of the

Jewish revolt, there would have been no way that the Jews would have easily taken it with six thousand trained men inside it. However, as it was, there were most likely only a few hundred soldiers there when the Jews took control. This also argues against the theory that the Temple Mount is Fort Antonia. The entire Tenth Legion did not stay there.

And when the Antonia finally fell to the Romans in AD 70, they destroyed it down to the foundations in only seven days. They did it so that they could move their siege machines into that area to finally take the Temple Mount. If the Temple was down the street in the City of David about a half a mile away, as many claim, then the Romans would not have destroyed a fort way back up on the Temple Mount to move their siege machines there. That would make no sense and does not agree with the historic record. And there is no way that the Romans could have torn down the gigantic stones of the retaining walls of the Temple Mount in seven days. Many of them weigh over three hundred tons.

This idea is also totally inconsistent with the many remaining retaining walls around the Temple Mount, like the Western Wall. The remaining walls testify against any theory that the Antonia is the Temple Mount because it was torn down to its foundation. Now, this, of course, reminds one again of Jesus' famous statement that "not one stone will be left upon another". So, how is the Western Wall still standing in light of Jesus' prophecy about not a single stone standing if the Temples were located on the Temple Mount? First of all, Jesus not only made this statement about the Temple, but he also made it a week earlier about all of Jerusalem. In Luke Jesus said this as he wept over Jerusalem:

> For the days shall come upon thee, that thine enemies shall cast a trench about thee, and compass thee round, and keep thee in on every side, And shall lay thee even with the ground, and thy children within thee; and they shall not leave in thee one stone upon another; because thou knewest not the time of thy visitation. Luke 19:43-44

Jesus said not one stone would be left on another in all of Jerusalem, not just the Temple. While the Western Wall stands in apparent opposition to this prophecy, an understanding of Jewish expressions and prophecy can help make sense of it. First, "not one stone upon another" was a Jewish idiom. It was a phrase that they used to describe a total destruction. It was not meant to be a one hundred percent literal statement. In other words, it was an intentional overstatement. It was a common phrase used by the Jews. Americans commonly say, "I have not seen you in a million years." They do not mean that literally. Jesus' statement "not one stone left on another" is the same kind of idiomatic overstatement. English and Hebrew both contain lots of idioms, and they are found throughout the Bible.

This passage is also a quote of Haggai who said the Temple was to be built stone upon stone (Haggai 2:15). That saying that one stone was left on another was Jesus' way of saying the building of the Temple would be undone in the same way it was built. It was always about the buildings, not the retaining walls. In the first verses of Matthew 24 the disciples were pointing out to Jesus the beautiful buildings, and it was these that Jesus said would not have a single stone left standing. However, when Josephus tells us the Antonia Fortress was torn down to its very foundation, that is entirely a different thing. That was a literal statement, and the reason was given was to move in the armies and the siege machines.

The Temple itself was destroyed, however, and the stones Jesus spoke of are littered on the streets around the Temple Mount. One of them that was found is a most unusual stone. On it was an inscription in Hebrew, "to the place of trumpeting", and consequently, it is called the Trumpeting Stone. Now, in the days of the Temple the sabbaths and the feasts were announced by trumpeting. So, such a stone is entirely consistent with the Temple. A Roman fort would not have had a stone with an inscription in Hebrew about trumpeting. This would be more consistent with the Temple being located on the Temple Mount.

Regarding those retaining walls, the retaining walls of the Temple Mount show the clear signs of multiple periods of construction. They are full of different stones, of different sizes, from different areas, and different construction techniques. This construction was something the Temple Mount underwent for over six hundred years, first with Nehemiah and then with the Hasmonean kings followed by Herod. But it is not consistent with a fort that was built at one time.

The Temple Mount construction took years to complete. That is known because of what was found under the Western Wailing Wall. The Western Wall is not the original retaining wall of Solomon's Temple. Rather, it was an expansion done by Herod. In order to do this expansion, the city of Jerusalem practiced eminent domain. In other words, they took over private property adjacent to the old Temple walls to expand the new ones. These were private homes and numerous baptismal baths. In the excavations under the wall in this area, they found two sealed jars that were sealed with cement. In the jars, they found coins that were from ten and twenty years after Herod had died. This makes it absolutely impossible to be the wall of a fort built a hundred and fifty years earlier by the Hasmonean kings and updated by Herod.

As noted earlier, a great deal of discussion centers around water on the Temple Mount. In the Middle East, water is very important, especially in the Temple due to the sacrifices being done there. Many will say that the Gihon Spring was the only source of running water in Jerusalem. So, to these scholars the Temple had to be over the spring. But that is not true. The Gihon may have been the only spring in Jerusalem, but it was not the only source of water on the Temple Mount. There are dozens of cisterns for water storage. They stored an incredible two hundred million gallons of water, and that was not all. An extensive aqueduct system ran twenty-one kilometers from the springs in Bethlehem, all the way to the Temple Mount. These were constructed one hundred years before the Romans occupied Israel, and they filled the *mikvahs* or baptismal baths. These baths or *mikvahs* required running water, not cistern water, to provide ritual purity. Only the aqueduct, coming from miles and miles away, had a water source high enough to provide running water to the Temple Mount. This aqueduct, built years prior to the Roman occupation, just to provide flowing water for ritual baths, demonstrates another false assumption in the Roman fort theory of the Temple.

On the southern side of the Temple Mount are the southern steps, the main entrance into the Temple Mount back in Jesus' day. Many believe this is the spot Peter gave his sermon in Acts 2 and Pentecost. But these are not just any old steps. The stairs are regular alternating wide steps with narrow ones which forced the faithful to pay attention as they ascended and to do so slowly. It prevented a hurried approach to the Temple and to God. This is very appropriate for a temple where reverence is required but not for a Roman fortress. The Roman commander would have wanted his soldiers to be able to come out or to go into the fortress in an instant, as quickly as possible. He would not have wanted his soldiers to be stuck on the steps and possibly even stumble coming out. This mounting evidence provides further support that the current Temple Mount was indeed the location of the Jewish Temple in biblical times and not a Roman fortress.

Now, if the Temple were to be built in the future on the Temple Mount, how would or could it be built with the Dome of the Rock already present there? Just where on the Temple Mount will the future Jewish Temple be built? Will the foundations be laid right in the middle of the Temple Mount as many suppose? This would necessitate the removal or destruction of the Dome of the Rock. Of course, this would be an earthshaking turn of events. The Dome is a revered Islamic site. Will the Dome of the Rock be destroyed? And is its removal even necessary? Just where did the original temple stand? Was it really in the center as seen in the paintings? Or was it situated to the north of the present location of the Dome of the Rock? Some Jewish authorities on the subject, notably Asher Kaufmann are saying precisely this. This is very interesting, since it opens up the very real possibility that the Third Jewish Temple will be constructed on the north side of the Mount without the necessity of removing the Dome.

There is evidence that the former Jewish temple was built north of the site where the Dome of the Rock presently sits. The Dome of the Spirits, a small cupola, is said by some to be the location of the Holy of Holies. This is well to the north and in direct alignment with the Eastern Gate. This fact along with some mounting archaeological evidence would seem to indicate that the former (Second) Temple was situated not in the center of the Temple Mount at all but rather on the north side of the Temple Mount, again directly opposite the Eastern Gate. This layout has been set forth by noted scholar Asher Kauffman.

This alignment of the future Jewish Temple with the Eastern Gate would only be appropriate. The architectural layout of the Temple would surely have been to allow the Messiah to come through the Eastern Gate and go straight ahead into the Holy City. He would not be doing any turning left and then right or any "jigs". He would enter the city and go straight ahead and up into the Temple. Such a zig zag route is, in fact, unthinkable. Surely Zerubbabel and Solomon before him were mindful of this when the Temple was designed. It was a magnificent temple laid out for a coming Messiah who was King of Kings. And surely the whole Temple Mount area was meticulously and tastefully laid out. YHVH, God Himself, was the true divine Architect here. He guided King David as the king set forth the plans and the materials.

Looking at the present situation, the Dome of the Rock occupies the center of the Temple Mount. The future Third Temple could, therefore, be rebuilt to the north of the Dome and would possibly be on the same site as the former temple. There would be room to provide an acceptable easement between the two buildings. There would, in fact, be a clearance of one hundred and fifty feet. This would allow the Dome to actually co-exist with the Third Jewish Temple provided the Temple is rebuilt straight across from the Eastern Gate. According to scholars such as Asher Kauffman, this is in fact the archaeologically correct position. The view of scholars like Kaufman is that the Temple stood about one hundred meters to the north of the Dome of the Rock, lining up with the current eastern gate (sometimes called the Golden Gate). If that were the case, then this view satisfies some comments in Revelation 11, because it puts the Dome of the Rock in the outer court:

> And there was given me a reed like unto a rod: and the angel stood, saying, Rise, and measure the temple of God, and the altar, and them that worship therein. But

the court which is without the temple leave out, and measure it not; for it is given unto the Gentiles: and the holy city shall they tread under foot forty and two months. Revelation 11:1-2

Still others propose that the Temple was located south and not north of the Dome of the Rock. Despite the uncertainty of its location, the Jewish Temple most likely can only be rebuilt under the covering of an all-encompassing world peace. This peace will most certainly involve Israel and her Islamic neighbors. Such a peace is something that we have not seen yet. Quite obviously it is out there in the future. To the current international political players, this peaceful coexistence of an Islamic Dome and a Jewish Temple would be quite acceptable as well. It would not be the architecture of the ultimate Messianic dominion in holiness expected by Jews and Christians, but the powers who rule in this present world would probably favor it. Such an arrangement would be "politically correct". The good news in all this, from the perspective of an interim pre-Messianic or non-Messianic world peace, is that building a third temple there would not require the destruction of an Islamic shrine, the Dome of the Rock. It could be constructed right next door to the Dome of the Rock without its removal.

Although this provides a simple solution for building the Temple on the Temple Mount without infringing on the Dome of the Rock, many others continue to believe that the Temple was indeed located directly over the rock in the Dome of the Rock. In fact, the scholar who has shed more light on this subject than anyone else in the world is Leen Ritmeyer, an archaeological architect, who discovered archaeological evidence for the location of Solomon's Temple with the emplacement of the Ark of the Covenant directly on the rock in the Dome of the Rock, the Foundation Stone. In his model, the location of the platform for the Temple Mount, as extended in the First Temple period probably during the time of Hezekiah, is described as a square of five hundred cubits. He has demonstrated that one of the steps leading to the Dome of the Rock is actually the top of a remaining stone course of the pre-Herodian Western Wall of the Temple Mount platform. This provides convincing evidence that not only was the Temple located on the Temple Mount but that it also was located directly on the site of the Dome of the Rock. Most importantly he has convinced the Jewish Sanhedrin, the Temple Institute, and the Jewish authorities that the site over the Dome of the Rock is the exact spot that Solomon's Temple and the Ark of the Covenant were located, which indicates that this is likely where the Third Temple would be built.

ARK OF THE COVENANT

Determining where the Temple might be built is challenging. But even if the Temple is constructed, there are other Temple articles and events that have to be in place before the Temple sacrifices could begin. The Tabernacle and the two Temples were representative types, where every part of them were symbolic and pointed to the Lord Jesus Christ. The gate pointed to Him as the Door; the altar pointed to the Cross; the laver, to His cleansing Word; the table of shewbread spoke of Him as the Bread of Life; the candlestick pointed to the Light of the World; and the altar of incense spoke of Him as the interceding High Priest. The ark of the covenant was a picture of Christ who by His blood redeemed us from the curse of the law. The linen in the Tabernacle spoke of His righteousness; the brass of the judgment He bore; the gold of His deity; the silver of His blood; the wood of His humanity. [De Haan, 1946, p. 297][7]

Of these items, the one Temple article that probably has received the most attention is the Ark of the Covenant which was initially kept in the Tabernacle, a model of the heavenly tabernacle where there is a heavenly Ark of the Covenant. Moses created the earthly version of the Ark of the Covenant based on what God revealed to him on Mount Sinai. The Ark has even been the subject of a series of movies (e.g., *Raiders of the Lost Ark* by director Steven Spielberg). As one of the most sacred objects in history, God's Shekinah glory dwelt above the gold mercy seat of the Ark. The Ark of the Covenant contained the tablets of the Law, a pot of manna, and Aaron's rod that budded with almonds. It was made of acacia wood overlaid with gold, within and without.

The Ark of the Covenant is sometimes called the Ark of the Testimony because that is where the tablets of the Law (i.e., the Ten Commandments, written on stone with "the finger of God") were located. The Ark, as noted earlier, is symbolic of Christ. The Ark itself was made of wood, symbolic of Christ being human. It was covered with gold, speaking of His divinity. The Ten Commandments showed that Christ perfectly fulfilled the Law. The pot of manna spoke of Christ as the Bread of Life, and Aaron's rod that budded is symbolic of the resurrection of Christ.

Early church father John Chrysostom notes that the symbols could also be interpreted as reminders [Stewart, 2016c]. The tablets of the law remind people of the rebellion, during which Moses broke the original tablets. The pot of manna reminds Israel of their complaining during the exodus from Egypt. Aaron's rod serves as a reminder of the rebellion of the Israelites when in jealousy they questioned Aaron's authority (Numbers 17:10-11).[6] The lid of the Ark was called the "Mercy Seat". Once per year, the high priest sprinkled blood on it, and this was symbolic of Jesus Christ eventually shedding His blood, to not just atone (cover) sin, but rather to remove sin.

But where now is the Ark of the Covenant and is it necessary for the rebuilding of the Third Temple? The Ark was housed initially in the Tabernacle, sometimes called "the tent of meeting" during the years of the Exodus. Wherever the Israelites travelled during the 40 years in the wilderness following the Exodus from Egypt, the Ark (and the rest of the Tabernacle) moved with them. Eventually, after entering the Promised Land, the Ark was moved from the Tabernacle to Solomon's Temple. The Levites had been given very specific instructions on how to transport the Ark. Yet, while moving the Ark, the men of Beth Shemesh opened the Ark, and over fifty thousand people died. King David made the mistake of forgetting how to carry the Ark, thus showing a lack of respect for the Ark, for God's holiness, and for God's specific instructions to the Levites. King Solomon finally brought the

Ark into the Temple amid great celebration, and over 120,000 sheep were sacrificed that day.

The Ark eventually disappeared from history, and it is unknown what happened to it. The Ark of the Covenant is not mentioned being carried away by the Babylonians when the first Temple was destroyed. It is not recorded as having been in the Second Temple, but it is believed to have been hidden by the Prophet Jeremiah before the sack of Jerusalem according to the Apocryphal book *Second Maccabees*. The last time it is mentioned in the Bible is in 2 Chronicles, during the time of King Josiah around 621 BC [Stewart, 2016c].

> And said unto the Levites that taught all Israel, which were holy unto the LORD, Put the holy ark in the house which Solomon the son of David king of Israel did build; it shall not be a burden upon your shoulders: serve now the LORD your God, and his people Israel, 2 Chronicles 35:3

This is shortly before the Babylonians invaded Jerusalem. The Ark may have been moved and hidden proactively in case of an invasion, and Don Stewart documents some theories about what may have happened to the Ark:

- Hidden somewhere underneath the Temple Mount
- Hidden by Jeremiah on Mount Nebo in Jordan
- Destroyed, possibly during the Babylonian invasion

And other proposed, but unlikely possibilities, include:

- Taken to Ethiopia by Solomon's son Menelik, the alleged son of King Solomon and the Queen of Sheba ... but the son left a replica in its place, in Jerusalem
- Taken to Ethiopia at a later time
- Taken to Babylon by King Nebuchadnezzar's armies
- Taken to Egypt by Pharaoh Shishak

- Taken from Judah to the northern kingdom of Israel, by King Jehoash (Joash) of Israel
- Taken to Rome by the Romans[7]

Chuck Missler provides additional insight to the conjecture that the Ark of the Covenant is being secretly stored in Ethiopia [Missler, 2005]. Tradition has it that the Ark was taken to Ethiopia (via Egypt) for safe storage by the Egyptian king Pharaoh Neco after the Levites sought protection from the evil Judean king Manasseh (2 Kings 21). Pharaoh Neco, incidentally, was Ethiopian. According to this hypothesis, the Ark was to be held by the Ethiopians and then was to be presented to the Messiah on Mount Zion (Isaiah 18:7; Zephaniah 3:10).

An interesting speculation is that perhaps the Ethiopian treasurer under Queen Candace (Acts 8:26-40) had been on his way to Jerusalem to see if it was the time to present the Ark to the Messiah (Jesus Christ). When the Ethiopian eunuch got to Jerusalem, however, he found out that the Messiah had been killed, and so the treasurer left in confusion. On his way home, the Holy Spirit moved Philip the evangelist to meet him on the road from Jerusalem to Gaza. The Ethiopian happened to be reading Isaiah (possibly Isaiah 53) at that time. Philip then explained the mission of the Messiah, and the Ethiopian rejoiced because of what he had heard and in the fact that the Messiah was going to come back.

> From beyond the rivers of Ethiopia my suppliants, even
> the daughter of my dispersed, shall bring mine offering.
> Zephaniah 3:10

So, according to this theory, the Ark could be in Ethiopia today. Bible prophecy teacher Grant Jeffrey also thought this could be the case [Jeffrey, 1988]. He reported that the majority of the northern Ethiopians have Semitic background and that the Ethiopian orthodox Coptic church traces its origin back to the times of King Solomon. There is very little information of the Ark of the Covenant after the time of Solomon. Recall that the Queen of Sheba travelled to meet King Solomon (1 Kings 10; 2 Chronicles 9). Jeffrey thought there may be a connection between the Ark, King Solomon, and the Queen of Sheba. Legend has it that the Queen of Sheba bore a son by Solomon. Incidentally, her palace is located near the Church of Zion in Aksum, Ethiopia. As a bit of trivia, recall that Moses married an Ethiopian woman (Numbers 12:1), and that an Ethiopian river, the Gihon, flowed through the Garden of Eden (Genesis 2:13).

The last mention of the Ark in the Old Testament is the story of Hezekiah when during the night the Angel of the Lord struck down 185,000 Assyrians. Sennacherib, the King of Assyria, never came against Jerusalem again. After the Babylonian captivity, there is no record of the Ark. Furthermore, although the Second Temple existed from about 515 BC to 70 AD, there is no evidence to suggest that the Ark was in the Second Temple, and there is no evidence to suggest that God met with the high priest in this Temple. David Hocking reminds us that, "God is not in the box." And the following Scripture passage suggests that during the Millennium, when Christ will literally reign from David's Throne in Jerusalem, there will be no need for the Ark of the Covenant.

> And it shall come to pass, when ye be multiplied and increased in the land, in those days, saith the Lord, they shall say no more, The ark of the covenant of the Lord: neither shall it come to mind: neither shall they remember it; neither shall they visit it; neither shall that be done any more. At that time they shall call Jerusalem the throne of the Lord; and all the nations shall be gathered unto it, to the name of the Lord, to Jerusalem: neither shall they walk any more after the imagination of their evil heart. Jeremiah 3:16-17

So, although discovering the Ark would cause excitement for a new temple, as far as rebuilding the Temple goes, it may not actually matter whether the Ark is found. After all, the Ark was possibly not present for the Second Temple. Ezekiel 41-44 explicitly mentions some articles used in the future Temple service; therefore, some authors conjecture that the Ark of the Covenant will once again be part of the worship of God in the rebuilt Temple [LaHaye & Hindson, 2004]. In particular, 2 Thessalonians 2:4 states that the Antichrist will take his seat in the Holy of Holies, implying the presence of the Ark of the Covenant (the "mercy seat") which historically occupied the Holy of Holies. Finding of the Ark would certainly stir national interest in Israel to build a temple, but its presence may not be absolutely required.[7]

RED HEIFER[8]

While the Ark of the Covenant has received quite a bit of notoriety, there is another part of Jewish worship that gathers very little attention, the sacrifice of the red heifer. This sacrifice is an important part of Jewish worship and bears a relationship with respect to the timeframe of a rebuilt Temple. In fact, the red heifer and a rebuilt Temple are very connected. The ashes of a perfect red heifer are needed to consecrate the Temple's furnishings and vessels. And just as locating the Ark could help bring about the building of a third Jewish temple, finding a red heifer may speed about the rebuilding of the Temple.

In Judaism, in order to purify a person who has become ritually contaminated, the only solution is to be washed with fresh water mixed with the ashes of a burnt red heifer. A priest absolutely cannot officiate in the Temple when he is ritually unclean, nor can the physical building of the Temple or even a Tabernacle tent be sanctified unless the blood ceremony of the heifer takes place. Even if Israel negotiated the right to build a temple or set up a tabernacle on the Temple Mount, the Temple would most likely not be built until they have a red heifer because the Temple and the priest would both be unclean from a Jewish perspective.

So, before officially sanctioned sacrifices can begin on the Temple Mount, or anywhere else, a red heifer sacrifice will have to take place. And in order for that to happen, a kosher red heifer has to be found. Here is what the Book of Numbers says about those who remain unclean and defile the Tabernacle.

> Whosoever toucheth the dead body of any man that is dead, and purifieth not himself, defileth the tabernacle of the Lord; and that soul shall be cut off from Israel: because the water of separation was not sprinkled upon him, he shall be unclean; his uncleanness is yet upon him. Numbers 19:13

This is why having a red heifer is so important. Before Jesus can return, official Jewish sacrifices have to be taking place in order for the Antichrist to terminate them. And before that can happen, a red heifer has to be sacrificed. It is an essential sign needed for the Antichrist to initiate the Great Tribulation.

But, finding a kosher red heifer is easier said than done. In the entire history of Israel, from Moses to the present day, there have only been nine kosher red heifers. The last one was sacrificed around 60 AD, and its ashes lasted about three hundred years but then ran out. So, for the last 1700 years, without the ashes of a red heifer, the Jews have felt that they are ritually unclean, and they are desperate for a heifer to make them clean again. Because of that, in the last twenty-five years a very impassioned search has been taking place to find one.

But first, what does being "ritually unclean" mean exactly? Unclean is not an issue of sin but is better thought of as not having access to God. If you are Jewish and ritually clean, then think of it as having an open door to the Father. But if you are unclean, think of the door as being closed. The ashes of the red heifer mixed in with fresh water gives a Jew this cleanliness and access to the Father.

A major way that someone becomes unclean is by coming in contact with a dead body. Now this contact not only includes touching a dead body but also walking over a grave of a dead body or even being in the same building as a dead body. From a Jewish perspective, just about everyone who has ever been in a hospital has been in the presence of a dead body. So, most Jews on the planet are ceremonially unclean in this way. You can see that this type of uncleanliness is not sin. It is just the closing of the door and closing of access to the Father. For the Christian, removing this uncleanliness is a type or picture of what Jesus already did for us because we were all dead and had no access to the Father until Jesus died on the cross. He opened the door for us.

An example of this red heifer purification is even found in the New Testament.

> And the Jews' passover was nigh at hand: and many went out of the country up to Jerusalem before the passover, to purify themselves. John 11:55

Those Jews were purifying themselves by the ashes of a red heifer. Notice this was taking place prior to the Passover. To this day Jews celebrate the Sabbath of the Red Heifer or Shabbat Parah which takes place on the Shabbat preceding Shabbat HaChodesh in preparation for Passover. During the Sabbath they read appropriate passages from the Old Testament about the red heifer. These are ancient texts that are read on this day to remind Jews to go to Jerusalem and purify themselves prior to the feast. That is what is seen happening in John's gospel.

Today, however, these passages simply remind the Jews that they are unclean, and this adds to the pressure and the desire to find a red heifer. Once they have one and sacrifice it, the pressure to begin sacrifices on the Temple Mount will increase. The pressure to build the Temple and start sacrifices right now in Israel is almost zero because they cannot. They do not have a red heifer. But once they get one, that pressure may become irresistible.

Examining the biblical texts about red heifers helps explain the symbolism behind the red heifer sacrifice. The first text is found in the Book of Numbers.

> This is the ordinance of the law which the LORD hath commanded, saying, Speak unto the children of Israel, that they bring thee a red heifer without spot, wherein is no blemish, and upon which never came yoke: And ye shall give her unto Eleazar the priest, that he may bring her forth without the camp, and one shall slay her before his face: Numbers 19:2-3

God commanded Moses and Aaron to find a red heifer with very specific requirements to be sacrificed. It had to be without defect or blemish and one where a yoke had never been placed. The rabbis, not surprisingly, have defined these simple restrictions extremely rigidly with their man-made laws in the Mishnah, a collection of Jewish oral tradition and laws. The rabbis have defined "without defect" as meaning that all the hairs in the cow have to be red. That is why, when a rabbi today examines a cow, he inspects it with a magnifying glass. They allow two, and only two, hairs to be a different color on the entire animal. This is what has disqualified all the potential red heifers in the past. When these heifers were examined, they had more than two white hairs. The red heifer also cannot have blemishes like warts or cysts or other marks, and they cannot have worn a yoke. The rabbis defined "wearing a yoke" as work, which strangely includes someone leaning against the heifer, because the rabbis believe that if you lean against it, the heifer has to lean back. This is the overly concern with minute details that has been added to the scripture and so frustrated Jesus during his ministry.

So, finding a kosher red heifer will have to almost take an act of God. The only way a perfect kosher one will be found, one that matches all these requirements, is if God permits it in His good timing. When it is announced that a red heifer has been sacrificed, know that it is God's doing, and His countdown will almost assuredly have begun. After finding a kosher red heifer, God then gave Moses these additional instructions.

> And ye shall give her unto Eleazar the priest, that he may bring her forth without the camp, and one shall slay her before his face: And Eleazar the priest shall take of her blood with his finger, and sprinkle of her blood directly before the tabernacle of the congregation seven times: Numbers 19:3-4

This was the only sacrifice commanded to be done outside of the camp and included God instructing a strange sprinkling of blood "seven times" toward the Tabernacle. After the Temple was built, this ceremony took place on the Mount of Olives. A bridge was built from the area of the Temple across the Kidron Valley to the Mount of Olives. The Kidron Valley is full of graves. So, this bridge allowed the priests and the cow to cross in a state of cleanliness and not be defiled. It can safely be assumed that the future red heifer sacrifice will take place on the Mount of Olives as well. Yet, additional unusual things were also required.

> And one shall burn the heifer in his sight; her skin, and her flesh, and her blood, with her dung, shall he burn: And the priest shall take cedar wood, and hyssop, and scarlet, and cast it into the midst of the burning of the heifer. Then the priest shall wash his clothes, and he shall bathe his flesh in water, and afterward he shall come into the camp, and the priest shall be unclean until the even. And he that burneth her shall wash his clothes in water, and bathe his flesh in water, and shall be unclean until the even. Numbers 19:5-8

Oddly, the one who does the sacrifice to make the nation clean becomes unclean himself. According to the rabbis this was the greatest of the mysteries. Rabbis simply did not understand. Those made unclean for seven days by the ceremony had to be purified on both the third day and the seventh day by being sprinkled with water mixed with the ashes. These numbers of days are also symbolic as will be seen. The other verse that is read on Shabbat Parah, the Sabbath of the Red Heifer, is in Ezekiel.

> For I will take you from among the heathen, and gather you out of all countries, and will bring you into your own land. Then will I sprinkle clean water upon you, and ye shall be clean: from all your filthiness, and from all your idols, will I cleanse you. A new heart also will I give you, and a new spirit will I put within you: and I

will take away the stony heart out of your flesh, and I will give you an heart of flesh. Ezekiel 36:24-26

This is speaking of the Messiah (Jesus) who will save all of Israel, at least those that survive the Great Tribulation upon his Second Coming. And notice the sprinkling of water to make them clean. That is red heifer language. Again, rabbis teach that there have been nine red heifers, and the next red heifer, the tenth, will accompany the building of the Third Temple and the coming of the Messiah. Israel believes that will be a sign to begin building the Temple.

Continuing to look at the imagery of the red heifer, the author of Hebrews wrote:

> For the bodies of those beasts (i.e. the red heifers), whose blood is brought into the sanctuary by the high priest for sin, are burned without the camp. Wherefore Jesus also, that he might sanctify the people with his own blood, suffered without the gate. Hebrews 13:11-12

The only sacrifice burned outside the camp was the red heifer. So, Jesus, as told in Hebrews, is our spiritual red heifer. In Hebrews the author further explained:

> For if the blood of bulls and of goats, and the ashes of an heifer sprinkling the unclean, sanctifieth to the purifying of the flesh: How much more shall the blood of Christ, who through the eternal Spirit offered himself without spot to God, purge your conscience from dead works to serve the living God? Hebrews 9:13-14

Jesus' blood sacrifice is the fulfillment of all the Old Testament sacrifices, including Passover, the red heifer, and Yom Kippur (Day of Atonement). All of them point to Jesus, and his sacrifice is the ultimate red heifer and never needs to be redone. There is no need to worry about running out of ashes. His sacrifice was once for all.

One might ask, why was it necessary for Jesus to be both our Passover lamb as well as our red heifer. Human thinking would ask, was not one symbol enough? Now, in the Jewish priesthood you needed to be baptized or *mikvahed* in water mixed with the red heifer ashes in order to put on the white robe and enter the Temple with an open door to the Father. So, it is Jesus' role as red heifer that gives us access to the Father and further, will allow us to put on white robes in heaven.

> After this I beheld, and, lo, a great multitude, which no man could number, of all nations, and kindreds, and people, and tongues, stood before the throne, and before the Lamb, clothed with white robes, and palms in their hands; Revelation 7:9

This provides answers to the questions that the Jewish scholars could not solve. Why is the heifer without spot or blemish? Jesus was our spotless lamb and at the same time our spotless red heifer, without sin. The heifer was examined by the priest for three years prior to sacrifice to make sure it was kosher, that it had less than those two white hairs. This three-year examination represents the three-year ministry of our Lord where he proved that he was sinless.

Did Jesus ever wear a yoke, since he worked hard his whole life? In Bible times, Jesus told us that a "yoke" was the yoke of the Pharisees. The yoke was their man-made religious law that they added to the Torah. Jesus never wore their yoke. He perfectly fulfilled God's law in the Torah but not their man-made laws. Additionally, as Jesus began to leave the city of Jerusalem to go to Calvary, he stumbled and from that point on his cross was carried by Simon of Cyrene. So, some consider this was also not wearing a yoke.

But why was the heifer red? You would think that if Jesus is the spiritual heifer, it would be a white heifer for his purity. But it is red for two reasons. First, Jesus was covered with blood during his crucifixion. It was a brutal murder. But more importantly, Paul stated:

For he hath made him to be sin for us, who knew no
sin; that we might be made the righteousness of God in
him. 2 Corinthians 5:21

The sinless one took on our sins to create a right relationship with
God. He made us clean. So, the red heifer is red, the color of sin, and
Jesus became sin for us.

The red heifer was purchased by the Temple for the purpose of
sacrifice. Jesus was bought for thirty pieces of silver from the Temple
Treasury which was paid to Judas.

When the sacrifice was finished, the Temple was opened, and
the high priest had to look inside the Holy of Holies. This made it an
official red heifer sacrifice. On the day of Jesus' crucifixion, a great
earthquake tore the veil of the Temple in two, and the high priest,
whether he was sitting on the Mount of Olives watching Jesus die or
in the Temple, heard the noise and looked into the Holy of Holies and
that authenticated the red heifer sacrifice.

After the red heifer was burned, its ashes were placed in a clean
place for three days. This clean place was a newly hewn stone container,
and after the three days, they would mix the ashes with living water,
which meant running water or fresh water. Jesus was placed in a clean,
never used grave, a newly hewn grave for three days. Prior to rising from
the dead and after three days, he was raised to life. So, there are multiple
similarities between Jesus and the red heifer.

With those questions answered, there are other even more puzzling
ones. First, why did the priest sprinkle the blood of the heifer seven
times toward the temple? An answer to that could be that there are
seven millennium, seven thousand years from Adam's fall to the end of
the Millennial Kingdom. So, Jesus died to make clean all of those who
died in faith in the Father and faith in Him during those thousand-year
periods, all seven of them.

These one thousand-year long days, the millennial days, also
explain the mysterious symbolism of the purification that takes place
on the third day and on the seventh day. On the third day, or after two
thousand years from creation, Moses did the initial red heifer sacrifice

for the purification of Israel. And on the seventh day, or after six thousand years, Jesus will return, and he himself will be our red heifer sprinkling at that time.

Another explanation for the seven sprinklings could be that Jesus also had seven wounds, one for each of those thousand years. His back was striped by the Roman whip. His head was pierced by a crown of thorns. Both of his hands were pierced by Roman spikes. Both of his feet were also pierced by spikes, and finally, his side was thrust through by a Roman spear, the final wound, and out flowed blood and water, the mixture of the red heifer ashes mixed with living water.

A second question is why was cedar wood, hyssop, and scarlet wool thrown into the fire when the red heifer was burned. This was not some sort of magic formula. Rather, it was a picture of Jesus on the cross, nailed to a wooden beam like cedar and offered sour wine on a stalk of hyssop. He was the scarlet Lamb of God, the red wool, a beautiful picture of the coming crucifixion that none of the onlookers at Calvary really understood.

But, one of the hardest questions concerns why the sacrifice makes all of Israel clean, yet it makes the one who burns the sacrifice (the one who starts out clean) into one who is unclean. The reason is because both the heifer and the priest start out clean, but in the process of the sacrifice, the heifer becomes unclean. This is a picture of Jesus taking on the sin of the world. So, the priests, who start out clean, become unclean as they touched the red heifer. And here is the spiritual analogy:

> For as many as are of the works of the law are under the curse: for it is written, Cursed is every one that continueth not in all things which are written in the book of the law to do them. Galatians 3:10

The Jewish priests were relying on the Torah to save them, but everyone who does not keep every single aspect of the Torah is cursed according to this verse. Obviously, only Jesus fulfilled all the Law. So, everyone relying on the Law alone is cursed. Only by abiding in Jesus, placing your full faith in him can you be saved. Then he can sprinkle you and make you righteous before God.

So, the priests and temple officials who oversaw the death of our Messiah became unclean because they relied solely on the Torah. That does not mean the Law and the prophets are done away with. It is just that we are not to rely on them for our salvation. Jesus, the red heifer, is salvation, and in fact, in Jewish, the name Yeshua (Jesus) literally means "salvation".

Attention now is turning to what many believe may transpire soon: the final red heifer sacrifice, the setting up of a temporary Tabernacle and/or the building of a third temple, and the beginning of animal sacrifices. It has already been indicated that the sacrifice of the red heifer will be a great sign that sacrifices are about to begin, because once the Jews have that heifer, the pressure to move forward and set up a Tabernacle will be overwhelming. Just to show how the rabbis already feel this pressure, the ancient site of the sacrifice on the Mount of Olives has been tentatively located by archaeologist Yonatan Adler. So, the place for the red heifer sacrifice can easily be prepared.

A practice run red heifer sacrifice has taken place to calculate exactly how much ash was created and how much of each type of wood provided through analysis of the ash would be needed. They have it down to a science and have figured out that they have not only enough to purify every Jew in the world but enough to go forward until another red heifer is found, in their opinion.

But a Tabernacle or tent must be in place first. An integral part of a sacrifice is sprinkling blood seven times in the direction of the Tabernacle. So, Israel has to have one, even if it is undedicated. It has to have one prior to the red heifer ceremony, and it is reported that there may be kosher red heifers in Israel right now, close to being ready for sacrifice. Even people who follow the red heifer closely have probably not noticed that the Jewish rabbis have moved the date up. They have redefined the method for determining how old the heifer has to be. Historically, it had to be three years old, but they have redefined it to be acceptable in the third year, which means two years plus at least one day.

So, the urgency to change the heifer's required age indicates that they are hoping to do the sacrifice soon. That could place it on a soon to come Shabbat Parah (the Sabbath of the Cow) which is the day set aside to remind Israelites to purify themselves before Passover. Yet, Jewish tradition gives the date of God providing Moses both the red heifer instructions and setting up the Tabernacle on Nisan 1, the beginning of the religious year. Shabbat Parah in the year 2030 occurs on Saturday March 23, 2030, and Nisan 1 lands on Thursday April 4, 2030. These are auspicious dates to consider on a timeline for the 70th Week. Remember, the timing is completely in God's hands. One way or the other, a kosher red heifer will be a miracle in light of all of the rabbi's regulations.

HANUKKAH AND WHEN WILL THE THIRD TEMPLE BE BUILT?[9]

When might the Temple be rebuilt and the daily sacrifices restarted? Most do not realize that Hanukkah is an extremely prophetic holiday that someday will greatly impact every single human alive on earth and provides some key information in determining the timing for the rebuilding of the Temple. Hanukkah, in fact, provides a hidden template for the Antichrist and the Great Tribulation.

Today's world thinks of Hanukkah as a nice happy little holiday, kind of like the Jewish Christmas where kids receive gifts, homes are lit with lights, and sweet potato pancakes are served. But it is not just a nice fun secular holiday. It is an amazingly prophetic revelation of the end times, the Antichrist, the abomination of desolation, the persecution of God's people, and Jesus' ultimate victory over the forces of darkness. In order to know what these things will look like in the future, knowing what they looked like in the original Hanukkah story is key.

But shockingly, Hanukkah is only mentioned by name in one place in the Bible. And that is in the New Testament where the only person seen celebrating it is Jesus. The Hebrew word *Hanukkah* means dedication, and the Gospel of John states:

> And it was at Jerusalem **the feast of the dedication**, and it was winter. And Jesus walked in the temple in Solomon's porch. John 10:22-23

So, when it says "the feast of the dedication", it is speaking of Hanukkah. It was at that time that Jesus' miracle of healing the blind man in John 9 and his teaching on the true and good shepherd in John 10 took place. All of these things happened at the time of the Feast of Dedication or Hanukkah. And John 10 is recounting Jesus' Hanukkah teaching.

> Verily, verily, I say unto you, He that entereth not by the door into the sheepfold, but climbeth up some other way, the same is a thief and a robber. The thief cometh not, but for to steal, and to kill, and to destroy: I am come that they might have life, and that they might have it more abundantly. John 10:1,10

Jesus contrasts himself with the thief who comes to steal, kill and destroy. Who is the thief? The ultimate coming thief is the Antichrist who is coming to steal the sheep. Speaking about the Antichrist at Hanukkah is very appropriate because historically the greatest foreshadow of the Antichrist, Antiochus IV Epiphanes, is the villain in the first Hanukkah account. His name Antiochus even sounds like Antichrist. That is why Jesus' teaching at this time is about his great end time enemy, the thief. And in order to know what the Antichrist is like, where he is from, and what he is going to do, a study of Hanukkah and Antiochus is essential because the historical accounts exactly match what is going to happen in the future according to prophecy.

This historic information is primarily found in the Book of Maccabees and also from Josephus, the greatest Jewish historian. Although the Book of Maccabees is not found in the canon of the Bible and is not inspired, it is part of what is called the Apocrypha, a history book that should be read like an historical account. These historical accounts parallel prophecies in the book of Daniel but do not imply that

Daniel was completely fulfilled by these ancient accounts. The historical information in the Book of Maccabees is a first fulfillment of Daniel and a first fulfillment only. To understand that, look at an example in the Daniel prophecy, then the historical account, and finally what Jesus said about the same thing. First, here is Daniel:

> And arms shall stand on his part, and they shall pollute the sanctuary of strength, and shall take away the daily sacrifice, and they shall place the abomination that maketh desolate. Daniel 11:31

Next, look at the historic record.

> Now on the fifteenth day of Chislev in the one hundred and forty-fifth year, they erected a desolating sacrilege upon the altar of burnt offerings. 1 Maccabee 1:54

Most likely those in Israel in the days of Jesus thought that this event in Maccabees had already fulfilled Daniel's prophecy of the abomination of desolation. However, look what Jesus had to say.

> When ye therefore shall see the abomination of desolation, spoken of by Daniel the prophet, stand in the holy place, (whoso readeth, let him understand:) Then let them which be in Judaea flee into the mountains: Matthew 24:15-16

He is referring back to Daniel 11, and the disciples were probably surprised, maybe even shocked, when they heard Jesus say this. They thought the abomination of desolation was over and completed back in the days of Antiochus. But Jesus was telling them that there was yet one more fulfillment of this abomination of desolation, a future fulfillment of this prophecy, and that the abomination of Antiochus was just a foreshadow. This type of dual fulfillment continues throughout the entire Hanukkah account. This is what makes the Hanukkah story the template for the Antichrist in the Great Tribulation, and there are some amazing things in the Hanukkah story not found in prophecy. If those things also happen, this account gives great insight into what is unknown strictly from Biblical prophecy.

So, beginning with this character Antiochus IV, he was called Antiochus Epiphanies which meant "God manifest" and sounds kind of like the Antichrist. His contemporaries, however, called him, of course behind his back, Antiochus Epimanes, which means Antiochus the Madman, because he was a little irrational. Now, Antiochus IV was the son of Antiochus III and a potential heir to the Seleucid Empire which was in the area of eastern Turkey, Syria, Iran and Iraq. This indicates that perhaps the future Antichrist will arise out of that same area, and Daniel 8:9 also seems to indicate that the little horn or Antichrist will come from this area.

However, unfortunately for Antiochus, his father lost some battles to the new empire on the block, the Roman Empire, and in the peace treaty between the two nations, Antiochus' father gave Antiochus to the Romans as a political prisoner. This was not uncommon in those days. The Romans figured that the Seleucids would keep their end of the treaty if the royal son was their prisoner. This, too, may have prophetic implication, indicating that the Antichrist might first be a political prisoner of the Western nations prior to rising to power. The former khalif of ISIS, al-Baghdadi, was just such a prisoner during the USA-Iraq war. In a parallel to the Hanukkah story, the Antichrist might follow a similar path. It is certainly something to keep in mind.

Antiochus was eventually released by the Romans and was living in Greece when the King of Pergamum (the same Pergamum with the throne of Satan from Revelation 2:13) secretly helped him enter the Seleucid Empire. Then, by means of intrigue, he became king, even killing his young nephew to assume total power. This correlates with Daniel's prophecy.

> And in his estate shall stand up a vile person, to whom they shall not give the honour of the kingdom: but he shall come in peaceably, and obtain the kingdom by flatteries. Daniel 11:21

This scripture has a dual fulfillment of both the historical Antiochus and the future Antichrist. Now, as soon as Antiochus came to power, the king of the South, i.e., the Ptolemaic Empire based in Egypt, decided to attack Antiochus, thinking his empire was still weak after all the political intrigue. But Antiochus was prepared, attacked first, and defeated the Egyptians.

> And he shall stir up his power and his courage against the king of the south with a great army; and the king of the south shall be stirred up to battle with a very great and mighty army; but he shall not stand: for they shall forecast devices against him. Yea, they that feed of the portion of his meat shall destroy him, and his army shall overflow: and many shall fall down slain. And both of these kings' hearts shall be to do mischief, and they shall speak lies at one table; but it shall not prosper: for yet the end shall be at the time appointed. Daniel 11:25-27

So, although this is primarily about the Antichrist, the parallels with Antiochus are almost perfect. Antiochus then led a second attack on Egypt, but a single elderly Roman ambassador directed Antiochus to withdraw his armies from Egypt, or Rome would attack the Seleucids. The Roman drew a circle in the sand around Antiochus and said, "Before you leave this circle, give me a reply that I can take back to the Roman senate." This is where the famous saying "a line in the sand" originated. Antiochus, afraid of the Romans, withdrew which parallels Daniel as well.

> At the time appointed he shall return, and come toward the south; but it shall not be as the former, or as the latter. For the ships of Chittim shall come against him: therefore he shall be grieved, and return, and have indignation against the holy covenant: so shall he do;

he shall even return, and have intelligence with them that forsake the holy covenant. Daniel 11:29-30

Once again, the eventual career of the Antichrist is paralleled by the historic account of Antiochus. Now, Antiochus was only opposed by a single individual, not a fleet of ships as the Antichrist will be, but the parallel is still there. Immediately after that, Antiochus undertook that for which he is most famous.

> For the ships of Chittim shall come against him: therefore he shall be grieved, and return, and have indignation against the holy covenant: so shall he do; he shall even return, and have intelligence with them that forsake the holy covenant. And arms shall stand on his part, and they shall pollute the sanctuary of strength, and shall take away the daily sacrifice, and they shall place the abomination that maketh desolate. And such as do wickedly against the covenant shall he corrupt by flatteries: but the people that do know their God shall be strong, and do exploits. And they that understand among the people shall instruct many: yet they shall fall by the sword, and by flame, by captivity, and by spoil, many days. Daniel 11:30-33

He entered Israel, took away the sacrifices, and set up the abomination of desolation. Maccabees tells us that the Israelites themselves actually began the apostasy. Previously, they had built a gymnasium in Jerusalem according to Gentile custom and removed the marks of circumcision and abandoned the holy covenant. They joined with the Gentiles and were trying to become like Greeks.

This is another one of the hidden gems in the Hanukkah account. A very large contingent of the Jews themselves were the ones forsaking the faith first, prior to the king committing the abomination and prior to Antiochus. That may very well happen in the future with the Antichrist. The Jews may adopt the Gentile practices of the Turkish

Syrian Antichrist willingly and on their own prior to the abomination since every other aspect has followed the historic account. Many say that the Jews will never accept a foreign non-Jewish Antichrist. But it has happened before, and it is likely that it will happen again.

Josephus, the historian, then tells what happened when the abomination was set up.

> The king went up to Jerusalem and by pretending to offer peace, overcame the city by treachery. But on this occasion, he did not spare even those who admitted him because of the wealth of the temple, but through greed he saw much gold in the temple and an array of very costly dedicatory offerings of other kinds and for the sake of taking this as spoil, he went so far as to violate the treaty which he had made with them. And so, he stripped the temple carrying out the vessels of God, the golden lampstands and the golden altar, and the table, and other altars, and not even forbearing to take the curtains which were made of fine linen and scarlet. He also emptied the Temple of its hidden treasures and left nothing at all behind, thereby throwing the Jews into deep mourning. Antiquity of the Jews (XII.5.4)

Notice that greed was an overwhelming motivation in the abomination then and likely will be again in the future. Josephus further tells us that Antiochus stopped the sacrifices for three and a half years, just like the Antichrist will in the future. In Daniel 9:27 it says that the sacrifices are stopped in the midpoint of seven years or at three and a half years. And in Revelation 11:2 it says that the holy place or temple is trampled for forty-two months. Again, this is about three and a half years, just like the original Antiochus account. Josephus continued:

> And when the king had built an idol altar upon God's altar, he slew swine upon it, and so offered a sacrifice

neither according to the law, nor the Jewish religious worship in that country. Antiquities of the Jews (XII.5.4)

This event was known as "the abomination of desolation" until the time of Jesus that is. Now we know an even greater event is coming and that this was just a foreshadowing of that future event. And immediately after this, Antiochus began a great persecution of the Jews.

> The books of the law, which they found, they tore to pieces and burned with fire. Where the book of the covenant was found in the possession of any one, or if anyone adhered to the law, the decree of the king condemned them to death. They kept using violence against Israel, against those found month after month in the cities. And on the twenty-fifth day of the month, they offered sacrifice on the altar which was the altar of burnt offering. According to the decree, they put to death the women who had their children circumcised, and their families and those who circumcised them; and they hung the infants from their mothers' necks. 1 Maccabees 1:56-61

Jesus tells us in Matthew 24:21 that in the same way, after the future abomination of desolation, a great tribulation or persecution of God's people will break out, but this time it will be one that affects the whole world and not just the nation of Israel. Maccabees details the resistance to the persecution that happened in the 2nd century BC.

> Then the king's officers who were enforcing the apostasy came to the city of Mo'de-in to make them offer sacrifice…. a Jew came forward in the sight of all to offer sacrifices upon the altar in Mo'de-in, according to the king's command. When Mattathi'as saw it, he burned with zeal and his heart was stirred. He gave vent to righteous anger; he ran and killed him upon the altar.

At the same time he killed the kings official who was forcing them to sacrifice, and he tore down the altar. Thus he burned with zeal for the law, as Phin'ehas did against Zimri the son of Salu. Then Mattathi'as cried out in the city with a loud voice, saying: "Let everyone who is zealous for the law and supports the covenant come out with me!" And he and his sons fled to the hills and left all that they had in the city. 1 Maccabees 2:15, 23-28

This also exactly parallels Jesus' command that in the future, those who refuse the Antichrist are to run to the mountains.

When ye therefore shall see the abomination of desolation, spoken of by Daniel the prophet, stand in the holy place, (whoso readeth, let him understand:) Then let them which be in Judaea flee into the mountains: Matthew 24:15-16

The parallels are clear, and it is why Hanukkah and the Hanukkah account is such an excellent source for those wanting to know what the end times will be like.

Mattathi'as' son Judah Maccabee then led the revolt against Antiochus, and after many battles in which they were greatly outnumbered, he finally defeated Antiochus and rededicated the Temple. That rededication is what is celebrated at Hanukkah. Here is how Maccabees records it:

He chose blameless priests devoted to the law, and they cleansed the sanctuary and removed the defiled stones to an unclean place. They deliberated what to do about the altar of burnt offering, which had been profaned. And they thought it best to tear it down, lest it bring reproach upon them, for the Gentiles had defiled it. So they tore down the altar, and stored the stones in a convenient place on the temple hill until there should come **a prophet** to tell them what to do with them. Then they took unhewn stones, as the law directs, and built a new altar like the former one. They also rebuilt the sanctuary and the interior of the temple, and consecrated the courts. They made new holy vessels, and brought the lampstand, the altar of incense, and the table into the temple. Then they burned incense on the altar and lighted the lamps of the lampstand, and these gave light in the temple. Maccabees 4:42-50

So, if every other aspect of the Hanukkah account is paralleled by future events, will this one be also? Will Jesus be the Prophet described here? Although he is the Messiah, the Jews of this era sometimes referred to the Messiah as the "Prophet that was greater than Moses". Will he show the priests where the old original altar stones are hidden and reconstruct the altar with them? It is certainly something to consider.

And, of course, the menorah or Jewish candelabra brings light to the Temple. Hanukkah revolves around the menorah oil. In the parable of the ten virgins recorded in Matthew 25, oil for their lamps is what determined the difference between the wise virgins and the foolish virgins. The miracle of the oil that did not run out for eight days is the most famous part of the Hanukkah story. Yet, there is nothing in Maccabees about it and nothing in Josephus. It is a rabbinic fable only. It could be true, but not necessarily. So, when celebrating Hanukkah, it is important to stress the rededication aspect. We are the temple of God on earth after all, and we use this temple to rededicate ourselves to the Lord, to keep our lamps burning, just like the wise virgins.

> Let your loins be girded about, and your lights burning; And ye yourselves like unto men that wait for their lord, when he will return from the wedding; that when he cometh and knocketh, they may open unto him immediately. Luke 12:35-36

Although its importance historically is undeniable, Hanukkah is just as critical in determining the timing of future prophetic end time events, especially in relation to the Third Jewish Temple. As noted earlier, Hanukkah may be the secret to understanding the mysterious number of days found in Daniel 12 and Revelation 11, including the numbers 1260, 1290, and 1335. The difference between 1335 days and 1260 days is exactly 75 days, and interestingly, there are exactly 75 days between the holidays of Yom Kippur and Hanukkah. So, Hanukkah is a very important holiday, and if Hanukkah actually is the 1335th day found in Daniel, that would aid in the timing of the reinstitution of the Temple sacrifices.

In the book of Daniel, there is another cryptic verse concerning the number "2300". It discusses how long is the vision concerning the regular burnt offering, the transgression that makes desolate, and the giving over the sanctuary and the host to be trampled. It states that these things would last for 2300 evenings and mornings.

> Then I heard one saint speaking, and another saint said unto that certain saint which spake, How long shall be the vision concerning the daily sacrifice, and the transgression of desolation, to give both the sanctuary and the host to be trodden under foot? And he said unto me, Unto two thousand and three hundred days; then shall the sanctuary be cleansed. Daniel 8:13-14

It appears that the 2300 evenings and mornings signify 2300 consecutive days. These consecutive evening and morning sacrifices in the Temple were what was known as the regular sacrifice. So, 2300 evening and mornings refer to 2300 days, and this time period marks three things: (1) the starting of the regular burnt offering, (2) the abomination of desolation which then takes away the sacrifice, and (3) the period that the sanctuary is trampled by the Gentiles before being cleansed during Hanukkah. That would mean that 2300 days before Hanukkah, the Temple sacrifices are reinstituted. In between those two events, the abomination of desolation occurs.

Assuming that the timeline outlined earlier is correct and that the year 2036 marks the final Hanukkah (Kislev 25 or December 15, 2036), then the sacrifices would be started 2300 days before this on August 29, 2030. This date matches Elul 1 on the Jewish calendar, which is the beginning of the Season of Repentance and also, amazingly to the precise date, corresponds exactly to 1960 years from when the Temple sacrifices ceased after the destruction of the Temple by the Romans on August 30, 70 AD.

In order for the sacrifices to be restarted, a temple or at least a temporary tabernacle would have to be in place. If the rebuilding of the Temple were to start at the beginning of the 70th Week, when a peace agreement was signed on Rosh Hashanah September 10, 2029, this would provide a time period of 353 days, or nearly one year, in which to build the Temple and begin the daily sacrifices. Chaim Richmond, who is the head of the Temple Institute, has estimated it will only take one year to construct the Temple based on the plans they have. This would also provide time for the red heifer sacrifice to be performed on Shabbat Parah, which falls on March 23, 2030, and would afford time for the ashes to be ready for use in the purification of the priests and the Temple.

There are other interpretations of the 2300-day prophecy that have been proposed. One possible explanation notes that the 2300 days are the total and exact number of days that the sanctuary is "trampled underfoot" by Gentiles. The Temple was made desolate by Antiochus IV Epiphanes from 168BC to 165BC. This desolation or trampling underfoot of the Temple by Antiochus in 168BC was said to last exactly three years or thirty-six months. Judah Maccabee cleansed the Temple on the three-year anniversary of its defilement according to Josephus. Twenty-three hundred days is seventy-eight lunar months (29.5 days per lunar month). Subtracting thirty-six months, i.e., the time that Antiochus defiled the Temple, from seventy-eight months leaves forty-two months remaining for the Temple to yet be trampled on by the Gentiles, which is the number of months that Revelation gives for the Gentiles to tread underfoot the Temple in the 70th Week of Daniel.

But the court which is without the temple leave out, and measure it not; for it is given unto the Gentiles: and the holy city shall they tread under foot forty and two months. Revelation 11:2

So, using this explanation of the 2300-day prophecy, the Temple will be trampled again by the Antichrist for forty-two months beginning at the midpoint of the 70th Week at Passover. And using the year 2029 as the beginning of the 70th Week, the abomination of desolation or the defilement of the Temple by the Antichrist would begin on April 30, 2033 and conclude on Rosh Hashanah, September 22, 2036 when Jesus proclaims His kingdom.

CONCLUSION

Eventually, there will have been four temples, the first two of which were destroyed long ago, and the last two are still future: (1) Solomon's Temple, (2) the Second Temple (aka Herod's Temple), (3) the Third Temple (the Temple of the 70th Week), and (4) the Millennial Temple. It seems clear that a third physical Jewish temple will be built and be present during the last 70th Week of Daniel. The only reason for a rebuilt Temple is to perform Old Testament ordinances, which include animal sacrifices. It is true that this is unnecessary for salvation because of Jesus Christ's ultimate and personal sacrifice. But remember that the 70th Week of Daniel specifically applies to the Jews—and the 70th Week is still in the future. It is only near the end of the 70th Week that the Jews realize that Jesus Christ has fulfilled this prophecy and that Jesus is the Son of God.

So, this Third Temple will satisfy one of the purposes of the Temple, to facilitate the offering of the required sacrifices, providing a way to purify the Israelites in order to allow them to be in the presence of a Holy God. However, it will not satisfy the main purpose of the Temple and that is to be a dwelling place for God to "tabernacle" with man.

The rebuilding of the Temple may be authorized and supervised by the Two Witnesses, possibly arriving on Cheshvan 29 rather than the traditional day of Passover. The daily sacrifices will then be reinstituted after the red heifer sacrifice on either Shabbat Parah or Nisan 1. The Antichrist will desecrate the Temple, likely on a Passover, and the Temple will be trodden under by the Gentiles for forty-two months before Jesus comes to reclaim His kingdom. The Temple will then be cleansed on Hanukkah, Kislev 25.

The book of Zechariah states that Christ ("the Branch") will build the Millennial Temple. We know that it is the Millennial Temple because Christ will rule and reign during that time period.

> And speak unto him, saying, Thus speaketh the LORD of hosts, saying, Behold the man whose name is The BRANCH; and he shall grow up out of his place, and he shall build the temple of the LORD: Even he shall build the temple of the LORD; and he shall bear the glory, and shall sit and rule upon his throne; and he shall be a priest upon his throne: and the counsel of peace shall be between them both. Zechariah 6:12-13

While a fourth temple, Ezekiel's Temple, will be present during the Millennium, no temple will be needed in New Jerusalem, since God Himself will be present, fulfilling His ultimate purpose, to dwell with man.

> And I saw no temple therein: for the Lord God Almighty and the Lamb are the temple of it. Rev 21:22

This, then, will be the ultimate fulfillment of God's desire to dwell with man, not just His shekinah glory but God Himself tabernacling with mankind.

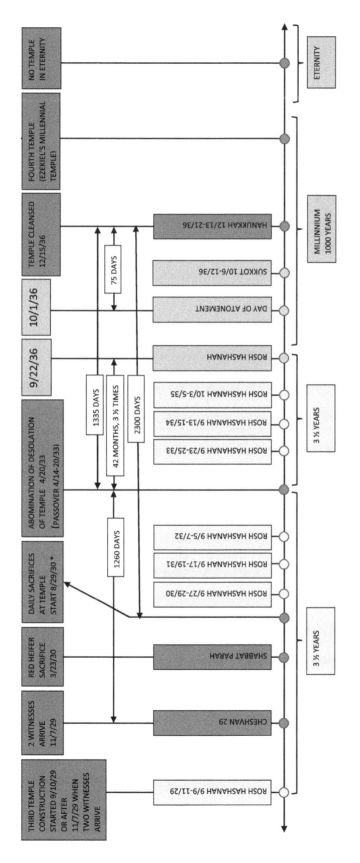

THE TEMPLE TIMELINE
2029-2036

*8/29/30 is exactly 1960 years from the destruction of the 2nd Temple when the daily sacrifices ceased on 8/30/70 AD

CHAPTER 8

The Second Coming of Christ

L ike much of eschatology, the topic of the second coming of Christ is surrounded with various opinions and disagreements. Especially controversial is whether the second advent occurs in one moment at a single event or is a series of events. As a result, there is much confusion regarding about those events associated with the Second Coming including the Rapture, the Day of the Lord, and the White Horse Return of Christ. While some conclude that these events are either the same exact event or at least overlap in time, it is the assertion here that these are three separate events that happen sequentially, each dealing primarily with a separate group of people. As seen earlier, God is dealing in the end times with three sets of people: the Church, the Jews, and the Gentiles. The premise here is that these events are separate actions of Christ where the Rapture concerns His coming for the Church; the Day of the Lord involves His coming for the Jews; and the White Horse Return of Revelation 19 entails His coming for the Gentiles. It is the sum total of these three acts of Christ occurring sequentially over a period of time (about one and a half years) that comprise his Second Coming.

These events will be shown to be clearly different and distinct actions. Although many Bible scholars believe that Jesus' Second Coming is a one-time event, it will be seen that just as Jesus' first coming included many events, the Second Coming of Christ will also include multiple events, including the Rapture which begins his second coming followed by the Day of the Lord. The final event in the Second Coming occurs after the end of the 70th week of Daniel, where Christ comes riding on a white horse to fight the battle of Armageddon, concluding His Second Coming and marking the start of the Millennium.

THE RAPTURE- CHRIST COMING FOR THE CHURCH

Again, many consider the coming (or the Greek term *parousia*) of Christ to be a single event. *Parousia* is a technical expression to denote the arrival or visit of a king or emperor. Every use of *parousia* in the New Testament refers to the Second Coming of Christ, except the one case in which it refers to the coming of the "Day of God" (2 Peter 3:12). The word *parousia* is found in the following verses: Matthew 24:3, 27, 37, 39; 1 Corinthians 15:23; 1 Thessalonians 2:19; 3:13; 4:15; 5:23; 2 Thessalonians 2:1,8,9; James 5:7,8; 2 Peter 1:16; 3:4,12; 1 John 2:28, and in each of these verses, it denotes the coming of Christ for the Church. So, in context, *parousia* signifies not only Christ's return but specifically his return for the Church at the Rapture.

The Rapture refers to the sudden, taking-away of believers from Earth to Heaven. The Rapture is a time of resurrection or bodily translation for believers (dead and alive) in Jesus Christ. The resurrected bodies are eternal—never subject to death, decay, disease, depression, etc. The idea of the Rapture is found throughout the New Testament. The Greek word used in 1Thessalonians 4:17 to describe the Rapture is *harpazo* (pronounced har-PAHD-zo) which means "forcibly snatch away" or "great snatch" [Missler, 2006]—or simply, "caught up" [Hitchcock, 2010].[3]

> But I would not have you to be ignorant, brethren, concerning them which are asleep, that ye sorrow not, even as others which have no hope For if we believe

that Jesus died and rose again, even so them also which sleep in Jesus will God bring with him. For this we say unto you by the word of the Lord, that we which are alive and remain unto the coming of the Lord shall not prevent them which are asleep. For the Lord himself shall descend from heaven with a shout, with the voice of the archangel, and with the trump of God: and the dead in Christ shall rise first: Then we which are alive and remain shall be **caught up** *(harpazo)* together with them in the clouds, to meet the Lord in the air: and so shall we ever be with the Lord. Wherefore comfort one another with these words. 1 Thessalonians 4:13-18

The Greek word *harpazo* appears fourteen times in the New Testament—in a total of seven different books of the New Testament. The English word *rapture* comes from *rapiemur* or *rapturo* which is a Latin translation of the Greek word *harpazo*. Recall that the New Testament was originally written in Greek. The Latin Vulgate was the only Bible used by Western civilization for twelve hundred years. It was the Bible that was in common use before the King James Version of 1611. *Vulgate* means "common language" of the people. Thus, the Latin Vulgate Bible contains the word for *rapture*. Although the actual word is not used in English translations, nevertheless, the concept has been in the Bible since the New Testament was written and as will be seen, even before in the Old Testament.[3]

In 1 Thessalonians, note the phrases "dead in Christ", "caught up" (*harpazo*), "we who are still alive", and "in the air". The "dead in Christ" refers only to Christians, those who have put their faith **in Christ**. Others who are righteous, including the Old Testament faithful and post-Rapture believers, are resurrected later during Christ's Second Coming. Thus, the resurrection of the saved takes place in stages. The resurrection of the unsaved dead, however, takes place in one event at the Great White Throne Judgment. This will be discussed in more detail in the chapter on "Judgments".

Thus, this Scripture teaches that there will be a "caught up" or "snatching away" event, which is called "the Rapture". The idea is that anyone, since the resurrection of Christ, who has placed their faith in Him for the forgiveness of their sins will be "caught up" to be with Him when He comes for His church. The dead in Christ will rise first. Then those who are alive at that time will be changed into incorruptible bodies in the twinkling of an eye.

> Behold, I shew you a mystery; We shall not all sleep, but we shall all be changed, In a moment, in the twinkling of an eye, at the last trump: for the trumpet shall sound, and the dead shall be raised incorruptible, and we shall be changed. 1 Corinthians 15:51-52

In so doing, God will spare Christians from His eschatological wrath as He has promised.

> And to wait for his Son from heaven, whom he raised from the dead, even Jesus, which **delivered us from the wrath to come**. 1 Thessalonians 1:10

> But of the times and the seasons, brethren, ye have no need that I write unto you. For yourselves know perfectly that the day of the Lord so cometh as a thief in the night. For when they shall say, Peace and safety; then sudden destruction cometh upon them, as travail upon a woman with child; and they shall not escape. But ye, brethren, are not in darkness, that that day should overtake you as a thief. Ye are all the children of light, and the children of the day: we are not of the night, nor of darkness. Therefore let us not sleep, as do others; but let us watch and be sober. For they that sleep sleep in the night; and they that be drunken are drunken in the night. But let us, who are of the day, be sober, putting on the breastplate of faith and love;

and for an helmet, the hope of salvation. **For God hath not appointed us to wrath**, but to obtain salvation by our Lord Jesus Christ, Who died for us, that, whether we wake or sleep, we should live together with him. 1 Thessalonians 5:1-10

Rapture in the New and Old Testament[4]

The key passages which explain the Rapture are found throughout the New Testament and include: John 14:1-3; 1Corinthians 15:50-57; 1Thessalonians 4:13-18; 2Thessalonians 2:1-7; and Revelation 7:9-17.

Let not your heart be troubled: ye believe in God, believe also in me. In my Father's house are many mansions: if it were not so, I would have told you. I go to prepare a place for you. And if I go and prepare a place for you, I will come again, and receive you unto myself; that where I am, there ye may be also. John 14:1-3

Now this I say, brethren, that flesh and blood cannot inherit the kingdom of God; neither doth corruption inherit incorruption. Behold, I shew you a mystery; We shall not all sleep, but we shall all be changed, In a moment, in the twinkling of an eye, at the last trump: for the trumpet shall sound, and the dead shall be raised incorruptible, and we shall be changed. For this corruptible must put on incorruption, and this mortal must put on immortality. So when this corruptible shall have put on incorruption, and this mortal shall have put on immortality, then shall be brought to pass the saying that is written, Death is swallowed up in victory. O death, where is thy sting? O grave, where is thy victory? The sting of death is sin; and the strength of sin is the law. But thanks be to God, which giveth us the victory through our Lord Jesus Christ. 1 Corinthians 15:50-57

But I would not have you to be ignorant, brethren, concerning them which are asleep, that ye sorrow not, even as others which have no hope For if we believe that Jesus died and rose again, even so them also which sleep in Jesus will God bring with him. For this we say unto you by the word of the Lord, that we which are alive and remain unto the coming of the Lord shall not prevent them which are asleep. For the Lord himself shall descend from heaven with a shout, with the voice of the archangel, and with the trump of God: and the dead in Christ shall rise first: Then we which are alive and remain shall be caught up together with them in the clouds, to meet the Lord in the air: and so shall we ever be with the Lord. Wherefore comfort one another with these words. 1 Thessalonians 4:13-18

Now we beseech you, brethren, by the coming of our Lord Jesus Christ, and by our gathering together unto him, That ye be not soon shaken in mind, or be troubled, neither by spirit, nor by word, nor by letter as from us, as that the day of Christ is at hand. Let no man deceive you by any means: for that day shall not come, except there come a falling away first, and that man of sin be revealed, the son of perdition; Who opposeth and exalteth himself above all that is called God, or that is worshipped; so that he as God sitteth in the temple of God, shewing himself that he is God. Remember ye not, that, when I was yet with you, I told you these things? And now ye know what withholdeth that he might be revealed in his time. For the mystery of iniquity doth already work: only he who now letteth will let, until he be taken out of the way. 2 Thessalonians 2:1-7

After this I beheld, and, lo, a great multitude, which no man could number, of all nations, and kindreds, and people, and tongues, stood before the throne, and before the Lamb, clothed with white robes, and palms in their hands; And cried with a loud voice, saying, Salvation to our God which sitteth upon the throne, and unto the Lamb. And all the angels stood round about the throne, and about the elders and the four beasts, and fell before the throne on their faces, and worshipped God, Saying, Amen: Blessing, and glory, and wisdom, and thanksgiving, and honour, and power, and might, be unto our God for ever and ever. Amen. And one of the elders answered, saying unto me, What are these which are arrayed in white robes? and whence came they? And I said unto him, Sir, thou knowest. And he said to me, These are they which came out of great tribulation, and have washed their robes, and made them white in the blood of the Lamb. Therefore are they before the throne of God, and serve him day and night in his temple: and he that sitteth on the throne shall dwell among them. They shall hunger no more, neither thirst any more; neither shall the sun light on them, nor any heat. For the Lamb which is in the midst of the throne shall feed them, and shall lead them unto living fountains of waters: and God shall wipe away all tears from their eyes. Rev 7:9-17

So, the concept of the Rapture is clearly defined throughout the New Testament. However, the idea that the Rapture is found neither in the Old Testament nor in the Gospels is such an ingrained idea in many churches that many are probably surprised to learn that, contrary to this opinion, there are over a dozen references to the Rapture in the Old Testament alone. The Rapture was no mystery when Jesus discussed it with his disciples. They knew exactly what he meant. Consider this statement of Jesus:

> In my Father's house are many mansions: if it were not so, I would have told you. I go to prepare a place for you. And if I go and prepare a place for you, I will come again, and receive you unto myself; that where I am, there ye may be also. John 14:2-3

Obviously, this is the Rapture, and just as obviously, it was presented to the disciples twenty years earlier than when Paul wrote about it. The Rapture was not a mystery, and this passage in John is a reference to the Old Testament. In fact, it is a reference to two passages in the Old Testament. But first, consider 1 Corinthians 15 that seems to say that the Rapture is a mystery.

> Behold, I shew you a mystery; We shall not all sleep, but we shall all be changed, In a moment, in the twinkling of an eye, at the last trump: for the trumpet shall sound, and the dead shall be raised incorruptible, and we shall be changed. 1 Corinthians 15:51-52

Paul does indicate a mystery, but the mystery Paul is describing here is not the Rapture. The mystery that Paul describes is that believers will be changed just prior to the Rapture, changed into resurrection bodies. That is what happens in a twinkling of an eye and not the Rapture. Even though Paul states that this change into resurrection bodies was a mystery, there is a passage in the Old Testament Prophets that describes what the resurrection bodies will be like. In fact, most if not all the New Testament rapture passages have a reference back in the Old Testament just as the Prophet Amos tells us.

> Surely the Lord God will do nothing, but he revealeth his secret unto his servants the prophets. Amos 3:7

The Old Testament passages prepare for what the New Testament reveals more fully. This Bible practice is something known as *progressive revelation*, which means that as time went on, more and more information about a subject became apparent. That is seen with Messiah Jesus where the Old Testament refers to Him throughout its pages, but it was not until the New Testament that all these references to the Messiah finally seemed to make sense. The same is true of the Rapture. The Bible reveals the who, what, when, where, and how of the Rapture in the Old Testament. And if all these references are put together, it is a fairly complete and convincing picture. But each passage on its own is not as detailed as 1 Thessalonians 4:16-17, which finally provides the definitive rapture passage in the New Testament.

From Genesis and throughout the Prophets, God revealed that he would protect His chosen people prior to punishing the wicked which is known as "the wrath of God". That relates to **who** is raptured. These references are clear that the protection of the righteous happens before the punishment of the wicked, providing the information on **when** the rapture would occur. A few of the references are clear that the Rapture takes the righteous all the way into heaven before the throne of the Father, which is remarkable because even the New Testament is vague on this point. That informs us **where** the rapture happens, and one or two of the references tell us **how** the Rapture takes place. They imply that angels gather the saints, but again, not all the New Testament passages are clear on that point either. In total, the references to the rapture from the Old Testament paint a picture, so that Bible literate Jews of the New Testament, including the disciples, were not at all surprised by Paul's or Jesus' rapture passages.

Historically, there were two examples of the Rapture in the Old Testament. Both Enoch and Elijah were raptured in representations of what the eventual eschatological rapture would be like. Enoch's translation is described in very simple terms.

And Enoch walked with God: and he was not; for God **took** him. Genesis 5:24

This word *took* actually means "translated" or "transferred" in the Greek. So, God translated him or transferred Enoch. The book of Hebrews gives us a more detailed description of this.

By faith Enoch was taken up so that he would not see death; and he was not found because God took him up; for before he was **taken up** *(metatithemi)*, he was attested to have been pleasing to God. Hebrews 11:5 (NASB)

The Greek word *taken* also has the meaning of "to transform", and it was used of Jesus in his transfiguration and by Paul in this passage about resurrection bodies.

For our conversation is in heaven; from whence also we look for the Saviour, the Lord Jesus Christ: Who shall change *(metatithemi)* our vile body, that it may be fashioned like unto his glorious body, according to the working whereby he is able even to subdue all things unto himself. Philippians 3:20-21

And the reason for Enoch's translation or rapture is that he was righteous. Also, he was taken **up**, which strongly implies that he was taken to heaven. The exact means of the Rapture was not given, however.

Some Jewish traditions say that Enoch was born on—and later was translated (or raptured) on—the Day of Pentecost (Sivan 6). The Day of Pentecost is also called the Feast of Weeks or Shavuot. It might be that Enoch is a foreshadowing or type of the Church. Recall that the Christian Church was also born on the Day of Pentecost. This also might suggest a future rapture on the Day of Pentecost, as discussed earlier regarding the end times timeline.

The other person who was raptured in the Old Testament is Elijah, and in this example, the means of his rapture was also given.

And it came to pass, as they still went on, and talked, that, behold, there appeared a chariot of fire, and horses of fire, and parted them both asunder; and Elijah went up by a whirlwind into heaven. And Elisha saw it, and he cried, My father, my father, the chariot of Israel, and the horsemen thereof. And he saw him no more: and he took hold of his own clothes, and rent them in two pieces. 2 Kings 2:11-12

Elijah seems to have been taken by a chariot of fire and its horsemen in a whirlwind. In this example, the horsemen were most likely angels. This is completely consistent with the New Testament where the rapture or "gathering together" uses angels as Jesus' agents of gathering. Consider the passage in John:

In my Father's house are many mansions: if it were not so, I would have told you. I go to prepare a place for you. And if I go and prepare a place for you, I will come again, and receive *(paralambano)* you unto myself; that where I am, there ye may be also. John 14:2-3

The word *paralambano* in this passage translated as "receive you unto myself" is the same Greek root word that Jesus uses in Matthew for *taken*:

Two women shall be grinding at the mill; the one shall be taken *(paralambano)*, and the other left. Matthew 24:40

The "taken" are taken into heaven just like Elijah was. Although these examples did not reveal God's plan to translate all the righteous someday into heaven, they explained to the ancient Jews that God was in the business of rapturing the righteous. After all, it had happened before.

The Lord then began to systematically reveal the details of the Rapture to his prophets. Isaiah was one who received numerous prophecies about the Rapture. The most famous one speaks of the same rooms that Jesus mentioned in John 14.

Thy dead men shall live, together with my dead body shall they arise. Awake and sing, ye that dwell in dust: for thy dew is as the dew of herbs, and the earth shall cast out the dead. Come, my people, enter thou into **thy**

chambers, and shut thy doors about thee: hide thyself as it were for a little moment, until the indignation be overpast. For, behold, the LORD cometh out of his place to punish the inhabitants of the earth for their iniquity: the earth also shall disclose her blood, and shall no more cover her slain. Isaiah 26:19-21

This passage lists the three events that occur on the day of the Rapture, all in the correct order: first, the resurrection of the dead; second, the entering into the rooms that Jesus talked about in his father's house; and then third, after the gathering, God will punish the wicked inhabitants of the earth. This passage reveals **who** is raptured. God calls those he raptures "my people". It shows **when** the rapture occurs, which is prior to the punishment of the wicked by the wrath of God. Finally, it shows **where** the rapture happens. God's people are taken into their rooms in heaven until the wrath of God is over. But it does not show **how** the gathering transpires. Perhaps Paul happened to consider this passage when writing 1 Thessalonians 4 since almost assuredly the dead in Christ will rise first, followed by their gathering together with the survivors of the great tribulation into the air to meet the Lord.

The Prophet Joel provided a similar prophecy.

The sun shall be turned into darkness, and the moon into blood, before the great and terrible day of the LORD come. And it shall come to pass, that whosoever shall call on the name of the LORD shall be delivered *(malat)*: for in mount Zion and in Jerusalem shall be deliverance, as the LORD hath said, and in the remnant whom the LORD shall call. Joel 2:31-32

Joel explained that the Rapture involves the righteous survivors of the Great Tribulation. He also gave a more exact timing for the Rapture which occurs after the sun and the moon go dark just as Jesus indicated in Matthew.

> Immediately after the tribulation of those days shall the sun be darkened, and the moon shall not give her light, and the stars shall fall from heaven, and the powers of the heavens shall be shaken: Matthew 24:29

It is then that God's people will escape. Two hundred years after Isaiah and Joel, the Prophet Daniel was given a very similar prophecy as well.

> And at that time shall Michael stand up, the great prince which standeth for the children of thy people: and there shall be a time of trouble, such as never was since there was a nation even to that same time: and at that time thy people shall be delivered *(malat)*, every one that shall be found written in the book. And many of them that sleep in the dust of the earth shall awake, some to everlasting life, and some to shame and everlasting contempt. And they that be wise shall shine as the brightness of the firmament; and they that turn many to righteousness as the stars for ever and ever. Daniel 12:1-3

Daniel was told that the righteous would be delivered. The Hebrew word *malat* translated as "delivered" also means "escape". In fact, it is the identical word used by the prophet Joel. It is the same escape, and it is also timed to happen during the Great Tribulation, the same timing that Joel gave. And like Isaiah, it is linked to the resurrection of the righteous dead. Also, notice in this passage that "the wise shall shine like the brightness of the firmament". This is almost assuredly a reference to the resurrection bodies glowing like the transfigured body of Jesus, for we shall be like him.

The prophet Zephaniah was given two rapture passages.

> Be silent before the Lord God! For the day of the LORD is near, For the LORD has prepared a sacrifice, He has consecrated *(qadas)* His guests. Zephaniah 1:7 (NASB)

Since God is in heaven, His consecrated guests must also be in heaven. The Hebrew word for consecrated here is *qadas* meaning "holy". Who will God make holy on the day of the Lord but the righteous, those who He is about to rapture? Just like Isaiah's prophecy, the rapture happens prior to the Lord's sacrifice or punishment of the wicked, and interestingly, it happens right before the silence in heaven. This is also seen in Revelation 7:9 where the raptured saints arrive in heaven as a great multitude that shocks John when he sees them. This happens just prior to the opening of the 7ᵗʰ seal, and once that seal is opened, there is silence in heaven for half an hour. This is then followed by the trumpet judgments which are the start of the wrath of God, His punishment of the wicked. So, the timing of these rapture events in the short verse of Zephaniah 1:7 confirms the description in Revelation.

Zephaniah then recorded a second rapture passage.

> **Gather yourselves together** *(sunachthete, LXX)*, yea, gather together, O nation not desired; Before the decree bring forth, before the day pass as the chaff, before the fierce anger of the LORD come upon you, before the day of the LORD's anger come upon you. Seek ye the LORD, all ye meek of the earth, which have wrought his judgment; seek righteousness, seek meekness: it may be ye shall be **hid** in the day of the LORD's anger. Zephaniah 2:1-3

Again, God tells Zephaniah that the righteous will be "gathered together". This is the identical Greek root word Jesus uses for the gathering together of the elect or the Rapture in Matthew.

> And he shall send his angels with a great sound of a trumpet, and they shall **gather together** *(episunago)* his elect from the four winds, from one end of heaven to the other. Matthew 24:31

Also notice that the righteous are hidden **prior** to the wrath of God. All the passages seen so far have had this similar message. There are several passages that speak of the disappearance of the righteous after the Rapture. The prophet Micah was speaking prophetically as if he was one enduring the wrath of God when he wrote:

> The good man is perished out of the earth: and there is none upright among men: they all lie in wait for blood; they hunt every man his brother with a net. Micah 7:2

Where did they go but in the Rapture? Psalms has an identical description.

> Help, Lord, for no one is faithful anymore; those who are loyal have **vanished** from the human race. Psalm 12:1 (NIV)

The choice of the word *vanish* gives a very appropriate depiction of the Rapture. A Psalm of Asaph also provides a picture of the Rapture.

> Our God shall come, and shall not keep silence: a fire shall devour before him, and it shall be very tempestuous round about him. He shall call to the heavens from above, and to the earth, that he may judge his people. **Gather** my saints together unto me; those that have made a covenant with me by sacrifice. Psalm 50:3-5

God judges first, and then gathers His people to Himself. That is a description of the Rapture, and then, of course, He pours out His tempest and fire after He gathers them. In a Psalm of David, the exact same thing is seen.

> The Lord also thundered in the heavens, and the Highest gave his voice; hail stones and coals of fire. Yea, he sent out his arrows, and scattered them; and he shot out lightnings, and discomfited them. Then the

channels of waters were seen, and the foundations of the world were discovered at thy rebuke, O Lord, at the blast of the breath of thy nostrils. He sent from above, he took me, he drew me out of many waters. He delivered me from my strong enemy, and from them which hated me: for they were too strong for me. Psalm 18:13-17

Notice that God took him and drew him out of many waters, delivering him from hailstones and coals of fire. This is what happens at the first trumpet in Revelation when God's wrath begins. Another passage from the Psalms, a psalm usually read in the month of Elul which is a time of repentance, alludes to the Rapture.

For in the time of trouble he shall hide me in his pavilion: in the secret of his tabernacle shall he hide me; he shall set me up upon a rock. And now shall mine head be lifted up above mine enemies round about me: therefore will I offer in his tabernacle sacrifices of joy; I will sing, yea, I will sing praises unto the Lord. Psalm 27:5-6

This describes a secret place of God's tabernacle where He will lift us above our enemies. In Revelation the raptured saints are seen in heaven immediately after the Rapture.

For this reason, they are before the throne of God; and they serve Him day and night in His temple; and He who sits on the throne will spread His tabernacle over them. Revelation 7:15 (NASB)

So, the imagery in Psalms and Revelation is the same.

The Rapture is seen in the Gospels as well as the Old Testament. In fact, there are two analogies of the Rapture that Jesus discussed in the Gospels: (1) Noah escaping the flood, and (2) Lot escaping Sodom and Gomorrah. In these events, not everyone who is given the chance to escape did escape. Lot's wife turned back and was turned into a pillar of salt, and Jesus warned us to remember Lot's wife. Why would He warn those in the Church to remember Lot's wife? Is there a chance of missing out on the escape, missing out on the Rapture? And what happens to one who misses out on the Rapture?

Left Behind, the Church after the Rapture

Will many of those attending our churches right now be left behind at the Rapture? Is Jesus' prophetic letter to the Church of Laodicea actually addressed to a massive group today sitting in church pews thinking that they are going with Jesus at the Rapture but in fact will be left to endure the most difficult time in human history, the wrath of God? And how can you know which side of this divide you are on?

Despite what our modern Christian culture teaches about the assurance of everyone who has said the sinner's prayer going with Jesus at the Rapture, Jesus Himself paints a very different picture in the Gospels, just as the apostles do in the Epistles and John in Revelation. Many of Jesus' parables and sermons speak of this separation of the righteous from the wicked, but in his teaching, the wicked are not who many imagine. They are not the idolaters, adulterers, or murderers. In the parable of the ten virgins (Matthew 25), all ten virgins are looking forward to the return of the bridegroom, and they are virgins, trying to keep themselves pure. All ten light their lamps, but only half get into the wedding feast.

In the parable of the Wheat and the Tares (Matthew 13), the weeds look identical to the wheat, who represent the truly saved. That means they look just like a true Christian, and it is not until the harvest when the fruit appears that the reapers, who are angels, know the difference. Even the angels do not know right now. Then the weeds are left behind to be burned while the wheat is taken into the barn.

In the Sermon on the Mount (Matthew 5-7), Jesus instructs that those who hear His words, yet do not put them into practice, will have their house destroyed. Those who hear His words today are those attending churches. They are those sitting in church pews right next to the righteous, fruit-bearing believers. This warning occurs in the same portion of scripture where Jesus gives this other incredible warning.

> Not every one that saith unto me, Lord, Lord, shall enter into the kingdom of heaven; but he that doeth the will of my Father which is in heaven. Many will say to me in that day, Lord, Lord, have we not prophesied in thy name? and in thy name have cast out devils? and in thy name done many wonderful works? And then will I profess unto them, I never knew you: depart from me, ye that work iniquity. Matthew 7:21-23

Jesus rarely spoke of those who were obviously unrighteous but rather focused primarily on the group that heard His words, including those who heard them in those days and those who hear them in churches today. Those who heard His words and did them are the saved, but those who did not act on them are the foolish virgins, the tares, the foolish builders building on the sand.

In Revelation, Jesus wrote to this foolish group in his letter to Laodicea. Jesus outlined the things that will not save. Calling Jesus Lord alone will not save. Doing amazing works in his name will not save. Yet, one thing condemns all these people. They practice or **continually** do unrighteous acts or lawlessness. With that in mind, in His letter to Laodicea, Jesus said:

> I know thy works, that thou art neither cold nor hot: I would thou wert cold or hot. So then because thou art lukewarm, and neither cold nor hot, I will spue thee out of my mouth. Revelation 3:15-16

Jesus divided people into three groups based not only on their faith but also on the deeds that they do. The first group are the "hot", i.e., those who are truly saved. They hear Jesus' words and do them. That is the sign of a true disciple: one who hears the teaching and then puts it into practice. The second group are the "cold", who are worldly and unrighteous and in reality, want nothing to do with Jesus. Jesus referred to this group in his message on the end times.

> Then shall they deliver you up to be afflicted, and shall kill you: and ye shall be hated of all nations for my name's sake. And then shall many be offended, and shall betray one another, and shall hate one another. And many false prophets shall rise, and shall deceive many. And because iniquity shall abound, the love of many shall wax **cold**. Matthew 24:9-12

This will in all likelihood include those who depart from the truth or fall away in the end times as stated by Paul.

> Let no man deceive you by any means: for that day shall not come, except there come a falling away first, and that man of sin be revealed, the son of perdition; 2 Thessalonians 2:3

> Now the Spirit speaketh expressly, that in the latter times some shall depart from the faith, giving heed to seducing spirits, and doctrines of devils; 1 Timothy 4:1

A third group are the "lukewarm", and although this group was a primary focus of Jesus' teaching, they are rarely discussed by our pastors. This last group, the lukewarm, are the tares, the foolish virgins, and the foolish builders. They are those who hear Jesus' words and yet do not put them into practice. They sit in church on Shabbat and Sundays or may be in a small group. They may be in your own family, or you may be lukewarm yourself. That is what makes Jesus' teaching critical to understand, because he promises to spit them out of his mouth. In fact, the Greek word in the original text actually implies that he will vomit them out of his mouth.

So, Jesus desires that they were either hot or cold. Why would Jesus prefer that they were unrighteous to being lukewarm? Well, the hot obviously will deserve their reward, and the cold obviously will deserve their punishment, having lived their lives in opposition to Jesus. But the lukewarm did not live in outright rebellion. They attended church. They heard sermons, and they thought they would be raptured. They thought they were saved, but they were not. They may have believed in Jesus, but they had not made Him Lord of their lives and been obedient to His commandments.

Jesus' letter to these lukewarm Christians, the Church of Laodicea, examines the whole idea of cheap grace. It observes how a person can attend a church and can say the sinner's prayer but still be absolutely lost. Many interpret the letter to Laodicea as a warning to the actual church in the first century while others consider it to be directed to one of the church ages, perhaps referring to our modern 21st century society. A more recent explanation of Revelation's letters to the churches considers that the letter to Laodicea is to those left behind at the future rapture. The answer as to which interpretation is correct may be that it refers to all three, with the primary focus being on the significance to the future church that appears after the Rapture.

In fact, each of the letters in Revelation 2 and 3 is addressed to the Church that will go through the 70th week of Daniel. Each letter provides information to help the end time church know how to overcome and endure the tribulation that it will experience during those apocalyptic events. The letters to the seven churches of Revelation, then, are prophetic instructions to Christians who will be enduring each of the seven seals of Revelation, purifying the Church prior to the Rapture as well as advising the post-Rapture church.

Each of the seven churches relates specifically to one of the seals in the 70th week of Daniel. The first letter to Ephesus concerns deception by false messiahs and prophets, the first seal. Smyrna involves the beginning of persecution, which corresponds to the second seal where there is bloodshed, war and chaos. Pergamum relates to economic collapse and famine with the return of Satan's throne and the mark of the beast, the third seal. Thyatira is about the abomination of desolation, death and the end time pestilence, the beginning of the Great Tribulation, the fourth seal. Sardis has to do with the martyrdom (physical death) and apostasy (spiritual death) of the saints in the Great Tribulation, the fifth seal. And the famous letter to Philadelphia is about the celestial signs and Rapture that takes place after the 6th seal. The seventh and final letter then concerns the wrath of God that falls upon the earth and those churchgoers who do not go with Jesus in the Rapture, the Church of Laodicea.

Correlation Between 7 Seals and 7 Letters to the End Time Churches

Seals in Matthew 24 & 25	Seals in Revelation 6-8	7 Churches in Rev 2 & 3
1-Deception 24:4-5	Conquering by deception 6:1-2	Ephesus- false prophets 2:2
2-War 24:6-7	Take peace; conflict 6:3-4	Smyrna- beginning of persecution 2:10
3-Famine 24:7	Scarcity 6:5-6	Pergamum- will be given hidden manna 2:17
4-Beginning of birth pains- 24:7-8	Widespread death 6:7-8	Thyatira-will kill with death 2:22
5-Tribulation 24:9	Martyrdom 6:9-11	Sardis- martyrdom in great tribulation 3:1-6
6-Cosmic signs before rapture 24:29	Cosmic disturbance before rapture 6:12-14	Philadelphia- kept from hour of trial by rapture 3:10
7-Faithful/evil servant; wise/foolish virgins 24:36-25:13	Silence 8:1	Laodicea- lukewarm; left behind 3:14-22

But why is Laodicea called a church at all, if its parishioners are left behind at the Rapture? The reason is that they were churchgoers. There is a difference between a pew sitter or a churchgoer and a true Christian, even though they all attend the same church. Both hear the same teaching, but only the true Christian obeys that teaching and puts it into practice.

So, before considering Laodicea and Jesus' instructions to the church that is left behind, take a moment to think about the bigger topic. What does is mean to be saved? Is it just saying a prayer once in your life and then continuing to act just like the world around us for the rest of your life? Here is what the Billy Graham Evangelistic Association says about how a person is saved:

> We cannot earn salvation; we are saved by God's grace when we have faith in his Son Jesus Christ. All you have to do is believe you are a sinner, that Christ died for your sins, and ask His forgiveness. Then turn from your sins- that is called repentance. BGEA

That is what faith is: belief combined with a turning from your sin. The problem many have in modern Christian churches is that they leave off the final part, the turning from sin. Grace is free, but it was not cheap. It cost the life of the most perfect son of God. Yet, many treat that sacrifice as if it was just some kind of "get out of jail free" card. Just say a prayer and get out of punishment in hell with that one prayer. But that is not the way it works. The writer of Hebrews, who some think may have even been Paul, had this to say:

> For if we sin wilfully after that we have received the knowledge of the truth, there remaineth no more sacrifice for sins, But a certain fearful looking for of judgment and fiery indignation, which shall devour the adversaries. Hebrews 10:26-27

So, those who go on in their previous sin, even after saying a sinner's prayer, can expect the fury of fire, the wrath of God. This is a crucial passage of scripture, and it continues:

> He that despised Moses' law died without mercy under two or three witnesses: Of how much sorer punishment, suppose ye, shall he be thought worthy, who hath

trodden under foot the Son of God, and hath counted the blood of the covenant, wherewith he was sanctified, an unholy thing, and hath done despite unto the Spirit of grace? Hebrews 10:28-29

Those who do not turn from sin insult the salvation of our Lord. This passage does not say that we can never sin and be saved, but rather states that if we **willfully** go on sinning in a perpetual pattern, then we were always unsaved. John had this to say:

If we say that we have no sin, we deceive ourselves, and the truth is not in us. If we confess our sins, he is faithful and just to forgive us our sins, and to cleanse us from all unrighteousness. 1 John 1:8-9

John says that all of us sin, and Jesus will forgive us. His blood has the power to save, but He forgives us if we repent. Although this is a famous and often memorized verse, the importance of turning away from sin and keeping Jesus' commandments is emphasized about three. verses later where it states:

And hereby we do know that we know him, if we keep his commandments. He that saith, I know him, and keepeth not his commandments, is a liar, and the truth is not in him. But whoso keepeth his word, in him verily is the love of God perfected: hereby know we that we are in him. 1 John 2:3-5

Not many Christian churches today are teaching this, and the reason might be that it is a whole lot easier to sell cheap grace than it is to sell a grace that requires repentance. This is the reason there is a letter to Laodicea, a letter to churchgoers who are left behind. They may have believed that Jesus was the Son of God and died for the sins of all, but they did not have the faith to act on it when the chips were down. Here's what Jesus' brother James says:

Even so faith, if it hath not works, is dead, being alone. Yea, a man may say, Thou hast faith, and I have works: shew me thy faith without thy works, and I will shew thee my faith by my works. Thou believest that there is one God; thou doest well: the devils also believe, and tremble. James 2:17-19

James is clear that belief alone does not save and that even the demons believe in God and Jesus. One cannot just pray a prayer and think they are saved without demonstrating a changed life. Real faith is living out what one believes. Steven Curtis Chapman, the Christian singer, put it this way:

I've got little Bible magnets on my refrigerator door; And a welcome mat to bless you before I walk across my floor; I got a Jesus bumper sticker and the outline of a fish stuck on my car; And even though this stuff's all well and good, yeah, I cannot help but ask myself: What about the change? What about the difference? What about the grace? What about forgiveness? What about a life that is showing I'm undergoing **the change**? SCC

Unfortunately, it is much easier for our modern churches to sell a cheap grace, one that allows salvation without a change. And that is exactly what many of our churches are doing, and that may be why Jesus indicates that fifty percent of those watching for his return, the five foolish virgins, will not be going with Him in the Rapture. Those are the ones Jesus wrote to and about in the letter to the Church of Laodicea.

To avoid the hour of trial after missing the Rapture, Jesus' sixth letter in Revelation, the letter to Philadelphia, concludes with a famous passage.

Because thou hast kept the word of my patience, I also will keep thee from the hour of temptation, which shall come upon all the world, to try them that dwell upon the earth. Revelation 3:10

There is a lot of controversy about what this trial is, but what very few realize is that the letter for Laodicea was written to those undergoing that trial. In fact, the word *Laodicea* means "trial of the people". They are the ones undergoing the trial. They are those who are not kept from it. And Jesus is the star witness who testifies that the foolish virgins of the Church of Laodicea never knew Him. That is repeated twice in the gospels.

> And then will I profess unto them, I never knew you: depart from me, ye that work iniquity. Matthew 7:23

> But he answered and said, Verily I say unto you, I know you not. Matthew 25:12

But Jesus is also their defense counsel.

> I counsel thee to buy of me gold tried in the fire, that thou mayest be rich; and white raiment, that thou mayest be clothed, and that the shame of thy nakedness do not appear; and anoint thine eyes with eyesalve, that thou mayest see. Revelation 3:18

So, the "wrath of God" time period will be a time of trial for those who are lukewarm. This means that they still have a chance to repent. Those left behind can still be saved. And later in Revelation there is direct evidence for this. Immediately prior to the return of Jesus, to rapture the wise virgins, in Revelation 14, a voice from heaven booms across the earth.

> And I heard a voice from heaven saying unto me, Write, Blessed are the dead which **die in the Lord from henceforth**: Yea, saith the Spirit, that they may rest from their labours; and their works do follow them. Revelation 14:13

It is immediately after this that Jesus comes on a cloud and harvests the earth, resurrecting and rapturing the righteous.

> And I looked, and behold a white cloud, and upon the cloud one sat like unto the Son of man, having on his head a golden crown, and in his hand a sharp sickle. And another angel came out of the temple, crying with a loud voice to him that sat on the cloud, Thrust in thy sickle, and reap: for the time is come for thee to reap; for the harvest of the earth is ripe. And he that sat on the cloud thrust in his sickle on the earth; and the earth was reaped. Revelation 14:14-16

Those who are going to die in Christ from then on are not those who have already been resurrected and raptured. Those who "die in the Lord from henceforth" must be some others. Obviously, it is those who are left behind. Since they are "in the Lord", it is clear that they can still repent and still be saved. In the letter to Laodicea, Jesus reinforces this idea.

> As many as I love, I rebuke and chasten: be zealous therefore, and repent. Behold, I stand at the door, and knock: if any man hear my voice, and open the door, I will come in to him, and will sup with him, and he with me. Revelation 3:19-20

What is very interesting in this passage is the mention of a door, the door of heaven. In the parable of the ten virgins, Jesus takes the wise five virgins through the door and into the wedding feast in heaven. But here in this passage, Jesus is offering to come back through the door to those in Laodicea and dine with them on the earth. Those left behind can still be saved, and Jesus will come back to be with them. But they have lost their chance to enter the door into heaven and spend time with the Father before His throne. Jesus concludes this letter speaking about this very throne.

> To him that overcometh will I grant to sit with me in
> my throne, even as I also overcame, and am set down
> with my Father in his throne. Revelation 3:21

So, obviously, there are two thrones, a heavenly one that the Father sits upon and an earthly one that Jesus will sit upon on the earth. And that is all that the Laodicean church is promised. They are to rule and reign with Jesus upon the earth if they overcome but will never enter heaven with the Father. They missed that opportunity when they were left behind at the Rapture.

This idea of being left behind at the Rapture creates other questions. For instance, when does the Rapture occur? How long is the period after the Rapture that the foolish virgins must endure? And what events happen during this hour of trial?

Timing of the Rapture

The timing of the Rapture, of course, is controversial. Many dates have been proposed, and, as has been suggested, the Day of Pentecost is one possibility. A major debate among evangelical Christians, however, is not the specific day, but rather revolves around the timing of the Rapture in relation to the 70th week of Daniel. Most fall into three camps: pretribulation (before the start of the 70th week), post-tribulation (after the end of the 70th week), or prewrath (somewhere in the middle of the 70th week before the start of God's wrath).

1 Thessalonians 4:16-17 clearly indicates that there will be a snatching away of living believers. Thus, there should not be any disagreement about the actual occurrence of the Rapture. In the Gospel of John, Jesus specifically says that He will take believers from the Earth to be with Him in Heaven:

> In my Father's house are many mansions: if it were not
> so, I would have told you. I go to prepare a place for
> you. And if I go and prepare a place for you, I will come

again, and receive you unto myself; that where I am, there ye may be also. John 14:2-3

Another important Scripture passage that is sometimes quoted as a Rapture passage is 1Corinthians 15:51-52. But it does not state whether or not the Rapture is pretribulation. Rather, it simply highlights the fact that at some point in the future, Christ will return and believers who are alive at that time will receive translated (perfected) bodies.

> Behold, I shew you a mystery; We shall not all sleep, but we shall all be changed, In a moment, in the twinkling of an eye, at the last trump: for the trumpet shall sound, and the dead shall be raised incorruptible, and we shall be changed. 1 Corinthians 15:51-52

So, the primary controversy focuses around the issue of the timing of the Rapture. Does it occur before the onset of the 70th week (pretribulation), at the end or after the 70th week (post-tribulation), or somewhere during the 70th week (prewrath)? To help answer this, Revelation points to the Rapture occurring between the sixth and seventh seals.

> After this I beheld, and, lo, a great multitude, which no man could number, of all nations, and kindreds, and people, and tongues, stood before the throne, and before the Lamb, clothed with white robes, and palms in their hands; And cried with a loud voice, saying, Salvation to our God which sitteth upon the throne, and unto the Lamb. Revelation 7:9-10

This would seem to confirm a prewrath interpretation, sometime during the 70th week. Interestingly, the letters to the Churches in Revelation, especially the one to Philadelphia the sixth church, has a lot to say about this issue and again supports the position of the Rapture occurring after the sixth seal, validating a prewrath view. The first question concerns who the Church of Philadelphia is. In order to know that, it is important to understand the promise that was given to them.

> Because thou hast kept the word of my patience, I also will keep thee from the hour of temptation, which shall come upon all the world, to try them that dwell upon the earth. Revelation 3:10

As noted earlier, there are different theories about what the letters to the Churches are about and who the Church of Philadelphia is. The most popular theory is that all seven of the letters to the Churches in Revelation are just historical letters to actual churches back in the first century. The letters happen to give good advice that is good advice for all times, back then and now. The second most common theory is that the letters represent various church ages. They reflect changes in the Universal Church over the last two thousand years that it has existed.

Yet, it has been shown that neither of these theories are completely correct, especially in regard to this promise to the Church of Philadelphia. If the letters to the seven churches were only historic back in the first century, then this promise means nothing. It would only be a tiny historic church that Jesus was telling would be kept from a trial. But notice that the trial was supposed to affect the whole world.

Additionally, what is very interesting is the difference between Jesus' letter in Revelation and a letter from the Church father Irenaeus to this same Church of Philadelphia. Jesus speaks of this church in glowing details and does not criticize them at all, while Irenaeus criticizes this same church for numerous ways that they were disobeying the way of Christ. So, if the letter from Jesus was only to this ancient church, then why is the letter different than the one Irenaeus sent them?

Second, if the Revelation letters refer to church ages, then this promise to the Church of Philadelphia belongs to the sixth church age. This would be an age that those believing in this theory think is historical and has already passed. If that is true, then this passage, about a promise to be kept from the hour of trial, also means nothing today, since most of those historical churches are boarded up and long forgotten.

So, a third theory about the letters is that they are addressed to Christians during the end times trial that impacts the entire world. This fits perfectly with the theory that all seven letters to the Churches of Revelation were written to advise the one and only end time church as it overcomes each of the seven seals in order. As discussed earlier regarding this theory, the first letter to Ephesus is about the first seal and false prophets; the second letter to Smyrna is about the beginning of persecution; the third the letter to Pergamum is about Satan's throne, the mark of the beast, and the end time famine; the fourth letter to Thyatira is about the abomination of desolation, end time pestilence, and the start of the Great Tribulation; and the fifth letter to Sardis is about the fifth seal and the martyrdom of the Saints during the Great Tribulation. Then comes the sixth seal and the letter to Philadelphia.

The letter begins with this description of Jesus.

> And to the angel of the Church in Philadelphia write;
> These things saith he that is holy, he that is true, he
> that hath the key of David, he that openeth, and no
> man shutteth; and shutteth, and no man openeth;
> Revelation 3:7

Jesus has the key of David and is in charge of who comes in and who goes out of this door that the key fits. But where is the door and where do the people go? Revelation refers to a door four times. As seen earlier, in the letter to Laodicea, the door is shut.

> Behold, I stand at the door, and knock: if any man hear
> my voice, and open the door, I will come in to him, and
> will sup with him, and he with me. Revelation 3:20

But in this letter to Philadelphia, it is an open door.

> I know thy works: behold, I have set before thee an open door, and no man can shut it: for thou hast a little strength, and hast kept my word, and hast not denied my name. Revelation 3:8

In the next chapter, the door is opened for the Apostle John to enter heaven.

> After this I looked, and, behold, a door was opened in heaven: and the first voice which I heard was as it were of a trumpet talking with me; which said, Come up hither, and I will shew thee things which must be hereafter. Revelation 4:1

And in Revelation 19:

> And I saw heaven opened, and behold a white horse; and he that sat upon him was called Faithful and True, and in righteousness he doth judge and make war. Revelation 19:11

So, there is obviously a door in heaven that Jesus, the Apostle John, and the saints go in and out. This is likely the same door that Jesus mentioned in the parable of the ten virgins.

> And while they went to buy, the bridegroom came; and they that were ready went in with him to the marriage: and the door was shut. Afterward came also the other virgins, saying, Lord, Lord, open to us. But he answered and said, Verily I say unto you, I know you not. Matthew 25:10-12

This parable describes how the door is used. The wise virgins enter the wedding feast by means of this door, and it is then shut on the foolish virgins who pound on the door to let them in. But it is too late for them. The letter to Philadelphia is all about the opening of the door of heaven for the wise virgins. It is a picture of the Rapture and the raptured Church that is portrayed by the wise virgins and also by the Philadelphia church.

This reinforces the idea that the Rapture happens after the 6th seal. That is why this letter is the 6th letter. Jesus opens the door of death and Hades, resurrects the righteous dead, and they are caught up together with the Church of Philadelphia in the air to meet Jesus and to go through the door of heaven.

Exploring the controversial issue on whether the escape from the hour of trial is pretribulational, prewrath, or post-tribulational, consider the reason Jesus gives for keeping the Church of Philadelphia out of the trial.

> Because thou hast kept the word of my patience *(hupomone)*, I also will keep thee from the hour of temptation, which shall come upon all the world, to try them that dwell upon the earth. Revelation 3:10

It is a conditional statement. The rescue requires them to have had "patient endurance". English Bibles translate the single Greek word *hupomone* as "patient endurance", and this word appears six other times in Revelation. Every single time it refers to Christians patiently enduring persecution. Here are just two examples from Revelation:

> He that leadeth into captivity shall go into captivity: he that killeth with the sword must be killed with the sword. Here is the patience *(hupomone)* and the faith of the saints. Revelation 13:10

> And the third angel followed them, saying with a loud voice, If any man worship the beast and his image, and receive his mark in his forehead, or in his hand, The same shall drink of the wine of the wrath of God, which is poured out without mixture into the cup of his indignation; and he shall be tormented with fire and

brimstone in the presence of the holy angels, and in the presence of the Lamb: And the smoke of their torment ascendeth up for ever and ever: and they have no rest day nor night, who worship the beast and his image, and whosoever receiveth the mark of his name. Here is the patience *(hupomone)* of the saints: here are they that keep the commandments of God, and the faith of Jesus. Revelation 14:9-12

Both passages refer to the Great Tribulation and fit with the model of the seven churches that has been presented. In other words, the sixth letter to Philadelphia concerns the Rapture that happens after the sixth seal, **after** the Great Tribulation. Thus, these saints will have endured the Great Tribulation, and it is their ability to patiently endure it with the assistance of the Holy Spirit that keeps them from the trial. The hour of trial will come only on the wicked, and the righteous will be kept from that period of God's wrath.

So, before he pours out His wrath on the unrepentant, God has promised that He will save those justified by the blood of Messiah Jesus, even those who have seriously transgressed His wishes at one point or another. But how will Christians be saved from the wrath to come? Will they be removed from the earth to heaven in the Rapture, or will they simply be protected on the earth and shielded from God's wrath? Scripture confirms that the Rapture is, in fact, a removal rather than simply a shielding.

And to wait for his Son **from heaven**, whom he raised from the dead, even Jesus, which **delivered** *(hruomai)* us from the wrath to come. 1 Thessalonians 1:10

Notice that Jesus delivers believers from God's wrath. He does not shield them from it. The Greek word translated "deliver" is *hruomai* which means "rescue, deliver, or snatch up". This is very similar in meaning to *harpazo*, which is where the word *rapture* comes from. So, as previously discussed, Jesus will come from heaven to earth and snatch up believers to heaven before God's wrath is poured out.

DAY OF THE LORD- CHRIST COMING FOR ISRAEL

After the Rapture of the Church, the wrath of God will begin. This is the period of time that the world, as well as the foolish virgins (the church goers who are left behind), will have to endure God's discipline. Like most end time events, Bible scholars differ on when the wrath of God begins and how long it will last. But before examining the timeline for God's wrath, what exactly is meant by His wrath? And then, how long does the Bible say that coming final eschatological wrath will be, and when will that day of wrath begin? Finally, what events occur during the Day of the Lord, the day of His wrath?

The Bible has much to say about the day of God's wrath which is when God will pour out his judgment and punishment on the unrepentant thereby changing the present world order. A New Testament book that has much to say about the coming eschatological wrath of God is surprisingly not Revelation but the book of Romans. This book reveals that God's wrath is poured out on those with hardened hearts, and that that wrath is unveiled on a single day.

> But after thy hardness and impenitent heart treasurest up unto thyself wrath against the day of wrath and revelation of the righteous judgment of God; Romans 2:5

God's wrath may last longer than a day, but it is revealed on that single day. So, why would a righteous and loving God inflict His wrath? Although we all merit God's wrath, certainly there are those who seem to be more deserving of the full measure of His wrath. For example, there are those prone to the vileness of human trafficking, drugs, terrorism, murder, torture, and abuse of all kinds. They all are worthy of judgment. Why then would God not bring an end to such things and judge those responsible, especially if they are unrepentant? And the short answer is that He will. But even those who are doing these vile acts have been given time to repent, at least for a time, right up until when God says, "enough". God in His mercy is patient towards them. He is patiently waiting for all those who will be saved to be saved. But one day He will finally say, "Enough!" And then He will begin to pour out His wrath.

How long is the Day of the Lord? And when does it begin and end?

The wrath of God will occur after the Rapture, once the final seal has been completed and God has finished dealing with the Church. On this proposed timeline His wrath will begin with the trumpet judgments directed at Israel during the Day of the Lord, a time of Jacob's trouble. But how long will that "day" be? Some, those who support a pretribulation model, insist that the wrath of God lasts for seven years, the entire 70th week of Daniel. Others claim it is only a single day, the Day of the Lord. Not surprisingly, the Bible has a very consistent answer to this debate. There are several passages in the Bible that seem to indicate that the "day" will actually be about a year long. Isaiah describes a yearlong period.

> For it is the **day** of the LORD's vengeance, and the **year** of recompences for the controversy of Zion. Isaiah 34:8

Isaiah says that God has a day of vengeance, the day His wrath starts. Then, His recompense or pay back for what the unrepentant did to Zion will take about a year. In other words, His wrath starts on a specific day but lasts for a year. During the last half of the tribulation period for three and a half years, the Antichrist and his kingdom will occupy the Temple and persecute God's people. The final year of Daniel's 70th week will bring recompense or payback for the cause of Zion. The final year is Jesus' pay back, His wrath, and this will start with the trumpet judgments.

Further, Isaiah states:

> For the **day** of vengeance is in mine heart, and the **year**
> of my redeemed is come. Isaiah 63:4

Here again, the day of vengeance is associated with a yearlong period. This time period lasts a year during which God will accomplish a redemption. He is going to save someone during this year. And those who will be saved are the unsaved Jews. It will be a year when they (and some Gentiles) come to faith in Jesus.

Finally, Isaiah once again declares a yearlong period:

> To proclaim the acceptable *(or desirable/favorable)* **year**
> of the Lord, and the **day** of vengeance of our God; to
> comfort all that mourn; Isaiah 61:2

This scripture was quoted by Jesus at least in part during his ministry (Luke 4:18-19). This day that vengeance begins is associated with a year of favor. Someone is being favored, while others are being punished. It is a year of favor or the acceptable year of the Lord. This indicates that Israel will be acceptable before God during that year. The Hebrew word *rason*, translated as "favor or acceptable", is also found in Exodus where a turban with a gold plate engraved with the words "Holy to the Lord" was placed on Aaron's head. This made him acceptable to the Lord.

> And it shall be upon Aaron's forehead, that Aaron may
> bear the iniquity of the holy things, which the children
> of Israel shall hallow in all their holy gifts; and it shall
> be always upon his forehead, that they may be accepted
> *(rason)* before the Lord. Exodus 28:38

So, some will experience acceptance before God in the final year of Daniel's 70th week. A seal or sign upon the forehead which makes someone acceptable before God is reminiscent of the seal of God placed upon the 144,000 Jews. It is in this acceptable year that Israel is made acceptable before Him.

The phrase "to comfort all that mourn" is also used in Isaiah 61:2. Zechariah uses this same word *mourn* to show who it is that will be mourning. It is those who had Him crucified, i.e., the Israelites.

> And I will pour upon the house of David, and upon the inhabitants of Jerusalem, the spirit of grace and of supplications: and they shall look upon me whom they have pierced, and they shall **mourn** for him, as one mourneth for his only son, and shall be in bitterness for him, as one that is in bitterness for his firstborn. Zechariah 12:10

And Jesus, speaking of the coming of the Son of Man, said:

> Immediately after the tribulation of those days shall the sun be darkened, and the moon shall not give her light, and the stars shall fall from heaven, and the powers of the heavens shall be shaken: And then shall appear the sign of the Son of man in heaven: and then shall all the tribes of the earth **mourn**, and they shall see the Son of man coming in the clouds of heaven with power and great glory. Matthew 24:29-30

It is when "all the tribes" mourn that they will see Jesus and experience His favor. In Job it says those that mourn are lifted to safety.

> To set up on high those that be low; that those which mourn may be exalted to safety. Job 5:11

The acceptable year of the Lord is when the righteous Jews, the 144,000, are lifted to safety, and it is proposed that all of these things will happen in that final year, the Day of the Lord.

So, there are three separate witness passages from Isaiah that associate the wrath of God with a yearlong period. And three things happen in this year: (1) recompense or payback, (2) favor, and (3) redemption.

Verse	Phrase	Meaning
Isa. 34:8, 61:2, 63:4	The day of vengeance	Day of the Lord
Isa. 34:8	Year of **recompense** for the cause of Zion	Year the wrath of God to be poured out
Isa. 61:2	**Favorable** Year of the Lord	Year the Raptured saints are in heaven
Isa. 63:4	Year of **redemption**	Year required to bring unsaved Jews to repentance and salvation

In writing to the Thessalonians, Paul uses these same descriptive terms when illustrating the fiery Day of the Lord that occurs after the saints have been raptured.

> Seeing it is a righteous thing with God to **recompense** tribulation to them that trouble you; And to you who are troubled rest with us, when the Lord Jesus shall be revealed from heaven with his mighty angels, In flaming fire taking **vengeance** on them that know not God, and that obey not the gospel of our Lord Jesus Christ: Who shall be punished with everlasting destruction from the presence of the Lord, and from the glory of his power; When he shall come to be glorified in his saints, and to be admired in all them that believe (because our testimony among you was believed) in that day. Wherefore also we pray always for you, that our God would count you worthy of this calling, and fulfil all the **good pleasure** *(delight or favor)* of his goodness, and the work of faith with power: 2 Thessalonians 1:6-11

Besides Isaiah and Paul there is still another witness. This is Daniel with his 70th week prophecy, perhaps the strongest witness of all. Daniel's 70th week mentions seven years or a "week" of years. This seven-year period is known as a *shabuah* or a seven-year sabbatical cycle.

All seventy of Daniels weeks are seven-year sabbatical cycles or weeks of years. So, this prophecy is seventy sets of seven-year cycles.

The last week of Daniel's 70th week, or as some call it "the Tribulation", is only one of these seven-year cycles. It is a week of years. A week of years is not just some random period of seven years. Just like a week of days has a sabbath day, a week of years has a sabbath year. The ancient Israelites were instructed to till and harvest their land for six years and then to rest on the seventh or sabbath year. The 70th week of Daniel is no different. It is a sabbatical cycle of six years of tilling and reaping, and a seventh Sabbath year that is set apart.

Consequently, this week of years is modeled on the Lord's week of days, resulting in six years of toil and then a sabbath year of rest. God's people are to sow and reap a harvest of souls for six years, bringing many to faith in Jesus, and then they have a separate year of rest. The final year is different than the first six. This final seventh year is the year of recompense, redemption, and favor that Isaiah identified. Correspondingly, the last year of the tribulation or Daniel's 70th week is the same year Isaiah referred to in the three passages that spoke of a day of vengeance linked to a period of time that will be one year long. So, this final year will in all likelihood be a sabbatical year.

However, it probably is not just any sabbatical year but is the sabbatical year right before a Jubilee year. This is illustrated from the account of Noah's flood, when the earth was punished by the first wrath of God and foreshadows His coming wrath. Dr. Joseph Lenard and Donald Zoeller introduced this idea in a book entitled *The Last Shofar*. In that book the authors calculated the exact number of days that Noah was in the Ark during the flood. They surmised that if the days of Noah are like the days of the Son of Man, just as Jesus tells us, then the number of days of the first wrath will be equal to the number of days of the coming second wrath.

In Genesis God tells us precisely when the flood started (on the 17th day of the second month), and it also tells us when Noah left the Ark (one year later in the second month on the 27th day). So, Noah was in the Ark exactly one year and ten days. The time that Noah was in the Ark, which is a picture of the 144,000 kept in safety during the Day of the

Lord, was not for a year. It was for one year and ten days, a very precise length of time. So, there are ten additional days added to a full year.

Hebraic years are only one year long except for one, the sabbatical year just before a Jubilee year. It is ten days longer to be exact. Hebraic secular years run from one Rosh Hashanah to the next Rosh Hashanah in the same way that the Gregorian calendar years run from one New Year's Day to another New Year's Day. This is true for all secular Hebraic years except the year before a Jubilee. That year runs from Rosh Hashanah to Yom Kippur, an extra ten days. This is the exact length of time that Noah was in the Ark, a traditional year plus ten days. God is a God of absolute precision. The pictures he provided in the accounts of the Old Testament are true and precise, even the extra ten days. This implies that the year of God's wrath lasts for not just for one year but for one year and ten days, the length of time for a sabbath year before a Jubilee year.

If this is the case, then the Day of the Lord will begin on a Rosh Hashanah, continue for one year and ten days, and conclude on the Day of Atonement, the start of a Jubilee year. On the proposed timeline this would be the year lasting from September 4, 2035 until October 1, 2036.

When do the Trumpet judgments start and how long do they last?

As noted, the Rapture occurs most likely on Pentecost between the 6th and 7th seals. Then, on Yom Teruah (Rosh Hashanah) of a sabbatical year, one year prior to the end, the 7th seal will be opened, after which there will be silence in heaven for half an hour.

> And when he had opened the seventh seal, there was silence in heaven about the space of half an hour. Revelation 8:1

This silence is in anticipation of the return of Jesus and the beginning of the trumpet judgments, as well as initiating the Day of the Lord, as described in Zephaniah.

> Be silent before the Lord God! For the day of the Lord
> is near, For the Lord has prepared a sacrifice, He has
> consecrated His guests. Zephaniah 1:7 (NASB)

At that future moment in time, it will be the realization in heaven that horrific judgment is about to fall upon the earth with the blowing of the seven trumpets that causes the silence. Believers in heaven will realize that God must first cleanse and purge the earth of all that has defiled it before Jesus Christ takes his rightful place as King of the earth at the inception of his millennial one-thousand-year kingdom.

> And cried with a loud voice, saying, Salvation to our
> God which sitteth upon the throne, and unto the Lamb.
> Revelation 7:10

But before He sits on His throne, it will be time for the trumpets to sound the battle cry. Everything will have been done and made ready. It will be time for the Son of God to go to war, for the Day of the Lord to begin on Rosh Hashanah. And it is proposed that this Day of the Lord will continue for one year and ten days, concluding on the following Day of Atonement. If that is the case, then the half hour of silence could correspond to the ten Days of Awe between Rosh Hashanah and the Day of Atonement at the beginning of the last year. At this point the trumpet judgments would start and be poured out.

If the trumpets do begin on the Day of Atonement in the final year of the 70th week, how long do they continue? They occur within the last year, so obviously the seven trumpets would have to last less than one year. Revelation 9:5 states that the results of the 5th trumpet lasts five months. Five months is a time period mentioned earlier in the Bible. In Genesis 8:4 the length of time the flood waters increased upon the earth during Noah's flood is given as that very amount of time, an identical five-month period. It was surmised previously that the second wrath of God in Revelation will be similar to the first wrath of God found in the Genesis flood, especially in terms of timing. If that is the case, then this five months of flooding in Noah's time might illustrate an approximate length of time for the trumpets. to be completed.

So, the trumpet judgments most likely take somewhere between five and twelve months. Since the fifth trumpet must begin at least five months before the end of the 70th week of Daniel, the first five trumpets must take less than seven months. Assuming that each trumpet judgment lasts one month and that the first trumpet will begin on the Day of Atonement (October 13, 2035), then the end of the trumpets, the seventh trumpet, would occur exactly six months later on Passover of the final year (April 12, 2036). This would permit the trumpet judgments to conclude in time for a second exodus led by Jesus, i.e., allowing six months for the exodus.

Events of the Day of the Lord

The Day of the Lord begins with a period of silence followed by the seven trumpet judgments. Then, just as Moses led the Israelites out of Egypt on Passover at the first Exodus, Jesus will deliver Israel on Passover and will lead them through their end time Exodus, from Egypt to Mount Sinai and finally to Jerusalem. He will fulfill His role as the New Moses and will defeat the Antichrist, the final Pharaoh. As Moses himself prophesied:

> God brought him forth out of Egypt; he hath as it were the strength of an unicorn: he shall eat up the nations his enemies, and shall break their bones, and pierce them through with his arrows. Numbers 24:8

> The LORD thy God will raise up unto thee a Prophet from the midst of thee, of thy brethren, like unto me; unto him ye shall hearken; According to all that thou desiredst of the LORD thy God in Horeb in the day of the assembly, saying, Let me not hear again the voice of the LORD my God, neither let me see this great fire any more, that I die not. And the LORD said unto me,

> They have well spoken that which they have spoken. I will raise them up a Prophet from among their brethren, like unto thee, and will put my words in his mouth; and he shall speak unto them all that I shall command him. Deuteronomy 18:15-18

And even Jesus indicated a distant Passover in a future kingdom of God.

> And he said unto them, With desire I have desired to eat this passover with you before I suffer: For I say unto you, I will not any more eat thereof, until it be fulfilled in the kingdom of God. Luke 22:15-16

This view, that when Jesus returns, He will retrace the whole first exodus specifically beginning in Egypt, is presented in the book *The Passover King* by Travis Snow. He also anticipates the second exodus taking place around the Passover, six months prior to the end of the 70th week.

In support of the trumpet judgments preceding a second exodus is the correlation of the trumpet judgments in Revelation to the ten plagues that occurred in Egypt during the time of Moses prior to the first exodus. The ten plagues occurred just before Israel's exodus from Egypt, prophetically foreshadowing the end time judgment before the final exodus of God's people. The following chart demonstrates this parallel.

TRUMPET JUDGMENTS In the book of Revelation	PLAGUES ON EGYPT In the book of Exodus
1st Trumpet: On the land; 1/3 earth, trees, grass burned (Rev 8:7)	Hail and fire (7th plague: Exodus 9:13-25)
2nd Trumpet: On the sea; 1/3 of sea becomes blood, 1/3 sea creatures die, 1/3 ships destroyed (Rev 8:8-9)	Waters become blood (1st plague: Exodus 7:17-21)

TRUMPET JUDGMENTS In the book of Revelation	PLAGUES ON EGYPT In the book of Exodus
3rd Trumpet: On rivers and springs;1/3 of waters become wormwood (Rev 8:10-11)	Waters become blood (1st plague: Exodus 7:17-21)
4th Trumpet: 1/3 of sun, moon, & stars darkened (Rev 8:12)	Darkness (9th plague: Exodus 10:21-23)
5th Trumpet: Demonic locusts tormenting mankind (Rev 9:1-12)	Locusts (8th plague: Exodus 10: 4-20)
6th Trumpet: Invasion of army from the river [Euphrates] kills 1/3 of mankind (Rev 9:13-21)	Invasion of frogs from the river [Nile] (2nd plague: Ex 8:2-4) (10th plague: Ex 12:29-30)
7th Trumpet: Voices, storm, earthquake, hail (Rev 11:15-19)	Hail storm (7th plague: Exodus 9:18-26)

Just as the ten plagues revealed God's power and destroyed Pharaoh's resources, so the trumpet judgments will do the same. And similar to Pharaoh and Egypt hardening their hearts to God's miracles, the Antichrist and his empire will harden their hearts against the Lord (Revelation 9:20-21). The message of the ten plagues will be the same message of the trumpets: "Let my people go."

So, it appears that the first exodus, where Moses led the Israelites out from bondage after the plagues, is another foreshadow of the second exodus. But in the second exodus, it is Jesus who returns to lead the Israelites once again out of captivity following the trumpet judgments.

Revelation 10 demonstrates that it is Jesus Himself who appears after the 6th trumpet and is described here portrayed as a strong angel or messenger that is descending from heaven.

> And I saw another mighty angel come down from heaven, clothed with a cloud: and a rainbow was upon his head, and his face was as it were the sun, and his feet as pillars of fire: And he had in his hand a little book open: and he set his right foot upon the sea, and his left foot on the earth, And cried with a loud voice, as when

a lion roareth: and when he had cried, seven thunders uttered their voices. Revelation 10:1-3

Many believe that this is Jesus because of his appearance. Everything about his appearance matches Jesus. His clothing is a cloud, and Jesus is the great cloud rider (Ex 13:21, Ps 68:4, Is 19:1, Dan 7:13, Acts 1:9, Rev 1:7). He has a rainbow over his head just as a rainbow is above God's throne in Revelation 4. His face is like the sun, and in Revelation 1:16 Jesus' face is like the sun. His legs are like polished bronze, just like in Revelation 1:15. And of course, this messenger roars like a lion.

The only reason some believe that it might not be Jesus is the use of the word *angel*. But in Greek *angelos* can be translated as "messenger" and not "angel". And if "messenger" is applied instead of "angel", then there is no problem identifying this as Jesus.

And although this is a very enigmatic part of Revelation, consider that this might be Jesus descending to the earth from heaven. If so, this is probably the same event described in Isaiah 19, where Jesus rides the clouds and comes to Egypt.

> The burden of Egypt. Behold, the LORD rideth upon a swift **cloud**, and shall come into Egypt: and the idols of Egypt shall be moved at his presence, and the heart of Egypt shall melt in the midst of it. Isaiah 19:1

This is a description of Jesus who will come to Egypt on a cloud after the 6th trumpet, and it is His kingdom that will be proclaimed at the blowing of the 7th trumpet, freeing the Israelite captives in Egypt in a replay of the first exodus.

Yet, as discussed earlier, many believe that Jesus' second coming is a one-time event, even though this passage clearly says that Jesus rides the clouds to Egypt which occurs after the trumpet judgments. In order to understand this scenario, Jesus is also seen descending on the clouds after the sixth seal at the Rapture.

And then shall appear the sign of the Son of man in heaven: and then shall all the tribes of the earth mourn, and they shall see the Son of man coming in the **clouds** of heaven with power and great glory. Matt 24:30

And Jesus also returns once more on His White Horse in Revelation 19. So, that implies more than one descending, as well as ascending, almost like Jacob's ladder. Christians have only assumed that Jesus rides the clouds once, but scripture shows that it is more than once as seen in the book of Daniel.

I kept looking in the night visions, And behold, with the clouds of heaven One like a son of man was coming, And He came **up** to the Ancient of Days And was presented before Him. Daniel 7:13 (NASB)

Notice the direction of Jesus' travel. He came on the clouds **up** to the Father and not from the Father **down** to the earth. To have come **up** to the Father implies that He had to have been on the earth. Also, Isaiah 19:1 says that Jesus rides the clouds to Egypt. Many would think that Jesus rode the clouds to the Mount of Olives and split it, but this verse says that he also rides the clouds to Egypt. This indicates that he rides the clouds more than one time, and his second coming involves more than one event.

After Jesus' return to rapture the Church, which occurs after the 6th seal, he ascends and descends from heaven at least two times, which is contrary to much of eschatological thought. Further New Testament scripture seems to support this idea of a multi-event Second Coming of Christ with the "ascending and descending" seen in John, which relates an encounter of Jesus with an amazed Nathaniel:

The day following Jesus would go forth into Galilee, and findeth Philip, and saith unto him, Follow me. Now Philip was of Bethsaida, the city of Andrew and Peter. Philip findeth Nathanael, and saith unto him,

We have found him, of whom Moses in the law, and the prophets, did write, Jesus of Nazareth, the son of Joseph. And Nathanael said unto him, Can there any good thing come out of Nazareth? Philip saith unto him, Come and see. Jesus saw Nathanael coming to him, and saith of him, Behold an Israelite indeed, in whom is no guile! Nathanael saith unto him, Whence knowest thou me? Jesus answered and said unto him, Before that Philip called thee, when thou wast under the fig tree, I saw thee. Nathanael answered and saith unto him, Rabbi, thou art the Son of God; thou art the King of Israel. Jesus answered and said unto him, Because I said unto thee, I saw thee under the fig tree, believest thou? thou shalt see greater things than these. And he saith unto him, Verily, verily, I say unto you, Hereafter ye shall see heaven open, and the angels of God **ascending and descending** upon the Son of man. John 1:43-51

After a future Passover during the last year of the 70th Week of Daniel, Jesus will trace the route of the first Exodus from Egypt to Mount Sinai and then on to Jerusalem. Jesus will lead His people out of Egypt, and just as the Red Sea (a tongue of the Egyptian sea) was split at the first Exodus, it will be split again.

And the LORD shall utterly destroy the tongue of the Egyptian sea; and with his mighty wind shall he shake his hand over the river, and shall smite it in the seven streams, and make men go over dryshod. Isaiah 11:15

Israel then heads to Mount Sinai, just as they did in the first exodus. Perhaps Psalm 68 depicts this multitude.

O God, when thou wentest forth before thy people, when thou didst march through the wilderness; Selah:

The earth shook, the heavens also dropped at the presence of God: even Sinai itself was moved at the presence of God, the God of Israel.... Kings of armies did flee apace: and she that tarried at home divided the spoil. Psalm 68:7-8, 12

This illustrates that during this time, as Jesus leads them to Mount Sinai, kings are fleeing before the throng of Israelites with Jesus in the lead. The Israelites then arrive at Mount Sinai. On that first Pentecost during the First Exodus account, God came down on the mountain in fire. Similarly, on Pentecost in the New Testament, tongues of fire and the Holy Spirit were poured out on believers. In the same way, at Mount Sinai on this future Pentecost, fifty days after Passover, God will again initiate the greatest outpouring of the Holy Spirit in all of history. Israel and the nations will be baptized in the Spirit, empowered to walk in God's ways, and given spiritual gifts in great abundance.

For I will take you from among the heathen, and gather you out of all countries, and will bring you into your own land. Then will I sprinkle clean water upon you, and ye shall be clean: from all your filthiness, and from all your idols, will I cleanse you. A new heart also will I give you, and a new spirit will I put within you: and I will take away the stony heart out of your flesh, and I will give you an heart of flesh. And I will put my spirit within you, and cause you to walk in my statutes, and ye shall keep my judgments, and do them. Ezekiel 36:24-27

And it shall come to pass afterward, that I will pour out my spirit upon all flesh; and your sons and your daughters shall prophesy, your old men shall dream dreams, your young men shall see visions: And also upon the servants and upon the handmaids in those days will I pour out my spirit. Joel 2:28-29

It is the opinion of Travis Snow in his book *The Passover King* that it is this day, Pentecost, when all Israel will be saved. And then they will continue on their way to Jerusalem.

From Mount Sinai, Jesus embarks on a military campaign to Jerusalem and Mount Zion where He establishes His kingdom. On the way He will continue to rescue the remnant of His people as described by Isaiah.

> And it shall come to pass in that day, that the Lord shall set his hand again the second time to recover the remnant of his people, which shall be left, from Assyria, and from Egypt, and from Pathros, and from Cush, and from Elam, and from Shinar, and from Hamath, and from the islands of the sea. Isaiah 11:11

This remnant that he frees is a mighty host of those from among Israel who will be prisoners of war.

> For, behold, in those days, and in that time, when I shall bring again the captivity of Judah and Jerusalem, Joel 3:1

> And the coast shall be for the remnant of the house of Judah; they shall feed thereupon: in the houses of Ashkelon shall they lie down in the evening: for the Lord their God shall visit them, and turn away their captivity. Zephaniah 2:7

As Jesus leads the procession from Sinai to Jerusalem, freeing the captives along the way as He goes, Habakkuk tells us something absolutely astounding.

> God comes from Teman, And the Holy One from Mount Paran. Selah. His splendor covers the heavens, And the earth is full of His praise. His radiance is like the sunlight; He has rays flashing from His

hand, And there is the hiding of His power. Before Him goes pestilence, And plague comes after Him. Habakkuk 3:3-5 (NASB)

Rays are actually coming out of his hands and pictures Jesus almost like a superhero. But it is because of these battles on the way to Jerusalem that Jesus' garments are already dipped in blood when he rides that White Horse at Armageddon later in Revelation.

And he was clothed with a vesture dipped in blood: and his name is called The Word of God. Rev 19:3

This great victory march will proceed up through Arabia and Edom (modern day Jordan) toward Jerusalem.

Who is this that cometh from Edom, with dyed garments from Bozrah? this that is glorious in his apparel, travelling in the greatness of his strength? I that speak in righteousness, mighty to save. Wherefore art thou red in thine apparel, and thy garments like him that treadeth in the winefat? I have trodden the winepress alone; and of the people there was none with me: for I will tread them in mine anger, and trample them in my fury; and their blood shall be sprinkled upon my garments, and I will stain all my raiment. For the day of vengeance is in mine heart, and the year of my redeemed is come. And I looked, and there was none to help; and I wondered that there was none to uphold: therefore mine own arm brought salvation unto me; and my fury, it upheld me. And I will tread down the people in mine anger, and make them drunk in my fury, and I will bring down their strength to the earth. Isaiah 63:1-6

Next, the procession reaches Jerusalem where it enters the Golden Gate.

> Open to me the gates of righteousness: I will go into them, and I will praise the LORD: This gate of the LORD, into which the righteous shall enter. I will praise thee: for thou hast heard me, and art become my salvation. Psalm 118:19-21

Psalm 24 describes this as well.

> Lift up your heads, O ye gates; and be ye lift up, ye everlasting doors; and the King of glory shall come in. Who is this King of glory? The LORD strong and mighty, the LORD mighty in battle. Psalm 24:7-8

In 1541 AD the Muslim caliph, Suleiman the Magnificent, who knew about these prophecies, sealed this gate to prevent the Jewish Messiah from entering it. However, the gate he sealed is a more modern gate that was built in the Middle Ages. In April 1969 American archaeologist James Fleming came to study the Golden Gate but fell into a hole and supposedly found a gate beneath the Golden Gate. If this is the true gate of mercy below Suleiman's gate, it gives new meaning to Psalm 24. "Lift up your heads, O ye gates."

Although Jesus will have already been proclaimed king at the 7th trumpet judgment, He now enters Jerusalem and is ready to be crowned king. Coincidentally, the next feast on the calendar is Yom Teruah, the Feast of Trumpets. This is the traditional day for coronating kings in Israel, after which their reign began immediately. The glorious ceremonies fulfilling thousands of years of ancient prophecies will then begin. Jesus will take His place as the rightful King Messiah on the throne of His father David.

> And when thy days be fulfilled, and thou shalt sleep with thy fathers, I will set up thy seed after thee, which

shall proceed out of thy bowels, and I will establish his kingdom. He shall build an house for my name, and I will stablish the throne of his kingdom for ever. I will be his father, and he shall be my son. If he commit iniquity, I will chasten him with the rod of men, and with the stripes of the children of men: But my mercy shall not depart away from him, as I took it from Saul, whom I put away before thee. And thine house and thy kingdom shall be established for ever before thee: thy throne shall be established for ever. 2 Samuel 7:12-16

And the seventh angel sounded; and there were great voices in heaven, saying, The kingdoms of this world are become the kingdoms of our Lord, and of his Christ; and he shall reign for ever and ever. And the four and twenty elders, which sat before God on their seats, fell upon their faces, and worshipped God, Saying, We give thee thanks, O Lord God Almighty, which art, and wast, and art to come; because thou hast taken to thee thy great power, and hast reigned. Revelation 11:15-17

Scripture states that the lights in the sky were placed to help man mark the times and seasons and to act as signs.

And God said, Let there be lights in the firmament of the heaven to divide the day from the night; and let them be for signs, and for seasons, and for days, and years: Genesis 1:14

One astronomical sign in the Bible was the Bethlehem star used to mark the birth of Jesus. Various theories as to the identity of this star have been proposed and have included labeling the Bethlehem star as a comet, a supernova, or one of several different planetary conjunctions. Perhaps another similar celestial event will mark and serve to confirm the second coming and coronation of Christ. Interestingly, on October

1-2, 2036, the Day of Atonement, there will be a conjunction of the planet Venus and the star Regulus. Venus, although a planet, is known as the Morning Star which is a name used for Jesus.

> I Jesus have sent mine angel to testify unto you these things in the churches. I am the root and the offspring of David, and the bright and **morning star**. Revelation 22:16

Regulus, which means "king" in Latin, is the brightest star in the constellation Leo the Lion, and Jesus also is described as "the lion of the tribe of Judah".

> And one of the elders saith unto me, Weep not: behold, **the Lion of the tribe of Judah**, the Root of David, hath prevailed to open the book, and to loose the seven seals thereof. Revelation 5:5

Every eight years, in late September and early October, the "king" star Regulus appears close enough to the bright morning star Venus that it appears to be crowning Venus. This event again occurs every eight years, and the next two conjunctions happen in 2028 and 2036. This celestial event then adds support to the possibility of Jesus' crowning occurring at His second coming on the proposed timeline in the year 2036.

This event, the crowning of Jesus, happens in heaven as already seen in Daniel 7.

> I saw in the night visions, and, behold, one like the Son of man came with the clouds of heaven, and came to the Ancient of days, and they brought him near before him. And there was given him dominion, and glory, and a kingdom, that all people, nations, and languages, should serve him: his dominion is an everlasting dominion,

which shall not pass away, and his kingdom that which shall not be destroyed. Daniel 7:13-14

Also, as indicated before, this is a moment where Jesus again ascends up into heaven. Perhaps he is ascending because only God the Father is worthy to crown Jesus as king. Certainly, no earthly man is worthy to do that. Psalm 47 alludes to this day, and looking at it as referring to the coronation of Jesus provides a new and different perspective.

God is gone up with a shout, the LORD with the sound of a trumpet. Psalm 47:5

Notice that God is seen ascending to the sound of trumpets and a shout perhaps on the Feast of Trumpets.

> For the LORD most high is terrible; he is a great King over all the earth. He shall subdue the people under us, and the nations under our feet…. Sing praises to God, sing praises: sing praises unto our King, sing praises. For God is the King of all the earth: sing ye praises with understanding. Psalm 47:2-3, 6-7

After the coronation, the Day of Atonement arrives at which the Bema Judgment will occur. This will be detailed further in the chapter on "Judgments". A great feast of celebration, the Feast of Tabernacles, then follows on Mount Zion,

> And in this mountain shall the LORD of hosts make unto all people a feast of fat things, a feast of wines on the lees, of fat things full of marrow, of wines on the lees well refined. And he will destroy in this mountain the face of the covering cast over all people, and the vail that is spread over all nations. Isaiah 25:6-7

It is a feast where God and his people "tabernacle" or commune together. This feast takes place after the completion of the 70th week of Daniel. It happens in the Millennial Kingdom at the beginning of the Jubilee year following the final sabbatical year. So, the Feast of Tabernacles happens in the next year, since it occurs after the Day of Atonement or Yom Kippur which is the end of the year before the Jubilee. It takes place in the Millennial Kingdom which completes the Day of the Lord.

WHITE HORSE RETURN- CHRIST COMING FOR THE GENTILES

As outlined, Christ comes first for the Church after the seal judgments and then for Israel after the trumpet judgments. Now, finally, He comes for the Gentiles after the bowl judgments. It has been demonstrated that Christ's Second Coming is a multi-step event, and the differences between the first step, the Rapture, and the last step, His coming on a white horse in Revelation 19, are clear. These events are separated by about one year, and the differences are outlined in the table below.

Difference between the Rapture and Christ Coming on a White Horse

Rapture	White Horse
Involves believers only (Church)	Includes all humanity (Gentiles)
Is a resurrection (translation) event—1 Cor 15:51-52	Is not a resurrection (translation) event
Christ comes in the air (not setting foot on Earth, yet)—1 Thessalonians 4:16-17	Christ comes to the Earth—Zechariah 14:4
Christ comes **for** His saints, meaning the Church is removed, i.e., believers (translated saints) are taken away to Heaven—John 14:2-3	Christ comes **with** His saints; that is, the Raptured saints return to Earth (No one is taken to Heaven)—1 Thess 3:13; Jude 14;
Believers will be taken away very quickly, in the blink of an eye, departing from the Earth—1 Cor 15:51-52	Unbelievers will be taken away as in the day of Noah—Matthew 24:39

Rapture	White Horse
Christ sends His angels to gathers the elect (saints)—Matthew 24:31	Christ comes with His armies in heaven (angels and saints—) Revelation 19:14
Unbelievers remain on Earth; however, some (probably many millions) become believers later on, and will enter the Millennial Kingdom in their earthly bodies	Unbelievers are taken away—Matthew 24:39
Occurs before the day of wrath (precedes the day of the Lord, aka the Tribulation)—1Thess 1:9-10; 4:18; 5:9; 2Thess 2:1-2; Rev 3:10-11	Occurs after the day of wrath during the Millennium which begins shortly thereafter.
Precedes the Bema Judgment Seat of Christ (where rewards are to be given); occurs about 1 year before the Battle of Armageddon and before the Millennial Kingdom	Occurs near the end with the Battle of Armageddon; precedes the judgment of the living Jews and Gentiles on Earth (Judgment of Nations) at the start of the Millennial Kingdom—Matt 25:31-46

Thomas Ice provides a table of Scripture passages that contrast the Rapture with the White Horse Second Coming of Christ, showing that they are different events [Ice, 2014c][3]:

Rapture		White Horse Second Coming	
John 14:1-3	2 Thessalonians 2:3	Daniel 2:44-45	2 Thessalonians 1:6-10
Romans 8:19	1 Timothy 6:14	Daniel 7:9-14	2 Thessalonians 2:8
1 Corinthians 1:7-8	2 Timothy 4:1	Daniel 12:1-3	1 Peter 4:12-13
1 Corinthians 15:51-53	2 Timothy 4:8	Zechariah 12:10	2 Peter 3:1-14
1 Corinthians 16:22	Titus 2:13	Zechariah 14:1-15	Jude 14-15
Philippians 3:20-21	Hebrews 9:28	Matthew 13:41	Revelation 1:7
Philippians 4:5	James 5:7-9	Matthew 24:15-31	Revelation 19:11-20:6

Rapture		White Horse Second Coming	
Colossians 3:4	1 Peter 1:7,13	Matthew 26:64	Revelation 22:7,12,20
1 Thessalonians 1:10	1 Peter 5:4	Mark 13:14-27	
1 Thessalonians 2:19	1 John 2:28-3:2	Mark 14:62	
1 Thess. 4:13-18	Jude 21	Luke 21:25-28	
1 Thessalonians 5:9	Revelation 2:25	Acts 1:9-11	
1 Thessalonians 5:23	Revelation 3:10	Acts 3:19-21	
2 Thessalonians 2:1		1 Thessalonians 3:13	

The final phase of Jesus' second coming, i.e., the judgment of the nations, begins with the bowl judgments and ends with His arrival to earth on a white horse. The psalmist envisions God subduing nations under Him and under His feet.

> The Lord said unto my Lord, Sit thou at my right hand,
> until I make thine enemies thy footstool. Psalm 110:1

Perhaps He is doing that by pouring out the bowl judgments on them. The shallow bowls described in the bowl judgments are meant to be poured out quickly and in rapid succession. So, it makes sense that this would take place over a very few days. The bowls are also incredibly severe, and the world would not last long if it took place over a much longer period.

It was proposed earlier that just like the first punishment of the world (Noah's flood) lasted forty days, the final punishment will also last forty days or approximately six weeks. A day for the commencement of the bowl judgments was also suggested as Cheshvan 10 (which in 2036 occurs on October 10). Cheshvan 10 is the day that God closed the door of the Ark. This is the day that God finally says, "Enough!" and all hope will be lost for unbelievers. Yet, up until this time God has granted time for them to repent and place their faith in Him. Despite this, those affected by the trumpet judgments still do not appear to repent of their sins but harden their hearts instead.

> And the rest of the men which were not killed by these plagues yet repented not of the works of their hands, that they should not worship devils, and idols of gold, and silver, and brass, and stone, and of wood: which neither can see, nor hear, nor walk: Neither repented they of their murders, nor of their sorceries, nor of their fornication, nor of their thefts. Revelation 9:20-21

Yet, it does appear that during this final judgment of Christ's return, a surviving remnant of the Gentile nations eventually will come to repent and serve Israel and Jesus her king.

> In that day will I raise up the tabernacle of David that is fallen, and close up the breaches thereof; and I will raise up his ruins, and I will build it as in the days of old: That they may possess the remnant of Edom, and of all the heathen, which are called by my name, saith the Lord that doeth this. Amos 9:11-12

> And it shall come to pass, that every one that is left of all the nations which came against Jerusalem shall even go up from year to year to worship the King, the Lord of hosts, and to keep the feast of tabernacles. Zechariah 14:16

It is interesting to note that one of the most repeated reasons given as to why Jesus will judge the nations is specifically because of their mistreatment of His people, Israel.

> For thy violence against thy brother Jacob shame shall cover thee, and thou shalt be cut off forever. In the day that thou stoodest on the other side, in the day that the strangers carried away captive his forces, and foreigners entered into his gates, and cast lots upon Jerusalem, even thou wast as one of them. But thou shouldest

not have looked on the day of thy brother in the day that he became a stranger; neither shouldest thou have rejoiced over the children of Judah in the day of their destruction; neither shouldest thou have spoken proudly in the day of distress. Thou shouldest not have entered into the gate of my people in the day of their calamity; yea, thou shouldest not have looked on their affliction in the day of their calamity, nor have laid hands on their substance in the day of their calamity; Neither shouldest thou have stood in the crossway, to cut off those of his that did escape; neither shouldest thou have delivered up those of his that did remain in the day of distress. For the day of the Lord is near upon all the heathen: as thou hast done, it shall be done unto thee: thy reward shall return upon thine own head. For as ye have drunk upon my holy mountain, so shall all the heathen drink continually, yea, they shall drink, and they shall swallow down, and they shall be as though they had not been. Obadiah 1:10-16

After the sixth bowl, Revelation describes Satan, the Antichrist, and the False Prophet's reaction to Jesus' absence from Jerusalem. They apparently noticed that Jesus was not in Jerusalem anymore.

And I saw three unclean spirits like frogs come out of the mouth of the dragon, and out of the mouth of the beast, and out of the mouth of the false prophet. For they are the spirits of devils, working miracles, which go forth unto the kings of the earth and of the whole world, to gather them to the battle of that great day of God Almighty. Revelation 16:13-14

At this point, since Jesus' return a year ago on Yom Teruah, the Antichrist's political power has been dramatically reduced. That may be why he needs demonic deceptive power to gather the kings of the earth.

He cannot just order them to assemble and try to retake Jerusalem. But King Jesus then gathers His heavenly armies, the raptured saints along with angels, for His glorious final return to the earth to defeat the forces of evil.

> And **the armies which were in heaven** followed him upon white horses, clothed in fine linen, white and clean. Revelation 19:14

The "armies which were in heaven" could refer to angels, believers, or both. Both angels and believers are described elsewhere in the book of Revelation as being clothed in clean linen garments (15:6; 19:8). However, in the verses that immediately precede Revelation 19:14, it is the saints who are said to wear "fine linen, bright and clean" (Revelation 19:7-8). Because of this and because of the earlier text in Revelation 17:14, which does in fact speak of believers returning with Jesus, the body of the Messiah (the Church that had been raptured) will be included in this host of heavenly armies that will accompany the "King of Kings" back to the earth. Based on all of the New Testament evidence, Jesus will return in glory with an army of both believers and angels. This army will form the core of His military force as He defeats the powers of darkness and ushers in the kingdom of God.

This is finally the moment Jesus mounts that White Horse.

> And I saw heaven opened, and behold a white horse; and he that sat upon him was called Faithful and True, and in righteousness he doth judge and make war. His eyes were as a flame of fire, and on his head were many crowns; and he had a name written, that no man knew, but he himself. And he was clothed with a vesture dipped in blood: and his name is called The Word of God. And the armies which were in heaven followed him upon white horses, clothed in fine linen, white and clean. Revelation 19:11-14

This battle, the Battle of Armageddon, that takes place at the beginning of the Millennium does not take long. Jesus will capture the Antichrist and False Prophet and will throw them into the Lake of Fire, while Satan is chained in the abyss. This ushers in a period of peace under the reign of Jesus until the end of the Millennium, when war will break out again.

So, the Second Coming of Christ includes several events, beginning with His coming for the Church in the Rapture (after the seals), followed by His coming for Israel (after the trumpets), and ending with His coming for the Gentile nations on a White Horse. Jesus will be leading the saints and armies of heaven once He has been crowned king at the start of the Millennium after the bowl judgments. This is outlined in the timeline below.

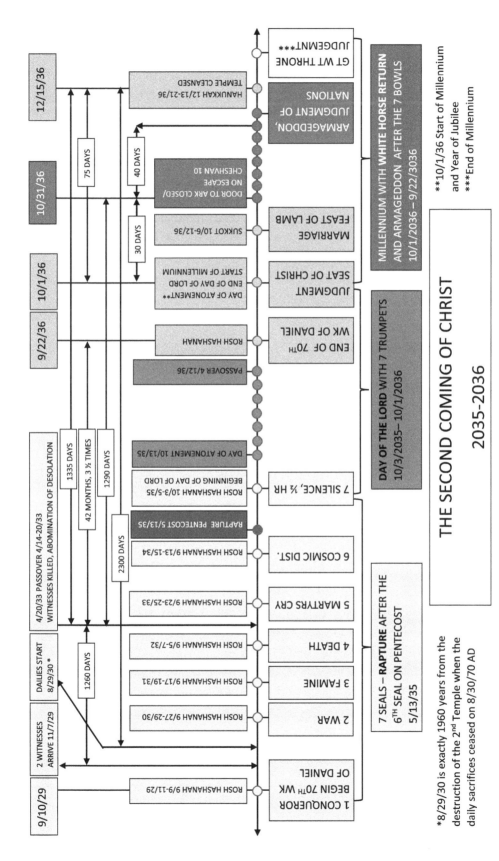

THE SECOND COMING OF CHRIST

2035-2036

*8/29/30 is exactly 1960 years from the destruction of the 2nd Temple when the daily sacrifices ceased on 8/30/70 AD

**10/1/36 Start of Millennium and Year of Jubilee
***End of Millennium

CHAPTER 9

Wars

GOG MAGOG WAR OF EZEKIEL [1,2,3,4]

W ars and rumors of wars are predicted throughout the Bible. Most people have heard of the Battle of Armageddon which is presented in scripture. Today all eyes are on the Middle East as armies from Russia and throughout the Middle East and Europe are on the move, and many Christians are wondering whether the Gog Magog battle of Ezekiel 38 and 39 could happen soon. Gog Magog is an end time battle between God and the enemies of God. Although it is accepted by nearly every Bible scholar that this is an end time battle, the question of who Gog and Magog are and exactly when the battle will occur is, as with most end times topics, very controversial.

All three Abrahamic religions, Jewish, Muslim, and Christian believe in a Gog Magog battle, although their views on this conflict differ. Christians base their views on the Old and New Testaments, while Jews base theirs solely on the Old Testament with much less information, and Muslims base theirs on a version of a battle from the Qur'an which is quite different from the Christian and Jewish beliefs. Additionally, some believe that there may be two battles of Gog and Magog instead of just one.

The most detailed account of this battle is found in Ezekiel 38 and 39, and many believe this conflict takes place around the time of Daniel's 70th week. Besides the source in Ezekiel, there is a second reference to a Gog Magog battle in Revelation.

> And when the thousand years are expired, Satan shall be loosed out of his prison, And shall go out to deceive the nations which are in the four quarters of the earth, Gog, and Magog, to gather them together to battle: the number of whom is as the sand of the sea. Revelation 20:7-8

From this passage it is clear that the Revelation 20 battle takes place after the one-thousand-year Millennial Kingdom and after Jesus has reigned on the earth for that period of time. It is only then that Satan is released from the abyss and deceives the nations one last time. Satan gathers the nations from the four corners of the earth, which the text calls Gog and Magog. Satan gathers them against the camp of the righteous which is in Jerusalem, but God destroys these armies.

> And they went up on the breadth of the earth, and compassed the camp of the saints about, and the beloved city: and fire came down from God out of heaven, and devoured them. And the devil that deceived them was cast into the lake of fire and brimstone, where the beast and the false prophet are, and shall be tormented day and night for ever and ever. Revelation 20:9-10

This battle puts the rebellion of Satan to rest forever. Satan was given the dominion of the earth after the fall in the Garden of Eden, and he has that dominion right now. But it will be taken from him at the seventh trumpet, when the kingdoms of this world become the kingdoms of Jesus. This final battle in Revelation is about Satan trying to regain that dominion.

So, the question is whether this final battle in Revelation 20 is the same battle described in Ezekiel 38 and 39, or is it actually a distinct battle. There are certainly parallels between the two. The first obviously is that they share the same name, Gog and Magog. Also, both demonstrate a large number of soldiers in the conflict. Ezekiel 38:4 notes "a great company" and Ezekiel 38:6 refers to "all its troops- many peoples with you". Also, Ezekiel 38:15-16 describes "a mighty army… like a cloud to cover the land". And in Revelation 20:8 "the number of them is like the sand of the seashore". Additionally, in both wars the battle occurs in Israel. Ezekiel locates the battle in "the land that is restored from the sword", an allusion to Israel, while Revelation references "the beloved city" that is Jerusalem. Finally, in both accounts, God supernaturally wins the victory with fire.

> And I will send a fire on Magog, and among them that dwell carelessly in the isles: and they shall know that I am the LORD. Ezekiel 39:6

> And they went up on the breadth of the earth, and compassed the camp of the saints about, and the beloved city: and fire came down from God out of heaven, and devoured them. Revelation 20:9

Yet, despite these similarities, there are differences that indicate they are not the same battle. First is the effect that the battle will have upon Israel in her relationship to God. In Ezekiel 39, it reports that after the battle, Israel and the nations will know that Jesus is Lord.

> So will I make my holy name known in the midst of my people Israel; and I will not let them pollute my holy name any more: and the heathen shall know that I am the LORD, the Holy One in Israel. Ezekiel 39:7

This verse eliminates the possibility of Ezekiel discussing the far future battle at the end of Revelation. Certainly, throughout the entire

Millennium, throughout the entire one thousand years, Jesus and God's name will already be known in Israel and throughout the world, and they will not be profaned. The nations will already know that Jesus is the Holy One in Israel, even if they do not place their faith in Him at that time. After all, Jesus will be reigning in Jerusalem at that time. These are not things that will happen after the Millennium and after the final battle. They must happen before it.

Second, look what else this passage says about Israel.

> And the heathen shall know that the house of Israel went into captivity for their iniquity: because they trespassed against me, therefore hid I my face from them, and gave them into the hand of their enemies: so fell they all by the sword. Ezekiel 39:23

Notice it states that Israel will be going into captivity for their treachery prior to the battle. In this end time prewrath timeline, that does not happen at the end of the Millennium but in the 70th Week of Daniel. So, for these reasons, the Gog Magog battle in Ezekiel is a separate battle from the one at the end of the Millennium.

Although this settles that the battle in Ezekiel 38 and 39 is prior to the beginning of the Millennial Kingdom, there is also disagreement regarding the time that it occurs during this premillennial period. Some believe that it occurs prior to or at the beginning of the 70th Week, while some hold to a midtribulational occurrence. Others place the battle at the end of the 70th Week. Again, this is highly controversial, but the vast number of scholars believe that the battle is pretribulational, occurring prior to the 70th Week of Daniel. This popular view holds that the Islamic nations and Russia combine to attack Israel, but God defeats them supernaturally. In the words of Dallas Seminary's most prominent historical scholar, John Walvoord:

> "With Russia (and Islam) out of the way, the head of the revived Roman Empire ... will be able to proclaim himself dictator of the whole world."

To those prophecy teachers who favor a Roman or papal Antichrist, this pretribulational view provides the means to eliminate the one and a half billion Muslims from their end time narrative. With Islam and Russia removed from the political scene, a European or American dictator could more easily rise to power.

Refuting this interpretation in his classic book *Mideast Beast*, Bible teacher Joel Richardson has written about multiple reasons that the battle of Gog and Magog in Ezekiel has to occur at the end of the 70th Week and is actually the Battle of Armageddon. The first reason given is that after the battle the name of the Lord will not be profaned anymore, as seen before in Ezekiel 39:7. It is impossible for a battle prior to the 70th Week to end up with this result, because the defining characteristic of the Antichrist is that he profanes the name of the Lord throughout his entire career. So, the battle cannot take place and result in the name of the Lord not being profaned anymore and then have the Antichrist profane it for another seven years. So, by itself, this point eliminates the popular view that the Gog and Magog war precedes the 70th Week or even that the battle concludes at the midpoint.

The second reason is that the survivors of Israel will dwell safely in their own land after this battle.

> Therefore thus saith the Lord GOD; Now will I bring again the captivity of Jacob, and have mercy upon the whole house of Israel, and will be jealous for my holy name; After that they have borne their shame, and all their trespasses whereby they have trespassed against me, when they dwelt safely in their land, and none made them afraid. Ezekiel 39:25-26

This again could not happen prior to the 70th Week. All scholars believe that a portion of the 70th Week is the time of Jacob's Trouble. The prophet Daniel tells us that that time will be the greatest time of distress that will ever come upon the nation of Israel. So, it is completely inconsistent for the battle, which results in the people of

Israel dwelling securely, to happen before the end of the 70ᵗʰ Week. In fact, it is impossible.

Third, the Lord will pour out his spirit on Israel after the battle, and they will know him forever more.

> Neither will I hide my face any more from them: for I have poured out my spirit upon the house of Israel, saith the Lord GOD. Ezekiel 39:29

> So the house of Israel shall know that I am the LORD their God from that day and forward. Ezekiel 39:22

Is that what scholars expect prior to the 70ᵗʰ Week of Daniel? Do they expect Israel to know Jesus is the Lord and that His spirit will be poured out on them? No, that requires that they would be saved in that period, and it is universally acknowledged that their total salvation only happens at the end of the 70ᵗʰ Week, when they see the one they had pierced. So, again, what is written in Ezekiel 39 is completely inconsistent with the battle taking place before the 70ᵗʰ Week, a battle which has to result in the salvation of Israel.

And fourth, Jesus will physically be on the land in Israel. Obviously, that is not something that happens prior to the 70ᵗʰ Week.

> So will I make my holy name known in the midst of my people Israel; and I will not let them pollute my holy name any more: and the heathen shall know that I am the LORD, the Holy One **in** Israel. Ezekiel 39:7

Notice that Jesus says he will be "the Holy One **in** Israel" not **of** Israel. The term *Holy One of Israel* is used multiple times in scripture, but the term used only here speaks of Jesus being **in** Israel after the battle. In other words, he is on the ground and physically present, and later God reinforces this idea.

Neither will I hide my face any more from them: for I have poured out my spirit upon the house of Israel, saith the Lord God. Ezekiel 39:29

They will see the literal face of Jesus after the battle. Obviously, this also precludes a battle prior to the 70ᵗʰ Week.

Fifth and finally, after the battle, the same Supper of the Lord takes place.

And, thou son of man, thus saith the Lord God; Speak unto every feathered fowl, and to every beast of the field, Assemble yourselves, and come; gather yourselves on every side to my sacrifice that I do sacrifice for you, even a great sacrifice upon the mountains of Israel, that ye may eat flesh, and drink blood. Ye shall eat the flesh of the mighty, and drink the blood of the princes of the earth, of rams, of lambs, and of goats, of bullocks, all of them fatlings of Bashan. Ezekiel 39:17-18

This is the same feast that Revelation 19 speaks of after Armageddon.

And I saw an angel standing in the sun; and he cried with a loud voice, saying to all the fowls that fly in the midst of heaven, Come and gather yourselves together unto the supper of the great God; That ye may eat the flesh of kings, and the flesh of captains, and the flesh of mighty men, and the flesh of horses, and of them that sit on them, and the flesh of all men, both free and bond, both small and great. Rev 19:17-18

So, in combination, these five similarities leave absolutely no doubt that the battle of Gog and Magog in Ezekiel 38 and 39 concludes at the same time as the battle of Armageddon, i.e., at the end of the 70ᵗʰ Week.

The battle seems to occur at or just after the 7ᵗʰ bowl judgment in Revelation which involves a "great earthquake".

And there were voices, and thunders, and lightnings; and there was a great earthquake, such as was not since men were upon the earth, so mighty an earthquake, and so great. Revelation 16:18

Similarly, at Ezekiel's battle there will surely be a great earthquake in the land of Israel.

For in my jealousy and in the fire of my wrath have I spoken, Surely in that day there shall be a great shaking in the land of Israel; So that the fishes of the sea, and the fowls of the heaven, and the beasts of the field, and all creeping things that creep upon the earth, and all the men that are upon the face of the earth, shall shake at my presence, and the mountains shall be thrown down, and the steep places shall fall, and every wall shall fall to the ground. Ezekiel 38:19-20

There are two other "great earthquakes" that occur in Revelation, including one at the 6th seal.

And I beheld when he had opened the sixth seal, and, lo, there was a great earthquake; and the sun became black as sackcloth of hair, and the moon became as blood; Revelation 6:12

The other "great earthquake" occurs when the Two Witnesses are resurrected at the middle of the 70th Week.

And the same hour was there a great earthquake, and the tenth part of the city fell, and in the earthquake were slain of men seven thousand: and the remnant were affrighted, and gave glory to the God of heaven. Revelation 11:13

However, the "great earthquake" in Ezekiel is also accompanied with "great hailstones" and the "mountains are thrown down".

> ...and the mountains shall be thrown down, and the steep places shall fall, and every wall shall fall to the ground. And I will call for a sword against him throughout all my mountains, saith the Lord GOD: every man's sword shall be against his brother. And I will plead against him with pestilence and with blood; and I will rain upon him, and upon his bands, and upon the many people that are with him, an overflowing rain, and great hailstones, fire, and brimstone. Ezekiel 38:22

Of the three "great earthquakes" in Revelation, the only one that occurs together with "great hailstones" and where the mountains are "thrown down" or "not found" is that which happens at the 7th bowl judgment.

> And every island fled away, and the mountains were not found. And there fell upon men a great hail out of heaven, every stone about the weight of a talent: and men blasphemed God because of the plague of the hail; for the plague thereof was exceeding great. Revelation 16:20-21

These scriptures all point to the Gog Magog War of Ezekiel occurring just before or at the beginning of the Millennium but after Jesus returns in the second half of the 70th Week at the 7th bowl judgment. Then a second Gog Magog War takes place at the end of the Millennium. The Ezekiel war then coincides with the War of Armageddon and therefore, should be considered one and the same.

Who and/or What are Gog and Magog?

As the alliance of nations that will be part of the battle of Gog and Magog seems to be gathering in the Middle East, Christians all over the world are also wondering who is the mysterious Gog (another name for the Antichrist as seen earlier) who will attack Israel, and where in the world is Magog. It seems as if there are as many guesses about who Gog is as there are Christian scholars. Nearly every recent US president has been a guess. Turkish president Erdogan and Russian president Putin are popular choices, too. And, of course, this only includes earthly leaders. Some believe that Gog might be a demonic power. Not only are US presidents considered candidates for Gog, but one president actually improperly evoked Gog and Magog to start a war. US President George Bush had this to say to the French leader Jacques Chirac prior to invading Iraq.

> "Gog and Magog are at work in the Middle East. This confrontation is willed by God, who wants to use this conflict to erase His people's enemies before a new age begins." George W. Bush[5]

That is one big reason why a proper understanding of the identity of Gog and Magog is important. Misapplication of scripture can lead to unwanted consequences.

As described in Ezekiel, Gog is an individual, and Magog is his country (Ezekiel 38:2). If Ezekiel's Gog Magog Battle is indeed Armageddon, as shown previously, then Gog is either the Antichrist himself or a demonic being. He cannot simply be a world leader who arises prior to the Antichrist. He is either the Antichrist or a demon. But identifying specifically who Gog is and where Magog is located are very great mysteries, and they have puzzled scholars for generations.

Identifying Magog, the country, narrows down the identity of Gog, since Gog is from Magog. Magog is found in the Bible as early as Genesis, where it is the name of a grandson of Noah and is who the nation was named for.

> Now these are the generations of the sons of Noah, Shem, Ham, and Japheth: and unto them were sons born after the flood. The sons of Japheth; Gomer,

and **Magog**, and Madai, and Javan, and Tubal, and Meshech, and Tiras. Genesis 10:1-2

The Bible states that the descendants of Noah's sons were divided into nations according to the languages at the tower of Babel.

These are the families of the sons of Noah, after their generations, in their nations: and by these were the nations divided in the earth after the flood. Genesis 10:32

There were seventy nations descended from Noah that are recorded in Genesis 10, and Magog is one of those original seventy nations. In fact, most, if not all of the nations fighting in the Gog Magog battle, are from these seventy nations. Ezekiel 38 compiles a list of those nations involved in the battle.

And say, Thus saith the Lord GOD; Behold, I am against thee, O Gog, the chief prince of Meshech and Tubal: And I will turn thee back, and put hooks into thy jaws, and I will bring thee forth, and all thine army, horses and horsemen, all of them clothed with all sorts of armour, even a great company with bucklers and shields, all of them handling swords: Persia, Ethiopia, and Libya with them; all of them with shield and helmet: Gomer, and all his bands; the house of Togarmah of the north quarters, and all his bands: and many people with thee. Ezekiel 38:3-6

So, all the nations listed as being involved in the Gog Magog battle are in the list of nations in Genesis 10, all except for what many consider the nation of Russia which is possibly called Rosh. This makes Russia and Rosh very controversial, and in fact, many doubt if Rosh is even a nation. In the Old Testament this word *rosh* is found hundreds of times, and it always means "chief or head". This would be the only instance in the entire Bible where the word *rosh* was used as a proper name.

Rosh is a familiar word and is found in the name of the holiday Rosh Hashanah which means "head of the year". It is the Jewish new year, and again the word is used in this way as "head or chief" throughout the Old Testament.

Now, since *rosh* means "head or chief", many translations like the King James, NIV, NLT and ESB translate *rosh* as if it is "chief or head". So, these translations use *rosh* to distinguish the prince as "the **chief** Prince of Meshach and Tubal", and they do not list Rosh as a nation at all. Rather, they consider it a title and, actually, this is the majority opinion of Christian scholars today.

However, the Septuagint, the Greek translation of the Hebrew Old Testament, was translated around 200 BC, and in it, the word *rosh*, which is a Hebrew word, is translated in the Greek as the name of a nation, not as "chief". The Septuagint Hebrew translators considered *rosh* a nation and not a title. As a result, some translations read "Gog Prince of Rosh, Meshach and Tubal" instead of "chief prince of Meshech and Tubal". So, the proper translation of *rosh* is ambiguous and makes it problematic to really tell if *rosh* is supposed to be a nation such as Russia or just a reference to "chief" prince.

There are either eight or nine nations involved in the invasion of Israel described in Ezekiel 38. These include Kush which is widely accepted as the area of Sudan and Ethiopia. Put is considered to be Libya, and, of course, Persia is Iran. But that leaves all of the more northern nations as somewhat enigmatic. Where these nations are located now depends on how one interprets the names of the nations. They could refer to the land mass i.e., the ground that the nation originally occupied at the time of the prophet Ezekiel, or they could also denote the people that lived on that land.

The first theory would indicate that Magog is the land where Magog originally was located during the time of Ezekiel. The second theory would point to Magog as anywhere that the people of Magog migrated to. There is a great deal of debate about which theory is correct. If the first theory is correct, i.e., that Ezekiel 38 refers to the original land mass of Magog in the days of Ezekiel, then Magog is the region right where it used to be. If it is the second theory, then Magog could be anywhere because the people living on that land mass have migrated and remigrated all over the earth. It has been suggested that Magog is Germany, Russia and even the USA for this very reason.

So, this second method, i.e., the migration method, is arduous, difficult, and as seen, leads to just about any result that the scholar desires. The first problem is that migration and intermarriage did not take place in one direction during the past 2500 years, from one location to another. Rather the people who originally inhabited Magog may have migrated and remigrated to numerous other countries. They are scattered to the winds of time.

Second, modern genetic tests cast serious doubt on this theory, too. For example, one USA presidential candidate claimed to be descended from American Indians, and her genetic test showed a positive correlation, but only 1%. This is the type of correlation one should expect to find for migrated Magog populations. Also, the people groups that existed at the time of Ezekiel do not really exist today. There are no identifiable Magog people.

Third, it is interesting that this migration theory is generally only applied to Magog. The other nations of the invasion force are thought to be in their original locations. Kush is thought to be Sudan and Ethiopia; Persia thought to be Iran; and Put is in Libya. It is inconsistent to only use the migration method for one nation like Magog.

So, this methodology, the migration method, is not reliable in determining where Magog is today. Instead, the historic method, i.e., defining where the land mass of Magog was located back in the days of Ezekiel, should prove more dependable. In order to do that, look at the passage from Ezekiel 38 in context, "Gog, the chief prince of Meshech and Tubal". This character Gog is from Magog and also rules the other territories, Meshech and Tubal. Gog is not from Rosh. But if Rosh is a nation and actually is Russia, then Gog is not from there but rules it. Many people assume that Gog is a Russian, but clearly from the passage, unless Magog is also Russia, that is impossible. However, it is likely that Magog and Meshach and Tubal are all close together since Gog rules them all. So, once Meshech and Tubal are located, Magog should be near them.

Magog is thought by most scholars to be the land of Gog, and the name "Gog" has been associated with a king who ruled Lydia or western Turkey. Numerous Bible dictionaries and commentaries all agree by placing Magog in western Turkey. Pliny the Elder, a first century Roman writer, placed it at the border of Turkey and modern-day Syria, as did Maimonides a Jewish sage. In referring to these writers, Sir Walter Raleigh specifically called this the Magog that Ezekiel referred to.

> "The scythians in old times coming out of the northeast wasted the better part of Asia minor and possessed Coele-Syria... which the Syrians called Magog and that to this Magog Ezekiel had referenced." Sir Walter Raleigh

All these academic and historical references point to Turkey. Yet, despite this overwhelming evidence that Magog is western Turkey, many Bible scholars continue to identify Magog as Russia. The reason for this is CI Scofield's 1909 Reference Bible which also promoted the pretribulation rapture position. Accordingly, there is a link between those who favor the pretribulation viewpoint and a Russian Gog/Magog, not because of a scriptural link but because of this older reference Bible that promoted both ideas.

So, why did Scofield suggest that Magog was Russia? He made this link because of the writing of Flavius Josephus, the famous first century Jewish writer, who identified Magog with the Scythians, and Scofield believed that the Scythians migrated to Russia. Note that this relies on the unreliable migration theory. However, modern historians believe that the word *scythians* was a catchall term for those living in Asia minor or Turkey. Even if some of these tribes did migrate north, which probably some did, only a few did. Equating Magog with all Scythians is like equating a single Native American tribe with all Native Americans. It does not make sense. But because of the Scofield Bible and its link to the popular pretribulation rapture theory, the idea has stuck in the minds of many Bible scholars to this day. However, the majority of modern Bible experts now agree that Magog is in western Turkey.

Concerning Meshech and Tubal, an even longer list of atlases equate Meshech and Tubal with Turkey as well. In fact, there is very little controversy about this. Nearly all Bible experts concur that Meshech and Tubal were located in modern Turkey, and this reinforces the idea that Magog was in Turkey, since Gog is the prince of these regions.

The same can be said about the nations of Gomer and Togarmah. Nearly every Bible expert places these nations in Turkey or the area just north of Turkey around the Black Sea. In regard to Togarmah, Ezekiel calls this area the uttermost parts of the North.

> Gomer with all its troops; Beth-togarmah from the remote parts of the north with all its troops—many peoples with you. Ezekiel 38:6 (NASB)

This also casts doubt on whether *rosh* even refers to Russia at all. If Togarmah is the utter most parts of the North and is located in Turkey, then Rosh or Russia would not, in all likelihood, be even further north. These nations surface again in Isaiah and in an end time context as well.

> I will set a sign among them and will send survivors from them to the nations: Tarshish, Put, Lud, Meshech, Tubal and Javan, to the distant coastlands that have neither heard My fame nor seen My glory. And they will declare My glory among the nations. Then they shall bring all your brethren from all the nations as a grain offering to the LORD, on horses, in chariots, in litters, on mules and on camels, to My holy mountain Jerusalem," says the LORD, "just as the sons of Israel bring their grain offering in a clean vessel to the house of the LORD. Isaiah 66:19-20 (NASB)

The same nations of Put, Meshach and Tubal are noted. And Lud is another name for Lydia which might be Magog. Also, notice this passage is the regathering of Israel scattered to the nations. They are brought back "on horses, in chariots, in litters and on mules and on camels". It is a great misunderstanding that the regathering of Israel after the Lord's return is by angels or supernatural means. Here is where the regathering of Israel is found in prophecy, and it is accomplished by natural means on horses and camels. The gathering by angels, rather, happens at the Rapture, the gathering of elect Christians. The regathering here involves Israelites in those nations where they were taken captive during the invasion and then placed in concentration camps.

This regathering of captives of Israel reinforces the idea that these places are included among the nations controlled by the Antichrist. The assembled list of nations involved in this invasion include Turkey, Iran, Libya, Sudan, most likely a few of the "stan" nations like Afghanistan and Kazakhstan, and maybe Russia. Knowing this aids in identifying Gog. Gog again is from Magog. So, he is almost assuredly from Turkey. Previously, the timing of this invasion of Israel was determined to be at the end of the 70th Week at the battle of Armageddon. This means that Gog, the leader of Armageddon, is either the Antichrist himself or a demon who possesses the Antichrist. Revelation asserts that the throne of Satan is in Pergamum, which also is in Turkey.

> And to the angel of the Church in **Pergamos** write; These things saith he which hath the sharp sword with two edges; I know thy works, and where thou dwellest, even **where Satan's seat is**: and thou holdest fast my name, and hast not denied my faith, even in those days wherein Antipas was my faithful martyr, who was slain among you, where Satan dwelleth. Revelation 2:12-13

The idea that Gog is a demon and not a man stems from the book of Daniel where it states that the nations have a demonic prince or ruler assigned to them. In Daniel 10 the archangel Michael restrains the princes of Persia (Iran) and Javan (better known as Greece). So, Gog is a prince, and some believe then that possibly he could be a demonic power or prince. The Hebrew word used for "prince" in Daniel, however, is not the same Hebrew word used in Ezekiel. In Daniel 10:13 the word used for prince is *sar* while in Ezekiel 38:2 the word *nasi* is employed. So, the fact that different words are used casts some doubt on this theory.

Yet, there is other scripture indicating that Gog is indeed a demon. The word *Gog* or the name "Gog" is found in the Septuagint translation of Amos.

> Thus the Lord showed me, and behold a swarm of locusts were coming, and behold, one of the young devastating locusts was Gog, the King. Amos 7:1 (LXX)

This links Gog with the invasion of locusts (as does the book of Joel) which many think alludes to Antichrist forces.

> And I will restore to you the years that the locust hath eaten, the cankerworm, and the caterpiller, and the palmerworm, my great army which I sent among you. Joel 2:25

Also, some connect locusts like those described in the 5th trumpet of Revelation with demons, supporting the idea that Gog himself is demonic.

Another possible connection to Gog is with an Old Testament character who has a similar name "Og" (without the "G"). Og is first mentioned in the book of Numbers where he is described as the King of Bashan which is the Golan Heights today. Deuteronomy states that he was a giant.

> For only Og king of Bashan remained of the remnant of giants; behold his bedstead was a bedstead of iron; is it not in Rabbath of the children of Ammon? nine cubits was the length thereof, and four cubits the breadth of it, after the cubit of a man. Deuteronomy 3:11

The Rephaites or Rephaim, were giants like the Nephilim. A nine cubic bed was probably twelve to fourteen feet long. In Ezekiel 39:18

Gog is also associated with this same region of Bashan. His army is compared to fatlings of Bashan when he is eaten by the birds. Bulls of Bashan of the same region encircled the Lord Jesus at his crucifixion as described in Psalm 22.

Many bulls have compassed me: strong bulls of Bashan have beset me round. Psalm 22:12

So, there is some connection between Og and Gog beyond the similar names as well as some link with the supernatural. But it is all very vague and not conclusive at all. Gog could be the name of the demon that possesses and empowers the Antichrist, but it is more likely that Gog is a man and that he is the Antichrist.

Earlier three men, Trump, Putin and Erdogan were considered as candidates for Gog or the Antichrist. Trump and Putin are not from Turkey. So, this seems to eliminate them from consideration of being Gog. Erdogan is from Turkey, but Daniel implies that the Antichrist will not be a current world leader but will seize power in the future.

> And in his estate shall stand up a vile person, to whom they shall not give the honour of the kingdom: but he shall come in peaceably, and obtain the kingdom by flatteries. Daniel 11:21

Notice that when this man arises, he is not a leader. Kingship will not have been conferred upon him. And since Erdogan is currently the leader of Turkey, this also seems to rule him out as a candidate for the Antichrist. So, although it is only speculation currently, it is likely that Gog is the Antichrist who is a shadowy person unknown to the world at large right now.

This brings up a common question about Gog: Why is Gog buried but the beast is thrown alive into the Lake of Fire?

> And it shall come to pass in that day, that I will give unto Gog a place there of graves in Israel, the valley of the passengers on the east of the sea: and it shall stop the noses of the passengers: and there **shall they bury**

> **Gog** and all his multitude: and they shall call it The valley of Hamongog. Ezekiel 39:11

> And **the beast** was taken, and with him the false prophet that wrought miracles before him, with which he deceived them that had received the mark of the beast, and them that worshipped his image. These both were **cast alive into a lake of fire** burning with brimstone. Revelation 19:20

Does this not preclude Gog from being the Antichrist? Although this is a puzzling question, it has a relatively simple explanation. As discussed earlier in the chapter on the Antichrist, the beast of Revelation has three natures. It is a man, the Antichrist. It is a kingdom or a nation at the same time. And finally, there is a demonic component who possesses the man, the Antichrist. In Daniel 7 the body of the beast is burned.

> I beheld then because of the voice of the great words which the horn spake: I beheld even till the beast was slain, and his body destroyed, and given to the burning flame. Daniel 7:11

This is the burning of the kingdom portion of the beast when Jesus and his angels throw fire and brimstone upon it. In Ezekiel 39, Gog, the human portion, is buried. And finally, in Revelation 19 the demon portion of the beast is thrown into the Lake of Fire. So, all three portions of the beast are disposed of in different ways. This is completely consistent with the three-part nature of the Antichrist.

Looking at Isaiah 14 brings this into perspective as well. This passage is a taunt that the Israelites will take up against someone known as the King of Babylon when God finally gives them their rest from their persecution which is at the end of the 70th Week of Daniel. Isaiah 14 is a highly confusing passage which has been ascribed as a reference to

Satan by most scholars. But on close examination it just does not seem possible for all of it to be about Satan.

> They that see thee shall narrowly look upon thee, and consider thee, saying, Is this the man that made the earth to tremble, that did shake kingdoms; That made the world as a wilderness, and destroyed the cities thereof; that opened not the house of his prisoners? Isaiah 14:16-17

First of all, notice it describes a man. And secondly, this man is buried.

> Thy pomp is brought down to the grave, and the noise of thy viols: the worm is spread under thee, and the worms cover thee. Isaiah 14:11

So, this passage cannot just be about Satan because it calls this individual a man, and it is a man who is buried. On the other hand, it cannot just simply be only about a human, either.

> How art thou fallen from heaven, O Lucifer, son of the morning! how art thou cut down to the ground, which didst weaken the nations! Isaiah 14:12

This can only be a fallen Angel or Satan. It is a man and a fallen spirit being that sounds similar to the beast who has a three-part nature, man, demon, and kingdom.

Earlier in the chapter on the Antichrist, it was determined that the beast or Antichrist would in all likelihood come from the area of the Grecian Empire which will be revived during the end times. Magog is located in Turkey or at least in the area of the Middle East north of Israel. This area includes Syria and Turkey, which were part of the Alexandrian or Grecian Empire. So, Gog the Antichrist is a man but also a man that is possessed by a demonic spirit who is cast down from heaven. He will come out of a Revived Grecian Empire, and more specifically he will originate from a region of the ancient Assyrian empire that includes the area of Turkey, Northern Iraq, and Northern Syria.

This is important, since knowing where the Antichrist will come from keeps us from being deceived in today's Christian culture. Just about everyone has been and continues to be fair game to be labeled as the Antichrist, from U.S. presidents, to popes, to Italians, to Asians, etc. But the most likely choice, not the only choice but the most likely choice, is that he is a Middle Eastern man who is not currently a world leader.

The Gog Magog War and Tish B'Av

Ezekiel mentions that after the Gog Magog War of Armageddon, the Land of Israel will be cleansed for "seven months" once Jesus returns.

> And **seven months** shall the house of Israel be burying of them, that they may cleanse the land. Yea, all the people of the land shall bury them; and it shall be to them a renown the day that I shall be glorified, saith the Lord GOD. And they shall sever out men of continual employment, passing through the land to bury with the passengers those that remain upon the face of the earth, to cleanse it: after the end of seven months shall they search. And the passengers that pass through the land, when any seeth a man's bone, then shall he set up a sign by it, till the buriers have buried it in the valley of Hamongog. And also the name of the city shall be Hamonah. Thus shall they cleanse the land. Ezekiel 39:12-16

Seven months after the Gog Magog War of Armageddon, which concludes with the cleansing of the Temple on Hanukkah (December 13-21, 2036), would be July 21, 2037. This date so happens to be Tish B'av. Tisha B'Av, the 9th day of the month of Av, is regarded as the saddest day in the Jewish calendar and is thus believed to be a day which is destined for tragedy. The observance of the day includes five prohibitions and includes a day of fasting. The Book of Lamentations, which mourns the destruction of Jerusalem is read in the synagogue.

According to Jewish tradition, five disastrous events have occurred on the ninth of Av that warrant fasting.

1. The twelve spies sent by Moses to observe the land of Canaan returned from their mission. Only two of the spies, Joshua and Caleb, brought a positive report, while the others spoke disparagingly about the land. The majority report caused the children of Israel to cry, panic and despair of ever entering the Promised Land. For this, they were punished by God so that their generation would not enter the land.
2. The First Temple built by King Solomon was destroyed by Nebuchadnezzar and the population of the Kingdom of Judah was sent into the Babylonian exile.
3. The Second Temple, built by Ezra and Nehemiah was destroyed by the Romans in 70 CE, scattering the people of Judea and commencing the Jewish exile from the Holy Land.
4. The Romans subsequently crushed and destroyed the Bar Kochba Revolt and the city of Betar, killing over 500,000 Jewish civilians (approximately 580,000) on August 4, 135 CE.
5. Following the Bar Kokhba revolt, Roman commander Turnus Rufus plowed the site of the Temple in Jerusalem and the surrounding area, in 135 CE.

The seven months following the Gog Magog War would be a time of mourning like none other and logically could culminate on Tish B'Av. This provides further confirmation that 2036 may be the final year in Daniel's 70th Week.

PSALM 83 WAR[6,7]

The war of Gog and Magog in Ezekiel leaves lots of unanswered questions. One of the most puzzling ones is: Why are not any of Israel's closest neighbors involved in Gog and Magog? Why are they not in the list of nations? Scholars like Bill Salus and Joel Richardson have given guesses, but in order to understand this, it is important to have a full grasp of Psalm 83 which was written by Asaph the Seer. Many believe that the prophet Asaph's Psalm 83 details some future war. Yet, there are others who claim that Psalm 83 is not a prophecy at all because they do not believe that Asaph was even a prophet. However, scripture actually shows that he was indeed a prophet or seer in King David's court three thousand years ago.

> Moreover Hezekiah the king and the princes commanded the Levites to sing praise unto the LORD with the words of David, and of Asaph the seer. And they sang praises with gladness, and they bowed their heads and worshipped. 2 Chronicles 29:30

Asaph also wrote 12 other Psalms, including Psalm 73-83 and 150, all of which have some prophetic elements. These twelve psalms make up what could be a twelve-chapter book of the Bible, but they were organized instead along with David's works in the book of Psalms. Psalm 83, however, is the capstone, detailing a history of war and conflict up until Armageddon. These details include nothing short of the planned genocide of the Jewish people in order to take their land. And what is detailed in this Psalm has never occurred in the history of Israel, that is up until the reformation of the nation in 1948. So, it is definitely prophetic.

Looking at the Psalm itself, it begins with Asaph's prayer to God for future generations of Israel.

> Keep not thou silence, O God: hold not thy peace, and be not still, O God. Psalm 83:1

The prophet here is crying out for justice and God's assistance because this is not an issue that Israel can handle on its own. That is because the Psalm describes an effort to abolish the nation and wipe it from the face of the earth.

> For, lo, thine enemies make a tumult: and they that hate thee have lifted up the head. They have taken crafty counsel against thy people, and consulted against thy hidden ones. They have said, Come, and let us cut them off from being a nation; that the name of Israel may be no more in remembrance. Psalm 83:2-4

This is why Asaph is pleading with God to get involved. The nations are attempting to destroy the nation of Israel and its people so that the name of Israel is remembered no more, and God cannot remain silent about that. God's very reputation is at stake, because He has big plans for Israel in the end times. If Israel is wiped out in the end times, God will have broken His promises to Israel, and that is not possible. No matter what Israel has done as a nation, God promises to let them stand.

That is one reason the Psalmist says "**thine** enemies" and "they that hate **thee**". They hate and attack Israel because they hate God Himself and because Israel is His chosen one. They strike out at God by attacking Israel. The psalmist then lists the specific people groups who conspire against the Lord and against Israel.

> The tabernacles of Edom, and the Ishmaelites; of Moab, and the Hagarenes; Gebal, and Ammon, and Amalek; the Philistines with the inhabitants of Tyre; Assur also is joined with them: they have holpen the children of Lot. Selah. Psalm 83:6-8

Understanding who all these groups are in today's world and then applying it to current conditions in our modern world will help in grasping the prophetic nature of this scripture. First, notice that there are eleven ancient names, and they are grouped mostly into groups of two or three. The tents of Edom and the Ishmaelites are the first grouping. Moab and the Hagarenes or Hagarites are the second grouping. Gebal, Ammon, and Amalek are the third group. The Philistines along with Tyre are the fourth group. Assur or Assyria is listed alone as are the children of Lot.

Beginning with the last group, the children of Lot, notice that all the other ancient ten peoples come to the aid of this group. This confederacy revolves around helping these children of Lot in their attempt to wipe out Israel. The sons of Lot were Moab and Ammon as seen in Genesis.

> And the first born bare a son, and called his name Moab: the same is the father of the Moabites unto this day. And the younger, she also bare a son, and called his name Benammi: the same is the father of the children of Ammon unto this day. Genesis 19:37-38

It would appear from this that the purpose of destroying the Hebrew people originated with the Moabites and Ammonites and that they had called for the help of the surrounding nations to carry out their plan. In today's world, Moab and Ammon are part of Jordan. So, what Jordanian people want Israel wiped off the map more than any other? It is the Palestinians. They are the ones desiring to control the entire land of Israel. In 2009, Mahmoud Abbas, president of the Palestinian State and Palestinian National Authority as well as chairman of the Palestine Liberation Organization (PLO), said:

"Call yourselves what you want but I will not accept it… the 'Jewish State'… I will not accept it."

This statement comes directly from the Palestinian Authority, a child of Lot originally of Jordanian descent, who desires the land of Israel. All these other groups are coming to their aid. One thing to remember while attempting to identify the other ten who remain is that this is based on the time period of the prophet Asaph. These are groups that existed in the days of Asaph, who was a contemporary of

King David. So, it is necessary to look at the political landscape of 1000 BC in order to locate them.

The first group is fairly straightforward, that is Assyria. During the days of King David, the Neo-Assyrian kingdom was reigning. This empire controlled parts of Syria, the northern parts of Iraq, and also included small parts of Turkey and Iran. Philistia is modern day Gaza, and Tyre is modern Lebanon. Iranian based terrorist organizations, Hezbollah and Hamas, are based in these two regions. Ancient Gebal denotes the same region cited also in Ezekiel and refers to Lebanon and more specifically to the modern Lebanese city of Jubal.

> The ancients of Gebal and the wise men thereof were in thee thy calkers: all the ships of the sea with their mariners were in thee to occupy thy merchandise. Ezekiel 27:9

Next are the nation states of Ammon and Amalek. Most scholars agree that Ammon and Moab are part of the current kingdom of Jordan, and Amalek was in the Sinai. This means that there is almost universal agreement about seven of the ten nations. However, there is disagreement about the remaining three.

Beginning with the Hagarites, they are also part of Jordan.

> And in the days of Saul they made war with the Hagarites, who fell by their hand: and they dwelt in their tents throughout all the east land of Gilead. 1 Chronicles 5:10

So, the Hagarites were located east of Gilead which is a part of Israel. But Bill Salus, one of the most prominent scholars in the Psalm 83 arena, looked at the same name (Hagarites) and noted that the spelling was similar to the name Hagar, the Egyptian maid of Abraham's wife Sarah. As a result, he claimed that the Hagarites were Egyptian. However, the Bible is clear that the Hagarites were Jordanians in the days of Asaph.

On the other hand, this does not mean that Egypt is still not part of the Psalm 83 Confederacy, just not in the way that Salus claimed.

The first grouping (the tabernacles of Edom and the Ishmaelites) are a very broad and comprehensive, wide-ranging group. Looking first at the Ishmaelites, Genesis 25 states that Ishmael had twelve sons. The Samaritan Book of Esther adds that they inhabited the region from the river of Egypt to the river of the Euphrates and that they built Mecca. Josephus states that they inhabited the land between the Euphrates and the Red Sea. So, the Arabian Peninsula is included in the area that was occupied by the Ishmaelites as well as southern Iraq, and possibly the western portion of Egypt.

In terms of Edom, these are the descendants of Esau who married one of the daughters of Ishmael, the son of Abraham and Hagar. So, their lands are similar to those of the Ishmaelites, but they predominantly inhabited the area of northern Saudi Arabia. Because Bill Salus' teachings have been so influential, it should be mentioned that he considers Edom to be the Palestinians today. He believes this because of the word *tents* or *tabernacles* that is used, which he thinks implies refugees. But the word *tents* can also be applied to other groups, including at least Edom and the Ishmaelites if not more of these groups, and 1 Chronicles 5:10 mentions the tents of the Hagarites. So, many of these people were nomadic in those days, and scholars are unified that the Edomites were living in northern Saudi Arabia in those days and not in the current site of today's Palestinians.

In conclusion, these lists of nations are **genetic** in origin. These people groups come from the line of Esau, Ishmael, the Jordanian children of Lot, and the Canaanites of Gaza and Lebanon. Looking at a map of the area that these people occupied shows a perfect ring encircling the nation of Israel. Nowhere in the Old Testament did these particular groups of nations all attack Israel all at the same time. So, that eliminates an historic fulfillment of this Psalm 83 prophecy, and therefore, it must be future.

Psalm 83 deals with an inner circle of countries that share common borders with Israel. These countries have all espoused an eternal hatred for Israel and include Lebanon, Gaza, Syria, Jordan, and the

Palestinians plus the Arabian Arabs as well as probably some Egyptian Arabs. Ezekiel in chapters 25-32 issued proclamations against these neighboring countries and in a prophecy against Sidon in Lebanon stated:

> And say, Thus saith the Lord GOD; Behold, I am against thee, O Zidon; and I will be glorified in the midst of thee: and they shall know that I am the LORD, when I shall have executed judgments in her, and shall be sanctified in her. For I will send into her pestilence, and blood into her streets; and the wounded shall be judged in the midst of her by the sword upon her on every side; and they shall know that I am the LORD. And there shall be no more a pricking brier unto the house of Israel, nor any grieving thorn of all that are **round about** (*sabiybah*) them, that despised them; and they shall know that I am the Lord GOD. Ezekiel 28:22-24

The Hebrew word for "round about" that is used here is *sabiybah* which means a "circle" or "neighbors". However, in contrast to the groups listed in Psalm 83, Ezekiel lists an entirely different group in chapter 38. They are an outer ring of countries, none of which are neighbors that share a common border with Israel. This outer group of countries include Turkey, Iran, Libya, Sudan, and maybe some of the breakaway republics of the Soviet Union. They were never Israel's historic enemies. Surprisingly, not one of the Psalm 83 nations is included in Armageddon, i.e., the Gog Magog war found in Ezekiel. Salus believes that this is not accidental, and it is beyond reasonable to think that the prophet Ezekiel chose not to list any of these inner ring nations by name without a reason for not listing them.

This evidence makes it overwhelmingly obvious that these two events (Armageddon and the Psalm 83 War) are not the same and do not occur at the same time. It is also clear that the two groups of nations in each war are exclusionary, one inner group and one outer group. This is not by random chance and eliminates the possibility that Jesus destroys both groups at one time on the Day of the Lord. Jesus will destroy both groups but at different times. Although confusing, the Bible lists two groups of nations and consequently limits the possibility that Psalm 83 relates solely to Armageddon and to the destruction of all of them on one day.

Timing of the Psalm 83 War

Now, if the Gog Magog War of Ezekiel is Armageddon and occurs at the end of the 70th Week and the Psalm 83 War is a separate and distinct conflict, then when does that Psalm 83 War occur? There are three main theories that currently exist about Psalm 83. Each theory according to the Psalm needs to meet the following criteria: (1) it must involve the nations described in Psalm 83, (2) the war must result in the described effect on these nations, i.e., in the nations being destroyed and put to shame forever by God alone (Psalm 83:13-17), and (3) these nations must know that He alone is God (Psalm 83:18).

The first theory is that Psalm 83 prophesized the 1948 Israeli War for Independence. In that war Egypt, Jordan, Syria, Lebanon, Gaza, and Iraq all attacked the newly formed state of Israel. These are exactly the nations listed in Psalm 83, and interestingly, the king of Jordan, who rules what is sometimes called the children of Lot, led the united effort against Israel, just as Psalm 83 predicted. So, from the aspect of the nations involved, Psalm 83 is an exact match with the Israeli war for dependence. However, the repercussions on the nations that follow the war do not match the description in Psalm 83.

> O my God, make them like a wheel; as the stubble before the wind. As the fire burneth a wood, and as the flame setteth the mountains on fire; So persecute them with thy tempest, and make them afraid with thy storm. Fill their faces with shame; that they may seek thy name, O LORD. Let them be confounded and troubled for ever; yea, let them be put to shame, and perish: Psalm 83:13-17

Obviously, God did not pursue the invading nations with His tempest, nor did He dismay them forever or destroy them. Also, they continue to worship a false god and do not know that He alone is God. So, the War for Independence then is not a perfect match on its own, and this first theory, the theory that Psalm 83 is about the 1948 War for Independence, matches the list of nations but does not match the fate of these aggressor nations.

The second theory concerning Psalm 83 was proposed by Bill Salus. His theory is that these same combined Muslim forces will once again invade Israel, but God will supernaturally empower the Israeli defense forces, who will completely destroy these nations. Israel will then expand its borders, overtake the land possessed by these other nations, and accomplish all of this prior to the 70th week or tribulation period. There are a couple of problems with this theory as a standalone theory. First, although Salus does not use this term, other scholars who agree with him, called this the War of Extermination, i.e., the extermination of the Arab peoples. Although the Bible does refer to the judgment of all these nations and even the complete extermination of one of the nations (Edom), Israel is not the one doing the judging but God and God alone. A passage about Edom's judgment makes this evident.

> Who is this that cometh from Edom, with dyed garments from Bozrah? this that is glorious in his apparel, travelling in the greatness of his strength? I that speak in righteousness, mighty to save. Wherefore art thou red in thine apparel, and thy garments like him that treadeth in the winefat? I have trodden the winepress alone; and of the people **there was none with me**: for I will tread them in mine anger, and trample them in my fury; and their blood shall be sprinkled upon my garments, and I will stain all my raiment. Isaiah 63:1-3

The scripture is clear that Edom will be judged, and that it is Jesus and Jesus alone who does the judging. Jesus was specific that "none was with me". Furthermore, Moab is seen to be judged in Numbers 24, Isaiah 25, and in Amos 2. Gaza, Moab, Syria, and Ammon are all judged and destroyed in Zephaniah 2, but again by the Lord Himself. Lebanon is destroyed in Joel 3, and Arabia is destroyed by the Lord in Ezekiel 30. All these righteous judgments belong to Jesus and Jesus alone. Nowhere in these passages, or in Psalm 83 for that matter, is Israel the agent of the destruction. Not only does this exclude this theory from Bill Salus, but it also places the timing of the judgment at the return of Christ.

A second problem associated with this theory is the vast expansion of Israel prior to the beginning of the 70th Week. Salus estimates that it will increase the size of Israel thirteen times after the Israeli victory which he envisions will achieve the borders God assigned in Genesis, from the Nile to the Euphrates. However, this land is promised to Jesus to distribute as he wishes.

> Now to Abraham and his seed were the promises made.
> He saith not, And to seeds, as of many; but as of one,
> And to thy seed, which is Christ. Galatians 3:16

So, this is an extremely premature, proposed expansion into the land, one without biblical backing, and one that if wrong will mislead the Church to watch for something that just will not happen.

The third and final theory is that the Psalm 83 War is an account of Armageddon, and that concept has already been discounted.

Despite all the problems that these theories have had determining when the Psalm 83 happens, it is possible to narrow down the timeframe within which the Psalm 83 War occurs and to even possibly pinpoint its timing. First, as noted earlier, it is Jesus and Jesus alone who brings this judgment, and consequently, it must occur during His second coming in the second half of the 70th Week. Second, the Bible is clear that the length of the wrath of God, when Jesus takes vengeance on the nations roundabout that he is promised to destroy, is one year, not a single day or a couple of days. Isaiah states the following regarding Edom, one of the nations that is in Psalm 83:

For my sword shall be bathed in heaven: behold, it shall come down upon Idumea *(Edom)*, and upon the people of my curse, to judgment. The sword of the LORD is filled with blood, it is made fat with fatness, and with the blood of lambs and goats, with the fat of the kidneys of rams: for the LORD hath a sacrifice in Bozrah, and a great slaughter in the land of Idumea. And the unicorns shall come down with them, and the bullocks with the bulls; and their land shall be soaked with blood, and their dust made fat with fatness. For it is **the day** of the LORD's vengeance, and **the year** of recompences for the controversy of Zion. And the streams thereof shall be turned into pitch, and the dust thereof into brimstone, and the land thereof shall become burning pitch. Isaiah 34:5-9

In this passage God has a day when His fire and brimstone is poured out, but this period of retribution or payback lasts an entire year. Here is another verse about Edom:

Who is this that cometh from Edom, with dyed garments from Bozrah? this that is glorious in his apparel, travelling in the greatness of his strength? I that speak in righteousness, mighty to save. Wherefore art thou red in thine apparel, and thy garments like him that treadeth in the winefat? I have trodden the winepress alone; and of the people there was none with me: for I will tread them in mine anger, and trample them in my fury; and their blood shall be sprinkled upon my garments, and I will stain all my raiment. For **the day** of vengeance is in mine heart, and **the year** of my redeemed is come. Isaiah 63:1-4

Again, Jesus is seen taking vengeance on Edom, and the day of vengeance starts on a single day but lasts an entire year. So, this Psalm 83

War likely takes place within the last year of the 70th Week, during the Day of the Lord.

Also, notice that this is where Jesus first stains his robes. In Revelation 19 his robes are already stained when he mounts the white horse to leave heaven and return to fight Armageddon.

> And he was clothed with a vesture dipped in blood: and his name is called The Word of God. And the armies which were in heaven followed him upon white horses, clothed in fine linen, white and clean. And out of his mouth goeth a sharp sword, that with it he should smite the nations: and he shall rule them with a rod of iron: and he treadeth the winepress of the fierceness and wrath of Almighty God. Rev 19:13-15

So, Jesus returns on the clouds, pours out his recompense on Edom and the other nations roundabout. This is where he stains his robes, and then he returns to heaven, gathers the army of the saints who were raptured, and together they return to the earth to fight Armageddon. The Psalm 83 War and the Gog Magog War of Ezekiel (Armageddon) are two separate events just as scripture shows.

Finally, Psalm 83 pinpoints even more precisely when this war takes place by relating how God will deal with these nations who oppress Israel.

> As the fire burneth a wood, and as the flame setteth the mountains on fire; Psalm 83:14

This is the same description that John gives of the first two trumpet judgments in Revelation where, first, a third of the trees are burned up which is then followed by a great burning mountain that is cast into the sea.

> The first angel sounded, and there followed hail and fire mingled with blood, and they were cast upon the

earth: and the third part of trees was burnt up, and all green grass was burnt up. And the second angel sounded, and as it were a great mountain burning with fire was cast into the sea: and the third part of the sea became blood; Revelation 8:7-8

This indicates that the timing of the Psalm 83 War is most likely to occur in conjunction with the trumpet judgments of Revelation.

As mentioned before, God typically deals first with His people Israel, and indeed this begins at the midpoint of the 70th Week with the time of Jacob's trouble. After this, He moves on to those who have persecuted His people. So, God next turns His attention to Israel's closest neighbors, the inner circle of nations detailed in the Psalm 83 War which takes place during the trumpet judgments. Finally, He deals with the nations of the outer circle at the Battle of Armageddon, Ezekiel's Gog Magog War, where the involved nations are destroyed and after which God's name will not be profaned.

RAM GOAT WAR

Although the Gog Magog War also known as Armageddon and the Psalm 83 War have received much attention, there is another war that is described by Daniel. A vision of this war was given to him and is detailed in Daniel 8, which shows that this war likely is a prelude to these other conflicts.

Then I lifted up mine eyes, and saw, and, behold, there stood before the river a ram which had two horns: and the two horns were high; but one was higher than the other, and the higher came up last. I saw the ram pushing westward, and northward, and southward; so that no beasts might stand before him, neither was there any that could deliver out of his hand; but he did according to his will, and became great. And as I was considering, behold, an he goat came from the west on the face of the whole earth, and touched not the ground: and the goat had a notable horn between his eyes. And he came to the ram that had two horns, which I had seen standing before the river, and ran unto him in the fury of his power. And I saw him come close unto the ram, and he was moved with choler against him, and smote the ram, and brake his two horns: and there was no power in the ram to stand before him, but he cast him down to the ground, and stamped upon him: and there was none that could deliver the ram out of his hand. Therefore the he goat waxed very great: and when he was strong, the great horn was broken; and for it came up four notable ones toward the four winds of heaven. And out of one of them came forth a little horn, which waxed exceeding great, toward the south, and toward the east, and toward the pleasant land. And it waxed great, even to the host of heaven; and it cast down some of the host and of the stars to the ground, and stamped upon them. Yea, he magnified himself even to the prince of the host, and by him the daily sacrifice was taken away, and the place of the sanctuary was cast down. And an host was given him against the daily sacrifice by reason of transgression, and it cast down the truth to the ground; and it practised, and prospered. Daniel 8:3-12

After he was given this vision, an interpretation of the vision was then provided to Daniel from Gabriel.

The ram which thou sawest having two horns are the kings of Media and Persia. And the rough goat is the king of Grecia: and the great horn that is between his eyes is the first king. Now that being broken, whereas four stood up for it, four kingdoms shall stand up out of the nation, but not in his power. And in the latter time of their kingdom, when the transgressors are come to the full, a king of fierce countenance, and understanding dark sentences, shall stand up. And his power shall be mighty, but not by his own power: and he shall destroy wonderfully, and shall prosper, and practise, and shall destroy the mighty and the holy people. And through his policy also he shall cause craft to prosper in his hand; and he shall magnify himself in his heart, and by peace shall destroy many: he shall also stand up against the Prince of princes; but he shall be broken without hand. Daniel 8:20-25

So, Daniel was given a vision, and two years later he was provided with an explanation of this vision by an angel. This passage in Daniel 8 is usually interpreted as having been fulfilled historically by Alexander the Great. However, although Alexander's reign and subsequent death and breakup of his kingdom appear to resemble these prophecies, it is not an exact match. For example, the goat (often interpreted as Alexander) is called the "first king", whereas Alexander was actually Alexander III. Also, at his death, Alexander's kingdom was broken into multiple parts, more than the four outlined in Daniel's vision. However, the various kingdoms eventually did coalesce into four major kingdoms. So, even though it is a close match, it is more likely a precursor or foreshadowing of a future event.

In addition, the passage makes it clear multiple times that these events occur at the **end time**, which makes the Alexander fulfillment not possible.

So he came near where I stood: and when he came, I was afraid, and fell upon my face: but he said unto me, Understand, O son of man: for **at the time of the end** shall be the vision. Now as he was speaking with me, I was in a deep sleep on my face toward the ground: but he touched me, and set me upright. And he said, Behold, I will make thee know what shall be **in the last end** of the indignation: for at the time appointed the end shall be. The ram which thou sawest having two horns are the kings of Media and Persia. And the rough goat is the king of Grecia: and the great horn that is between his eyes is the first king. Now that being broken, whereas four stood up for it, four kingdoms shall stand up out of the nation, but not in his power. And **in the latter time** of their kingdom, when the transgressors are come to the full, a king of fierce countenance, and understanding dark sentences, shall stand up. Daniel 8:17-23

So, clearly this is an end time prophecy of future yet to occur events, even though it does foreshadow the life and events surrounding Alexander.

The passage also identifies who the participants are in this end time confrontation. It clearly names the ram as Media and Persia, which is modern day Iran. The opponent is a male goat that is called Javan, and many translations label it as Greece. However, most scholars believe that Javan is actually the territory of Turkey along with parts of Greece. So, an end time battle between Turkey and Iran is predicted, with Turkey being the ultimate victor. The kingdom that Javan or Turkey establishes is then broken up into four kingdoms, which are the horns described in Daniel chapter 8. It is at this point that Daniel 8 parallels Daniel 7 which depicts the four beasts.

These four beasts in Daniel 7 are plainly the same as the four horns in Daniel 8. Both quartets are groups of four end time kingdoms. Daniel 7 implies this, and Daniel 8 states it directly. They are each four in number, unlike the goat and ram which are two in number. So, the goat and ram in Chapter 8 are not part of the beasts described in Chapter 7. Their emergence is related to the four winds of heaven.

Daniel spake and said, I saw in my vision by night, and, behold, **the four winds of the heaven** strove upon the great sea. Daniel 7:2

> Therefore the he goat waxed very great: and when he was strong, the great horn was broken; and for it came up four notable ones toward **the four winds of heaven**. Daniel 8:8

Both chapters also speak of the arrival of the little horn or Antichrist as coming from amongst the horns.

> I considered the horns, and, behold, there came up among them another little horn, before whom there were three of the first horns plucked up by the roots: and, behold, in this horn were eyes like the eyes of man, and a mouth speaking great things. Daniel 7:8

> And out of one of them came forth a little horn, which waxed exceeding great, toward the south, and toward the east, and toward the pleasant land. Daniel 8:9

So, it is clear that the goat and ram are not part of the four beasts and horns. What then would cause the goat (Turkey) to attack the ram (Iran) since both Iran and Turkey are Islamic nations? The answer may lie in the divisions among the Islamic faith, Shiite and Sunni. Iran is the center for the Shiites while Turkey is the heart of the Sunni branch. In fact, Istanbul (formerly Constantinople) in Turkey is considered among many Islamic clerics to be the capital of an Islamic caliphate.

These two Islamic divisions began soon after the death of Muhammad on June 8, AD 632. Immediately following his death, two major traditions emerged, divided over who should succeed the great prophet. Muhammad had united all the once warring tribes of the broad plains of Arabia, around the city of Mecca, near the banks of the Red Sea in what today is known as the Arabian Peninsula. Shiites agree with Sunnis in most areas of Islamic theology, including belief in Muhammad as the final prophet, the Qur'an as God's final book replacing what came before it, and Islam as God's final and perfect religion. Sunnis are by far the largest group, making up approximately eighty-five to ninety percent of Islam, whereas the Shiites make up the remaining ten to fifteen percent living primarily in Iran, Pakistan, and Iraq. However, there are minority Shia groups residing in most Muslim countries.

Where Sunnis and Shias differ is on who is a rightful successor to Muhammad. Sunni Islam argues that the true successors to Muhammad do not need to be descended from the immediate family of Muhammad and emphasizes tradition in religious life, i.e., the way the Prophet and his followers lived. Thus, the Qur'an is the fundamental authority, along with the Hadith (the various collected accountings of the words, actions, and habits of the Prophet Muhammad during his lifetime) and the consensus of the community. Today, Saudi Arabia, including Mecca, is the center of power for Sunni Islam. Yet, as noted, many believe that Istanbul is and will be the capital of the Islamic caliphate as it once was.

Shia Islam, on the other hand, argues that the true successors to Muhammad descend directly from Muhammad's family. Although there is disagreement within Shiism on the number of Imams (who lead Muslim worshippers in prayer) and their exact progression, most Shiites assume that the spiritual power of the Imams works through and guides Shiite leaders. They assume that the last Imam will return to restore true Islam and inaugurate a new age in world history. Mainstream Shiites have long believed in the eventual return of the Mahdi, who will be the Twelfth Imam and who is believed to be a direct bloodline descendant of Muhammad's son-in-law Ali. Shias believe that Ali's family constitute the only legitimate successors to Muhammad. The Twelfth Imam will allegedly return in the future as the Mahdi ("The rightly guided One") who will bring about a messianic-like era of global order and justice for Shiites in which Islam will be victorious and reign supreme. It is believed that the time of the appearance of the Twelfth Imam can be hastened through apocalyptic chaos and violence—that is, by unleashing an apocalyptic holy war against Christians and Jews.

All Muslim theology holds to a return of Isa, the Islamic Christ, and a return of Muhammad. According to Islam, Christ will return, marry, have children, destroy all crosses and pigs, deny His crucifixion, His deity, and the Trinity, and then will die. Iranian Shiites, however, believe that the Twelfth Imam, the Mahdi, was removed by God at the age of four or five in AD 873 and is in a miraculous state of hiddenness. They believe that occasionally the Mahdi appears and speaks with special people and that following much conflict and war he will reappear with Christ. The return of Christ is very close in concept to the Muslim's return of the Mahdi. In order to explain Iranian terrorism, many believe that political and religious leaders in Iran want to stir conflict in order to bring the Mahdi back sooner than later.

With so much animosity between the two factions, it is not unlikely that a military conflict between them could erupt. If Shiite Iran were to claim that the Mahdi had arrived, then it is possible that this would enrage the Turkish Sunnis, who believe that the Mahdi will be Sunni and that his capital will be in Istanbul. Whatever the cause, it is plain that something will enrage Turkey to cause them to attack and destroy Iran.

> And I saw him come close unto the ram, and he was moved with choler against him, and smote the ram, and brake his two horns: and there was no power in the ram to stand before him, but he cast him down to the ground, and stamped upon him: and there was none that could deliver the ram out of his hand. Daniel 8:7

After its victory, the male goat (Turkey) then becomes very great but later is broken up into four kingdoms.

> Therefore the he goat waxed very great: and when he was strong, the great horn was broken; and for it came up four notable ones toward the four winds of heaven. Daniel 8:8

Out of one of these kingdoms arises the little horn or Antichrist, who moves to consolidate his kingdom into a ten-nation confederacy. The Antichrist will most likely originate from one of the northern kingdoms since he is also called the "king of the north" in Daniel 11.

> And out of one of them came forth a little horn, which waxed exceeding great, toward the south, and toward the east, and toward the pleasant land. Daniel 8:9

Since these events happen prior to the emergence of the Antichrist, it demonstrates that the Ram Goat War occurs prior to the beginning of the 70th Week, which is when the Antichrist will help broker a Mideast peace deal at the first seal. Also, Daniel 8 gives a time frame of 2300 days from the restart of the daily sacrifices to the cleansing of the Temple at the end.

> Then I heard one saint speaking, and another saint said unto that certain saint which spake, How long shall be the vision concerning the daily sacrifice, and the transgression of desolation, to give both the sanctuary and the host to be trodden under foot? And he said unto me, Unto two thousand and three hundred days; then shall the sanctuary be cleansed. Daniel 8:13-14

This localizes these events of Daniel 7 and 8 prior to the first half of the 70th Week when the Temple sacrifices will be reinstituted. Consequently, a war between Iran and Turkey should be one of the first upcoming events that indicate that the 70th Week is soon to follow.

Ramadan and the Timing of the Ram Goat War[8]

Although Ramadan is a Muslim holiday, it may provide some insight as to when this Ram Goat War might occur. Ramadan is the ninth and holiest month on the Muslim calendar, and to most Muslims it is a month of repentance. Yet worldwide terrorist organizations like ISIS and al-Qaeda like to call for terrorist attacks during this time, and historically places like Israel see a marked increase in extremist incidents during this month. This is not surprising since from the terrorist perspective, they expect to receive a double reward in heaven if they do something during this month.

According to their traditions, the Qur'an was revealed to the prophet Muhammad during Ramadan. It is a floating month that shifts by approximately ten days each year. For instance, in the year 2023 it will begin on March 22, and in 2024 it begins on March 10. That is because, like the Jewish calendar, the Islamic calendar is based on a lunar cycle and not a solar cycle like the Western calendar. The lunar cycle is about ten days shorter than a solar cycle. That means that Ramadan can and does take place in any season of the year.

In addition to Muslims believing that the Qur'an was given to them during Ramadan, five of their historically greatest military victories were all won during that month as well. This includes the Battle of Badr where Muhammad waged his first jihad which again links terrorism and Islamic war with this month of Ramadan.

Also, caliphs, who are Muslim leaders, may be appointed, and caliphates that are Muslim empires may form during Ramadan. Although the last caliph faded with the fall of the Ottoman empire in 1923, the final caliph, the Islamic messiah known as the Mahdi, will emerge during Ramadan according to their prophecies. Two Muslim predictions are: (1) for the Mahdi to arrive during Ramadan and (2) that a double eclipse, one of the moon and one of the sun, will occur during that month. In this prophecy the lunar eclipse should occur on the first of the eclipse nights with the occurrence of the solar eclipse in the middle of the eclipse days. Any new caliph wanting to be declared the Mahdi would want to be declared caliph during a month that has these two eclipses.

Interestingly, there are two years between now and 2029 that fit the prophetic criteria for the twin eclipses during Ramadan, 2024 and 2025. In 2024 Ramadan occurs from March 10 to April 8. During this time frame a lunar eclipse takes place on March 24-25 and a solar eclipse on April 8. Similarly, in 2025 Ramadan transpires from February 28 to March 29 with a lunar eclipse happening on March 13-14 and a solar eclipse falling on March 29.[9] So, these two years could be the time when the Mahdi makes his appearance.

Just like many of the Christian end time events happen during the Jewish month of Tishri, the month that God has ordained for these events, Islamic nations may want events to happen during the month that they consider holy, the month of Ramadan. Besides the appearance of the Mahdi, one of these events is the reformation of the Ottoman Empire with its capital in Istanbul where a revived Sunni caliphate will likely arise. Modern Turks are looking to reform that caliphate in 2023 on the one hundredth anniversary of the breakup of the Ottoman Empire after World War I. The "prominent horn" listed in Daniel 8:21 is likely to be the first caliph or sultan of this new empire. The Bible does not give any specifics on when a revived Ottoman Empire might occur, but of course, this caliph would want to be appointed during Ramadan since this would make him a candidate to be their Mahdi.

So, perhaps a revived Ottoman Empire will be established in 2023, one hundred years from it being disbanded. Of course, this is speculation but certainly this date is one to keep in mind. And once a Sunni caliphate is reestablished, any attempt by Iran to name a Shiite Mahdi, perhaps in a year of twin eclipses during Ramadan, e.g., 2024 or 2025, could be met with hostilities leading to the Ram Goat War.

SUMMARY

Wars and rumors of wars continue to increase in frequency as the end times near. There are four major end time wars that are outlined in scripture. Their basic characteristics and differences are outlined in the chart below detailing who is involved, when these battles occur, who wins, and how the battle was won. This is then followed by locating these events on the proposed end time's timeline.

SUMMARY OF END TIMES BATTLES

	Ram Goat	Psalm 83	Armageddon	Gog Magog
Reference	Daniel 8	Psalm 83	Ezekiel 38-39	Revelation 20
Nations involved	Turkey vs Iran	Lebanon, Gaza, Syria, Jordan, Palestinians, Arabian Arabs, Egyptian Arabs vs Israel	Turkey, Iran, Libya, Sudan, Ethiopia, Afghanistan, Kazakhstan, & ?Russia vs Israel	The nations vs the saints & the beloved city
Timing	Prior to beginning of 70th Week	During last year of 70th Week, during the Day of the Lord	At end of the 70th Week	At end of the Millennium
Means of Victory	Turkey with furious power tramples Iran	Jesus alone brings judgment	God supernaturally wins victory with fire & brimstone	God supernaturally wins victory with fire
Outcome	Turkey wins & then is broken into 4 kingdoms; Arrival of little horn (Antichrist) out of 4 kingdoms	Judgment of all these nations & complete extermination of Edom in northern Saudi Arabia	Lord pours out his spirit on Israel; Israel & nations know that Jesus is Lord; Jesus' name will not be profaned; Israel dwells safely in their own land; Supper of the Lord takes place; Antichrist & False Prophet cast into lake of fire; Satan bound 1000 years	Puts rebellion of Satan to rest forever; Devil cast into lake of fire

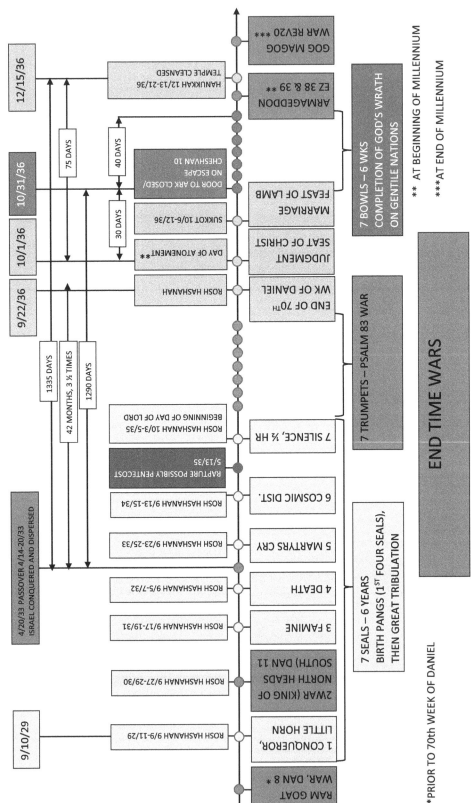

END TIME WARS

*PRIOR TO 70th WEEK OF DANIEL

** AT BEGINNING OF MILLENNIUM

*** AT END OF MILLENNIUM

Timeline labels (bottom to top of image):

- RAM GOAT WAR, DAN 8 *
- 9/10/29
- 1 CONQUEROR, LITTLE HORN — ROSH HASHANAH 9/9-11/29
- 2 WAR (KING OF NORTH HEADS SOUTH) DAN 11 — ROSH HASHANAH 9/27-29/30
- 3 FAMINE — ROSH HASHANAH 9/17-19/31
- 4 DEATH — ROSH HASHANAH 9/5-7/32
- 4/20/33 PASSOVER 4/14-20/33 (ISRAEL CONQUERED AND DISPERSED)
- 5 MARTYRS CRY — ROSH HASHANAH 9/23-25/33
- 6 COSMIC DIST. — ROSH HASHANAH 9/13-15/34
- RAPTURE POSSIBLY PENTECOST 5/13/35
- 7 SILENCE, ½ HR — ROSH HASHANAH 10/3-5/35 BEGINNING OF DAY OF LORD
- 7 SEALS – 6 YEARS BIRTH PANGS (1ST FOUR SEALS), THEN GREAT TRIBULATION
- 7 TRUMPETS – PSALM 83 WAR
- 1335 DAYS
- 42 MONTHS, 3 ½ TIMES
- 1290 DAYS
- 9/22/36
- END OF 70TH WK OF DANIEL — ROSH HASHANAH
- 10/1/36
- JUDGMENT SEAT OF CHRIST — DAY OF ATONEMENT **
- 30 DAYS
- MARRIAGE FEAST OF LAMB — SUKKOT 10/6-12/36
- 10/31/36
- 40 DAYS
- DOOR TO ARK CLOSED/ NO ESCAPE CHESHVAN 10
- 75 DAYS
- 7 BOWLS – 6 WKS COMPLETION OF GOD'S WRATH ON GENTILE NATIONS
- ARMAGEDDON EZ 38 & 39 **
- 12/15/36
- TEMPLE CLEANSED — HANUKKAH 12/13-21/36
- GOG MAGOG WAR REV 20 ***

CHAPTER 10

Judgments

Standing before a judge to be sentenced is nobody's idea of fun. Yet, the Bible is clear that all will be judged by God.

> Marvel not at this: for the hour is coming, in the which **all** that are in the graves shall hear his voice, And shall come forth; they that have done good, unto the resurrection of life; and they that have done evil, unto the resurrection of damnation. John 5:28-29

> For we must **all** appear before the judgment seat of Christ; that every one may receive the things done in his body, according to that he hath done, whether it be good or bad. 2 Corinthians 5:10

> And as it is appointed unto men once to die, but after this the judgment: Hebrews 9:27

Everyone, that is everyone who ever was, is, or will be, will undergo judgment. But when will that judgment occur? And does judgment occur at the same time for each person and group of people. Four different judgments will be discussed, including: (1) judgment of the Church, (2) judgment of Israel, (3) judgment of the Nations, and (4) the final Great White Throne judgment.

But first of all, why must judgment even occur? Although the Bible seems to leave some questions unanswered, it does provide insight into the judgment that is coming. God must judge, because if there is to be justice, then there must be a judgment. There often is no immediate justice in this world, but we are promised that there will be justice after we die. If there were no ultimate justice, then there is no reason to live a holy and righteous life. But God must judge because He is righteous and holy. God's holiness is emphasized throughout scripture.

> And the four beasts had each of them six wings about him; and they were full of eyes within: and they rest not day and night, saying, Holy, holy, holy, LORD God Almighty, which was, and is, and is to come. And the four beasts had each of them six wings about him; and they were full of eyes within: and they rest not day and night, saying, Holy, holy, holy, Lord God Almighty, which was, and is, and is to come. Rev 4:8

And because God is holy, He cannot look at sin.

> Thou art of purer eyes than to behold evil, and **canst not look on iniquity**: wherefore lookest thou upon them that deal treacherously, and holdest thy tongue when the wicked devoureth the man that is more righteous than he? Habakkuk 1:13

Although standing before God and His judgment is a frightful and horrible concept, it should have some positive results in our lives. First, it should cause us to fear God and to consider our actions before carrying them out. Second, it should instigate a reevaluation in the way we have been living our lives and consequently change our priorities. Next, it should humble us since God's judgment removes our self-righteousness and prompts us to remember how sinful we are. It reminds us that we are not really in control of our lives and how dependent we are on God. Finally, the fact that there will be a final judgment reassures us that there is justice in the world. The wicked will be held accountable for what they have done, and it is encouraging to know ultimately there will be justice.[1]

Who Does the Judging?

So, if there will be a final judgment, who will do the judging? The Bible says that the Lord Jesus Himself will be the judge. Jesus said:

> For the Father judgeth no man, but hath committed all judgment unto the Son: And hath given him authority to execute judgment also, because he is the Son of man. John 5:22,27

And Paul confirmed that Jesus will be the judge of mankind.

> Because he hath appointed a day, in the which he will judge the world in righteousness by that man whom he hath ordained; whereof he hath given assurance unto **all** men, in that he hath raised him from the dead. Acts 17:31

> In the day when God shall judge the secrets of men by Jesus Christ according to my gospel. Romans 2:16

The claim made by Jesus Christ is that He will be the one who will judge humanity. As opposed to His first coming when He came as a suffering savior of mankind, at His second coming Jesus will come as a conquering king who will rule with a rod of iron. This rod will be used for discipline, chastisement and wrath on the wicked.

> I will declare the decree: the LORD hath said unto me, Thou art my Son; this day have I begotten thee.

> Ask of me, and I shall give thee the heathen for thine inheritance, and the uttermost parts of the earth for thy possession. Thou shalt break them with a rod of iron; thou shalt dash them in pieces like a potter's vessel. Psalm 2:7-9

> But with righteousness shall he judge the poor, and reprove with equity for the meek of the earth: and he shall smite the earth: with the rod of his mouth, and with the breath of his lips shall he slay the wicked. Isaiah 11:4

> And he shall rule them with a rod of iron; as the vessels of a potter shall they be broken to shivers: even as I received of my Father. Revelation 2:27

The Lord will strike the nations with the rod, meting out the fierceness and wrath of God's judgment to those that are deserving. However, rods were also used for protection. In one of his psalms, King David wrote,

> Yea, though I walk through the valley of the shadow of death, I will fear no evil: for thou art with me; thy rod and thy staff they comfort me. Psalm 23:4

This passage demonstrates how the rod was used for protection by a shepherd just like David did. In this case the rod was applied for the keeping of the sheep, not their discipline or chastisement. The use of the rod of iron by the Lord is not spoken of negatively for use on the Lord's sheep, His people. Rather, He will use the rod to smite the evil ones who harmed and wanted to destroy His sheep.[2]

Will Christians also judge?

If Jesus is responsible for judging all things, will Christians also participate in that judging? 1 Corinthians states:

> Do ye not know that the saints shall judge the world? and if the world shall be judged by you, are ye unworthy to judge the smallest matters? Know ye not that we shall judge angels? how much more things that pertain to this life? 1 Corinthians 6:2-3

Jesus in the Book of Revelations says to the saints:

> To him that overcometh will I grant to sit with me in my throne, even as I also overcame, and am set down with my Father in his throne. Revelation 3:21

If the saints have any role in judgment at all, it will be as a participant in the rights and the authority of Jesus, and Jesus gives a specific example with a promise.

> And he that overcometh, and keepeth my works unto the end, to him will I give power over the nations: Revelation 2:26

Paul puts it like this:

> If we suffer, we shall also reign with him: if we deny him, he also will deny us: 2 Timothy 2:12

The spectacular thing about being told that the saints will judge the world and angels is not mainly the specific ways that it will take place, but the inexpressible greatness of the status, the position given to ordinary people of God, who actually share in the functions of the judge of the universe.

When will God's judgments occur?

Although Jesus will judge everyone, the time and location of their judgment depends on their faith and righteousness, as well as their state of mortality, i.e., whether they have died. There are three groups that

God deals with throughout time: The Church, Israel and the Gentile nations, and each group will be judged differently and at separate times. The first group to be judged will be the Church after they are raptured into heaven. They will appear before the Bema Seat of Christ to receive their rewards. The second group to undergo sentencing is Israel, who will be judged by Christ at His second coming. The third group to be judged will include the Gentile nations at the end of the 70th week, after God's wrath has been completed. And the final judgment occurs at the Great White Throne Judgment, at the end of the Millennium, where all the dead who have not yet been judged will be judged. The righteous will go into eternal life while the unrighteous will perish.

> For God so loved the world, that he gave his only begotten Son, that whosoever believeth in him should not perish, but have everlasting life. John 3:16

How does God judge? On what basis does He judge?

Before discussing each of these judgments in more detail, exactly how does God arrive at these verdicts. On what basis does He sentence each individual? What are His criteria? And in fact, does God use different criteria for each of the different groups?

First of all, it must be noted that judgment will be fair. The psalmist wrote:

> Before the Lord: for he cometh, for he cometh to judge the earth: he shall judge the world with righteousness, and the people with his truth. Psalm 96:13

As seen earlier, the Apostle Paul also emphasized the truth of God's righteous judgment.

> Because he hath appointed a day, in the which he will judge the world in righteousness by that man whom he hath ordained; whereof he hath given assurance unto

all men, in that he hath raised him from the dead. Acts 17:31

Jeremiah quoted God as saying:

> I the LORD search the heart, I try the reins, even to give every man according to his ways, and according to the fruit of his doings. Jeremiah 17:10

Not only will it be fair, but humanity will be judged according to God's standards, not ours. The benchmark for measurement will be Christ, not one another. Jesus said:

> Also I say unto you, Whosoever shall confess me before men, him shall the Son of man also confess before the angels of God: But he that denieth me before men shall be denied before the angels of God. Luk 12:8-9

And those who reject Jesus Christ will be judged by the one they rejected.

> He that rejecteth me, and receiveth not my words, hath one that judgeth him: the word that I have spoken, the same shall judge him in the last day. John 12:48

The basis of God's judgment will be their relationship to Christ.

> He that believeth on him is not condemned: but he that believeth not is condemned already, because he hath not believed in the name of the only begotten Son of God. And this is the condemnation, that light is come into the world, and men loved darkness rather than light, because their deeds were evil. John 3:18-19

Salvation, therefore, is not a matter of our good deeds, not what we have done, but is based upon what Christ has done for us. Paul wrote:

For **by grace** are ye saved through faith; and that not of yourselves: it is the gift of God: Not of works, lest any man should boast. Ephesians 2:8-9

Not by works of righteousness which we have done, but **according to his mercy** he saved us, by the washing of regeneration, and renewing of the Holy Ghost; Titus 3:5

But, although our salvation will be based on our faith in Christ, the Bible clearly says that each of us will still be judged according to our works. Paul wrote:

Who will render to every man **according to his deeds**: But glory, honour, and peace, to every man that worketh good, to the Jew first, and also to the Gentile: For there is no respect of persons with God. Romans 2:6,10,11

And the Book of Revelation states:

And I will kill her children with death; and all the Churches shall know that I am he which searcheth the reins and hearts: and I will give unto every one of you **according to your works**. Revelation 2:23

In case we might think that God will weigh our good deeds against our bad deeds, He has told us of what the work of God consists.

Then said they unto him, What shall we do, that we might work the works of God? Jesus answered and said unto them, This is the work of God, that **ye believe on him whom he hath sent**. John 6:28-29

The work of God is to believe in Him whom He has sent, Jesus Christ, and to demonstrate that work in the way we live in obedience to God.

But what about those who have never heard the gospel message of Christ or had an opportunity to respond to that good news? Each will be judged according to the information they have received. Jesus said:

> Woe unto thee, Chorazin! woe unto thee, Bethsaida! for if the mighty works, which were done in you, had been done in Tyre and Sidon, they would have repented long ago in sackcloth and ashes. But I say unto you, It shall be more tolerable for Tyre and Sidon at the day of judgment, than for you. And thou, Capernaum, which art exalted unto heaven, shalt be brought down to hell: for if the mighty works, which have been done in thee, had been done in Sodom, it would have remained until this day. But I say unto you, That it shall be more tolerable for the land of Sodom in the day of judgment, than for thee. Matthew 11:21-24

The scriptural truth is that to whom much has been given, much will be required.

> But he that knew not, and did commit things worthy of stripes, shall be beaten with few stripes. For unto whomsoever much is given, of him shall be much required: and to whom men have committed much, of him they will ask the more. Luke 12:48

And in fact, teachers and those leaders responsible for guiding the Church will undergo a stricter judgment.

> My brethren, be not many masters, knowing that we shall receive the greater condemnation. James 3:1

Summary

So, the Bible is clear on this issue of God's judgment. God is fair, but where a person spends eternity depends upon how they view Jesus Christ. Those who receive Him as Savior will not be condemned. However, those who reject His free gift of salvation will be condemned for all eternity. God's judgment will be fair. There will be no partiality. We can accept God's Son and His **mercy** (God not giving us the punishment that we deserve) and also receive His **grace** (God giving us gifts that we do not deserve). Or we can deny His Son and thereby choose instead to receive God's **justice** (God giving us what we deserve). By selecting to do the work of God and electing to believe on Jesus Christ, we are choosing His grace and mercy, sparing us from His justice.

JUDGMENT OF THE CHURCH

God's judgment begins first with the Church, those who have accepted God's grace and mercy through His son. And although judgment will begin with the New Testament Church, the judgment itself is actually introduced and described in the Old Testament.

> Our God shall come, and shall not keep silence: a fire shall devour before him, and it shall be very tempestuous round about him. He shall call to the heavens from above, and to the earth, that he may **judge** his people. Gather my saints together unto me; those that have made a covenant with me by sacrifice. Psalm 50:3-5

Here it indicates that the saints are raptured to heaven so that they may be judged by God. This principle of judgment of the righteous continues in the New Testament with the Doctrine of Rewards and the Judgment Seat of Christ. It is a doctrine often ignored, or when taught, is misrepresented because of the term *judge* that is used in translating the Greek text. Commenting on this, Samuel Hoyt writes:

Within the Church today there exists considerable confusion and debate regarding the exact nature of the examination at the judgment seat of Christ. The expression "the judgment seat of Christ" in the English Bible has tended to cause some to draw the wrong conclusion about the nature and purpose of this evaluation. A common misconception which arises from this English translation is that God will mete out a just retribution for sins in the believer's life, and some measure of retributive punishment for sins will result.

Though it is tremendously serious with eternal ramifications, the Judgment Seat of Christ is not a place and time when the Lord will mete out punishment for sins committed by the child of God. Rather, it is a place where rewards will be given or lost depending on how one has used his or her life for the Lord. In 1Thessalonians, the Apostle Paul drew courage and was motivated by the fact of rewards at the return of the Lord for the Church which he mentions in every chapter in this epistle and then becomes the primary subject of 2 Thessalonians.

> For what is our hope, or joy, or crown of rejoicing? Are not even ye in the presence of our Lord Jesus Christ at his coming? For ye are our glory and joy. 1 Thessalonians 2:19-20,

The Lord's return and what this means not only to the world but to us individually is a very prominent subject throughout the New Testament. It is significant that the final words of Revelation, the last book of the Bible, include these words of the Lord:

> And, behold, I come quickly; and my **reward** is with me, to give every man according as his work shall be. Revelation 22:12

Salvation is a gift, and there are rewards given for faithfulness in the Christian life and loss of rewards for unfaithfulness. The promise of rewards becomes (or should become) one of the great motives in the Christian's life. But understanding the nature of these rewards is needed in order to understand the nature of this motivation. Some people are troubled by the doctrine of rewards because it seems to suggest merit instead of grace, works in place of faith. Also, it is pointed out that we should only serve the Lord out of love and for God's glory, not our own reward.

Of course, we should serve the Lord out of love and for God's glory, and understanding the nature of rewards will help us do that. But the fact still remains that the Bible promises us rewards. God gives us salvation which is a gift through faith. But He also will reward us for good works, and God graciously supplies the means by which we do those works as we serve Him. Indeed, He works in us both to will and to do works of His good pleasure as we willingly accept His grace.

> Wherefore, my beloved, as ye have always obeyed, not as in my presence only, but now much more in my absence, work out your own salvation with fear and trembling. For it is God which worketh in you both to will and to do of his good pleasure. Philippians 2:12-13

But the decision to serve and the diligence employed in doing so are our responsibility and our contribution which God sees as rewardable. Compare the following passages:

> But by the grace of God I am what I am: and his grace which was bestowed upon me was not in vain; but I laboured more abundantly than they all: yet not I, but the grace of God which was with me. 1 Cor 15:10

> Whereunto I also labour, striving according to his working, which worketh in me mightily. Colossians 1:29

The Judgment (*Bema*) Seat

Where does the judgment of the Church by Christ occur? The following verses speak of the "judgment seat of Christ".

> But why dost thou judge thy brother? or why dost thou set at nought thy brother? for we shall all stand before the judgment seat *(bema)* of Christ. Romans 14:10

> Wherefore we labour, that, whether present or absent, we may be accepted of him. For we must all appear before the judgment seat *(bema)* of Christ; that every one may receive the things done in his body, according to that he hath done, whether it be good or bad. 2 Corinthians 5:9-10

"Judgment seat" is a translation of one Greek word, the word *bema*. The word *bema* is used in the gospels and Acts of the raised platform where a Roman magistrate or ruler sat to make decisions and pass sentence.

> When he *(Pilate)* was set down on the judgment seat *(bema)*, his wife sent unto him, saying, Have thou nothing to do with that just man: for I have suffered many things this day in a dream because of him. Matthew 27:19

> When Pilate therefore heard that saying, he brought Jesus forth, and sat down in the judgment seat *(bema)* in a place that is called the Pavement, but in the Hebrew, Gabbatha. John 19:13

Because of his many allusions to the Greek athletic contests, Paul used the word *bema* more in keeping with its original use among the Greeks. This word was taken from Isthmian games where the contestants would compete for the prize under the careful scrutiny of judges who would make sure that every rule of the contest was obeyed. The victor of a given event who participated according to the rules was led by the judge to the platform called the *Bema*. There the laurel wreath was placed on his head as a symbol of victory.[9]

> Know ye not that they which run in a race run all, but one receiveth the prize? So run, that ye may obtain. And every man that striveth for the mastery is temperate in all things. Now they do it to obtain a corruptible crown; but we an incorruptible. 1 Corinthians 9:24-25

So, the judge at the *Bema* bestowed prizes or crowns to the victors. He did not whip the losers. In other words, it is a reward seat and portrays a time of rewards or loss of rewards following examination. But it is not a time of punishment where believers are judged for their sins. Such would be inconsistent with the finished work of Christ on the Cross because He totally paid the penalty for our sins.

The Participants at the *Bema*

All the passages dealing with the *Bema* or rewards are addressed to believers or pertain to believers in the Church (Romans 14:10-12; 1 Corinthians 3:12f; 2 Corinthians 5:9f; 1 John 2:28; 1 Thessalonians 2:19-20; 1 Timothy 6:18-19; Titus 2:12-14). All believers, regardless of their spiritual state, will be raptured and will then stand before the *Bema* to give an account of their lives, receiving or losing rewards.

The examiner or judge at the Bema, as we have seen, is none other than the Lord Jesus who is even now examining our lives and will bring to light the true nature of our walk and works when we stand before Him at the *Bema* (Revelation 1-2; 1 Corinthians 4:5f; 2 Corinthians 5:10; 1 John 2:28). In Romans 14:10 Paul called this examining time the *Bema of God*, while in 2 Corinthians 5:10 he called it the *Bema of Christ*. The point is that Jesus will be our examiner and rewarder.[9]

Basis of the Judgment

In regards to **sin**, Scripture teaches that the child of God under grace shall **not** come into judgment.

> He that believeth on him is not condemned: but he that believeth not is condemned already, because he hath not believed in the name of the only begotten Son of God. John 3:18

> Verily, verily, I say unto you, He that heareth my word, and believeth on him that sent me, hath everlasting life, and shall not come into condemnation; but is passed from death unto life. John 5:24

> All that the Father giveth me shall come to me; and him that cometh to me I will in no wise cast out. John 6:37

> Therefore being justified by faith, we have peace with God through our Lord Jesus Christ: Romans 5:1

> There is therefore now no condemnation to them which are in Christ Jesus, who walk not after the flesh, but after the Spirit. Romans 8:1

> But when we are judged, we are chastened of the Lord, that we should not be condemned with the world. 1 Corinthians 11:32

God's child stands before God on the grounds that the penalty for all sin—past, present, and future—has been borne by Christ as the perfect substitute.

> And you, being dead in your sins and the uncircumcision of your flesh, hath he quickened together with him, having forgiven you all trespasses; Colossians 2:13

The believer is not only placed beyond condemnation, but being in Christ is accepted in the perfection of Christ.

> But of him are ye in Christ Jesus, who of God is made unto us wisdom, and righteousness, and sanctification, and redemption: 1 Corinthians 1:30

> To the praise of the glory of his grace, wherein he hath made us accepted in the beloved. Ephesians 1:6

> And ye are complete in him, which is the head of all principality and power: Colossians 2:10

> For by one offering he hath perfected for ever them that are sanctified. Hebrews 10:14

And being accepted, the believer is loved of God as Christ is loved.

> I in them, and thou in me, that they may be made perfect in one; and that the world may know that thou hast sent me, and hast loved them, as thou hast loved me. John 17:23

So, this judgment is emphatically unrelated to the problem of sin. The believer's salvation is secure before Christ, and this judgment consequently is for the bestowing of rewards rather than the rejection for failure.

Timing of the *Bema*

At some time in the future, the Lord will come back for those who have believed upon Him. He will resurrect them, changing their bodies from corruptible to incorruptible which is a description of the Rapture.

> But I would not have you to be ignorant, brethren, concerning them which are asleep, that ye sorrow not,

even as others which have no hope. For if we believe that Jesus died and rose again, even so them also which sleep in Jesus will God bring with him. For this we say unto you by the word of the Lord, that we which are alive and remain unto the coming of the Lord shall not prevent them which are asleep. For the Lord himself shall descend from heaven with a shout, with the voice of the archangel, and with the trump of God: and the dead in Christ shall rise first: Then we which are alive and remain shall be caught up together with them in the clouds, to meet the Lord in the air: and so shall we ever be with the Lord. Wherefore comfort one another with these words. 1 Thessalonians 4:13-18

After this event, believers in Christ will go to the judgment seat of Christ. Supporting this view is the idea that rewards for the righteous are linked with the resurrection.

Then said he also to him that bade him, When thou makest a dinner or a supper, call not thy friends, nor thy brethren, neither thy kinsmen, nor thy rich neighbours; lest they also bid thee again, and a recompence be made thee. But when thou makest a feast, call the poor, the maimed, the lame, the blind: And thou shalt be blessed; for they cannot recompense thee: **for thou shalt be recompensed at the resurrection of the just.** Luke 14:12-14

So, since rewards are connected with the resurrection (and the Rapture is when the Church is resurrected), then the position that the judgment of the Church follows the Rapture is backed. Further supporting the idea that the sequence of events will be the Rapture followed by judgment are scriptures in 2 Timothy and 1 Corinthians. In these passages rewards are again associated with "that day" and with the Lord's coming, which for the Church means the event seen in 1Thessalonians 4:13-18, that is the Rapture.

> Henceforth there is laid up for me a crown of righteousness, which the Lord, the righteous judge, shall give me **at that day**: and not to me only, but unto all them also that love his appearing. 2 Timothy 4:8

> Therefore judge nothing before the time, until **the Lord come**, who both will bring to light the hidden things of darkness, and will make manifest the counsels of the hearts: and then shall every man have praise of God. 1 Corinthians 4:5

So, the likely order of events will be (1) the Rapture which includes the glorification or resurrection of the saint's bodies, (2) exaltation into the heavens with the Lord, (3) examination before the *Bema*, and (4) compensation or rewards.

Location of the *Bema* Judgment

The judgment of the Church saints will occur somewhere in the heavenlies in the presence of the Lord. This is evident in 1 Thessalonians.

> Then we which are alive and remain shall be caught up together with them **in the clouds**, to meet the Lord **in the air**: and so shall we ever be with the Lord. 1 Thessalonians 4:17

Basis of the *Bema* Judgment

There will be three parts to this judgment:

(1) Evaluation of the quality of every believer's work whether it is good or bad, i.e., acceptable and thus worthy of rewards, or unacceptable, to be rejected and unworthy of rewards.

(2) Destruction and removal of unacceptable production portrayed in the symbols of wood, hay, and stubble. All sinful deeds, thoughts, and motives, as well as all good deeds done in the strength of the flesh will be consumed like wood, hay, and stubble before a fire because they are unworthy of reward.

(3) Rewarding of the believer for all the good he or she has done as portrayed by the symbols of gold, silver, and precious stones, that which is valuable and can stand the test of fire without being consumed.[3]

> For other foundation can no man lay than that is laid, which is Jesus Christ. Now if any man build upon this foundation gold, silver, precious stones, wood, hay, stubble; Every man's work shall be made manifest: for the day shall declare it, because it shall be revealed by fire; and the fire shall try every man's work of what sort it is. If any man's work abide which he hath built thereupon, he shall receive a reward. If any man's work shall be burned, he shall suffer loss: but he himself shall be saved; yet so as by fire. 1 Corinthians 3:11-15

As noted, entrance into this examination or judgment has already been determined by the examinees faith in Christ, resulting in their salvation. So, in fact, this phase of the judgment is completed before even arriving at the bema. Everyone at this judgment is saved, and the next stage of the judgment will provide rewards in accordance with one's works and motives. This part of the evaluation will be a review of "examination questions" that have been given to us in advance through Biblical principles, and may include:

- How we treated other believers
- How we employed our God-given talents and opportunities
- How we used our money
- How well we accepted mistreatment and injustice

- How we endured suffering and trial in this life
- How we spent our time (e.g., the choices that we made with our hours)
- How we ran the particular "race" that God has set before us; each person's "race" to run is different
- How we controlled our fleshly appetites
- How many souls we witnessed to, and won for Christ
- How faithful we were to God's Word and to God's people
- How hospitable we were to strangers
- How faithful we were in our vocation
- How we used our tongue

How a person answers these and other questions on what they have done with their life will determine his or her reward.[14]

Many Christians will have little to show for their lives, even though they may have accepted Jesus Christ as Lord and Savior many years before they died. Perhaps because of indifference, lack of desire, or enchantment with the world, the rest of their lives are symbolically represented as "wood, hay or straw". This will probably also include "good" works that were performed for selfish reasons such as drawing attention or praise to themselves.

Finally, there are many others who worked hard for the Lord, and perhaps sacrificed greatly (the persecuted church comes to mind).

> Therefore, my beloved brethren, be ye stedfast, unmoveable, always abounding in the work of the Lord, forasmuch as ye know that your labour is not in vain in the Lord. 1 Corinthians 15:58

> And whatsoever ye do, do it heartily, as to the Lord, and not unto men; Knowing that of the Lord ye shall receive the reward of the inheritance: for ye serve the Lord Christ. Colossians 3:23-24

For the Son of man shall come in the glory of his Father with his angels; and then he shall reward every man according to his works. Matthew 16:27

And, behold, I come quickly; and my reward is with me, to give every man according as his work shall be. Revelation 22:12

So, while your belief or faith determines **where** you will spend eternity, your behavior determines **how** you will spend eternity. Note that some people will have few rewards because, although they believed in Christ, they did little on this earth to show for it. They may have been choked with worldly pleasures. There is a sense of shame in this, even though they are admitted to Heaven.

And now, little children, abide in him; that, when he shall appear, we may have confidence, and not be ashamed before him at his coming. 1 John 2:28

So, it appears that the good works survive, and the bad works are burned up. The consequences of sin exist in this life, meaning that it is likely that fewer good works follow one's pursuit into a sinful lifestyle; therefore, there are fewer rewards to claim at the Bema judgment than might otherwise be had. Even King David, a man after God's heart, stumbled, resulting in consequences during his later life; but Scripture tells us that David will still be rewarded mightily by God. Once the bad works have been burned up, the good works are ready to be rewarded in the final part of the judgment.

Rewards

Only the work of God, the "good" works, that you carried out will determine your richness in heaven and the type of crown or reward you will receive. What are these rewards and how are they described in Scripture? They are described in terms of generalities. So, what we know about rewards is given in terms that are more general than specific and include the following:

(1) The Promise of Crowns. This seems to be used as a symbol of victory, authority, and responsibility.[3] Arnold Fruchtenbaum explains the five crowns of rewards:

> The Greek language has two words meaning "crown". One is the word *diadem*, which is a king's crown. It is the crown of a sovereign and of a person who is royal by his nature and by his position—a king. This is the kind of crown that Jesus wears. The second Greek word is *stephanos*, which is a crown given to an overcomer, a victor, one who has won a race. These are the kinds of crowns available to believers because they overcame in the spiritual warfare and now crowed at the Judgment Seat of the Messiah. There are five such crowns mentioned in the Scriptures.

a) The first such crown is called the **incorruptible crown** given to those who have learned to live a Spirit-controlled life.

> Know ye not that they which run in a race run all, but one receiveth the prize? So run, that ye may obtain. And every man that striveth for the mastery is temperate in all things. Now they do it to obtain a corruptible crown; but we an incorruptible. 1 Corinthians 9:24-25

b) A second crown is called the **crown of rejoicing** given to those who win souls for Jesus.

> For what is our hope, or joy, or crown of rejoicing? Are not even ye in the presence of our Lord Jesus Christ at his coming? 1 Thessalonians 2:19

David Jeremiah comments on this crown:

I suspect [the Crown of Rejoicing] is not just reserved for those who actually lead another person to Christ. I think it will be shared by all those who play a role in bringing others to Christ. It is a team effort. Whenever I have the opportunity of leading others to receive Jesus as Savior, I almost always find someone else has already planted the seed of the Gospel in their hearts. Paul wrote: I have planted, Apollos watered; but God gave the increase. 1 Corinthians 3:6 [Jeremiah, 2017, p. 126]

c) 2 Timothy speaks of a third crown, the **crown of righteousness** for those who have kept the faith both doctrinally and morally in spite of adverse circumstances. It is a crown given to those who love his appearing, those who look longingly for the return of the Messiah.

I have fought a good fight, I have finished my course, I have kept the faith: Henceforth there is laid up for me a crown of righteousness, which the Lord, the righteous judge, shall give me at that day: and not to me only, but unto all them also that love his appearing. 2 Timothy 4:7-8

d) A fourth crown is called the **crown of life** and is mentioned in two passages. In James 1:12, it is a crown for those who endure trials. In Revelation 2:10, it is given to those who suffer martyrdom for their faith.

Blessed is the man that endureth temptation: for when he is tried, he shall receive the crown of life, which the Lord hath promised to them that love him. James 1:12

Fear none of those things which thou shalt suffer: behold, the devil shall cast some of you into prison, that ye may be tried; and ye shall have tribulation ten days: be thou faithful unto death, and I will give thee a crown of life. Revelation 2:10

Martyrdom is something thought of as occurring in the past, and we are fortunate in North America to be free for now to practice our faith without persecution. However, quite a few countries in the world today experience persecution—even to the point of torture and death—for their Christian faith. Likewise, during the end times, Christians will especially be faced with this.

e) A fifth and final crown mentioned in the Scriptures is a **crown of glory** for faithfully feeding the flock of God. It is available to those pastors, elders and others who feed the sheep with the milk and meat of the Word of God.

> Feed the flock of God which is among you, taking the oversight thereof, not by constraint, but willingly; not for filthy lucre, but of a ready mind; Neither as being lords over God's heritage, but being examples to the flock. And when the chief Shepherd shall appear, ye shall receive a crown of glory that fadeth not away. 1 Peter 5:2-4

This crown seems especially designed for Christian leaders and for those who are faithful shepherds of the people of God. Now, you do not necessarily have to be an official pastor on the staff of the Church. You might be the shepherd of a small group. Your flock might be your family and your children. It might be your Sunday school class or small group. The Lord often gives us responsibility for the spiritual well-being and nurturing of others, and what an opportunity to serve him! [Jeremiah, 2017, p. 133][14]

(2) The Promise of Heavenly Treasure. This stresses their eternal value and security.[3]

> But lay up for yourselves treasures in heaven, where neither moth nor rust doth corrupt, and where thieves do not break through nor steal: Matthew 6:20

> To an inheritance incorruptible, and undefiled, and that fadeth not away, reserved in heaven for you, 1 Peter 1:4

(3) The Promise of Accolades or Commendations. This is seen in those passages where a reward is administered in the form of something like "well done thou good and faithful servant …" [3]

> His lord said unto him, Well done, thou good and faithful servant: thou hast been faithful over a few things, I will make thee ruler over many things: enter thou into the joy of thy lord. Matthew 25:21

> And he said unto him, Well, thou good servant: because thou hast been faithful in a very little, have thou authority over ten cities. Luke 19:17

> Therefore judge nothing before the time, until the Lord come, who both will bring to light the hidden things of darkness, and will make manifest the counsels of the hearts: and then shall every man have praise of God. 1 Corinthians 4:5

(4) The Promises to Overcomers. These could refer to special blessings or rewards to those believers who overcome special trials and tests rather than a general promise to all believers.[3]

> He that hath an ear, let him hear what the Spirit saith unto the Churches; To him that overcometh will I give to eat of the tree of life, which is in the midst of the paradise of God. Revelation 2:7

He that hath an ear, let him hear what the Spirit saith unto the Churches; He that overcometh shall not be hurt of the second death. Revelation 2:11

He that hath an ear, let him hear what the Spirit saith unto the Churches; To him that overcometh will I give to eat of the hidden manna, and will give him a white stone, and in the stone a new name written, which no man knoweth saving he that receiveth it. Revelation 2:17

And he that overcometh, and keepeth my works unto the end, to him will I give power over the nations: Revelation 2:26

He that overcometh, the same shall be clothed in white raiment; and I will not blot out his name out of the book of life, but I will confess his name before my Father, and before his angels. Revelation 3:4-5

(5) The Promise of Special Responsibilities and Authority of the Lord's Possessions.[3]

And Jesus said unto them, Verily I say unto you, That ye which have followed me, in the regeneration when the Son of man shall sit in the throne of his glory, ye also shall sit upon twelve thrones, judging the twelve tribes of Israel. Matthew 19:28

Who then is a faithful and wise servant, whom his lord hath made ruler over his household, to give them meat in due season? Blessed is that servant, whom his lord when he cometh shall find so doing. Verily I say unto you, That he shall make him ruler over all his goods. Matthew 24:45-47

His lord said unto him, Well done, thou good and faithful servant: thou hast been faithful over a few things, I will make thee ruler over many things: enter thou into the joy of thy lord. His lord said unto him, Well done, good and faithful servant; thou hast been faithful over a few things, I will make thee ruler over many things: enter thou into the joy of thy lord. Matthew 25:21,23

And he said unto him, Well, thou good servant: because thou hast been faithful in a very little, have thou authority over ten cities. And the second came, saying, Lord, thy pound hath gained five pounds. And he said likewise to him, Be thou also over five cities. Luke 19:17-19

And I appoint unto you a kingdom, as my Father hath appointed unto me; That ye may eat and drink at my table in my kingdom, and sit on thrones judging the twelve tribes of Israel. Luke 22:29-30

The Negative Aspects of the *Bema*

Despite the joy of the rewards, there are a number of passages that refer to the negative aspects of the *Bema* which need to be mentioned and explained. In these passages we read such things as "give account of himself", "suffer loss", "shrink away from Him in shame", and "recompense for his deeds ... whether good or bad".[3] Will believers experience shame, grief, remorse at the Bema? If so, how do we reconcile this with passages like:[3]

And God shall wipe away all tears from their eyes; and there shall be no more death, neither sorrow, nor crying, neither shall there be any more pain: for the former things are passed away. Revelation 21:4

For, behold, I create new heavens and a new earth: and the former shall not be remembered, nor come into mind. Isaiah 65:17

How is a believer made to feel shame? The believer, who fails to abide, experiences shame by the revelatory nature of Christ's presence at the *Bema*. This is caused by the realization of what his own failure and sin has cost him in terms of the loss of rewards and loss of glory to the Lord. But this will only be momentary or short-lived at best in view of passages like:

For the Lamb which is in the midst of the throne shall feed them, and shall lead them unto living fountains of waters: and God shall wipe away all tears from their eyes. Revelation 7:17

And God shall wipe away all tears from their eyes; and there shall be no more death, neither sorrow, nor crying, neither shall there be any more pain: for the former things are passed away. Revelation 21:4

Thus saith the LORD, Keep ye judgment, and do justice: for my salvation is near to come, and my righteousness to be revealed. Isaiah 56:1

Hoyt has a good summary of what these passages are talking about and involve:

The Bible suggests that there will be shame at the judgment seat of Christ to a greater or lesser degree, depending on the measure of unfaithfulness of each individual believer. Therefore, it should be each believer's impelling desire to be well-pleasing to the Lord in all things. Although Christians apparently will reflect on this earthly life with some regret, they will also realize what is ahead for them in the heavenly life. This latter realization will be the source of boundless joy.

E. Schuyler English also strikes a proper balance on this subject.

> Joy will indeed be the predominant emotion of life with the Lord; but I suspect that, when our works are made manifest at the tribunal, some grief will be mixed with the joy, and we shall know shame as we suffer loss. But we shall rejoice also as we realize that the rewards given will be another example of the grace of our Lord; for at best we are unprofitable servants. (E. Schuyler English, "The Church At the Tribunal", in Prophetic Truth Unfolding Today, ed. Charles Lee Feinberg [Old Tappan, NJ: Fleming H. Revell Co., 1968], p. 29)

The elements of remorse, regret, and shame cannot be avoided in an examination at the judgment seat of Christ. But this sorrow must be somewhat relative because even for the finest of Christians there will be some things worthy of unceasing remorse in the light of God's unapproachable holiness. This would mean that the best of Christians could be sorrowful throughout eternity. However, this is not the picture that the New Testament gives of eternity. The overwhelming emotion is one of joyfulness and gratefulness. Although there is undeniably some measure of remorse or regret, this is not the overriding emotion to be experienced throughout the eternal state.[3]

The emotional condition of the redeemed is that of complete and unending happiness. Emotion proceeds from the realization of facts in personal experience. Hope will at last become reality for all those who are delivered from the bondage of corruption into the glorious liberty of the children of God.[3]

> For I reckon that the sufferings of this present time are not worthy to be compared with the glory which shall be revealed in us. For the earnest expectation of

the creature waiteth for the manifestation of the sons of God. For the creature was made subject to vanity, not willingly, but by reason of him who hath subjected the same in hope, Because the creature itself also shall be delivered from the bondage of corruption into the glorious liberty of the children of God. For we know that the whole creation groaneth and travaileth in pain together until now. And not only they, but ourselves also, which have the firstfruits of the Spirit, even we ourselves groan within ourselves, waiting for the adoption, to wit, the redemption of our body. For we are saved by hope: but hope that is seen is not hope: for what a man seeth, why doth he yet hope for? But if we hope for that we see not, then do we with patience wait for it. Romans 8:18-25

Elimination of the curse, pain and death will also remove sorrow, tears and crying.

And God shall wipe away all tears from their eyes; and there shall be no more death, neither sorrow, nor crying, neither shall there be any more pain: for the former things are passed away. Revelation 21:4

Summary

The judgment seat of Christ is a time of examination and reward. From Scripture we can conclude the following concerning the judgment seat of Christ, the Bema. First, the Lord will resurrect the bodies of the saints who have died during the Church age, as well as change the bodies of those still alive. Then they will meet the Lord in the air and proceed to the judgment seat of Christ in heaven. This judgment will consist of **rewards** for faithful service. There will be no condemnation of anyone. Any remorse or sorrow will be short-lived, and joy and happiness will follow the rewards of crowns, treasure, and commendations given to believers based upon their faithful service to Him.

JUDGMENT OF ISRAEL

While the *Bema* judgment is taking place in heaven (with the Church in the Lord's presence) a series of terrible judgments will begin to unfold on the earth for a period of about one and a half years beginning at the midpoint of the 70th Week of Daniel. This will culminate with the return and manifestation of Christ to earth as the Great White Horse Rider of Revelation 19.

The main point to see here is that this entire one-and-a-half-year period is the expression of God's wrath, first towards Israel and then towards the "nations". This will occur in increasingly severe degrees of judgment to be poured out eventually on the entire world. The world will seek to find answers to its problems through the one world movement of the last days, apart from the true God as He has revealed Himself in Christ. Much as Romans 1:18f explains, God turns the world over to the consequences of its choices. It will begin with an apparent time of prosperity and peace created under the deceptions of the man of lawlessness. But even this will be God's judgment and the expression of His wrath. While people are saying peace and safety, then sudden destruction will come as birth pains upon a woman in travail. The judgments of this time will grow in intensity and conclude with an awesome display of God's wrath against a Christ-rejecting world.

The Judgment and Reward of Resurrected Old Testament and Tribulation Saints

While many would place the resurrection and judgment of Old Testament saints along with that of the Church at the time of the Rapture, a number of factors favor their resurrection after the Rapture. One proposed timetable places this judgment at the conclusion of the 70th week of Daniel, at the same time as the resurrection and reward of the tribulation saints mentioned in Revelation.

> And I saw thrones, and they sat upon them, and judgment was given unto them: and I saw the souls of them that were beheaded for the witness of Jesus, and for the word of God, and which had not worshipped the beast, neither his image, neither had received his mark upon their foreheads, or in their hands; and they lived and reigned with Christ a thousand years. Revelation 20:4

Daniel, who wrote concerning the God's program for Israel, places the resurrection of the righteous in Israel as occurring after "a time of trouble such as never was …"

> And at that time shall Michael stand up, the great prince which standeth for the children of thy people: and there shall be a time of trouble, such as never was since there was a nation even to that same time: and at that time thy people shall be delivered, every one that shall be found written in the book. Daniel 12:1

Clearly this is the "the time of Jacob's Trouble" mentioned by Jeremiah and occurs in the second half of Daniel's 70th week.

> Alas! for that day is great, so that none is like it: it is even the time of Jacob's trouble, but he shall be saved out of it. Jeremiah 30:7

Resurrection can be viewed in Scripture as an event that terminates one program and initiates another. Consequently, one would not expect Israel's resurrection to come until God has completed His program for the Jews, the seventy-year plan decreed for His people and outlined in Daniel.

> Seventy weeks are determined upon thy people and upon thy holy city, to finish the transgression, and to make an end of sins, and to make reconciliation for iniquity,

and to bring in everlasting righteousness, and to seal up the vision and prophecy, and to anoint the most Holy. Know therefore and understand, that from the going forth of the commandment to restore and to build Jerusalem unto the Messiah the Prince shall be seven weeks, and threescore and two weeks: the street shall be built again, and the wall, even in troublous times. And after threescore and two weeks shall Messiah be cut off, but not for himself: and the people of the prince that shall come shall destroy the city and the sanctuary; and the end thereof shall be with a flood, and unto the end of the war desolations are determined. And he shall confirm the covenant with many for one week: and in the midst of the week he shall cause the sacrifice and the oblation to cease, and for the overspreading of abominations he shall make it desolate, even until the consummation, and that determined shall be poured upon the desolate. Daniel 9:24-27

Since the events mentioned in Daniel 9:26 (the cutting off of Messiah and the destruction of city and sanctuary) have to occur after the sixty-nine weeks of years had run their course but before the 70th week begins, there has to be a space of time, the parenthesis of the Church age, between the conclusion of the 69th week and the beginning of the 70th week. The resurrection (rapture) and *Bema* judgment of the Church concludes this parenthesis, the Church age. But Old Testament saints (the righteous dead) will not be resurrected and rewarded until the 70th week is finished when God concludes His program with Israel concerning the seventy weeks of Daniel.

So, the order of God's resurrection program which includes the judgment of rewards would seem to occur in the following order. First, the resurrection of Christ occurred as the beginning of the resurrection program.

But every man in his own order: Christ the firstfruits; afterward they that are Christ's at his coming. 1 Corinthians 15:23

Next to happen will be the resurrection of the Church age saints at the Rapture.

For the Lord himself shall descend from heaven with a shout, with the voice of the archangel, and with the trump of God: and the dead in Christ shall rise first: 1 Thessalonians 4:16

Finally, the resurrection of Old Testament saints will occur.

And many of them that sleep in the dust of the earth shall awake, some to everlasting life, and some to shame and everlasting contempt. Daniel 12:2

Thy dead men shall live, together with my dead body shall they arise. Awake and sing, ye that dwell in dust: for thy dew is as the dew of herbs, and the earth shall cast out the dead. Isaiah 26:19

This will likely happen together with the resurrection of tribulation-period saints.[3]

And cast him into the bottomless pit, and shut him up, and set a seal upon him, that he should deceive the nations no more, till the thousand years should be fulfilled: and after that he must be loosed a little season. And I saw thrones, and they sat upon them, and judgment was given unto them: and I saw the souls of them that were beheaded for the witness of Jesus, and for the word of God, and which had not worshipped the beast, neither his image, neither had received his mark upon their foreheads, or in their hands; and they lived and reigned with Christ a thousand years. But the rest of the dead lived not again until the thousand years were finished. This is the first resurrection. Revelation 20:3-5

After each of these resurrections, judgment occurs.

Timing of the Judgment of Israel

The Scripture teaches that before the Messiah can begin to reign, there must be a judgment to determine who will enter into His kingdom since "they are not all Israel (spiritually regenerated believers who put their trust in Jesus Christ as their Messiah) which are of Israel (physical descendants only)".[3]

> Not as though the word of God hath taken none effect. For they are not all Israel, which are of Israel: Romans 9:6

When this judgment of Israel occurs is not clearly defined in scripture. However, by using scripture, some possible, if not reasonable, deductions can be formulated. First, it was noted earlier that Zechariah asserted that two-thirds of the Jews will be killed near the midpoint of the 70th week when the Antichrist begins his reign.

> And it shall come to pass, that in all the land, saith the LORD, two parts therein shall be cut off and die; but the third shall be left therein. And I will bring the third part through the fire, and will refine them as silver is refined, and will try them as gold is tried: they shall call on my name, and I will hear them: I will say, It is my people: and they shall say, The LORD is my God. Zechariah 13:8-9

The Day of the Lord with the trumpet judgments then follow, which certainly will cause judgment to fall on many of the remaining unrighteous Jews. Christ's return to lead the second Exodus will purge the remaining unrighteous rebels, just as in the first Exodus where the rebels were removed before Israel entered the Promised Land. This judgment is described in Ezekiel.

> And I will bring you out from the people, and will gather you out of the countries wherein ye are scattered, with a mighty hand, and with a stretched out arm, and with fury poured out. And I will bring you into the wilderness of the people, and there will I plead with you face to face. Like as I pleaded with your fathers in the wilderness of the land of Egypt, so will I plead with you, saith the Lord God. And I will cause you to pass under the rod, and I will bring you into the bond of the covenant: And I will purge out from among you the rebels, and them that transgress against me: I will bring them forth out of the country where they sojourn, and they shall not enter into the land of Israel: and ye shall know that I am the Lord. Ezekiel 20:34-38

Jesus also illustrated this judgment in the parables of the ten virgins.

> Then shall the kingdom of heaven be likened unto ten virgins, which took their lamps, and went forth to meet the bridegroom. And five of them were wise, and five were foolish. They that were foolish took their lamps, and took no oil with them: But the wise took oil in their vessels with their lamps. While the bridegroom tarried, they all slumbered and slept. And at midnight there was a cry made, Behold, the bridegroom cometh; go ye out to meet him. Then all those virgins arose, and trimmed their lamps. And the foolish said unto the wise, Give us of your oil; for our lamps are gone out. But the wise answered, saying, Not so; lest there be not enough for us and you: but go ye rather to them that sell, and buy for yourselves. And while they went to buy,

the bridegroom came; and they that were ready went in with him to the marriage: and the door was shut. Afterward came also the other virgins, saying, Lord, Lord, open to us. But he answered and said, Verily I say unto you, I know you not. Watch therefore, for ye know neither the day nor the hour wherein the Son of man cometh. Matthew 25:1-13

Jesus then followed this parable with another parable concerning judgment, the parable of the ten talents.

For the kingdom of heaven is as a man travelling into a far country, who called his own servants, and delivered unto them his goods. And unto one he gave five talents, to another two, and to another one; to every man according to his several ability; and straightway took his journey. Then he that had received the five talents went and traded with the same, and made them other five talents. And likewise he that had received two, he also gained other two. But he that had received one went and digged in the earth, and hid his lord's money. After a long time the lord of those servants cometh, and reckoneth with them. And so he that had received five talents came and brought other five talents, saying, Lord, thou deliveredst unto me five talents: behold, I have gained beside them five talents more. His lord said unto him, Well done, thou good and faithful servant: thou hast been faithful over a few things, I will make thee ruler over many things: enter thou into the joy of thy lord. He also that had received two talents came and said, Lord, thou deliveredst unto me two talents: behold, I have gained two other talents beside them. His lord said unto him, Well done, good and faithful servant; thou hast been faithful over a few things, I will make thee ruler over many things: enter thou into the joy of thy lord. Then he which had received the one talent came and said, Lord, I knew thee that thou art an hard man, reaping where thou hast not sown, and gathering where thou hast not strawed: And I was afraid, and went and hid thy talent in the earth: lo, there thou hast that is thine. His lord answered and said unto him, Thou wicked and slothful servant, thou knewest that I reap where I sowed not, and gather where I have not strawed: Thou oughtest therefore to have put my money to the exchangers, and then at my coming I should have received mine own with usury. Take therefore the talent from him, and give it unto him which hath ten talents. For unto every one that hath shall be given, and he shall have abundance: but from him that hath not shall be taken away even that which he hath. And cast ye the unprofitable servant into outer darkness: there shall be weeping and gnashing of teeth. Matthew 25:14-30

Christ (the bridegroom, a man travelling into a far country) returns to Jerusalem with the righteous remnant of Israel, proclaims His kingdom, and is crowned king at the end of the 70th week of Daniel (most likely on Rosh Hashana). It is only then that the bema judgment of Israel will follow. A likely day for this judgment is on the Day of Atonement which is a day for judgment, but one where judgment is paused and forgiveness for Israel is provided by the High Priest, Jesus Christ, who has made atonement for the nation. The righteous of Israel, with faith in Jesus, survived the Great Tribulation and are found written in the Book of Life. Now they will be judged at the earthly Judgment Seat (Bema) of Christ in Jerusalem. It is also most likely here and at this time that the Old Testament saints and tribulation saints are also resurrected and judged.

Basis of the Judgment of Israel

The Book of Revelation confirms that salvation for Israel in the Tribulation (just as in the Church age) is through faith in the person and work of Jesus Christ as the Lamb of God.[3]

> And I said unto him, Sir, thou knowest. And he said to me, These are they which came out of great tribulation, and have washed their robes, and **made them white in the blood of the Lamb**. Revelation 7:14

This is further validated by the message in the book of Romans where Paul illustrates Israel's problem to be one of seeking to establish her own righteousness by keeping the Law rather than accepting God's righteousness by faith in Christ (Romans 9-11). The parables of the ten virgins and ten talents in Matthew 25:1-30 showed that God will judge living Israel in order to separate the saved from the unsaved. As seen above in Ezekiel 20:37-38 and reinforced by Malachi, the individual's works will be brought into judgment. However, this is not because they are saved by their works, but because their works demonstrate that they are rebels who have failed to trust in Jesus.

> But who may abide the day of his coming? and who shall stand when he appeareth? for he is like a refiner's fire, and like fullers' soap: And he shall sit as a refiner and purifier of silver: and he shall purify the sons of Levi, and purge them as gold and silver, that they may offer unto the LORD an offering in righteousness. And I will come near to you to judgment; and I will be a swift witness against the sorcerers, and against the adulterers, and against false swearers, and against those that oppress the hireling in his wages, the widow, and the fatherless, and that turn aside the stranger from his right, and fear not me, saith the LORD of hosts. Malachi 3:2,3,5

JUDGMENT OF THE NATIONS
(SHEEP GOAT JUDGMENT)

Just as Christ will judge the Jews still alive at the end of the Tribulation and the Old Testament saints when He personally returns to earth, so Christ will also judge those Gentiles who remain and are still alive at the end of the 70th week. This judgment begins with the bowl judgments which end with the Battle of Armageddon. The Judgment of Nations then concludes this evaluation and sentencing of the Gentiles. Jesus discussed this judgment of the Gentiles in Matthew's Gospel right after the parables of the ten virgins and the ten talents that concern the judgment of the Jews:

> When the Son of man shall come in his glory, and all the holy angels with him, then shall he sit upon the throne of his glory: And before him shall be gathered all nations: and he shall separate them one from another, as a shepherd divideth his sheep from the goats: And he shall set the sheep on his right hand, but the goats on the left. Then shall the King say unto them on his right hand, Come, ye blessed of my Father, inherit the kingdom prepared for you from the foundation of the world: For I was an hungred, and ye gave me meat: I was thirsty, and ye gave me drink: I was a stranger, and ye took me in: Naked, and ye clothed me: I was sick, and ye visited me: I was in prison, and ye came unto me. Then shall the righteous answer him, saying, Lord, when saw we thee an hungred, and fed thee? or thirsty, and gave thee drink? When saw we thee a stranger, and took thee in? or naked, and clothed thee? Or when saw we thee sick, or in prison, and came unto thee? And the King shall answer and say unto them, Verily I say unto you, Inasmuch as ye have done it unto one of the least of these my brethren, ye have done it unto me. Then shall he say also unto them on the left hand, Depart

from me, ye cursed, into everlasting fire, prepared for the devil and his angels: For I was an hungred, and ye gave me no meat: I was thirsty, and ye gave me no drink: I was a stranger, and ye took me not in: naked, and ye clothed me not: sick, and in prison, and ye visited me not. Then shall they also answer him, saying, Lord, when saw we thee an hungred, or athirst, or a stranger, or naked, or sick, or in prison, and did not minister unto thee? Then shall he answer them, saying, Verily I say unto you, Inasmuch as ye did it not to one of the least of these, ye did it not to me. And these shall go away into everlasting punishment: but the righteous into life eternal. Matthew 25:31-46

Here Jesus spoke of judging the living Gentile (non-Jewish) nations at His Second Coming. When the Son of Man comes in His glory, and all the angels with Him, then He will sit on the throne of His glory. All the Gentile nations will be gathered before Him, and He will separate people one from another as a shepherd separates the sheep from the goats. These Gentiles are people who are still alive upon the earth after the Great Tribulation. They are the living, not the dead. The dead will be raised to judgment in the future at the Great White Throne Judgment. The prophet Isaiah wrote of these who are still alive at the end of the 70th Week.

Behold, the nations are as a drop of a bucket, and are counted as the small dust of the balance: behold, he taketh up the isles as a very little thing. All nations before him are as nothing; and they are counted to him less than nothing, and vanity. Isaiah 40:15,17

Most people imagine that God will judge them only after they die, and for the vast majority that will be true. However, the Judgment of the Nations is a judgment of the living. Jesus said that "before him shall be gathered all the nations" (Matthew 25:32). This event has

---

been called the Judgment of the Nations to distinguish it from God's other judgments. The dreadful events of the Tribulation will cause the deaths of many who live on the earth. In addition, a large number of armed forces will die in the final campaign of Armageddon when the Lord Jesus Christ conquers His enemies. However, there will be those from around the world who did not participate in the conflict and will survive. It is these who will be judged at this time.

Although this judgment is called the "Judgment of the Nations", it is not a judgment of national groups of people. The Greek word translated "nations" implies Gentiles; and the context indicates that individuals, not groups, will be evaluated: "He shall separate them one from another," [Matthew 25:32]. Jesus "shall set the sheep on his right hand, but the goats on the left" [Matthew 25:33]. Both sheep and goats graze together during the day; but when night falls, the shepherd separates the two groups. At this judgment of the Gentiles, Christ will separate the sheep, representing the saved, from the goats, symbolizing the lost.

Place and Time of the Judgment of the Nations

At this judgment, the nations will be brought to the city of Jerusalem and judged in the valley of Jehoshaphat.

> For, behold, in those days, and in that time, when I shall bring again the captivity of Judah and Jerusalem, I will also gather all nations, and will bring them down into the valley of Jehoshaphat, and will plead with them there for my people and for my heritage Israel, whom they have scattered among the nations, and parted my land. And they have cast lots for my people; and have given a boy for an harlot, and sold a girl for wine, that they might drink. Joel 3:1-3

The righteous will enter into God's Millennial Kingdom while the unrighteous will be taken to judgment. Like the unbelievers from the nation Israel, they will probably be killed at this time, and their final judgment will still be future.

It is when Jesus is sitting on His throne in Jerusalem at the beginning of His Millennial Kingdom that He will judge the nations. Jesus declared, "When the Son of man shall come in his glory, . . . then shall he sit upon the throne of his glory" (Matt. 25:31). This verse clearly describes our Lord's kingship beginning at the end of the seven-year Tribulation period, at the beginning of the Millennial reign of Christ. This climactic event will display His powerful reign over the earth. For centuries believers have longed for this visible manifestation of their Savior's glory; and they still cry, "Even so, come, Lord Jesus" (Rev. 22:20).

This New Testament truth finds roots in Old Testament prophecy. For generations the people of Israel longed for a godly king who would reign on Earth and reverse the curse of the serpent (Gen. 3:15; 49:10). David received God's promise that, through David's own line, God would raise up such a ruler (2 Sam. 7). This Davidic Covenant became the bedrock of Jewish faith for the future:

> Behold, the days come, saith the LORD, that I will raise
> unto David a righteous Branch, and a King shall reign
> and prosper, and shall execute justice and righteousness
> in the earth. Jeremiah 23:5

Although Jesus did come once, His reign of justice on this earth has not yet begun. Yet, he did speak of His return when that reign will finally commence. Then all the prophet's prophecies will find fulfillment when the Messiah, the son of David, reigns in Jerusalem (Isa. 9:6–7; Hos. 3:4–5; Dan. 7:13–14; Zech. 9:9–10).

The Basis of the Judgment of the Nations

Once the Gentiles who survive the Tribulation are gathered to the throne of King Jesus, their guilt or innocence will be revealed. No attorney will be able to intercede. Jesus will be the prosecutor, the judge, and the jury. Only this One, with infallible knowledge of both actions and motives, is able to disclose the truth. And He will reveal His decision by separating these people as a shepherd divides the sheep from the goats.

After the separation, Jesus will provide the reason for the division. It will be their treatment of Jesus Himself. When both groups hear this explanation, they will not understand that His judgment was based not necessarily on their personal treatment of Him, but of His brethren, that is Israel, who He considered to be part of Himself.[12]

> Then shall the righteous answer him, saying, Lord, when saw we thee an hungred, and fed thee? or thirsty, and gave thee drink? When saw we thee a stranger, and took thee in? or naked, and clothed thee? Or when saw we thee sick, or in prison, and came unto thee? Matthew 25:37-39

How could Jesus evaluate these Gentiles when they never personally met Him on Earth? His answer to them is surprising. [12]

> Inasmuch as ye have done it unto one of the least of these my brethren, ye have done it unto me. Matt 25:40

Who are the people whom Jesus calls "my brethren"? Since the context indicates the time immediately following the Tribulation, they apparently constitute a third group in addition to the Gentile sheep and goats. These "brethren" of Jesus are the Jewish people. And only Gentile believers in Jesus will have dared to provide for their physical needs (food, clothing, and housing) and even visited them in prison.

The true faith of Gentiles who survive the Tribulation will be evidenced by their treatment of Jewish people during the Tribulation period. This mark of true salvation shows the spiritual union of Jesus Christ with His people, their union with Him, and their union with one another. That is why, when the Lord confronted Saul of Tarsus on the Damascus Road, He described Saul's attack on Christians by saying:[12]

> And he fell to the earth, and heard a voice saying unto him, Saul, Saul, why persecutest thou **me**? Acts 9:4

Again, salvation is not contingent upon good works. Nowhere does Scripture uphold such a teaching, but in fact, just the opposite.

> Therefore we conclude that a man is justified by faith without the deeds of the law. Romans 3:28

Since the faith that brings salvation comes by God's free grace, it is no wonder that believers actually are destined and created to do good works.[12]

> For by grace are ye saved through faith; and that not of yourselves: it is the gift of God: Not of works, lest any man should boast. For we are his workmanship, created in Christ Jesus unto good works, which God hath before ordained that we should walk in them. Ephesians 2:8-10

Believers are admonished to be concerned for the physical welfare of other Christians.

> If a brother or sister be naked, and destitute of daily food, And one of you say unto them, Depart in peace, be ye warmed and filled; notwithstanding ye give them not those things which are needful to the body; what doth it profit? Even so faith, if it hath not works, is dead, being alone. James 2:15-17

Anti-Semitism will run rampant during the Tribulation. Apart from genuine faith in the Jewish Messiah, no Gentile will dare to befriend a Jew. Yet the bond between believers in Christ runs deeper than race. True Christianity and anti-Semitism are as opposite as righteousness and sin.[12]

> We know that we have passed from death unto life, because we love the brethren. He that loveth not his brother abideth in death. 1 John 3:14

Selfless love for fellow Christians and Jewish people is an act of love for our Savior and Lord and will determine the Gentiles fate at their judgment.

The Results of the Judgment of the Nations

Jesus said that the righteous will "inherit the kingdom" (Matt 25:34) as well as enjoy "life eternal" (Matt 25:46). These righteous Gentile believers who survive the Tribulation will enter the initial phase of God's Kingdom, the Millennium, with natural, unresurrected bodies. This generation of believing Gentiles also will begin to populate the earthly Kingdom. They will form the Gentile nations that will worship God in Jerusalem, as prophesied by Isaiah:[12]

> And it shall come to pass in the last days, that the mountain of the Lord's house shall be established in the top of the mountains, and shall be exalted above the hills; and all nations shall flow unto it. And many people shall go and say, Come ye, and let us go up to the mountain of the Lord, to the house of the God of Jacob; and he will teach us of his ways, and we will walk in his paths: for out of Zion shall go forth the law, and the word of the Lord from Jerusalem. Isaiah 2:2-3

At the conclusion of Christ's one-thousand-year earthly reign, these believing Gentiles will live for eternity with glorified bodies in the new heavens and Earth.[12]

The goats, whose lack of true faith in Christ will have been evidenced in their persecution of His "brethren", will be condemned to "everlasting fire", the same eternal punishment "prepared for the devil and his angels" (Matt 25:41).

Long ago God promised Abram:

> And I will bless them that bless thee, and curse him that
> curseth thee: and in thee shall all families of the earth
> be blessed. Genesis 12:3

These words find their fulfillment in the judgment of the nations.
Gentiles who bless the Jewish people during the coming Tribulation
will themselves be blessed. And those who do not will regret it forever.[12]

THE GREAT WHITE THRONE JUDGMENT

A final judgment of mankind will occur before a great white throne and
is described in Revelation.

> But the rest of the dead lived not again until the thousand
> years were finished. This is the first resurrection.
> Revelation 20:5

> And I saw a great white throne, and him that sat on it,
> from whose face the earth and the heaven fled away;
> and there was found no place for them. And I saw the
> dead, small and great, stand before God; and the books
> were opened: and another book was opened, which is
> the book of life: and the dead were judged out of those
> things which were written in the books, according to
> their works. And the sea gave up the dead which were in
> it; and death and hell delivered up the dead which were
> in them: and they were judged every man according to
> their works. And death and hell were cast into the lake
> of fire. This is the second death. And whosoever was
> not found written in the book of life was cast into the
> lake of fire. Revelation 20:11-15

This is an awesome and solemn scene, and one which should cause everyone to stop and think about the eternal implications of this future event. For the non-Christian, the one who has never trusted in the person and work of Jesus Christ, it should cause him to want to search out the truth regarding Jesus Christ, to embrace Him in faith as the Savior from his sin and eternal doom. For the Christian, the future reality of this event should cause deep concern because of the many (including some of our friends and relatives) who will face this throne of judgment because they never received the Savior by faith.[3] All who have scoffed at God, denied His being, rebelled at His rule, or rejected His sovereignty—and in the process, also rejected His Son, the Lord Jesus Christ—must now stand before this throne to be condemned to eternal judgment. May the reality of this judgment cause us to carefully reflect on the serious consequences of this passage on a Christ-rejecting world.

The Time and Place of the Great White Throne Judgment

Revelation 20:5 and 20:11-15 show that this judgment takes place at the conclusion of the Millennium after Satan is cast into the lake of fire and brimstone. Heaven and earth are seen fleeing from the face of Him who sits on this throne (Revelation 20:11). In other words, they are destroyed and dissolved as seen in 2 Peter.[3]

> But the heavens and the earth, which are now, by the same word are kept in store, reserved unto fire against the day of judgment and perdition of ungodly men. But the day of the Lord will come as a thief in the night; in the which the heavens shall pass away with a great noise, and the elements shall melt with fervent heat, the earth also and the works that are therein shall be burned up. Seeing then that all these things shall be dissolved, what manner of persons ought ye to be in all holy conversation and godliness, Looking for and hasting unto the coming of the day of God, wherein

the heavens being on fire shall be dissolved, and the elements shall melt with fervent heat? 2 Peter 3:7,10-12

The point is that the Great White Throne Judgment does not occur on earth or in heaven as we know it, but most likely somewhere beyond. It is also clear that it does not occur in the new heavens and earth which are not created until after this event (compare Revelation 20:11 with Revelation 21:1).[3]

In other words, God has removed Satan and his demons, the False Prophet and the Beast, and is about to judge the rest of the unbelieving dead. So, it is only fitting that He also judge the old earth and heavens that have been the arena of Satan's activity and man's sin and rebellion. This evidently takes place after the resurrection of the unbelieving dead from the grave and Hades. They are resurrected, gathered before the throne and actually behold the dissolution of heaven and earth as a foreboding preparation for their judgment. All their hopes and dreams had been placed in an earth and system that was passing away, and now they see it dissolve before their very eyes.[3]

> And the world passeth away, and the lust thereof: but he
> that doeth the will of God abideth for ever. 1 John 2:17

"And no place was found for them", (Revelation 20:11) i.e., for heaven and earth. In the eternal state there will be no place for that which reminds men of the rebellions of Satan and man with all its wickedness and sorrow.[3]

> And there shall be no more curse: but the throne of God
> and of the Lamb shall be in it; and his servants shall
> serve him: Revelation 22:3

> And God shall wipe away all tears from their eyes; and
> there shall be no more death, neither sorrow, nor crying,
> neither shall there be any more pain: for the former
> things are passed away. Revelation 21:4

> For, behold, I create new heavens and a new earth: and
> the former shall not be remembered, nor come into
> mind. Isaiah 65:17

The Participants in the Great White Throne Judgment

Like the other judgments, the judge, as seen at the Great White Throne
is the Lord Jesus Christ.[3]

> For the Father judgeth no man, but hath committed all
> judgment unto the Son: That all men should honour the
> Son, even as they honour the Father. He that honoureth
> not the Son honoureth not the Father which hath sent
> him. And hath given him authority to execute judgment
> also, because he is the Son of man. John 5:22-23,27

All judgment has been placed into His hands as the perfect
Son of man, Son of God, the one qualified to judge by virtue of
his sinless humanity and defeat of Satan and sin through the cross
(Revelation 5:1-14).[3]

Those who will be judged at the Great White Throne are "the dead,
great and small", those who had no part in the first resurrection.[3]

> But the rest of the dead lived not again until the thousand
> years were finished. This is the first resurrection. Blessed
> and holy is he that hath part in the first resurrection: on
> such the second death hath no power, but they shall be
> priests of God and of Christ, and shall reign with him
> a thousand years. Revelation 20:5-6

> And I saw the dead, small and great, stand before God;
> and the books were opened: and another book was
> opened, which is the book of life: and the dead were
> judged out of those things which were written in the
> books, according to their works. And the sea gave up
> the dead which were in it; and death and hell delivered

up the dead which were in them: and they were judged every man according to their works. And death and hell were cast into the lake of fire. This is the second death. Revelation 20:12-14

And shall come forth; they that have done good, unto the resurrection of life; and they that have done evil, unto the resurrection of damnation. John 5:29

Specifically, this is the judgment of the dead from the second resurrection, the resurrection of the unjust, the resurrection unto the second death mentioned in Revelation and John. "The dead, great and small" emphasizes that no one is exempt. All who have died without faith in Jesus Christ regardless of their status in human history—religiously, politically, economically, or morally—must stand before this throne of judgment.[3]

The Basis of the Great White Throne Judgment

The basis for the Great White Throne judgment is found in two sets of books: (1) the books which are opened, and (2) the Book of Life.[3]

And I saw the dead, small and great, stand before God; and the **books** were opened: and another book was opened, which is the **book of life**: and the dead were judged out of those things which were written in the books, according to their works. And the sea gave up the dead which were in it; and death and hell delivered up the dead which were in them: and they were judged every man according to their works. And death and hell were cast into the lake of fire. This is the second death. And whosoever was not found written in the **book of life** was cast into the lake of fire. Revelation 20:12-15

Note that the text in verse 12 says "and the books (plural) were opened, and another book (singular) was opened, which is the Book of Life". There are two sets, the books and the book of life which is mentioned again in verse 15a.[3]

The Books: The identity of the books is not specifically revealed, but from a comparison of other passages of Scripture and from the nature of these verses a conjecture can be made. Of course, the use of the plural indicates that there are at least two books here.

The first book opened will probably be the Scripture, the Word of God, which contains the revelation of God's holy character, the moral law, the declaration of man's sinfulness, and God's plan of salvation through faith in Christ. This book also reveals that even when men do not have the written Word, they have the law of God written in their hearts (Romans 2:14-16) and the revelation of God-consciousness in creation so that they are without excuse (Romans 1:18-21; 2:12).[3]

> For when the Gentiles, which have not the law, do by nature the things contained in the law, these, having not the law, are a law unto themselves: Which shew the work of the law written in their hearts, their conscience also bearing witness, and their thoughts the mean while accusing or else excusing one another;) In the day when God shall judge the secrets of men by Jesus Christ according to my gospel. Rom 2:14-16

> For the wrath of God is revealed from heaven against all ungodliness and unrighteousness of men, who hold the truth in unrighteousness; Because that which may be known of God is manifest in them; for God hath shewed it unto them. For the invisible things of him from the creation of the world are clearly seen, being understood by the things that are made, even his eternal power and Godhead; so that they are without excuse: Because that, when they knew God, they glorified him not as God, neither were thankful; but became

vain in their imaginations, and their foolish heart was darkened. Romans 1:18-21

For as many as have sinned without law shall also perish without law: and as many as have sinned in the law shall be judged by the law; Romans 2:12

Undoubtedly, then, the Scripture will be used to demonstrate the clarity of the plan of God and that man is without excuse. John 12:48 is very pertinent here.[3]

He that rejecteth me, and receiveth not my words, hath one that judgeth him: the word that I have spoken, the same shall judge him in the last day. John 12:48

The second book will be the book of works or deeds. Revelation 20:13-14 states that the unbelieving dead will be judged according to their deeds (works). Certainly then, one of the books will be the book of works which contains a record of every person's deeds as a witness of the true nature of their spiritual condition.

The principle here is that Jesus Christ died for their sins, no matter how evil, that He might forgive them and give them a righteousness from God so that they may have a perfect standing before God. As Paul declares:[3]

Therefore being justified by faith, we have peace with God through our Lord Jesus Christ: By whom also we have access by faith into this grace wherein we stand, and rejoice in hope of the glory of God. Romans 5:1-2

But when men reject the knowledge of God and His plan of salvation, they, in essence, determine to stand on their own merit or in their own righteousness. So, the book of works will contain a record of all the unbeliever's deeds, good and bad, to demonstrate the truth.[3]

For all have sinned, and come short of the glory of God; Romans 3:23

In other words, "for all have sinned and continually miss the mark, short of the glory and perfect holiness of God". All fall short of God's perfect righteousness and, therefore, have no basis upon which to stand accepted and justified before a holy God. This judgment proves them sinners and in need of the righteousness which God freely gives through faith in Jesus Christ.

The Book of Life: This book contains the names of all believers, of all who have put their faith in Christ and God's plan of salvation or righteousness through the substitutionary death of Christ. Or, to put it another way, it is a record of those who have not rejected God's plan of salvation and have responded to Christ in faith; for these their faith is reckoned for righteousness and their sins have not been imputed to them.[3]

> Now to him that worketh is the reward not reckoned of grace, but of debt. But to him that worketh not, but believeth on him that justifieth the ungodly, his faith is counted for righteousness. Even as David also describeth the blessedness of the man, unto whom God imputeth righteousness without works, Rom 4:4-6
>
> And therefore it was imputed to him for righteousness. Romans 4:22

At the Great White Throne Judgment, the Book of Life is produced to show that the participant's name was not found written in the Book of Life because of their rejection of Jesus Christ. They, therefore, have no righteousness and cannot be accepted before God, but must be cast into the eternal Lake of Fire. The Book of Life contains the names of believers, those justified by faith and who have a righteousness from God credited to their account. These and only these are accepted by God and will spend eternity with Him.[3]

Brethren, my heart's desire and prayer to God for Israel is, that they might be saved. For I bear them record that they have a zeal of God, but not according to knowledge. For they being ignorant of God's righteousness, and going about to establish their own righteousness, have not submitted themselves unto the righteousness of God. For Christ is the end of the law for righteousness to every one that believeth. Romans 10:1-4

And be found in him, not having mine own righteousness, which is of the law, but that which is through the faith of Christ, the righteousness which is of God by faith: Philippians 3:9

Judgment and Punishment

So, the real issue is whether one's name is in the Book of Life, not one's deeds. The deeds of the unbeliever are only examined to show that the person, no matter how much good he may have done, falls short of God's holy demands. Paul shows us in Romans that all people—good and bad—are on their way to eternal separation from God. Obviously, most see that the immoral bad person deserves the wrath of God, as the Apostle describes in Romans 1:18-32. But he also shows us that the same applies to the good and moral person (Romans 2:1-3:23). No one is perfect, no matter how good they may appear to men. In the face of the awesome holiness of God, they are sinners and cannot stand in the presence of God on their own merit.

Fortunately, the awesome fact is that salvation is through faith in Jesus Christ and not through our deeds. The loss of salvation, and ultimately the one sin that separates a person from God and confines him to the eternal Lake of Fire, is because of failure to trust in the Lord Jesus Christ for forgiveness which results in a perfect righteous standing before God.

For God so loved the world, that he gave his only begotten Son, that whosoever believeth in him should not perish, but have everlasting life. For God sent not his Son into the world to condemn the world; but that the world through him might be saved. He that believeth on him is not condemned: but he that believeth not is condemned already, because he hath not believed in the name of the only begotten Son of God. John 3:16-18

He that believeth on the Son hath everlasting life: and he that believeth not the Son shall not see life; but the wrath of God abideth on him. John 3:36

Since the Savior has died for the sin of the world, the ultimate issue is the sin of unbelief and rejection of Christ. So, judgment is for unbelievers at the Great White Throne Judgment, at the end of the Millennium. It involves two sets of books: The Book of Life (which shows that the person is not saved, if his/her name is not written in it) and the other "books" which document the individual's works while on Earth.

CONCLUSION

The study of judgment creates as many questions as it answers. Yet, scripture is clear that every person will be judged. None can escape judgment. But there is a choice that can be made as to which judgment one will undergo, for the righteous who are born again and the unrighteous who are not born again in Christ will appear in different judgment seats for judgment. By accepting Christ as your Lord and Savior you can choose to be judged at Christ's Bema Seat where there will be no condemnation but only rewards, or you can reject Christ and appear before the Great White Throne. Are you going to stand before the judgment seat of Christ or at the Great White Throne judgment? God has given you the freedom to choose.

Below is a summary of this one theory on the different judgments followed by a proposed time when they might occur on the end time's timeline.

SUMMARY OF END TIMES JUDGMENTS

	JUDGMENT OF THE CHURCH	JUDGMENT OF ISRAEL	JUDGMENT OF NATIONS	GREAT WHITE THRONE JUDGMENT
WHO IS JUDGED	The Church (NT saints)	Israel (OT saints and Jews who survived Tribulation)	Gentiles alive at end of God's wrath	The remaining dead
WHO IS THE JUDGE	Jesus	Jesus	Jesus	Jesus
WHERE IS THE JUDGMENT	Bema Seat in Heaven	Bema Seat in Jerusalem	Jesus' Throne on Millennial Earth	Great White Throne
WHEN IS THE JUDGMENT	After the Rapture	After the Great Tribulation	Beginning of Millennium	End of Millennium
BASIS OF THE JUDGMENT	Faith(salvation) Works (rewards)	Acceptance of Jesus as their Lord	How they treated the Jews	Works according to Law of God & Book of Life
WHAT IS THE JUDGMENT	Loss or gain of rewards	Reign with Jesus as priests	Entry (or not) into the Millennial Kingdom	Eternal life or lake of fire (second death)
BIBLE VERSES	Luke 14:12-14 Romans 14:20-22 1Cor 3:11-15;4:1-5 2Cor 5:9-10 1Thess 4:13-18 2Tim 4:8 Rev 22:12	Ez 20:34-38 Dan 7:18,22,27 Zech 13:8-9 Matt 25:1-13 (10 Virgins) Matt 25:14-30 (Parable of Talents) Luke 19:17-19	Matt 25:31-46 (Sheep and Goat) Matt 13:24-30 (Wheat and Tares)	Rev 20:1-15

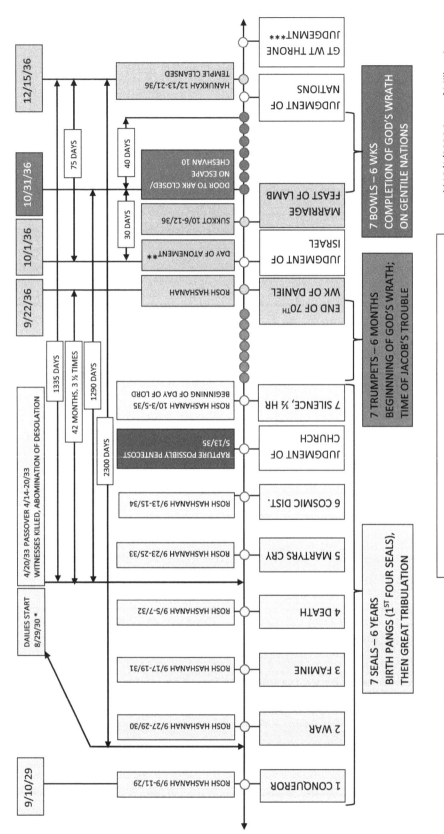

END TIME JUDGMENTS

9/10/29

ROSH HASHANAH 9/9-11/29 — 1 CONQUEROR

ROSH HASHANAH 9/27-29/30 — 2 WAR

ROSH HASHANAH 9/17-19/31 — 3 FAMINE

ROSH HASHANAH 9/5-7/32 — 4 DEATH

ROSH HASHANAH 9/23-25/33 — 5 MARTYRS CRY

ROSH HASHANAH 9/13-15/34 — 6 COSMIC DIST.

RAPTURE POSSIBLY PENTECOST 5/13/35 — JUDGMENT OF CHURCH

ROSH HASHANAH 10/3-5/35 BEGINNING OF DAY OF LORD — 7 SILENCE, ½ HR

7 SEALS – 6 YEARS BIRTH PANGS (1ST FOUR SEALS), THEN GREAT TRIBULATION

DAILIES START 8/29/30 *

4/20/33 PASSOVER 4/14-20/33 WITNESSES KILLED, ABOMINATION OF DESOLATION

1335 DAYS
42 MONTHS, 3 ½ TIMES
1290 DAYS
2300 DAYS

ROSH HASHANAH — END OF 70TH WK OF DANIEL

DAY OF ATONEMENT** — JUDGMENT OF ISRAEL

SUKKOT 10/6-12/36 — MARRIAGE FEAST OF LAMB

DOOR TO ARK CLOSED/ NO ESCAPE CHESHVAN 10

HANUKKAH 12/13-21/36 TEMPLE CLEANSED — JUDGMENT OF NATIONS

GT WT THRONE JUDGMENT*** — GT WT THRONE JUDGMENT***

7 TRUMPETS – 6 MONTHS BEGINNING OF GOD'S WRATH; TIME OF JACOB'S TROUBLE

7 BOWLS – 6 WKS COMPLETION OF GOD'S WRATH ON GENTILE NATIONS

9/22/36
10/1/36
10/31/36
12/15/36

30 DAYS
40 DAYS
75 DAYS

*8/29/30 is exactly 1960 years from the destruction of the 2nd Temple when the daily sacrifices ceased on 8/30/70 AD

**10/1/2036 Start of Millennium, Year of Jubilee
***End of Millennium

CHAPTER 11

The Millennium

The Millennium begins at the end of Daniel's 70th week after Jesus has been crowned king and begins His reign on earth. It is, as the name implies, one thousand years, the final dispensation to occur on earth at the end times or "the fulness of times".

> That in the dispensation of the fulness of times **he might gather together in one** *(anakefalaiomai)* all things in Christ, both which are in heaven, and which are on earth; even in him: Ephesians 1:10

This period is our future hope and the culmination of everything that has occurred before in history. At this time God will "gather together in one all things in Christ". This phrase comes from the Greek word *anakefalaiomai*, which is a compound word. The root word is *kefalaiomai* which means to bring everyone and everything under the submission of one person, the head, and to gather around him. In this context, the head is Jesus who is going to be the focal point of this dispensation. The prefix to this word is *ana* which means "again" and implies that it was like this once before. So, the prefix *ana* implies that there was a time once before when everyone and everything on the earth was under the submission of Jesus Christ and gathered around Him. And when was that time? It was before the fall of man in the Garden of Eden. So, this verse indicates that at the final dispensation, everything is going to return to the way it was before the fall. Everything will be brought back into submission to Jesus and gathered around him. Jesus will restore not only man but nature to its pre-fall state.

Jesus will return at some time to rule the earth, and upon his return to earth, Jesus will defeat the then current world-ruler, the Antichrist and his armies. After Jesus' victory at the Battle of Armageddon, He then can set up His government, the Kingdom of God. This thousand-year period of His rule is commonly referred to as the Millennium. On the proposed timeline, the Millennium begins in a Jubilee year which represents freedom, restoration, and renewal, a time when the earth will be restored to its pre-fall state.

> And I saw thrones, and they sat upon them, and judgment was given unto them: and I saw the souls of them that were beheaded for the witness of Jesus, and for the word of God, and which had not worshipped the beast, neither his image, neither had received his mark upon their foreheads, or in their hands; and they lived and reigned with Christ a thousand years. Revelation 20:4

Some believe that the one thousand years is not really literal, but is merely figurative language for an unspecified long time. Nevertheless, Revelation 20 uses the phrase "the one thousand years" **six times** to refer to this period. Furthermore, other verses also mention this same one thousand years and point to the Millennium as being a fulfillment of the seventh day Sabbath, a day ancient Israel was commanded to rest from their labors. In other words, the Sabbath day is a foreshadow or type of the coming "Sabbath millennium" following six millennia that the previous six days of the week foreshadow or typify.

So, the Millennium could well parallel the 7th day of creation. Under a young earth creation model, this means that there would be about six thousand years from Adam until the present (i.e., approximately four thousand years before Christ, and two thousand more years until now). Then there will be one thousand years (the Millennium) when we will live in His presence. Thus, the total of seven thousand years could parallel the seven days of creation—as per Hosea 6:2 and 2 Peter 3:8:

> I will go and return to my place, till they acknowledge their offence, and seek my face: in their affliction they will seek me early. Come, and let us return unto the LORD: for he hath torn, and he will heal us; he hath smitten, and he will bind us up. After two days will he revive us: in the third day he will raise us up, and we shall live in his sight. Hosea 5:15-6:2

> But, beloved, be not ignorant of this one thing, that one day is with the Lord as a thousand years, and a thousand years as one day. 2 Peter 3:8

During this final thousand-year period, Satan is bound and Christ will rule (Revelation 20:1-6), beginning the restoration of creation by reestablishing peace on earth and true worship, as well as beginning the renewal of even nature itself. After this period of peace, Satan is released and deceives the nations once again (Revelation 20:7-10). The Millennium then ends with the final battle of Gog Magog, followed by the Great White Throne Judgment and the end of Death and Hades (Revelation20:11-15).

After the Millennium, a new heaven and a new Earth appear.

> And I saw a new heaven and a new earth: for the first heaven and the first earth were passed away; and there was no more sea. Revelation 21:1

The word *new*, however, should be replaced with a word such as *renewed*, *cleansed*, *purified*, or *transformed* [Jeremiah, 2017]. God never gives up on His original plan for human beings to dwell on Earth. In fact, the climax of history will be the creation of a new heaven and a New Earth, a resurrected universe inhabited by resurrected people living with the resurrected Jesus (Revelation 21:1-4). [Alcorn, 2004, p. xx] The New Earth will not be a non-Earth but a real Earth. The Earth spoken of in Scripture is the Earth we know – with dirt, water, rocks, trees, flowers, animals, people, and a variety of natural wonders. And Earth without these would not be Earth. ... We're told the "first Earth" will pass away (Revelation 21:1). The word for *first* is *prote*, suggesting a vital connection between the two Earths. The first Earth serves as the prototype or pattern for the New Earth. There's continuity between new and old. [Alcorn, 2004, p. 158][1]

> And I saw a **new** *(renewed)* heaven and a **new** *(renewed)* earth: for the first heaven and the first earth were passed away; and there was no more sea. And I John saw the holy city, new Jerusalem, coming down from God out of heaven, prepared as a bride adorned for her husband. And I heard a great voice out of heaven saying, Behold, the tabernacle of God is with men, and he will dwell with them, and they shall be his people, and God himself shall be with them, and be their God. And God shall wipe away all tears from their eyes; and there shall be no more death, neither sorrow, nor crying, neither shall there be any more pain: for the former things are passed away. Revelation 21:1-4

God will not entirely destroy what He has created in order to start completely over. It is a restored or renewed earth, back to its pre-fall conditions that God has promised to bring about as well as a restored Israel which will occur at the Millennium.

> And he said, It is a light thing that thou shouldest be my servant to raise up the tribes of Jacob, and to **restore** the preserved of Israel: I will also give thee for a light to

the Gentiles, that thou mayest be my salvation unto the end of the earth. Isaiah 49:6

Who is present during the Millennium and what events occur?

In His restoration plan for creation, God will continue to work on and through the various groups of people that He has dealt with throughout time. The Millennium is a time when mortals will co-exist with immortals on Earth. The resurrected people entering the Millennium are the raptured believers, i.e., the Church, and the Old Testament saints. They will return in their resurrected, immortal bodies to reign with Christ. Believers who are alive at the time of Christ's return will enter the Millennium in their natural bodies. Jesus Christ freely associated with the disciples (and others) following His resurrection and even ate with them. Similarly, the resurrected individuals will be able to interact with those in their natural bodies, even though they will have permanent, perfected bodies.

After Christ's Second Coming, the living Gentiles and Jews will enter the Millennium with unresurrected bodies, and it is they who will populate the Earth during the Millennium. Babies will be born post-Second Coming, during the Millennium but only to those people who have not had resurrected bodies at that point in time. The living saints who go into the Millennium in their natural bodies will beget children throughout the age. Those born in this age will have to deal with sin, and some of these children may be unbelievers. So, salvation will be required. [Pentecost, 1958, p. 489][1]

> Their children also shall be as aforetime, and their congregation shall be established before me, and I will punish all that oppress them. Jeremiah 30:20

> In those days they shall say no more, The fathers have eaten a sour grape, and the children's teeth are set on edge. Jeremiah 31:29

> And it shall come to pass, that ye shall divide it by lot for an inheritance unto you, and to the strangers that sojourn among you, which shall beget children among you: and they shall be unto you as born in the country among the children of Israel; they shall have inheritance with you among the tribes of Israel. Ezekiel 47:22

> I will hiss for them, and gather them; for I have redeemed them: and they shall increase as they have increased. Zechariah 10:8

During the Millennium the population will greatly increase. In fact, the number of unbelievers born during the Millennium will alone be large.

> And when the thousand years are expired, Satan shall be loosed out of his prison, And shall go out to deceive the nations which are in the four quarters of the earth, Gog, and Magog, to gather them together to battle: the number of whom is as the sand of the sea. Revelation 20:7-8

RESTORATION OF PEACE

The Millennium, again, is a time of restoration. Although it begins and ends with war, the world will finally experience absence of war in the interim. Furthermore, Christ will be in charge, ruling over the nations on the Earth.

> And he shall judge among the nations, and shall rebuke many people: and they shall beat their swords into plowshares, and their spears into pruninghooks: nation shall not lift up sword against nation, neither shall they learn war any more. Isaiah 2:4

> And he shall judge among many people, and rebuke strong nations afar off; and they shall beat their swords into plowshares, and their spears into pruninghooks: nation shall not lift up a sword against nation, neither shall they learn war any more. Micah 4:3

The world longs for peace, but only Jesus Christ can provide true peace.

> For unto us a child is born, unto us a son is given: and the government shall be upon his shoulder: and his name shall be called Wonderful, Counsellor, The mighty God, The everlasting Father, The Prince of Peace. Of the increase of his government and peace there shall be no end, upon the throne of David, and upon his kingdom, to order it, and to establish it with judgment and with justice from henceforth even for ever. The zeal of the LORD of hosts will perform this. Isaiah 9:6-7

1. The New Form of Government: "Glorified Monarchy"

Ever since Adam left the Garden of Eden, man has been ruled by other men with very bad results. The problem with men ruling is twofold: First, humanity's natural inclination is evil. We're all familiar with the horrors of despots and dictators of the past and present. Even good men are still corruptible with time. Power corrupts and absolute power corrupts absolutely. King Solomon, the wisest man who ever lived, still turned away from God.

Second, even when a ruler is good and avoids corruption, there is still the problem that he is mortal. When he dies, he will most likely be replaced by somebody wicked. The Book of Kings bears out this pattern. Chuck Missler made the observation that "the people of God are always one generation away from apostasy" for this very reason. This sums up well the problem of the mortality of righteous rulers. This, by the way, is why Jesus told us to pray:

> Thy kingdom come, Thy will be done in earth, as it is in heaven. Matthew 6:10

The Kingdom of God is God's government. The Bible's most frequent use of the word *kingdom* refers to Christ's political, ethnic, Israel-centered kingdom that will begin in the last days. This kingdom has several names including: Messianic Kingdom, Davidic Kingdom, and Eschatological Kingdom. The kingdom is referred to as the Messianic Kingdom because Messiah Jesus will return to establish the specific will of God on earth (Isa.11; Dan. 7; Zech. 14; Rev. 19). It is also called the coming Davidic Kingdom because it will fulfill God's promise to King David in the Davidic Covenant to send the Messiah to reign forever from David's throne in Jerusalem (2 Sam. 7; Ps. 89; Amos 9:11-15). And it is sometimes called the Eschatological Kingdom because Christ will establish it in the last days. Currently it only rules in heaven. In the past it ruled on earth, too, but only for a short time when Adam and Eve were obedient to God in the Garden of Eden. Once they rebelled, they effectively rejected His rule and were cast out of the resulting utopia that God's Kingdom creates and into a dystopia that Satan's kingdom or rule creates.[1]

> In whom the god of this world hath blinded the minds of them which believe not, lest the light of the glorious gospel of Christ, who is the image of God, should shine unto them. 2 Corinthians 4:4

When Jesus comes back to reestablish the Kingdom of God on earth, the pattern of apostasy described above will be broken forever. The righteous saints who were glorified in the rapture and first resurrection will come back from heaven to become the rulers in the Kingdom of God with Jesus.

> And I saw thrones, and they sat upon them, and judgment was given unto them: and I saw the souls of them that were beheaded for the witness of Jesus, and for the word of God, and which had not worshipped the beast, neither his image, neither had received his mark upon their foreheads, or in their hands; and they lived and reigned with Christ a thousand years. Revelation 20:4

However, those rewarded saints who reign with Christ will have glorified bodies instead of the physical ones they had in their previous life. The lust of the flesh will be gone along with their mortality. This means they will not be corruptible nor will they ever die and be replaced by a wicked ruler. The benevolent rule of Jesus and his saints will be continuous. The resulting peace and prosperity will be unprecedented and ever increasing.

So, the Millennium will be characterized by "good government" compared to the many failed attempts at peaceful rule by governments of all kinds—democratic and dictatorship—all over the world, for decades, centuries, and indeed millennia.

2. The New Government Structure and Hierarchy of Rulers

Scripture is clear throughout the Old and New Testament that Christ will rule over the Kingdom of God as king.

> For unto us a child is born, unto us a son is given: and the government shall be upon his shoulder: and his name shall be called Wonderful, Counsellor, The mighty God, The everlasting Father, The Prince of Peace. Of the increase of his government and peace there shall be no end, upon the throne of David, and upon his kingdom, to order it, and to establish it with judgment and with justice from henceforth even for ever. The zeal of the LORD of hosts will perform this. Isaiah 9:6-7

He shall be great, and shall be called the Son of the Highest: and the Lord God shall give unto him the throne of his father David: And he shall reign over the house of Jacob for ever; and of his kingdom there shall be no end. Luke 1:32-33

And the Lord shall be king over all the earth: in that day shall there be one Lord, and his name one. Zechariah 14:9

Behold, the days come, saith the Lord, that I will raise unto David a righteous Branch, and a King shall reign and prosper, and shall execute judgment and justice in the earth. In his days Judah shall be saved, and Israel shall dwell safely: and this is his name whereby he shall be called, The Lord Our Righteousness. Jeremiah 23:5-6

Even King David in the Psalms announced the Messiah's reign and that the Messiah would rule over him.

The Lord [God the father] said unto my [David's] Lord [Jesus], Sit thou at my right hand, until I make thine enemies thy footstool. Psalm 110:1

And Psalm 72, also written by David, looked forward to the Messiah's (Jesus') literal reign on the entire Earth:

He shall judge thy people with righteousness, and thy poor with judgment. The mountains shall bring peace to the people, and the little hills, by righteousness. He shall judge the poor of the people, he shall save the children of the needy, and shall break in pieces the oppressor. They shall fear thee as long as the sun and moon endure, throughout all generations. He shall come down like rain upon the mown grass: as showers that water the earth. In his days shall the righteous flourish; and abundance of peace so long as the moon endureth. He shall have dominion also from sea to sea, and from the river unto the ends of the earth. They that dwell in the wilderness shall bow before him; and his enemies shall lick the dust. The kings of Tarshish and of the isles shall bring presents: the kings of Sheba and Seba shall offer gifts. Yea, all kings shall fall down before him: all nations shall serve him. For he shall deliver the needy when he crieth; the poor also, and him that hath no helper. He shall spare the poor and needy, and shall save the souls of the needy. He shall redeem their soul from deceit and violence: and precious shall their blood be in his sight. And he shall live, and to him shall be given of the gold of Sheba: prayer also shall be made for him continually; and daily shall he be praised. There shall be an handful of corn in the earth upon the top of the mountains; the fruit thereof shall shake like Lebanon: and they of the city shall flourish like grass of the earth. His name shall endure for ever: his name shall be continued as long as the sun: and men shall be blessed in him: all nations shall call him blessed. Psalm 72:2-17

Zechariah, as well, tells us that His kingdom will encompass the entire earth.

And I will cut off the chariot from Ephraim, and the horse from Jerusalem, and the battle bow shall be cut off: and he shall speak peace unto the heathen: and his dominion shall be from sea even to sea, and from the river even to the ends of the earth. Zechariah 9:10

In order to accomplish His rule, Jesus instructed us on who would be ruling with Him during His kingdom using various parables. In Matthew 25:14-29, Jesus tells a parable about three individuals to whom a master had given different amounts of resources, and the master wanted to see how well they did with the resources he gave them. He commended those who were faithful and used their resources to gain even more. Similarly, in Luke 19:11-27, in the Parable of the Ten Minas (coins), the master commended those who had invested wisely, and rewarded them by putting them in charge of several cities. However, the master rebuked the man who hid his original mina and did not create any wealth from it, sending him away without any reward. The point is that whoever uses their resources wisely in the service of the master, in this life, will be rewarded with more responsibility in the age to come. In other words, the wise use of talents and resources in this life will be appropriately rewarded in the resurrected bodies of the future, specifically in reigning with Christ. Several verses state that we will rule with Christ, implying that we will be judging and ruling in the Millennium which will extend into the eternal state.[1]

> Do ye not know that the saints shall judge the world? and if the world shall be judged by you, are ye unworthy to judge the smallest matters? Know ye not that we shall judge angels? how much more things that pertain to this life? 1 Corinthians 6:2-3

> If we suffer, we shall also reign with him: if we deny him, he also will deny us: 2 Timothy 2

> And there shall be no night there; and they need no candle, neither light of the sun; for the Lord God giveth them light: and they shall reign for ever and ever. Revelation 22:5

Revelation 20:4 says that those who refused to take the mark of the beast during the Tribulation will rule with Christ throughout the Millennium:

> And I saw thrones, and they sat upon them, and judgment was given unto them: and I saw the souls of them that

were beheaded for the witness of Jesus, and for the word of God, and which had not worshipped the beast, neither his image, neither had received his mark upon their foreheads, or in their hands; and they lived and reigned with Christ a thousand years. Revelation 20:4

So, those who use their talents more wisely will have greater positions of authority in the Millennium. After that, it is not quite as clear regarding the order of the rulers who will serve under Jesus. The following hierarchy of rulers is taken from Fruchtenbaum, 2004. In his model there are two branches in the kingdom, a Gentile and a Jewish branch, which Jesus Christ rules over the world during the Millennium. The Jewish branch rules the land of Israel with its extended borders, as per the original Promised Land; the Gentile branch governs the rest of the world. The Gentile branch most likely will be ruled over by the Church and Tribulation saints in resurrected bodies (Revelation 20:4-6). King David will be resurrected, and will rule over Israel during the Millennium (but under Jesus Christ). Regarding David's throne, the following passages were written well after King David died. Note that it says that David will be resurrected.[1]

But they shall serve the LORD their God, and David their king, whom I will raise up unto them. Jer 30:9

And I will set up one shepherd over them, and he shall feed them, even my servant David; he shall feed them, and he shall be their shepherd. And I the LORD will be their God, and my servant David a prince among them; I the LORD have spoken it. Ezekiel 34:23-24

And David my servant shall be king over them; and they all shall have one shepherd: they shall also walk in my judgments, and observe my statutes, and do them. And they shall dwell in the land that I have given unto Jacob my servant, wherein your fathers have dwelt; and they shall dwell therein, even they, and their children, and their children's children for ever: and my servant David shall be their prince for ever. Ezekiel 37:24-25

Afterward shall the children of Israel return, and seek the LORD their God, and David their king; and shall fear the LORD and his goodness in the latter days. Hosea 3:5

The twelve apostles, as promised by Jesus, in their resurrected bodies will rule over the twelve tribes of Israel who are in their natural bodies.

And Jesus said unto them, Verily I say unto you, That ye which have followed me, in the regeneration when the Son of man shall sit in the throne of his glory, ye also shall sit upon twelve thrones, judging the twelve tribes of Israel. Matthew 19:28

Ye are they which have continued with me in my temptations. And I appoint unto you a kingdom, as my Father hath appointed unto me; That ye may eat and drink at my table in my kingdom, and sit on thrones judging the twelve tribes of Israel. Luke 22:28-30

The Old Testament saints will finally inherit the Promised Land. These events will fulfill the writings of the prophets of long ago, and will also fulfill the covenants made by God to Israel. Unlike the many centuries following King Solomon, Israel will be joined as one nation; there will not be a separation of Israel and Judah. Zerubbabel (of the times of Nehemiah, Ezra, and Haggai) may be one of the princes ruling over part of Israel.

And again the word of the LORD came unto Haggai in the four and twentieth day of the month, saying, Speak to Zerubbabel, governor of Judah, saying, I will shake the heavens and the earth; And I will overthrow the throne of kingdoms, and I will destroy the strength of the kingdoms of the heathen; and I will overthrow the chariots, and those that ride in them; and the horses and their riders shall come down, every one by the sword of his brother. In that day, saith the LORD of hosts, will I take thee, O Zerubbabel, my servant, the son of Shealtiel, saith the LORD, and will make thee as a signet: for I have chosen thee, saith the LORD of hosts. Haggai 2:20-23

In summary, a structure for the Millennial governmental hierarchy might look something like this, with Christ on the throne governing a Gentile and Jewish branch.[1]

Jesus Christ on the Throne of David (Isaiah 9:6-7; Luke 1:30-33; Zechariah 14:9; Jeremiah 23:5-6)	
Gentile Branch	**Jewish Branch**
Church and Tribulation Saints—in resurrected bodies (Revelation 20:4-6)	David—in his resurrected body (Jeremiah 30:9; Ezekiel 34:23-24; 37:24-25; Hosea 3:5)
Kings of the Gentile Nations—in their natural bodies (Psalm 72)	12 Apostles—in their resurrected bodies—ruling over the 12 Tribes who are in their natural bodies (Matthew 19:28; Luke 22:28-30)
who rule over the Gentile nations	Princes (e.g., possibly Zerubbabel) (Isaiah 32:1; Ezekiel 45:8; Haggai 2:20-23)
	Judges and Counselors (Isaiah 1:26).
	.. who rule over Israel (Deuteronomy 15:6; Deuteronomy 28:1).
	who in turn rule over the Gentiles

3. Nations and Borders

ISRAEL

From each nation, with Israel at the head, will thus come a remnant to rebuild their devastated countries. Israel, of course, will be the chief nation of the world during the Millennium.

> And many nations shall come, and say, Come, and let us go up to the mountain of the Lord, and to the house of the God of Jacob; and he will teach us of his ways, and we will walk in his paths: for the law shall go forth of Zion, and the word of the Lord from Jerusalem.
> Micah 4:2

Bible prophecy points to a soon-coming age (the Millennium) when the people of Israel (Abraham's descendants, the Jews) live at peace within the boundaries promised unconditionally to Abraham. Those boundaries span from the river Jordan in the east to the Mediterranean in the west, and embrace the disputed territories of the West Bank and Gaza.

God promised that He would give all the land of Canaan to Abraham and his descendants. He made a covenant with Abraham.

> And I will set thy bounds from the Red sea even unto the sea of the Philistines, and from the desert unto the river: for I will deliver the inhabitants of the land into your hand; and thou shalt drive them out before thee.
> Exodus 23:31

Despite Israel's future disobedience, this promise was **unconditional** in that the land was to be theirs forever with no conditions or strings attached.

> And I will give unto thee, and to thy seed after thee, the land wherein thou art a stranger, all the land of Canaan,

for an everlasting possession; and I will be their God.
Genesis 17:8

In Numbers 34:1-12 the boundaries given to Moses are found as he was about to divide up Canaan for the twelve tribes. These borders are:

- Western: the Mediterranean Sea
- Eastern: from Kadesh-barnea, via Zin and the salt sea to Zedad and Hamath in the north
- Southern: from Kadesh Barnea to the Brook of Egypt (probably not the Nile)
- Northern: from the Mediterranean Sea (Mount Hor) to Hamath to Zedad

In Ezekiel 47:13-20 there is more boundary detail which confirms these boundaries. It is clearly stated that the Jordan is the eastern boundary (v18) and the western boundary (the Mediterranean Sea) goes north as far as 'opposite Hamath' (v20). The southern boundary is defined by a 'brook' in Numbers 34:5 and Ezekiel 47:19 and by a 'river' in Genesis 15:18. Note that this is most likely *not* the Nile. The significant point here is that many understand Ezekiel 47 (in fact, Ezekiel 40-48) to describe Millennial Israel. And it is interesting to observe that the boundaries given to Moses as he was about to divide up Canaan for the twelve tribes (Numbers 34) correlate well with the Millennial boundaries given in Ezekiel 47.

Not only will the borders of Israel be expanded in the Millennial Kingdom but also the divisions of the land among the tribes will be changed. Under Moses, the land was divided according to the size of each tribe (Joshua 13) and consequently resulted in a very unequal division (e.g., the tribe of Manasseh took a large share). In contrast, Ezekiel 47 and 48 state that the land in Millennial Israel will be divided *equally* between the tribes, and in an east-west way (parallel sections).

Thus saith the Lord GOD; This shall be the border, whereby ye shall inherit the land according to the twelve tribes of Israel: Joseph shall have two portions. And ye shall inherit it, one as well as another: concerning the which I lifted up mine hand to give it unto your fathers: and this land shall fall unto you for inheritance. Ezekiel 47:13-14

So, each tribe will have one portion, starting with Dan in the north and ending with Gad in the south, with all sections run from east to west.

In addition, there will be a portion of land between the section for the tribe of Judah and the section for the tribe of Benjamin that is "set apart for the LORD" (Ezekiel 45:1-5, 48:8-22). In the Millennial age, the law will emanate from Zion (Micah 4:2). In the Old Testament, Zion came to mean Jerusalem, and the Temple area in particular. This indicates that Christ will rule from some future temple and its surrounding area, and a graphic description of such a temple is found in Ezekiel 40-48.

A return of the tribes of Israel to the Promised Land begins with the Second Exodus led by Jesus, and this repatriation continues in the Millennium.

And say unto them, Thus saith the Lord GOD; Behold, I will take the children of Israel from among the heathen, whither they be gone, and will gather them on every side, and bring them into their own land: And I will make them one nation in the land upon the mountains of Israel; and one king shall be king to them all: and they shall be no more two nations, neither shall they be divided into two kingdoms any more at all. Neither shall they defile themselves any more with their idols, nor with their detestable things, nor with any of their transgressions: but I will save them out of all their dwelling places, wherein they have sinned, and will cleanse them: so shall they be my people, and I will be their God. And David my servant shall be king over them; and they all shall have one shepherd: they shall also walk in my judgments, and observe my statutes, and do them. And they shall dwell in the land that I have given unto Jacob my servant, wherein your fathers have dwelt; and they shall dwell therein, even they, and their children, and their children's children for ever: and my servant David shall be their prince for ever. Ezekiel 37:21-25

We know that the Messiah's rule during the Millennium will usher in a time of peace unknown since the Garden of Eden (or possibly the early days of the post-Noahic period). But, what about the nations surrounding Israel? Will animosity turn to peace? Indeed, the Millennial period appears to be a time of peace and prosperity between Egypt, Israel, and Assyria.[1]

In that day shall there be a highway out of Egypt to Assyria, and the Assyrian shall come into Egypt, and the Egyptian into Assyria, and the Egyptians shall serve with the Assyrians. In that day shall Israel be the third with Egypt and with Assyria, even a blessing in the midst of the land: Whom the LORD of hosts shall bless, saying, Blessed be Egypt my people, and Assyria the work of my hands, and Israel mine inheritance. Isaiah 19:23-25

EGYPT

Large parts of Egypt may be desolate for forty years, quite possibly the first forty years of the Millennium, in accordance with the prophets Joel and Ezekiel. Chapter 3 of Joel concerns the latter stages of the Tribulation and the first part of the Millennium.

Egypt shall be a desolation, and Edom shall be a desolate wilderness, for the violence against the children of Judah, because they have shed innocent blood in their land. Joel 3:19

And the land of Egypt shall be desolate and waste; and they shall know that I am the LORD: because he hath said, The river is mine, and I have made it. Behold, therefore I am against thee, and against thy rivers, and I will make the land of Egypt utterly waste and desolate, from the tower of Syene even unto the border of Ethiopia. No foot of man shall pass through it, nor foot of beast shall pass through it, neither shall it be inhabited forty years. And I will make the land of Egypt desolate in the midst of the countries that are desolate, and her cities among the cities that are laid waste shall be desolate forty years: and I will scatter the Egyptians among the nations, and will disperse them through the countries. Yet thus saith the Lord GOD; At the end of forty years will I gather the Egyptians from the people whither they were scattered: And I will bring again the captivity of Egypt, and will cause them to return into the land of Pathros, into the land of their habitation; and they shall be there a base kingdom. Ezekiel 29:9-14

Thus saith the LORD; They also that uphold Egypt shall fall; and the pride of her power shall come down: from the tower of Syene [from Migdol to Aswan (NIV)] shall they fall in it by the sword, saith the Lord GOD. Ezekiel 30:6

This prophecy was issued by the prophet Ezekiel around 570 BC and has not yet been fulfilled. It is possible that Ezekiel 29 will be fulfilled in the time leading up to Armageddon, suggesting that large parts of Egypt will be uninhabited during the first forty years of the Millennium [LaHaye, et al., 2001]. It is also possible that it will occur prior to the Tribulation, and prior to the Magog invasion of

Ezekiel 38-39 [Stearman, 2019]. This would explain why Egypt is not one of the invading countries, yet Libya and Sudan (Egypt's neighbors) are invaders.

Although Egypt is strangely absent from the Gog and Magog passage of Ezekiel 38-39, the prophet Isaiah writes that many Egyptians will turn to the Lord and that they will be blessed.[1] In the millennial situation, Egypt is to have a prominent place. Israel will be regathered from Egypt to their Promised Land, but Egypt will be a prominent nation in the millennial situation. That Egypt will be blessed is mentioned specifically in Isaiah 19:25, and that it will be a prominent nation along with Israel and Assyria is indicated in the same passage.

> In that day shall there be an altar to the Lord in the midst of the land of Egypt, and a pillar at the border thereof to the Lord. And it shall be for a sign and for a witness unto the Lord of hosts in the land of Egypt: for they shall cry unto the Lord because of the oppressors, and he shall send them a saviour, and a great one, and he shall deliver them. And the Lord shall be known to Egypt, and the Egyptians shall know the Lord in that day, and shall do sacrifice and oblation; yea, they shall vow a vow unto the Lord, and perform it. And the Lord shall smite Egypt: he shall smite and heal it: and they shall return even to the Lord, and he shall be intreated of them, and shall heal them. In that day shall there be a highway out of Egypt to Assyria, and the Assyrian shall come into Egypt, and the Egyptian into Assyria, and the Egyptians shall serve with the Assyrians. In that day shall Israel be the third with Egypt and with Assyria, even a blessing in the midst of the land: Whom the Lord of hosts shall bless, saying, Blessed be Egypt my people, and Assyria the work of my hands, and Israel mine inheritance. Isaiah 19:19-25

Egypt is also singled out for special warning in Zechariah 14:18, 19.

> And if the family of Egypt go not up, and come not, that have no rain; there shall be the plague, wherewith the Lord will smite the heathen that come not up to keep the feast of tabernacles. This shall be the punishment of Egypt, and the punishment of all nations that come not up to keep the feast of tabernacles Zechariah 14:18-19

God will punish them unless they keep the feast of tabernacles in the millennial kingdom. What is revealed in respect to Egypt has reference to the world-wide rule of Christ and indicates that all people will necessarily be required to serve Him.

In summary, peace will come between Israel and Egypt by means of conversion. Only when the Egyptians worship the same God as Israel, through Jesus the Messiah, will peace finally come. For the first forty years of the Kingdom, the land of Egypt will be desolate and the Egyptians will be dispersed all over the world. But afterwards, the Egyptians will be regathered, becoming a kingdom again. [Fruchtenbaum, 2009, p. 501][1]

ASSYRIA

The importance of Assyria in the Bible is borne out by more than 140 references including over twenty references to its principal city Nineveh. It was the kingdom that rose to power and eventually conquered Israel. Today, ancient Assyria corresponds to most parts of modern-day Iraq as well as parts of Iran, Kuwait, Syria, and Turkey.

From the standpoint of prophecy, the history of Assyria is important because along its path numerous prophecies were fulfilled. Isaiah the prophet, for instance, solemnly warned the children of Israel of the coming invasion of the Assyrians and their ultimate captivity (Isaiah 7:17-20; 8:4-7) and predicted that Assyria would be punished in due time and brought down (Isaiah 11:12-16). The entire book of Nahum relates to the downfall of Nineveh, and the book of Jonah records the remarkable experience of repentance of the people of Nineveh at the preaching of Jonah which delayed their ultimate destruction one hundred and fifty years later.

Most of the prophecies concerning Nineveh have already been fulfilled. A few references, however, are subject to fulfillment in the millennial reign and events relating to it. That Assyria is to be recognized in the millennial situation, however, is indicated in several passages. According to Isaiah 11:11, 16, the regathering of Israel at the beginning of the millennium will be from Assyria as well as from other nations, and a highway will stretch from Egypt to Assyria through the land of Israel as a major transportation link in the millennial kingdom. A similar prophecy is found in Isaiah 19:23-25 in reference to the future millennial kingdom: "In that day shall there be a highway out of Egypt to Assyria, and the Assyrian shall come into Egypt, and the Egyptian into Assyria, and the Egyptians shall serve with the Assyrians. In that day shall Israel be the third with Egypt and with Assyria, even a blessing in the midst of the land: Whom the Lord of hosts shall bless, saying, Blessed be Egypt my people, and Assyria the work of my hands, and Israel mine inheritance."

It is evident from this passage that Israel's two most important neighbors in the millennial kingdom will be the peoples who inhabit the area of ancient Assyria to the northeast and Egypt to the southwest. In that day both Assyria and Egypt will be blessed along with Israel. The fact that Israel is called "third" in the light of other prophecies should not be interpreted, however, as meaning that Israel is less than these nations, but rather that it will be spoken of in the same breath as a prominent world power of that day. Another reference to Israel's regathering from Assyria is found in Isaiah 27:13. Zechariah adds his contribution in Zechariah 10:10-11 where the destruction of the pride of Assyria and the scepter of Egypt is predicted and the regathering of Israel from these lands is anticipated. Assyria, the great nation of the past which antedated the Babylonian Empire and successive dominions of the Gentiles, will have its echo in the prophetic future and its place in the divine program of the millennial kingdom.

JORDAN (Edom, Moab, and Ammon)

Throughout the Millennial Kingdom, while the whole earth is beautified and blossoming as the rose, the area of Edom will be a place of continual burning pitch and burning brimstone. The smoke will rise and be visible for the entire one thousand years. [Fruchtenbaum, 2004][1] So, while Israel, Egypt and Assyria prosper, the destruction of Jordan is predicted. The prophets Jeremiah and Obadiah describe the destruction of Edom, which is present day southern Jordan.

> And the streams *(of Edom)* thereof shall be turned into pitch, and the dust thereof into brimstone, and the land thereof shall become burning pitch. It shall not be quenched night nor day; the smoke thereof shall go up for ever: from generation to generation it shall lie waste; none shall pass through it for ever and ever. Isaiah 34:9-10

Note that this has not happened yet. Obadiah states rather clearly that this destruction of Edom will come by means of the children of Israel (v. 18), for the two houses of Israel will be like fire, while Edom will be like stubble that quickly catches fire when exposed to the flame. The destruction will be total, so that nothing will remain of Esau's descendants, while the descendants of brother Jacob will own and possess the mountains of Edom (vv. 19-20). It is out of Mount Zion that judgment will fall on Edom (v. 21).

As for Moab, which is present-day central Jordan, it, too, will suffer destruction (Jer. 48:1-46), but it will not be total. Those who survive will come to repentance and a remnant of Moab will return, according to Jeremiah 48:47.

Concerning Ammon, or modern northern Jordan, it will also undergo a partial destruction and become a possession of Israel, as seen in Jeremiah 49:1-2. As with Moab, it will not be a total destruction, and those who survive will turn to the Lord, for a remnant of Ammon will also be found in the Kingdom according to Jeremiah 49:6. Thus, peace comes between Israel and northern Jordan by means of a partial destruction which is followed by conversion. So, there will be a saved nation called Ammon in the Kingdom. [Fruchtenbaum, 2004, pp. 495-496][1]

4. One Language Again - Tower of Babel in Reverse?

Everyone can relate to the frustration of not being able to understand people around you because they are speaking a foreign language. It leads to confusion, misunderstanding, alienation, conflict and even, at times, violence. Imagine how great a world it would be without this source of friction holding back progress and the ready sharing of information.

It is easy to forget today, but mankind was not always divided by myriad languages. Genesis records how the whole world was of one language (Genesis 11:1). But the unity and information-sharing benefits of one common language caused a problem. The progress of man was so great and rapid that God knew nothing would be impossible to man (Genesis 11:6). The Tower of Babel ascending to heaven was evidence of this fact. So, God went down and confused the languages. But Bible prophecy may indicate a reversal of the Tower of Babel event.

> For then will I turn to the people a pure language, that they may all call upon the name of the LORD, to serve him with one consent. Zephaniah 3:9

Admittedly, it is not one hundred percent clear from Zephaniah that a return to a common tongue is what is being predicted, and another prophet Zechariah may indicate that different languages continue into the Millennium.

> Thus saith the LORD of hosts; In those days it shall come to pass, that ten men shall take hold out of all languages of the nations, even shall take hold of the skirt of him that is a Jew, saying, We will go with you: for we have heard that God is with you. Zechariah 8:23

But it is not unlikely that a wise and godly government would establish at least a universal language to make things easier. Under such a system, everyone would learn their native nation or culture's tongue and one other language, a universal language. In the spirit of a "restoration of all things", this language could be Hebrew, the language everyone may have spoken before the Tower of Babel. So, a restoration to a pre-fall state would probably include a return to one common language.

5. New Jerusalem

New Jerusalem is described in Revelation 21 and 22, the last two chapters of the Bible. In order to understand these concluding chapters, one question that needs to be addressed is whether these two chapters chronologically follow Chapter 20 which outlines the timeline of the Millennium. In that event Revelation 21 and 22 would be describing a post-millennial eternal state. However, that is not necessarily the case. Since chapter 21 begins with "And I saw", it indicates that this is a new vision and does not necessarily follow chapter 20 in time.

> **And I saw** a new heaven and a new earth: for the first heaven and the first earth were passed away; and there was no more sea. Revelation 21:1

Just as Revelation has other parenthetical passages (10:1-11:14 and 12:1-15:4) that add information to what has happened before, it is not only possible but also likely that Revelation 21:1-22:5 is a parenthetical passage that provides additional information to the scripture previously related to the Millennium. If this is the case, then the city of New Jerusalem described in Revelation 21 would be present during the Millennium, the same time frame for the Millennial temple in Jerusalem portrayed in Ezekiel 40-48. The question then becomes whether New Jerusalem is a restored earthly Jerusalem or a completely new and different city.

Many scholars believe that the New Jerusalem of Revelation is simply a restored Jerusalem on earth, whereas others, and probably most Christians, contend that it is a heavenly city where Christians live for eternity. It is proposed here that the two cities are separate and distinct. Jerusalem is the restored earthly Jerusalem, the capital of the millennial

Israel, whereas New Jerusalem is a heavenly city that descends to earth and is the place where God resides with resurrected saints. When the two cities, the Jerusalem with the millennial temple described primarily in Ezekiel and the New Jerusalem of Revelation, are compared, it is clear that they are similar but also completely different. As will be seen, Ezekiel's Jerusalem concerns a restored Israel populated by Jews, while New Jerusalem will be inhabited by the nations of the righteous who made up the Church.

> And the man said unto me, Son of man, behold with thine eyes, and hear with thine ears, and set thine heart upon all that I shall shew thee; for to the intent that I might shew them unto thee art thou brought hither: declare all that thou seest to the house of **Israel**. Ezekiel 40:4

> And he said unto me, Son of man, the place of my throne, and the place of the soles of my feet, where I will dwell in the midst of the children of **Israel** for ever, and my holy name, shall the house of Israel no more defile, neither they, nor their kings, by their whoredom, nor by the carcases of their kings in their high places. Eze 43:7

> And the **nations** of them which are saved shall walk in the light of it: and the kings of the earth do bring their glory and honour into it. Revelation 21:24

First of all, the names of the two cities are different. Ezekiel's city of Jerusalem will be called "The LORD is there" (Ezekiel 48:35) while in Revelation the city is called New Jerusalem. Also, Ezekiel's Jerusalem is specifically located in Israel on the physical earth as described in Ezekiel 40-48. Yet, New Jerusalem is shown descending from heaven to earth with no specific location given.

Additionally, the size of the two cities is completely different. Ezekiel's city measures either one mile x one mile (if cubits of about twenty-four inches are used) or about ten miles x ten miles (if a rod or reed of six cubits or twelve feet is used).

> Now when he had made an end of measuring the inner house, he brought me forth toward the gate whose prospect is toward the east, and measured it round about. He measured the east side with the measuring reed, five hundred reeds, with the measuring reed round about. He measured the north side, five hundred reeds, with the measuring reed round about. He measured the south side, five hundred reeds, with the measuring reed. He turned about to the west side, and measured five hundred reeds with the measuring reed. Ezekiel 42:15-19

However, New Jerusalem measures much larger at about 1500 miles x 1500 miles on each side with a height of 1500 miles. This assumes that a furlong measures about one eighth of a mile.

> And the city lieth foursquare, and the length is as large as the breadth: and he measured the city with the reed, twelve thousand furlongs. The length and the breadth ad the height of it are equal. Revelation 21:16

The height is given for New Jerusalem, indicating that the shape could either be a cube or a pyramid and also suggesting that it might be an enclosed city as opposed to Ezekiel's Jerusalem. Both cities have a wall with twelve gates, but New Jerusalem's wall additionally has twelve foundations of precious stones.

> And the wall of the city had twelve foundations, and in them the names of the twelve apostles of the Lamb. Revelation 21:14

Ezekiel's Jerusalem has a temple where sacrifices are performed (Ezekiel 40-44), whereas New Jerusalem has no temple since God and the Lamb are its temple.

> And I saw no temple therein: for the Lord God Almighty and the Lamb are the temple of it. Rev 21:22

God's throne is in the Temple of Ezekiel's Jerusalem where the glory of the LORD is, and Jesus is sitting on that throne. But in New Jerusalem there is a throne of God and the Lamb that is in the city (not in a temple) where God Himself will be present, perhaps indicating that the entire city is the Temple of God.

> And the glory of the LORD came into the house by the way of the gate whose prospect is toward the east. So the spirit took me up, and brought me into the inner court; and, behold, the glory of the LORD filled the house. And I heard him speaking unto me out of the house; and the man stood by me. And he said unto me, Son of man, the place of my throne, and the place of the soles of my feet, where I will dwell in the midst of the children of Israel for ever, and my holy name, shall the house of Israel no more defile, neither they, nor their kings, by their whoredom, nor by the carcases of their kings in their high places. Ezekiel 43:4-7

> And he shewed me a pure river of water of life, clear as crystal, proceeding out of the throne of God and of the Lamb. In the midst of the street of it, and on either side of the river, was there the tree of life, which bare twelve manner of fruits, and yielded her fruit every month: and the leaves of the tree were for the healing of the nations. And there shall be no more curse: but the throne of God and of the Lamb shall be in it; and his servants shall serve him: Revelation 22:1-3

> And I heard a great voice out of heaven saying, Behold, the tabernacle of God is with men, and he will dwell with them, and they shall be his people, and God himself shall be with them, and be their God. Revelation 21:3

In New Jerusalem, light comes from the glory of God so that there is no need for a lamp or the moon and sun. No mention of light coming from the glory of God is mentioned in Eze 40-48.

> And the city had no need of the sun, neither of the moon, to shine in it: for the glory of God did lighten it, and the Lamb is the light thereof. Revelation 21:23

> And there shall be no night there; and they need no candle, neither light of the sun; for the Lord God giveth them light: and they shall reign for ever and ever. Revelation 22:5

There is a river in both cities. The river in Ezekiel's Jerusalem flows east from the Temple, originating south of the Temple's altar. It flows to the Dead Sea, restoring it to life. New Jerusalem's river flows from the throne of God and the Lamb, down the middle of the street, providing the water of life. No destination for it is given.

> Afterward he brought me again unto the door of the house; and, behold, waters issued out from under the threshold of the house eastward: for the forefront of the house stood toward the east, and the waters came down from under from the right side of the house, at the south side of the altar. Then said he unto me, These waters issue out toward the east country, and go down into the desert, and go into the sea: which being brought forth into the sea, the waters shall be healed. Ezekiel 47:1,8

> And he shewed me a pure river of water of life, clear as crystal, proceeding out of the throne of God and of the

Lamb. In the midst of the street of it, and on either side of the river, was there the tree of life, which bare twelve manner of fruits, and yielded her fruit every month: and the leaves of the tree were for the healing of the nations. Revelation 22:1-2

Both rivers have trees on either side. Ezekiel's river has many trees on both sides of the river. Each tree bears fruit every month without fail, and the fruit is used for food. However, New Jerusalem's river has only one tree of life on each side of the river. The tree yields twelve fruits every month, but no mention is made of the fruit being used for food.

Now when I had returned, behold, on the bank of the river there were very many trees on the one side and on the other. And by the river on its bank, on one side and on the other, will grow all kinds of trees for food. Their leaves will not wither and their fruit will not fail. They will bear fruit every month because their water flows from the sanctuary, and their fruit will be for food and their leaves for healing. Ezekiel 47:1,12 (NASB)

In the midst of the street of it, and on either side of the river, was there the tree of life, which bare twelve manner of fruits, and yielded her fruit every month: and the leaves of the tree were for the healing of the nations. Revelation 22:2

As noted in the verses above, the leaves on the trees in Ezekiel's Jerusalem will not wither and are used for medicine. In New Jerusalem the leaves are used for the healing of the nations.

And finally, in Ezekiel's Jerusalem the sea is present, while in Revelation's New Jerusalem there is no more sea.

Then said he unto me, These waters issue out toward the east country, and go down into the desert, and go into the sea: which being brought forth into the sea, the waters shall be healed. And it shall come to pass, that every thing that liveth, which moveth, whithersoever the rivers shall come, shall live: and there shall be a very great multitude of fish, because these waters shall come thither: for they shall be healed; and every thing shall live whither the river cometh. And it shall come to pass, that the fishers shall stand upon it from Engedi even unto Eneglaim; they shall be a place to spread forth nets; their fish shall be according to their kinds, as the fish of the great sea, exceeding many. Ezekiel 47:8-10

And I saw a new heaven and a new earth: for the first heaven and the first earth were passed away; and there was no more sea. Revelation 21:1

In summary, the differences between the two cities are outlined in the chart below:

Differences Between Ezekiel's Jerusalem and Revelation's New Jerusalem

	Ezekiel's Jerusalem	Revelation's New Jerusalem
Name of the City	The Lord is There (YHWH Shammah) Ez 48:35	New Jerusalem Rev 21:2
Location	Specific location in Israel (**on** earth) Ez 40-48	Not specific; comes down from heaven **to** earth Rev 3:12; 21:2,10
City Dimensions	1 sq mi using cubits or about 10mi x 10mi using a rod of 12ft; no height specified Ez 42:15-19	Square with 1500 mi on each side and 1500 mi high Rev 21:16
Wall Foundation	None	12 Foundations Rev 21:14-21

	Ezekiel's Jerusalem	Revelation's New Jerusalem
Temple present	Yes, with sacrifices Ez 40	None; God and the Lamb are its temple Rev 21:22
Throne	God's throne in Temple with Jesus sitting on it Ez 43:4-7	Throne of God and Lamb in the city (not in a temple) Rev 22:1,3
God's presence	Glory of the LORD in the Temple Ez 43:4	God Himself will be present Rev 21:3
Light/Day	No light from the glory of God mentioned in Ez 40-48	Light from glory of God and no need for lamp or moon/sun; No night Rev 21:23, 22:5
Pain/Death/ Sorrow	Present Ez 44:25	None Rev 21:4
Sin	Sin offering required Ez 40:39; 44:27,29; 45:17,20,23; 46:20	No sin, no curse, and no unrighteous al- lowed in Rev 22:5
Residents	All the tribes of Israel, Levites, priests and sons of Zadok; the prince (?David) Ez 40-48; 43:7	The nations; Only the righteous whose names are written in the Lamb's Book of Life; Angels; God Rev 21:12,24-27; 22:14-15
River, source	Flowing east from the temple south of the altar Ez 47:1-8	From the throne of God and the Lamb down the middle of the street Rev 22:1-2
River, destination	Dead Sea Ez 47:8	None given
River, purpose	Restores and heals the Dead Sea Ez 47:8-10	Provide water of life Rev 21:6, 22:1-2
River, trees	Many trees along both sides of river Ez 47:7	One tree of life on each side of the river Rev 22:2
Tree, fruit	Trees bear fruit every month without fail and fruit will be for food Ez 47:12	One tree yields 12 fruits every month (not men- tioned for food) Rev 22:2

	Ezekiel's Jerusalem	Revelation's New Jerusalem
Tree, leaves	Will not wither and used for medicine Ez 47:12	For the healing of the nations Rev 22:2
Sea	Present Ez 47:8-10,15-20; 48:28	None Rev 21:1

It is clear from this comparison that these are two similar but very different cities, one an earthly city for the Israelites in their Promised Land and still dealing with sin and death, while the other is a city from heaven for the Church, made completely holy, righteous, and pure in order to be allowed into God's presence in New Jerusalem. Jewish believers who survive the Great Tribulation will live in Israel during the Millennium while believing Gentile survivors will populate the nations. They and their children will live on Earth during the Millennium. The Church will inhabit the New Jerusalem, and that is likely where the mansions are that Jesus spoke of in John.

> Let not your heart be troubled: ye believe in God, believe also in me. In my Father's house are many mansions: if it were not so, I would have told you. I go to prepare a place for you. And if I go and prepare a place for you, I will come again, and receive you unto myself; that where I am, there ye may be also. John 14:1-3

New Jerusalem is seen coming down from heaven in Revelation 21 but is never described as actually landing on earth. Truth be told, it would not really fit anywhere unless geographical changes, that will be discussed shortly, occur. Far bigger than all of Israel it will have a foot print as big as western Europe, or all of the Eastern US from the Atlantic coast to the Mississippi River and Maine to Florida. Besides that, it is 1500 miles tall. Compare that to the tallest building on earth today at 1800 feet. In volume it is one sixth the size of Earth.

So, New Jerusalem during the Millennium may be near the earth, but not actually on it. Of course, this is only speculation but can be inferred because it says that sinners cannot go there, only the redeemed.

The "no more death", etc., of Revelation 21:4 refers to the Church in the New Jerusalem, not to people on Earth. We know this because Revelation 21:24-27 shows the kings of the earth bringing their splendor to the New Jerusalem. Nothing impure is allowed to enter, nor will any sinner, but only those whose names have been written in the Lamb's book of life. However, New Jerusalem apparently must at least be close to earth, since angels guard its gates to keep out anything that might defile it.

> And there shall in no wise enter into it any thing that defileth, neither whatsoever worketh abomination, or maketh a lie: but they which are written in the Lamb's book of life. Revelation 21:27

Now, if you had always thought that the destiny of the righteous was to live up in heaven with Jesus, this idea may come as a surprise. It turns out that "the meek shall inherit the earth" (Psalm 37:11, Matthew 5:5) is indeed literal and not poetic.

> And hast made us unto our God kings and priests: and we shall reign on the earth. Revelation 5:10

The glorified saints of God, with residence in New Jerusalem with God Himself, will rule with King Jesus **on the earth**, not in heaven. Jesus, though, has thrones both in Jerusalem on earth and New Jerusalem. Of course, much of this is theoretical but with some scriptural basis. It is simply a best guess at applying scripture. So, in summary:

- Only redeemed, resurrected individuals enter the New Jerusalem during the Millennium. [Pentecost, 1958]
- The New Jerusalem is to be inhabited by God, the Church, the unfallen angels, and the redeemed of all ages.
- At the time of Christ's Second Coming, the living Gentiles and Jews enter the Millennium with unresurrected bodies. They

will populate the Earth during the Millennium. They are not permitted to enter the New Jerusalem in their unresurrected bodies.

- The Old Testament saints will have access to New Jerusalem after Christ's Second Coming, where they join the Church saints who are already there (because they were taken there at the Rapture). However, they most likely live and reign in Israel, along with the 12 Apostles, where they receive their promised land inheritance
- The New Jerusalem appears possibly to be suspended over the earth during the Millennium and serves not only as residence quarters but a base from where Christ with His saints rules the world.[1]

RESTORATION OF TRUE WORSHIP

The corruption and failure of not only Israel but of all the nations to worship the one true God will be corrected in the Millennium. Other nations will be expected to honor Israel and to center their worship there.

> And it shall come to pass, that every one that is left of all the nations which came against Jerusalem shall even go up from year to year to worship the King, the LORD of hosts, and to keep the feast of tabernacles. And it shall be, that whoso will not come up of all the families of the earth unto Jerusalem to worship the King, the LORD of hosts, even upon them shall be no rain. Zechariah 14:16-17

Evil Spirits Gone (Not Just Satan)

Stopping evil men from ruling the world is a crucial change for the Millennium, but it only addresses one source of the evil control of the world today. The Bible says that we do not fight against flesh and blood but against spiritual forces of evil.

> For we wrestle not against flesh and blood, but against principalities, against powers, against the rulers of the darkness of this world, against spiritual wickedness in high places. Ephesians 6:12

To what spiritual forces of darkness is this referring? Satan, the fallen angel, is the main culprit as the leader of the dark spirits and is responsible for actively deceiving the world.

> And the great dragon was cast out, that old serpent, called the Devil, and Satan, which deceiveth the whole world: he was cast out into the earth, and his angels were cast out with him. Revelation 12:9

However, Satan will finally be bound for one thousand literal years, so that he cannot deceive people during that time.

> And I saw an angel come down from heaven, having the key of the bottomless pit and a great chain in his hand. And he laid hold on the dragon, that old serpent, which is the Devil, and Satan, and bound him a thousand years, And cast him into the bottomless pit, and shut him up, and set a seal upon him, that he should deceive the nations no more, till the thousand years should be fulfilled: and after that he must be loosed a little season. Revelation 20:1-3

Some contend that Satan has already been bound, but it is clear that this has not happened yet; this event is still in the future. One look at the evil in today's world—and looking back for many centuries—makes it clear that Satan has not been bound. If Satan were already bound, then the Church should not be undergoing persecution, and there should not be much evil in the world—but there clearly is. Furthermore, if Satan were already chained by the death of Christ on the Cross, then why does Revelation 2:13 state that he is living in Pergamos? Some authors argue that if Satan is currently chained, then "his chain is too long". In fact, it appears that Satan has been more active in the past two thousand years than he was before Christ [Morris, 1983]. Timothy describes "the last days"—and arguably, our world's current social situation—as follows:[1]

> This know also, that in the last days perilous times shall come. For men shall be lovers of their own selves, covetous, boasters, proud, blasphemers, disobedient to parents, unthankful, unholy, Without natural affection, trucebreakers, false accusers, incontinent, fierce, despisers of those that are good, Traitors, heady, highminded, lovers of pleasures more than lovers of God; Having a form of godliness, but denying the power thereof: from such turn away. 2 Timothy 3:1-5

> Yea, and all that will live godly in Christ Jesus shall suffer persecution. But evil men and seducers shall wax worse and worse, deceiving, and being deceived. 2 Timothy 3:12-13

Although amillennialists and postmillennialists argue that Satan was bound at the Cross, scripture says that he is not bound yet [Hitchcock, 2012]. In fact, Satan is said to be:

- The prince of this world (John 12:31; 14:30)
- The god of this age (2 Corinthians 4:4)
- The ruler of the kingdom of the air (Ephesians 2:2)
- A roaring lion looking for someone to devour (1 Peter 5:8)[1]

Even though Satan has not been bound yet, there is coming a time (the Millennium) when he will be chained, and the deception that he and the demons are responsible for will be eliminated from the world for a period of time. This helps usher in a time when man, without the

burden of Satan the Accuser, will worship the King of Kings. And that
king, King Jesus, will rule with an iron hand, so that anyone that does
not honor Him will be punished.

> Thou shalt break them with a rod of iron; thou shalt
> dash them in pieces like a potter's vessel. Psalm 2:9

> And if the family of Egypt go not up, and come not,
> that have no rain; there shall be the plague, wherewith
> the LORD will smite the heathen that come not up to
> keep the feast of tabernacles. Zechariah 14:18

The Millennial Temple sacrifices

Jesus will rule from Jerusalem where a great temple will be
established as described in Ezekiel 40-46, and a form of the ancient
worship instituted again, complete with priestly orders and sacrificial
animal offerings.

In addition, as noted earlier, there will be a portion of land between
the section for the tribe of Judah and the section for the tribe of
Benjamin that is "set apart for the LORD" (Ezekiel 45:1-5, 48:8-22).
In the Millennial age, the law will emanate from Zion.

> And many nations shall come, and say, Come, and let
> us go up to the mountain of the LORD, and to the house
> of the God of Jacob; and he will teach us of his ways,
> and we will walk in his paths: for the law shall go forth
> of Zion, and the word of the LORD from Jerusalem.
> Micah 4:2

In the Old Testament, Zion came to mean Jerusalem and the Temple
area in particular. This indicates that Christ will rule from some future
temple and its surrounding area, and a graphic description of such a
temple is found in Ezekiel 40-48.

So, the land "set apart" must include a holy place for the LORD's
temple or sanctuary. Its precise dimensions are given in Ezekiel 45:1-5,

and it is in the center of this special section of land. It is the place of Christ's throne on earth – a glorious place in the midst of the children of Israel. This is the place described as "THE LORD IS THERE" (Ezekiel 48:35).

> Son of man, the place of my throne, and the place of the soles of my feet, where I will dwell in the midst of the children of Israel for ever... Ezekiel 43:7

> The glory of Lebanon shall come unto thee, the fir tree, the pine tree, and the box together, to beautify the place of my sanctuary; and I will make the place of my feet glorious. Isaiah 60:13

The purpose for a temple throughout Scripture has been to establish a location upon earth (which is under the curse of sin) for the presence of God that reveals through its ritual God's great holiness. God's plan for Israel, His earthly people, includes a relationship with them through a temple. Currently the Church is God's spiritual temple made of living stones (1Corinthians 3:16-17; Ephesians 2:19-22), until the rapture. The Millennium will return to a focus upon Israel but will continue to be a time in which sin will be present upon the earth. Thus, God will include a new temple, a new priesthood, a new Law, etc., at this future time because He will be present in Israel and still desires to teach that holiness is required to approach Him.[3]

It must be remembered that the Levitical sacrifices of the Mosaic system are said by the Bible to "make atonement" (Leviticus 4:20, 26, 31, 35, etc.). If these sacrifices in the past actually atoned for the people's sins, which of course they did not, then they would be equally blasphemous in light of Christ's perfect sacrifice. Hebrews 10:4 tells us, "It is impossible for the blood of bulls and goats to take away sins." Furthermore, there would have been no need for Christ's once and for all atoning sacrifice if these past acts did the job.

The sacrifices of the Millennial Temple will not be a return to the Mosaic Law, since that Law has forever been fulfilled through Christ

(Romans 6:14-15; 7:1-6;1 Corinthians 9:20-21; 2 Corinthians 3:7-11; Galatians 4:1-7; 5:18; Ephesians 2-3; Hebrews 7:12; 8:6-7, 13; 10:1-14). Instead, it will be a new Law, containing a mixture of Mosaic type new laws under the jurisdiction of the New Covenant (Hebrews 7:12). The millennial system will have Jesus the Messiah physically present as well as the Shechinah glory presence; a new Law instead of the Mosaic Law; a new priestly order from the sons of Zadok (Ezekiel 40:46; 43:19; 48:11) instead of the Levites; a new Temple measuring one mile square (Ezekiel 40:48-41:26) instead of the much smaller Solomonic model.[2]

Millennial sacrifices are mentioned as a "matter of fact" by the major prophets of the Old Testament as future occurrences. At least four other prophets join Ezekiel in affirming a sacrificial system in a millennial Temple (Isaiah 56:7; 66:20-23; Jeremiah 33:18; Zechariah 14:16-21; Malachi 3:3-4). This further supports the literal interpretation of Ezekiel. Why would five of Israel's prophets mention these sacrifices if they will not take place? Many who take a literal interpretation of the Millennial Temple and sacrifices believe that one aspect of these acts will serve as a memorial to Christ's once-for-all atoning work at His first coming. Yet, critics believe this to be a flawed conclusion. Support for a future memorial aspect can be seen in the fact that our current observation of the Lord's Supper includes this aspect (1 Corinthians 11:23-26). Under the Mosaic system, various Temple sacrifices are many times specifically called "memorials" (Exodus 30:16; Leviticus 2:2, 9; 5:12; 6:15; 24:7; Numbers 5:15,18, 26). Such terminology could in fact be the basis for our current church age understanding of remembering the Lord's death adopted by Paul. The Mosaic memorial aspect would clearly support viewing future temple sacrifices in this way, as millennial believers look back upon Christ's sacrificial provision.

Critics of future millennial sacrifices seem to assume that all sacrifices, past and future, always depict Christ's final sacrifice for sin, but this is not necessarily so. There were various purposes for sacrifice in the Bible. An overwhelming majority of sacrifices under the Mosaic system were for purification of the priests and objects used in various rites. This is why atonement can be said in the past to be effective, yet still need Christ's future sacrifice, because many of the sacrifices did atone ceremonially, cleansing participants and objects in Temple ritual. Just as we never finish the task of washing cloths, ceremonial cleansing was an ongoing need. The same is clearly the case in Ezekiel. In Ezekiel 43:20 and 26, the atonement is specifically directed at cleansing the altar in order to make it ritually fit for sacrifice. The only other use of atonement also refers to cleansing objects so that ritual purity may be maintained for proper function of further worship (Ezekiel 45:15, 17, 20).[2]

Dr. Jerry Hullinger has worked through the related issues involved in an interpretation of the millennial sacrifices and tells us the following:

> . . . a solution that maintains dispensational distinctives, deals honestly with the text of Ezekiel, and in no way demeans the work Christ did on the cross. This study suggests that animal sacrifices during the millennium will serve primarily to remove ceremonial uncleanness and prevent defilement from polluting the temple envisioned by Ezekiel. This will be necessary because the glorious presence of Yahweh will once again be dwelling on earth in the midst of a sinful and unclean people. Because of God's promise to dwell on earth during the millennium (as stated in the New Covenant), it is necessary that He protect His presence through sacrifice . . . It should further be added that this sacrificial system will be a temporary one in that the millennium (with its partial population of unglorified humanity) will last only one thousand years. During the eternal state all inhabitants of the New Jerusalem will be glorified and will therefore not be a source of contagious impurities to defile the holiness of Yahweh.[2]

Since all the sacrifices of Ezekiel relate to purification of the priests for Temple service, they do not specifically depict or represent Christ's atoning sacrifice. The presence and purpose of sacrifices neither diminishes the finished work of Christ, nor violates the normal and "literal" interpretation of the prophetic passages. Nothing in Ezekiel 40-48 conflicts with the death of Christ or New Testament teaching at any point.

The supposed contradictions between a literal understanding of Ezekiel and New Testament doctrine evaporate when examined specifically. The literal interpretation of the Bible and Bible prophecy stands, especially when one considers the fact that the critics cannot tell us, based upon a textual interpretation, what Ezekiel does mean if not taken literally. Instead of becoming an embarrassing problem, the millennial sacrifices issue becomes an argument and demonstration for consistent literal interpretation of Bible prophecy by demonstrating that the details of the text can only be harmonized with the rest of biblical teaching by taking them to mean what they say. Although there will be millennial sacrifices, the focus of all worship will remain on the person and work of the Savior. The Millennial Temple and its ritual will serve as a daily reminder of fallen man's need before a Holy God and lessons about how this same God lovingly works to remove the obstacle of human sin for those who trust Him.[2]

So, the nation of Israel must maintain a status of ceremonial purity. As argued above, this kind of sacrificial "atonement" is not for salvation nor for inward sanctification, but to preserve outward corporate "sanctification" (or ceremonial purification) so that a holy God can remain in the midst of an unholy people.

The Millennial feasts

In addition to sacrifices, there will be festivals in the Millennium. Scripture does not clearly define which of the seven festivals, except for Tabernacles and Passover, will be celebrated.

> And it shall come to pass, that every one that is left of all the nations which came against Jerusalem shall even go up from year to year to worship the King, the LORD of hosts, and to keep the feast of tabernacles. Zechariah 14:16

> In the first month, in the fourteenth day of the month, ye shall have the passover, a feast of seven days; unleavened bread shall be eaten. Ezekiel 45:21

So, in the Messianic kingdom of the Millennium, the observance of Sukkot (Feast of Tabernacles) will be obligatory not only for Jews, but for all the Gentiles as well. Every year, each Gentile nation will have to send a delegation to Jerusalem. And although Passover and the Feast of Tabernacles are mentioned in Ezekiel 40-48, there is no explicit reference to the third major feast, namely, Pentecost (the Feast of Weeks). It does appear that from Ezekiel chapters 44-46 there is some confusion of exactly which Festivals of the original seven will be carried out in the Millennium.

In conclusion, there is no doubt of the importance of the people of Israel during the Millennium, not only politically as seen earlier, but spiritually in regards to worship.

> Behold, the days come, saith the LORD, that I will **make a new covenant with the house of Israel, and with the house of Judah**: Not according to the covenant that I made with their fathers in the day that I took them by the hand to bring them out of the land of Egypt; which my covenant they brake, although I was an husband unto them, saith the LORD: But this shall be the covenant that I will make with the house of Israel; After those days, saith the LORD, I will put my law in their inward parts, and write it in their hearts; and will be their God, and they shall be my people. Jeremiah 31:31-33

It is imperative to notice how this passage specifically states that this covenant is made with Israel and Judah, not the Church. It also is clear that the Law is again part of the covenant. However, unlike with the previous Old Covenant of Moses, this time the Law will be written on people's hearts so that they can succeed in keeping it, honoring God with true worship and bringing that worship to the rest of the world and nations.

As noted before, Jesus will rule the earth with a "rod of iron" (Psalm 2:9; Revelation 2:27, 12:5, 19:15). Also, as already seen, the nations that do not obey the Torah command to go up to the Festival of Tabernacles or Booths will be punished with drought (Zechariah 14:19). This is a pretty harsh correction, indeed, but it accomplishes two things. It not only corrects the bad behavior, but it also demonstrates the supernatural power behind the government and its laws. That type of evidence of God and his power is why in time the "religions "of atheism, agnosticism or skepticism will disappear. There will be no denying the supernatural or God anymore, and the nations will worship the one true God.

> And they shall teach no more every man his neighbour, and every man his brother, saying, Know the LORD: for they shall all know me, from the least of them unto the greatest of them, saith the LORD: for I will forgive their iniquity, and I will remember their sin no more. Jeremiah 31:34

RESTORATION OF MAN AND NATURE

Just as there will be a spiritual restoration in the Millennium, there will also be a physical restoration of man and nature. Creation itself is now groaning and expectantly waiting for the restoration that will occur when Christ returns and ushers in His Millennial Kingdom.

> For the anxious longing of the creation waits eagerly for the revealing of the sons of God. For the creation was subjected to futility, not willingly, but because of Him who subjected it, in hope that the creation itself also will be set free from its slavery to corruption into the freedom of the glory of the children of God. Romans 8:19-21 (NASB)

Life Span/Age

Even though the initial population of each nation will be small, the conditions and incentives will be present to encourage large families, and the populations will grow rapidly. Furthermore, antediluvian or pre-flood longevity will be restored.

> There shall be no more thence an infant of days, nor an old man that hath not filled his days: for the child shall die an hundred years old; but the sinner being an hundred years old shall be accursed. Isaiah 65:20

This may be accomplished partially by the restoration of antediluvian climatologic and agricultural conditions and partially by new technologies developed by millennial scientists.

As noted previously, there will be fruit trees in the Millennium as recorded in Ezekiel:

> And by the river upon the bank thereof, on this side and on that side, shall grow all trees for meat, whose leaf shall not fade, neither shall the fruit thereof be consumed: it shall bring forth new fruit according to his months, because their waters they issued out of the sanctuary: and the fruit thereof shall be for meat, and the leaf thereof for medicine. Ezekiel 47:12

By improving the food supply and providing medicine, these trees help explain the increased life spans seen during the Millennium. Not only is the food supply improved qualitatively but also quantitatively. Note the agricultural productivity during the Millennium:

> Behold, the days come, saith the LORD, that the plowman shall overtake the reaper, and the treader of grapes him that soweth seed; and the mountains shall drop sweet wine, and all the hills shall melt. And I will bring again the captivity of my people of Israel, and they

shall build the waste cities, and inhabit them; and they shall plant vineyards, and drink the wine thereof; they shall also make gardens, and eat the fruit of them. And I will plant them upon their land, and they shall no more be pulled up out of their land which I have given them, saith the LORD thy God. Amos 9:13-15

Additionally, life spans will be increased due to the lack of dangerous predators. The carnivorous animals that would be a threat to living out a nice enhanced long millennial life span are domesticated.

The wolf also shall dwell with the lamb, and the leopard shall lie down with the kid; and the calf and the young lion and the fatling together; and a little child shall lead them. And the cow and the bear shall feed; their young ones shall lie down together: and the lion shall eat straw like the ox. And the sucking child shall play on the hole of the asp, and the weaned child shall put his hand on the cockatrice' den. They shall not hurt nor destroy in all my holy mountain: for the earth shall be full of the knowledge of the LORD, as the waters cover the sea. Isaiah 11:6-9

And in that day will I make a covenant for them with the beasts of the field and with the fowls of heaven, and with the creeping things of the ground: and I will break the bow and the sword and the battle out of the earth, and will make them to lie down safely. Hosea 2:18

When Jesus comes back, the "lion will lay down with the lamb". Many have considered this phrase to be poetic, but in fact it is quite literal. It also indicates that the nature of the animals will change so that they do not fear men like they do today, changing them back to how they were in the Garden of Eden.

Randy Alcorn writes:

I realize that if there was no food chain, then the animal world of Eden was different from the animal world we know today. Indeed, our entire ecosystem was likely changed more by the Fall than we can imagine. We do not know what the animals in Eden looked like. Did God change their form as part of the Curse—or as a way to help them survive after the Curse? Is it possible that originally cheetahs ran for the sheer joy of it rather than to chase their prey? Could a lion have been capable of tearing apart other animals but have no desire to do so? Could he be powerful, even with sharp teeth, without being a killer? I think so. There was a special beauty and great power that refrains from doing harm, as Jesus himself demonstrated. ... It is no coincidence that the first two chapters of the Bible (Genesis 1-2) begin with the creation of the heavens and the earth and the last two chapters (Revelation 21-22) begin with the re-creation of the heavens and the earth. All that was lost at the beginning will be restored at the end. And far more will be added besides. [Alcorn, 2004, pp. 124-126][4]

Geographical Changes

Besides the changes in the animal world, many kinds of tectonic, topographic, or geographical changes can also be expected for the Millennium and especially around Jerusalem. These changes occur in the area around Jerusalem in order to fulfill the prophecies about the Millennial Temple given in Ezekiel 40-48. At the onset of the Millennium, the Messiah will rebuild Jerusalem on a reconfigured, post-tribulational landscape. A forceful tectonic upthrust will have elevated the area around Jerusalem to form a plateau some fifty miles square.[1]

And it shall come to pass in the last days, that the mountain of the LORD's house shall be established in the top of the mountains, and shall be exalted above the hills; and all nations shall flow unto it. Isaiah 2:2

But in the last days it shall come to pass, that the mountain of the house of the LORD shall be established in the top of the mountains, and it shall be exalted above the hills; and people shall flow unto it. And many nations shall come, and say, Come, and let us go up to the mountain of the LORD, and to the house of the God of Jacob; and he will teach us of his ways, and we will walk in his paths: for the law shall go forth of Zion, and the word of the LORD from Jerusalem. Micah 4:1-2

And his feet shall stand in that day upon the mount of Olives, which is before Jerusalem on the east, and the mount of Olives shall cleave in the midst thereof toward the east and toward the west, and there shall be a very great valley; and half of the mountain shall remove toward the north, and half of it toward the south. Zech 14:4

All the land shall be turned as a plain from Geba to Rimmon south of Jerusalem: and it shall be lifted up, and inhabited in her place, from Benjamin's gate unto the place of the first gate, unto the corner gate, and from the tower of Hananeel unto the king's winepresses. Zechariah 14:10

On the northern end of the plateau will be the earthly city of Jerusalem, ten miles square and housing the center of government for the Messianic Kingdom, with the Millennial Temple at the heart of the city (Ezek. 48:1-28). (As seen earlier, the rebuilt city of Jerusalem should not be confused with the New Jerusalem that descends from heaven after the creation of the new heaven and Earth, cf. Rev. 21:2, 10.) [McCracken, 2011, p. 25][1]

In addition to the area around Jerusalem, at the Second Coming of Christ other significant geological changes in the Middle East will occur. For example, the Red Sea (*the tongue of the Egyptian sea*) will be dried up, perhaps when Jesus leads the Second Exodus out of Egypt.

> And the LORD shall utterly destroy **the tongue of the Egyptian sea**; and with his mighty wind shall he shake his hand over the river, and shall smite it in the seven streams, and make men go over dryshod. And there shall be an highway for the remnant of his people, which shall be left, from Assyria; like as it was to Israel in the day that he came up out of the land of Egypt. Isaiah 11:15-16

And another body of water that is dried up during this time is the Euphrates River at the sixth bowl judgment. So, while the Euphrates served as a boundary for David and Solomon, it virtually ceases to be a landmark in the Millennium.

> And the sixth angel poured out his vial upon the great river Euphrates; and the water thereof was dried up, that the way of the kings of the east might be prepared. Revelation 16:12

Although much will be different about creation, it will greatly be the same. And much will need to be learned and explored. In his excellent book called Heaven, Randy Alcorn states:

> When we open our eyes for the first time on the New Earth, will it be unfamiliar? Or will we recognize it as home? [Alcorn, 2004, pp. 153-154]

Learning will take place, too, because unlike God, we will not be omniscient (knowing everything). In Eden God commanded Adam and

Eve to take dominion over the Earth, including fish, birds, and animals (Genesis 1:28). Adam and Eve had roles and responsibilities. They had work to do in the Garden of Eden, and almost certainly there was learning and exploration along the way. Similarly, in the Millennium and the eternal state, we will most likely be able to explore the universe, learn about science, invent things, understand mathematics, create literary works or art or music, and probably do all kinds of physical activities including sports, some of which are not invented yet. Since we will have physical bodies that will function perfectly, and keen minds and memories, it seems natural that we will be able to do many, if not all, of these things. We will glorify God as we search the wonders of God's creation.

> Culture will not regress to Eden, where musical instruments had not yet been invented or where metalworking and countless other skills had not yet been developed (Genesis 4:20-22). The fact that God mentions in Scripture these and other examples of technological progress suggests that he approved of the use of creativity and skills to develop society, even though people were hampered by the Curse.
>
> Some people expect the New Earth to be a return to Eden, with no technology or the accomplishments of civilization. But that does not fit the biblical picture of the great city, the New Jerusalem. Nor is it logical. Would we expect on the New Earth a literal reinvention of the wheel? [Alcorn, 2004, p. 234]
>
> The stated reference point for understanding the future destruction of the world is the Flood. The Flood was certainly cataclysmic and devastating. But did it obliterate the world, making it cease to exist? No. Noah and his family and the animals were delivered from God's judgment in order to reinhabit a new world made

ready for them by God's cleansing judgment. Flooding the whole world did not destroy all the mountains (Genesis 8:4). Though many people believe that the Tigris and Euphrates rivers near Eden (Genesis 2:14) were not the same rivers as those we know today, the fact that they were given the same names as the original suggest some continuity.

... The New Earth will be the same as the old Earth, just as a new Christian is still the same person he was before. Different? Yes. But also the same. [Alcorn, 2004, pp. 148-149][4]

CONCLUSION

While much may look familiar during the Millennium when Jesus returns to claim His kingdom, much will be changed. Christ's second coming will bring about a renewal of the earth and man to a pre-fall state. With the restoration will come a return of peace and fellowship between man, God, and nature that has been absent since the fall.

CHAPTER 12

Epilogue

So, what happens after the story is finished, once the end times narrative is completed? More importantly, what happens to you? It has been my attempt to provide one possible timeline for the 70th week of Daniel and the Biblical end times. It is not meant to be prophetic, but only an effort to analyze the scriptures, in order to arrive at a timeline that is consistent throughout the Bible. Hopefully, this has provided those who are watching and waiting for Christ's Second Coming a new and encouraging picture of what to expect in the future. However, this brings to mind something John F. Walvoord once said when he commented, "Anyone who thinks his or her prophetic position has no problems simply has not studied prophecy very carefully."

> "To be sure, extremists have taken unhealthy paths as a result of their understanding of prophecy. To avoid such extreme decisions, good advice is for people to live their lives as if the Rapture could happen today but to plan their lives as if they'll be here their entire lifetime expectancy. That way they are prepared for time and eternity. Scripture says that we should seek to be accurate observers of the times. Of course, some

people today utterly ignore biblical prophecy. Other people have been misled by anti-prophecy Christians (preterists) who teach that most biblical prophecies were fulfilled in the first century and that we should not look for any future fulfillments of Bible prophecies relating to the tribulation or the Rapture. This viewpoint is as unfortunate as it is unbiblical. Scripture indicates that just as biblical prophecies about the first coming of Christ were fulfilled in a quite literal way (see, for example, Isaiah 7:14; Micah 5:2; Zechariah 12:10), so the prophecies about the second coming (and related events, like the Ezekiel invasion) will also be literally fulfilled. In view of this, we do well to stay aware of what Scripture teaches about the end times and to be accurate observers of the times. We should not be sensationalists or alarmists, for such behavior is not becoming of our God (1 Peter 4:7-10). But we should be accurate observers of the times." [Rhodes, 2008, pp. 199-200][1]

It is my hope that those who read this will study it, knowing that as we do approach the end times our knowledge of the Bible is increasing and our understanding of Biblical prophecy is getting clearer. Certainly, current news headlines have been indicating that Biblical, prophetic events are being fulfilled right before our eyes. So, as time passes and specific time markers seen in the Bible transpire, our understanding of the Revelation of Jesus Christ will come into much sharper focus. Obviously, when the Antichrist commits the abomination of desolation at the midpoint of the 70th Week of Daniel, we will know exactly where we are on the prophetic end time's timeline.

Until then much about prophecy can seem vague and murky, but what is clear is that Jesus is coming back for the Church, and when He comes, He has made promises that He will absolutely fulfill. Promises were made to the overcomers in the Church through seven letters given to John and are seen in the 2nd and 3rd chapters of Revelation. These promises were made to the first century church as well as to the Church universal, and some believe that these churches represent seven periods of the Church down through history. But like the entire Book of Revelation, these letters were written not only for the first century church but even more importantly for the church that will be undergoing the tribulation of the end times. And if the timeline outlined here is correct, then we are quickly approaching that time. This can be both exciting and frightening at the same time, but John has included words of encouragement for the end time's church in each of his seven letters as outlined here.

Church	Promise
Ephesus	**To him that overcometh** will I give to eat of the tree of life, which is in the midst of the paradise of God. Rev 2:7
Smyrna	**He that overcometh** shall not be hurt of the second death. Rev 2:11
Pergamos	**To him that overcometh** will I give to eat of the hidden manna, and will give him a white stone, and in the stone a new name written, which no man knoweth saving he that receiveth it. Rev 2:17
Thyatira	**And he that overcometh**, and keepeth my works unto the end, to him will I give power over the nations: And he shall rule them with a rod of iron; as the vessels of a potter shall they be broken to shivers: even as I received of my Father. And I will give him the morning star. Rev 2:26-28
Sardis	**He that overcometh**, the same shall be clothed in white raiment; and I will not blot out his name out of the book of life, but I will confess his name before my Father, and before his angels. Rev 3:5
Philadelphia	**Him that overcometh** will I make a pillar in the temple of my God, and he shall go no more out: and I will write upon him the name of my God, and the name of the city of my God, which is new Jerusalem, which cometh down out of heaven from my God: and I will write upon him my new name. Rev 3:12
Laodicea	**To him that overcometh** will I grant to sit with me in my throne, even as I also overcame, and am set down with my Father in his throne. Rev 3:21

These are some amazing promises given to those who overcome in the end times. But what does it mean to be an overcomer? Joel Richardson in his internet series on Revelation notes that most think of an overcomer or victor as someone who is very strong, who preaches boldly and confidently to the pagan, and who is beheaded while standing firm in the faith. And certainly, there are those today in the Church who are undergoing severe persecution and standing firm. Even John calls overcomers those who "loved not their lives unto the death".

> And they overcame him by the blood of the Lamb, and by the word of their testimony; and they **loved not their lives unto the death**. Revelation 12:11

Yet, for the vast majority of Christians down through history, being an overcomer means simply this:

> Who is he that overcometh the world, but he that believeth that Jesus is the Son of God? 1 John 5:5

This is something that people who are not confident in their own strength and who are poor in spirit can relate to much better.

So, throughout history, what does it mean to overcome? Well, usually it does not look like Mel Gibson at the end of Braveheart, disemboweled nobly for the one he loves. It is not usually being beheaded for preaching to the pagans. For most, it means simply staying faithful when their child dies in a car accident or of an overdose; when your spouse dies of cancer; or whatever tragedy life brings you that does not even seem related to the gospel. Despite that pain and despite that agony, you do not curse God. You do not give up the faith, and you faithfully endure to the end, even in brokenness. Even if you make it to the end and at the judgment get a grade of C+ and looked horrible doing it, you nevertheless stayed faithful and endured.

Overcomers are those who believe that Jesus is the Son of God, believing and holding on to the very end, despite all of the pain and all of the difficulty and all of the trauma and catastrophe that life throws our way. Despite this, an overcomer is able to say:

> Though he slay me, yet will I trust in him: but I will maintain mine own ways before him. Job 13:15

We are overcomers not by our own strength but by the blood of the Lamb according to 1 John 5:5. Overcoming is something most often done in weakness. It is not done in strength. If we are proud of our strength, this usually leads to a fall.

> But he giveth more grace. Wherefore he saith, God resisteth the proud, but giveth grace unto the humble. James 4:6

So, we need to be in touch with our poverty and our weakness but confident in Him to preserve us through all these things, especially with the trials and tribulations that are sure to come during Daniel's 70th week. And we need to be assured that we will be overcomers, not because we're more committed or somehow more superior, but by merely saying, "Lord, by Your grace, we're going to endure patiently to the end."

The gospel message is for the poor, the weak, the downtrodden, the forgotten, and the needy. It is for the average person throughout the earth and throughout history, and it is by clinging to Him through our weakness that we are the overcomers, the victors.[2]

So, what happens to you at the end of the story, after that Christmas yet to come, when Christ returns in all His glory? Well, you can actually determine that. First, be **in Christ** by accepting Him as the savior of the world and of yourself. Then, just stay strong **in Christ**, trusting in His power and remaining obedient to His commands. Stay faithful and endure to the end. Be an overcomer, and by God's grace we'll see each other in New Jerusalem.

APPENDIX A

Genealogy Timeline from Adam to Abraham*

NAME	LIFE-SPAN	AGE AT SON'S BIRTH	BORN AM**	REFERENCES
1. ADAM	929.5	129.5 (130)	1	Genesis 5:3-5
2. SETH	911.5	104.5 (105)	129.5	Genesis 5:6-8
3. ENOS	904.5	89.5 (90)	234	Genesis 5:9-11
4. CAINAN	909.5	69.5 (70)	323.5	Genesis 5:12-14
5. MAHALALEL	894.5	64.5 (65)	393	Genesis 5:15-17
6. JARED	961.5	161.5 (162)	457.5	Genesis 5:18-20
7. ENOCH	364.5	64.5 (65)	619	Genesis 5:21-24
8. METHUSELEH	968.5	186.5 (187)	683.5	Genesis 5:25-27
9. LAMECH	776.5	181.5 (182)	870	Genesis 5:28-31
10. NOAH	949.5	503	1051.5	Genesis 5:32, 7:11, 10:21, 11:10-11
11. SHEM	599.5	99.5 (100)	1554.5	Genesis 11:10-11
FLOOD	1	(599.5)	1651-1652	Genesis 7:11
12. ARPHAXAD	437.5	34.5 (35)	1654	Genesis 11:12-13
13. SALAH	432.5	29.5 (30)	1688.5	Genesis 11:14-15
14. EBER	463.5	33.5 (34)	1718	Genesis 11:16-17
15. PELEG	238.5	29.5 (30)	1751.5	Genesis 11:18-19
16. REU	238.5	31.5 (32)	1781	Genesis 11:20-21
17. SERUG	229.5	29.5 (30)	1812.5	Genesis 11:22-23
18. NAHOR	147.5	28.5 (29)	1842	Genesis 11:24-25
19. TERAH	204.5	129.5 (130)	1870.5	Genesis 11:26-32, 12:4; Acts 7:4
20. ABRAM	174.5		2000	Genesis 25:7

*Tim Warner. *The Time of the End.* (2012)
**Anno Mundi (The Year of the World from Creation)

APPENDIX B

Creation Timeline*

(Using only Biblical data and no secular dates)

CREATION YEAR	EVENT	YEAR	JUBILEE
1	ADAM CREATED	3964 BC	
930	ADAM DIED	3034 BC	
1550	GOD ANNOUNCES TO NOAH LIMIT OF 120 YEARS; GEN 5:32-6:3	2414 BC	31 ST
1650	FLOOD OF NOAH	2314 BC	33 RD
2000	ABRAM'S BIRTH AND NOAH'S DEATH	1964 BC	40 TH
2070	ABRAHAMIC COVENANT, 430 YEARS BEFORE THE EXODUS/LAW GAL 3:17	1894 BC	
2100	ISAAC'S BIRTH (400 YEARS BEFORE THE EXODUS) GEN 15:13; ABRAHAM 100 YEARS OLD GEN 21:5	1864 BC	42 ND
2420	MOSES' BIRTH	1544 BC	
2500	EXODUS AND MOSAIC COVENANT (THE LAW), JUBILEE OF JUBILEES	1464 BC	50 TH
2540	MOSES DEATH AND ISRAEL ENTERS THE PROMISED LAND	1424 BC	
2550	FIRST JUBILEE IN PROMISED LAND, LAND DIVIDED, 450 YEARS FROM ISAAC; ACTS 13:16-19	1414 BC	51 ST
2600	FIRST JUBILEE CELEBRATED IN PROMISED LAND	1364 BC	52 ND
2950	DAVIDIC COVENANT	1014 BC	59 TH
2976	DAVID'S DEATH AND SOLOMON'S REIGN BEGINS	988 BC	

CREATION YEAR	EVENT	YEAR	JUBILEE
2980	BEGIN SOLOMONS TEMPLE; 480 YEARS AFTER EXODUS; I KINGS 6:1-8, 2 CHRON 3:2	984 BC	
3000	TEMPLE DEDICATED (7+13=20 YEARS TO COMPLETE TEMPLE AND PALACE) 2 CHRON 7:11-22	964 BC	60 TH
3016	SOLOMON'S DEATH	948 BC	
3250	ISAIAH'S VISION, UZZIAH'S DEATH; ISAIAH 6	714 BC	65 TH
3300	ISAIAH/HEZEKIAH'S JUBILEE (HEZEKIAH'S 15TH YEAR); ISAIAH 37:30-32	664 BC	66 TH
3430	JUDAH AND JERUSALEM FALL, TEMPLE DESTROYED; 390+70=430 YEARS EZEKIEL 4	534 BC	
3500	CYRUS' 1ˢᵗ YEAR DECREE TO RESTORE JERUSALEM AND TEMPLE(70 YRS AFTER FALL)2 CHRON 36:17-21	464 BC	70 TH
3550	DANIEL'S 7 "WEEKS" TO RESTORE JERUSALEM/TEMPLE REBUILT AND DEDICATED BY NEHEMIAH	414 BC	71 TH
3961	YESHUA BORN 9/22/4 BC	4 BC	
3990	YESHUA BAPTIZED AND STARTS MINISTRY IN 15TH YEAR OF TIBERIUS; LUKE 3:1-2	27 AD	
3993	YESHUA'S DEATH, TEMPLE SPIRITUALLY DEAD (DANIEL'S 69 "WEEKS" FROM CYRUS DECREE) 4/6/30 AD	30 AD	
4033	2ND TEMPLE PHYSICALLY DESTROYED (40 YEARS FROM YESHUA'S DEATH) AV 9, 70 AD or 8/29/70 AD	70 AD	

CREATION YEAR	EVENT	YEAR	JUBILEE
4098	JERUSALEM PLOWED UP (A SABBATICAL YEAR BEFORE THE 82ND JUBILEE IN 136 BC) MICAH 3:12	135 AD	
5911	ISRAEL BECOMES A NATION AGAIN	1948 AD	
5930	ISRAEL RECAPTURES TEMPLE MOUNT (SIX DAY WAR)	1967 AD	
5993	3RD TEMPLE REBUILT (1960 YEARS FROM 2ND TEMPLE DESTRUCTION)	2030 AD	
6000	YESHUA RETURNS, MILLENIUM BEGINS	2036 AD	

*Tim Warner. *The Time of the End.* (2012)

APPENDIX C

Sabbath and Jubilee Years

SABBATH YEARS (CREATION YEAR 3964 BC)							JUBILEE YR	JUBILEE #
-3957	-3950	-3943	-3936	-3929	-3922	-3915	-3914	1
-3907	-3900	-3893	-3886	-3879	-3872	-3865	-3864	2
-3857	-3850	-3843	-3836	-3829	-3822	-3815	-3814	3
-3807	-3800	-3793	-3786	-3779	-3772	-3765	-3764	4
-3757	-3750	-3743	-3736	-3729	-3722	-3715	-3714	5
-3707	-3700	-3693	-3686	-3679	-3672	-3665	-3664	6
-3657	-3650	-3643	-3636	-3629	-3622	-3615	-3614	7
-3607	-3600	-3593	-3586	-3579	-3572	-3565	-3564	8
-3557	-3550	-3543	-3536	-3529	-3522	-3515	-3514	9
-3507	-3500	-3493	-3486	-3479	-3472	-3465	-3464	10
-3457	-3450	-3443	-3436	-3429	-3422	-3415	-3414	11
-3407	-3400	-3393	-3386	-3379	-3372	-3365	-3364	12
-3357	-3350	-3343	-3336	-3329	-3322	-3315	-3314	13
-3307	-3300	-3293	-3286	-3279	-3272	-3265	-3264	14
-3257	-3250	-3243	-3236	-3229	-3222	-3215	-3214	15
-3207	-3200	-3193	-3186	-3179	-3172	-3165	-3164	16
-3157	-3150	-3143	-3136	-3129	-3122	-3115	-3114	17
-3107	-3100	-3093	-3086	-3079	-3072	-3065	-3064	18
-3057	-3050	-3043	-3036	-3029	-3022	-3015	-3014	19
-3007	-3000	-2993	-2986	-2979	-2972	-2965	-2964	20
-2957	-2950	-2943	-2936	-2929	-2922	-2915	-2914	21
-2907	-2900	-2893	-2886	-2879	-2872	-2865	-2864	22
-2857	-2850	-2843	-2836	-2829	-2822	-2815	-2814	23
-2807	-2800	-2793	-2786	-2779	-2772	-2765	-2764	24
-2757	-2750	-2743	-2736	-2729	-2722	-2715	-2714	25

SABBATH YEARS (CREATION YEAR 3964 BC)							JUBILEE YR	JUBILEE #
-2707	-2700	-2693	-2686	-2679	-2672	-2665	-2664	26
-2657	-2650	-2643	-2636	-2629	-2622	-2615	-2614	27
-2607	-2600	-2593	-2586	-2579	-2572	-2565	-2564	28
-2557	-2550	-2543	-2536	-2529	-2522	-2515	-2514	29
-2507	-2500	-2493	-2486	-2479	-2472	-2465	-2464	30
-2457	-2450	-2443	-2436	-2429	-2422	-2415	-2414	31
-2407	-2400	-2393	-2386	-2379	-2372	-2365	-2364	32
-2357	-2350	-2343	-2336	-2329	-2322	-2315	-2314	33
-2307	-2300	-2293	-2286	-2279	-2272	-2265	-2264	34
-2257	-2250	-2243	-2236	-2229	-2222	-2215	-2214	35
-2207	-2200	-2193	-2186	-2179	-2172	-2165	-2164	36
-2157	-2150	-2143	-2136	-2129	-2122	-2115	-2114	37
-2107	-2100	-2093	-2086	-2079	-2072	-2065	-2064	38
-2057	-2050	-2043	-2036	-2029	-2022	-2015	-2014	39
-2007	-2000	-1993	-1986	-1979	-1972	-1965	-1964	40
-1957	-1950	-1943	-1936	-1929	-1922	-1915	-1914	41
-1907	-1900	-1893	-1886	-1879	-1872	-1865	-1864	42
-1857	-1850	-1843	-1836	-1829	-1822	-1815	-1814	43
-1807	-1800	-1793	-1786	-1779	-1772	-1765	-1764	44
-1757	-1750	-1743	-1736	-1729	-1722	-1715	-1714	45
-1707	-1700	-1693	-1686	-1679	-1672	-1665	-1664	46
-1657	-1650	-1643	-1636	-1629	-1622	-1615	-1614	47
-1607	-1600	-1593	-1586	-1579	-1572	-1565	-1564	48
-1557	-1550	-1543	-1536	-1529	-1522	-1515	-1514	49
-1507	-1500	-1493	-1486	-1479	-1472	-1465	-1464	50
-1457	-1450	-1443	-1436	-1429	-1422	-1415	-1414	51
-1407	-1400	-1393	-1386	-1379	-1372	-1365	-1364	52
-1357	-1350	-1343	-1336	-1329	-1322	-1315	-1314	53
-1307	-1300	-1293	-1286	-1279	-1272	-1265	-1264	54
-1257	-1250	-1243	-1236	-1229	-1222	-1215	-1214	55

SABBATH YEARS (CREATION YEAR 3964 BC)							JUBILEE YR	JUBILEE #
-1207	-1200	-1193	-1186	-1179	-1172	-1165	-1164	56
-1157	-1150	-1143	-1136	-1129	-1122	-1115	-1114	57
-1107	-1100	-1093	-1086	-1079	-1072	-1065	-1064	58
-1057	-1050	-1043	-1036	-1029	-1022	-1015	-1014	59
-1007	-1000	-993	-986	-979	-972	-965	-964	60
-957	-950	-943	-936	-929	-922	-915	-914	61
-907	-900	-893	-886	-879	-872	-865	-864	62
-857	-850	-843	-836	-829	-822	-815	-814	63
-807	-800	-793	-786	-779	-772	-765	-764	64
-757	-750	-743	-736	-729	-722	-715	-714	65
-707	-700	-693	-686	-679	-672	-665	-664	66
-657	-650	-643	-636	-629	-622	-615	-614	67
-607	-600	-593	-586	-579	-572	-565	-564	68
-557	-550	-543	-536	-529	-522	-515	-514	69
-507	-500	-493	-486	-479	-472	-465	-464	70
-457	-450	-443	-436	-429	-422	-415	-414	71
-407	-400	-393	-386	-379	-372	-365	-364	72
-357	-350	-343	-336	-329	-322	-315	-314	73
-307	-300	-293	-286	-279	-272	-265	-264	74
-257	-250	-243	-236	-229	-222	-215	-214	75
-207	-200	-193	-186	-179	-172	-165	-164	76
-157	-150	-143	-136	-129	-122	-115	-114	77
-107	-100	-93	-86	-79	-72	-65	-64	78
-57	-50	-43	-36	-29	-22	-15	-14	79
-7	0	7	14	21	28	35	36	80
43	50	57	64	71	78	85	86	81
93	100	107	114	121	128	135	136	82
143	150	157	164	171	178	185	186	83
193	200	207	214	221	228	235	236	84
243	250	257	264	271	278	285	286	85

SABBATH YEARS (CREATION YEAR 3964 BC)							JUBILEE YR	JUBILEE #
293	300	307	314	321	328	335	336	86
343	350	357	364	371	378	385	386	87
393	400	407	414	421	428	435	436	88
443	450	457	464	471	478	485	486	89
493	500	507	514	521	528	535	536	90
543	550	557	564	571	578	585	586	91
593	600	607	614	621	628	635	636	92
643	650	657	664	671	678	685	686	93
693	700	707	714	721	728	735	736	94
743	750	757	764	771	778	785	786	95
793	800	807	814	821	828	835	836	96
843	850	857	864	871	878	885	886	97
893	900	907	914	921	928	935	936	98
943	950	957	964	971	978	985	986	99
993	1000	1007	1014	1021	1028	1035	1036	100
1043	1050	1057	1064	1071	1078	1085	1086	101
1093	1100	1107	1114	1121	1128	1135	1136	102
1143	1150	1157	1164	1171	1178	1185	1186	103
1193	1200	1207	1214	1221	1228	1235	1236	104
1243	1250	1257	1264	1271	1278	1285	1286	105
1293	1300	1307	1314	1321	1328	1335	1336	106
1343	1350	1357	1364	1371	1378	1385	1386	107
1393	1400	1407	1414	1421	1428	1435	1436	108
1443	1450	1457	1464	1471	1478	1485	1486	109
1493	1500	1507	1514	1521	1528	1535	1536	110
1543	1550	1557	1564	1571	1578	1585	1586	111
1593	1600	1607	1614	1621	1628	1635	1636	112
1643	1650	1657	1664	1671	1678	1685	1686	113
1693	1700	1707	1714	1721	1728	1735	1736	114
1743	1750	1757	1764	1771	1778	1785	1786	115

SABBATH YEARS (CREATION YEAR 3964 BC)							JUBILEE YR	JUBILEE #
1793	1800	1807	1814	1821	1828	1835	1836	116
1843	1850	1857	1864	1871	1878	1885	1886	117
1893	1900	1907	1914	1921	1928	1935	1936	118
1943	1950	1957	1964	1971	1978	1985	1986	119
1993	2000	2007	2014	2021	2028	2035	2036	120

APPENDIX D
Timeline For Mid-week Events

(Passover Week 30 AD AND 2033 AD)
(Satan Mimics God's Passover Timeline During 70th Week)

	30 AD		2033 AD	
Nisan 10	SUN 4/2-3	Jesus rides into Jerusalem on Palm Sunday	SUN 4/10-11	The Beast rides into Jerusalem
Nisan 14	THURS 4/6-7	Jesus is crucified	THUR 4/14-15	The Beast is killed with a deadly head wound
Nisan 17	SUN 4/9-10	Jesus is resurrected	SUN 4/17-18	The Beast rises from the dead
Nisan 18			MON 4/18-19	The Beast kills the Two Witnesses
Nisan 19			TUES 4/19-20	Abomination of Desolation, image set up, saints flee
Nisan 21			THUR 4/21-22	Two witnesses arise from the dead

APPENDIX E
Chronological Summary of Dates/Events on Timeline

Gregorian Date	Jewish Holiday/ Date	Events
Present-9/10/2029		Ram Goat War between Turkey and Iran
9/10/2029	Rosh Hashanah	1st Seal; Seven-year peace deal with Israel
11/7/2029	Cheshvan 29	Two witnesses arrive
3/23/2030	Shabbat Parah	Red heifer sacrifice
8/29/2030	Rosh Chodesh Elul	Daily sacrifices at the Temple start
9/28/2030	Rosh Hashanah	2nd Seal; War
9/18/2031	Rosh Hashanah	3rd Seal; Famine, inflation
9/6/2032	Rosh Hashanah	4th Seal; Death
4/10/2033	Nisan 10	The Antichrist rides into Jerusalem
4/14/2033	Passover	The Antichrist is killed with deadly head wound
4/17/2033	Passover	The Antichrist is resurrected from the dead
4/18/2033	Passover	The Antichrist kills the two witnesses
4/19/2033	Passover	Abomination of Desolation; image of the Beast set up; saints flee
4/21/2033	Nisan 21	Two witnesses arise from the dead
9/24/2033	Rosh Hashanah	5th Seal; Martyr's cry
9/14/2034	Rosh Hashanah	6th Seal; Cosmic disturbances (great earthquake, sun darkened, blood moon, stars fall)
5/13/2035	Pentecost	The Rapture
10/4/2035	Rosh Hashanah	7th Seal; Silence in heaven; beginning of the Day of the Lord
10/13/2035	Day of Atonement	1st Trumpet; 1/3 of vegetation struck

11/12/2035	Cheshvan 10	2nd Trumpet; 1/3 sea turned to blood; 1/3 sea creatures die; 1/3 ships destroyed
12/12/2035	Kislev 11	3rd Trumpet; Star called Wormwood falls; 1/3 water turned bitter
1/11/2036	Tevet 11	4th Trumpet; Darkness with 1/3 sun, moon and stars struck
2/10/2036	Shevat 12	5th Trumpet; Locusts from the bottomless pit
3/11/2036	Adar 12	6th Trumpet; Angels from Euphrates released who release fire, smoke and brimstone
4/11-19/2036	Passover	7th Trumpet; Kingdom of the Lord proclaimed
9/22/2036	Rosh Hashanah	End of 70th Week of Daniel
10/1/2036	Day of Atonement	End of the Day of the Lord; Beginning of the Millennium
10/6-12/2036	Sukkot	Marriage Feast of the Lamb
10/31/2036	Cheshvan 10	1st Bowl; Door of ark closed, i.e., no more escape; foul and loathsome sores on men
11/7/2036	Cheshvan 17	2nd Bowl; Sea turns to blood
11/14/2036	Cheshvan 24	3rd Bowl; Rivers and springs turn to blood
11/21/2036	Kislev 2	4th Bowl; Men are scorched with fire
11/28/2036	Kislev 9	5th Bowl; Kingdom of the Antichrist full of darkness
12/5/2036	Kislev 16	6th Bowl; Euphrates River dried up
12/12/2036	Kislev 23	7th Bowl; Great earthquake; great hail
12/12-15/2036		The Battle of Armageddon
12/15/2036	Hanukkah	The Temple cleansed
3036		Gog Magog War at end of the Millennium
3036		The Great White Throne Judgment; End of the Millennium

REFERENCES

CHAPTER 1: Date Setting and the Tribulation

1. Ed Knorr, PhD. (2021, Feb 21). *Revelation and Bible Prophecy, A Comparison of Eschatological Views: Dispensationalism and Preterism.* https://www.cs.ubc.ca/~knorr/public/comparison_ of_eschat_models.pdf, pg. 137-149.

2. RD Davis (1986). *The Heavenly Court Scene of Revelation 4-5.* https://digitalcommons.andrews.edu/cgi/viewcontent.cgi? article=1030&context=dissertations.

CHAPTER 2: The Timeline

1. The Incredible Journey. (2021, Dec 3). *Walking with Reindeer* [Video]. https://www.youtube.com/watch?v=t8rN2_durDM&t=1509s.

2. Francisco Ursini, Alfredo De Giorgi, […], and Roberto Manfredini. *Chronobiology and Chronotherapy in Inflammatory Joint Diseases.* https://www.ncbi.nim.nih.gov/pmc/articles/ PMC8621834/.

3. Ed Knorr, PhD. (2021, Feb 21). *Revelation and Bible Prophecy, A Comparison of Eschatological Views: Dispensationalism and Preterism.* https://www.cs.ubc.ca/~knorr/public/comparison_ of_eschat_models.pdf, pg 88-91, 464.

4. Tim Warner. *The Time of the End.* (2012).

5. Robin Sampson & Linda Pierce. *A Family Guide to the Biblical Holidays.* (Stafford, VA: Heart of Wisdom Publishing, Inc., 2004).

CHAPTER 3: Two Witnesses

1. Nelson Walters. (2019, Apr 8). *Two Witnesses Documentary| Who What When?* [Video]. https://www.youtube.com/watch?v=cfhWpTKDOQg&t=1503s.

2. Ed Knorr, PhD. (2021, Feb 21). *Revelation and Bible Prophecy, A Comparison of Eschatological Views: Dispensationalism and Preterism.* https://www.cs.ubc.ca/~knorr/public/comparison_of_eschat_models.pdf, pg 530-535.

3. Jim Springer [Life Hope & Truth]. *Two Witnesses of Revelation 11.* https://lifehopeandtruth.com/prophecy/revelation/two-witnesses/.

4. Tim Warner. (2021, May 15). *The Revelation of Jesus the Anointed, Last Generation Version. Translation and notes by Tim Warner.* https://www.4windsfellowships.net/LGV/LGV_Revelation.pdf, pg 21.

CHAPTER 4: The Beasts of Revelation

1. Thomas Ice [Rapture Ready]. (2016, Oct 10). *The Ethnicity of the Antichrist.* https://www.raptureready.com/2015/07/10/the-ethnicity-of-the-antichrist-by-thomas-ice/

2. Joel Richardson. *Mideast Beast.* Washington, D.C., WND Books, 2012.

3. David Rosenthal [Zion's Hope]. (2019, Mar 5). *Four Kingdoms and a Fierce King Will Arise* [Video]. https://www.youtube.com/watch?v=AapNmX-aOxA.

4. Nelson Walters. (2019, Dec 29). *The Antichrist Explained in Detail by Scripture* [Video]. https://www.youtube.com/watch?v=gJwapS5TrKE.

5. [NeverThirsty]. *What does the Bible say about the idolatrous tribe of Dan?* https://www.neverthirsty.org/bible-qa/qa-archives/question/what-does-bible-say-about-tribe-dan/.

6. https://en.wikipedia.org/wiki/Dan_(son_of_Jacob).

7. [Shalach Ministries]. *The NUMBER 666 and the NAME of the BEAST Without Using GEMATRIA.* http://shalach.org/

Antichrist/Number%20666%20and%20Name%20of%20
the%20Beast.htm

CHAPTER 5: Mystery Babylon

1. Joel Richardson. *Mystery Babylon*. Washington, D.C., WND Books, 2017.
2. David Rosenthal [Zion's Hope]. (2017, May 22). *What Is Mystery Babylon-Part 1* [Video]. https://www.youtube.com/watch?v=AapNmX-aOxA.
3. David Rosenthal [Zion's Hope]. (2017, Jul 26). *What Is Mystery Babylon-Part 2* [Video]. https://www.youtube.com/watch?v=BG1ALbGNoIs&t=1388s.
4. David Rosenthal [Zion's Hope]. (2017, Oct 5). *What Is Mystery Babylon- Part 3* [Video]. https://www.youtube.com/watch?v=RF9fF928pBM.
5. [End Times Truth]. *The Beast with Seven Heads and Ten Horns.* https://endtimestruth.com/new-world-order/the-beast-with-seven-heads-and-ten-horns/.

CHAPTER 6: The Church, Israel, and Gentiles

1. Ed Knorr, PhD. (2021, Feb 21). *Revelation and Bible Prophecy, A Comparison of Eschatological Views: Dispensationalism and Preterism.* https://www.cs.ubc.ca/~knorr/public/comparison_of_eschat_models.pdf, pg 262-8, 342.
2. Sam Storm [crosswalk.com]. (2017, Apr 13). *10 Things You Should Know About the New Covenant.* https://www.crosswalk.com/faith/spiritual-life/10-things-you-should-know-about-the-new-covenant.html.
3. [Compelling Truth]. *During the Millennial Kingdom, will there be animal sacrifices?* https://www.compellingtruth.org/millennial-sacrifices.html.
4. David M. Levy [Israel My Glory]. (2019, Mar/Apr). *Q: Why will people offer animal sacrifices in the Millennial Temple?* https://

israelmyglory.org/article/q-why-will-people-offer-animal-sacrifices-in-the-millennial-temple/.

5. Clarence Larkin. *Dispensational Truth. Chapter 26.* https://www.blueletterbible.org/study/larkin/dt/26.cfm

6. Paul M. Sadler [Berean Bible Society]. *The Bride of Christ.* https://www.bereanbiblesociety.org/the-bride-of-christ/.

7. [doctrine.org]. *The Bride of Christ.* https://doctrine.org/the-bride-of-christ.

8. [Facts About Israel]. *God's Purpose for Israel: Why do the nations concern themselves over tiny Israel?* https://www.factsaboutisrael.uk/gods-purpose-for-israel/.

9. Jesper Svartvik. *Supersessionism.* https://www.bibleodyssey.org:443/en/passages/related-articles/supersessionism.

10. Alan Kurschner. (2021, May 5). *Why Isaiah 26:19-21 Supports the Prewrath View.* [Video]. https://www.youtube.com/watch?v=437MPcBB4Rw&t=1304s.

11. John F. Walvoord [Bible.org]. (2008, Jan 1). *The Times of the Gentiles.* https://bible.org/article/times-gentiles.

12. Ken Symes [Jewish Awareness Ministries]. (2018, May 25). *The Fullness of the Gentile.* http://www.jewishawareness.org/the-fullness-of-the-gentiles/.

CHAPTER 7: The Temple

1. The Messianic Prophecy Bible Project. *End-Time Prophecy: Why is the Third Temple so Important?* https://free.messianicbible.com/feature/end-time-prophecy-why-is-the-third-temple-so-important/.

2. *The Tabernacle, Temple, Synagogue & Church – What is the House of God?* https://biblethingsinbibleways.wordpress.com/2016/11/25/the-tabernacle-temple-synagogue-church-what-is-the-house-of-god/.

3. *Update on the Building of the Third Temple.* https://www.jewishvoice.org/read/article/update-building-third-temple

4. Thomas D. Ice (May 2009). *Ready to Rebuild.* https://digitalcommons.liberty.edu/cgi/viewcontent.cgi?article=1054&context=pretrib_arch.

5. Nelson Walters. (2020, Jan 5). *Who Builds the Third Temple & the SHOCKING Reason Why* [Video]. https://www.youtube.com/watch?v=hHI1Gcq4E4Y&t=1656s.

6. Nelson Walters. (2020, May 16). *When Will The Third Temple Be Built In Israel: The Two Witnesses' Role* [Video]. https://www.youtube.com/watch?v=CGB4fbbnwBk.

7. Ed Knorr, PhD. (2021, Feb 21). *Revelation and Bible Prophecy, A Comparison of Eschatological Views: Dispensationalism and Preterism.* https://www.cs.ubc.ca/~knorr/public/comparison_of_eschat_models.pdf, pg 379, 398-401.

8. Nelson Walters. (2020, May 13). *Third Temple in Jerusalem Requires a Red Heifer: How Soon Will One be Ready?*[Video]. https://www.youtube.com/watch?v=5LqZ3EqP0gE.

9. Nelson Walters. (2020, Dec 12). *Hanukkah is the Hidden Template of the Great Tribulation and ANTICHRIST*[Video]. https://www.youtube.com/watch?v=WWBlHbrPTa4&t=1238s.

10. [My Olive Tree]. (2019, Jan28). *What Was the Importance of the Temple in Jerusalem?* https://www.myolivetree.com/what-was-the-importance-of-the-temple-in-jerusalem/.

11. Brian Brodersen [Back to Basics]. (2018, Dec 3). *The Tabernacle of God Is With Men.* https://backtobasicsradio.com/the-tabernacle-of-god-is-with-men/.

CHAPTER 8: The Second Coming of Christ

1. Joel Richardson. *Sinai to Zion.* Leawood, KS, Winepress Media, 2020.

2. Travis M. Snow. *The Passover King.* Dallas, TX, Voice of Messiah, Inc., 2020.

3. Ed Knorr, PhD. (2021, Feb 21). *Revelation and Bible Prophecy, A Comparison of Eschatological Views: Dispensationalism and Preterism.* https://www.cs.ubc.ca/~knorr/public/comparison_of_eschat_models.pdf, pg 275-292, 301-318.

4. Nelson Walters. (2020, Oct 14). *SURPRISING Rapture Details from the OLD Testament - Who, Where, When, and How* [Video]. https://www.youtube.com/watch?v=tlcp1CO3OZI.

CHAPTER 9: Wars

1. Nelson Walters. (2019, Nov 24). *Gog and Magog (How Soon Can It Happen?)* [Video]. https://www.youtube.com/watch?v=qfmg4-zsos8&t=41s.

2. Nelson Walters. (2020, Jan 24). *Psalm 83 War- Israel's Next Wars Predicted* [Video]. https://www.youtube.com/watch?v=dJ2RPI2NdLA&t=12s.

3. J. Paul Tanner [JETS 39/1]. (1996, Mar). *Rethinking Ezekiel's Invasion by Gog.* https://www.etsjets.org/files/JETS-PDFs/39/39-1/39-1-pp029-046_JETS.pdf.

4. Renald Showers [The Friends of Israel Gospel Ministry]. (2012, Jul 24). *Gog of Magog.* https://www.foi.org/free_resource/gog-magog/.

5. *Gog and Magog.* https://en.m.wikipedia.org/wiki/Gog_and_Magog.

6. Bill Salus. *Psalm 83: The Missing Prophecy Revealed.* La Quinta, CA, Prophecy Depot Ministries, 2013.

7. Nelson Walters. (2020, Jan 27). *Gog and Magog Explained by Psalm 83- A NEW Revolutionary Theory* [Video]. https://www.youtube.com/watch?v=lxj8qbhftqs.

8. Nelson Walters. (2022, Apr 25). *Are Temple Mount Riots (AND Some END TIME Events) Linked to Ramadan?* [Video]. https://www.youtube.com/watch?v=RJqljw7AI8Y&t=204s.

9. *Eclipses During The Month Of Ramadan: 2001-2100 CE / 1422-1524 AH.* https://www.geocities.ws/muslimapocalyptic/eclipses_during_the_month_of_ram.htm.

CHAPTER 10: Judgments

1. Greg Laurie [The Christian Post]. (2013, Apr 16). *Why Does God Judge?* https://www.christianpost.com/news/why-does-god-judge.html.

2. [The Truth Stands Forever]. (2017). *The Lord Will Rule With a Rod of Iron.* https://www.thetruthstandsforever.com/the-lord-will-rule-with-a-rod-of-iron.html.

3. J. Hampton Keathly III [Bible.org]. (2004, May 14). *The Judgments- (Past, Present, and Future.* https://bible.org/article/judgments-past-present-and-future.

4. [Got Questions]. *What does the Bible say about when God will judge us?* https://www.gotquestions.org/judgment.html. *judge*

5. [Got Questions]. *How does God judge those who were raised in non-Christian cultures?* https://www.gotquestions.org/God-judge-religions.html.

6. John Walvoord [Bible.org]. (2008, Jan 1). *7. The Judgment of the Nations.* https://bible.org/seriespage/7-judgment-nations.

7. J. Hampton Keathly III [Bible.org]. (2004, May 25). *The Doctrine of Rewards: The Judgment Seat (Bema) of Christ.* https://bible.org/article/doctrine-rewards-judgment-seat-bema-christ.

8. Watchman Nee [Living Stream Ministry]. *Four Judgments.* https://www.ministrysamples.org/excerpts/FOUR-JUDGMENTS.HTML.

9. Don Stewart [Blue Letter Bible]. *What Is the Judgment Seat of Christ? (The Bema).* https://www.blueletterbible.org/faq/don_stewart/don_stewart_144.cfm.

10. Don Stewart [Blue Letter Bible]. *Whom Will Christ Judge at His Second Coming?* https://www.blueletterbible.org/faq/don_stewart/don_stewart_145.cfm.

11. [Bibleline Ministries]. *Judgment of the Nations.* http://www.biblelineministries.org/articles/basearch.php?action=full&mainkey=JUDGMENT+OF+THE+NATIONS.

12. William Krewson [Israel My Glory]. (2001, July/August). *The Judgment of the Nations.* https://israelmyglory.org/article/the-judgment-of-the-nations/.

13. [Got Questions]. *What is the Great White Throne Judgment?* https://www.gotquestions.org/great-white-throne-judgment.html.

14. Ed Knorr, PhD. (2021, Feb 21). *Revelation and Bible Prophecy, A Comparison of Eschatological Views: Dispensationalism and Preterism.* https://www.cs.ubc.ca/~knorr/public/comparison_of_eschat_models.pdf, pg. 209, 328-340.

15. [Got Questions]. *What does it mean that we will judge angels?* https://www.gotquestions.org/judge-angels.html.

CHAPTER 11: The Millennium

1. Ed Knorr, PhD. (2021, Feb 21). *Revelation and Bible Prophecy, A Comparison of Eschatological Views: Dispensationalism and Preterism.* https://www.cs.ubc.ca/~knorr/public/comparison_of_eschat_models.pdf, pg. 617-658, 659-675, 695-759.
2. Thomas D. Ice [Liberty University]. (2009, May]. *Literal Sacrifices in the Millennium.* https://core.ac.uk/download/pdf/58821959.pdf.
3. Thomas D. Ice [Liberty University]. (2009, May]. *Why Sacrifices in The Millennium.* https://digitalcommons.liberty.edu/cgi/viewcontent.cgi?article=1059&context=pretrib_arch.
4. Randy Alcorn. *Heaven.* Carol Stream, IL, Tyndale House Publishers, Inc., 2004.

CHAPTER 12: Epilogue

1. Ed Knorr, PhD. (2021, Feb 21). *Revelation and Bible Prophecy, A Comparison of Eschatological Views: Dispensationalism and Preterism.* https://www.cs.ubc.ca/~knorr/public/comparison_of_eschat_models.pdf, pg. 52-53.
2. Joel Richardson. (2021, Feb 5). *The Son of Man's Messages to the Seven Churches: Maranatha Global Bible Study #9* [Video]. https://www.youtube.com/watch?v=Y0POOlLDLb4&t=13s.

RECOMMENDED RESOURCES

1. Marvin Rosenthal. *The Pre-Wrath Rapture of the Church.* Nashville, TN, Thomas Nelson, Inc., 1990.
2. Nelson Walters. *Revelation Deciphered.* Ready for Jesus Publications, 2016.
3. Alan Kurschner. *Antichrist Before the Day of the Lord.* Pompton Lakes, NJ, Eschatos Publishing, 2013.

Lightning Source UK Ltd.
Milton Keynes UK
UKHW012232060223
416577UK00003B/274/J